World
Mirrors
1650 – 1900

Graham Child

Sotheby's Publications

To my wife Melanie

First published 1990 for Sotheby's Publications
by Philip Wilson Publishers Limited
26 Litchfield Street
London WC2H 9NJ

British Library Cataloguing in Publication Data
Child, Graham
World mirrors 1650–1900.
1. Mirrors, history
I. Title
749.3

ISBN 0 85667 355 2

LC 90-060782

Distributed in the USA and Canada by
Rizzoli International Publications, Inc
300 Park Avenue South
New York
NY 10010

Designed by Andrew Shoolbred
Typeset by Wyvern Typesetting Ltd, Bristol
Printed and bound by Singapore National Printers Ltd, Singapore

Frontispiece illustration French
Mirror, Napoleon III, *c.*1865
(see 421)

Contents

Acknowledgements

The preparation of this book could not have been possible without the help and encouragement of many friends and colleagues. I am particularly grateful to Sally Prideaux and Jane Bennett for all the trouble and care they have taken in editing the work. Among the many helpers Iola Lenzi has been wonderful in assisting with the photographic research and has given great enthusiasm and encouragement. My colleagues in the furniture department at Sotheby's have always been generous with their support and advice, particularly Jonathan Bourne and Christopher Payne. Many hands have helped with typing the manuscript from longhand, but without Caroline Hurlock the task would have been almost impossible. My thanks go to the photographic department at Sotheby's especially Ken Adeard, Clarissa Bruce, Paul Kinchen, David Grollman and to Keith Lloyd for allowing them to assist me. I am especially grateful to those who allowed photographs to be taken in their workshops and studios: Clifford Wright and George Bird and the staff at Clifford Wright. Salvador Titian, his son Rodrigo, Lizzie Porter and the staff at Titian's Studio. To Robert and Vivian Dunn of the old established firm of A. Dunn & Son who, together with Chris and Catherine Webber helped with the marquetry photographs and technique. To Tony Howells of the even older established firm of G. Jackson and to Ray Hitching and Ron Wood. A number of photographs have been kindly supplied by Fischer-Bölher of Munich and by Arne Bruun Rasmussen of Copenhagen. There have been many who have been very kind in giving me their time, experience and encouragement and I would particularly like to thank Paul Barry Liss for his help with research, Clifford Wright, Francesco Morroni, Laura Rogge, Alicia Henriquez de Luna, Hans Reichart, Amanda Deitsch, Claire Edwards, Anne Pollen, Mette Tang Simpson, Roberta Hughes, Thierry van Ophem, William Stahl, Geoffrey Wills, Monica Sandes, Jeanette Hayhurst, Bob Huffman and all the others who have helped in so many ways, especially my family who have put up with so much. Thank you all.

Foreword

The majority of the photographs of mirrors in this book have been taken from the catalogues of Sotheby's and other auctioneers in Great Britain, the United States, Germany, Monaco, Spain and Denmark. I have often relied on the original catalogue entries for my information, since to have examined every piece would clearly have been impossible. As research and knowledge have improved, and continues to do so, there may well be differing opinions as to the country of origin and date of some examples.

The definite emphasis placed upon English mirrors, in relation to the other sections in this book, directly reflects the amount of relevant auction activity in the countries concerned.

Introduction

The word 'mirror' is understood today to describe both reflective glass and the surrounding frame. The dictionary describes a mirror thus: 'A polished surface (usually of amalgam coated glass or metal), reflecting images; looking-glass that gives a faithful reflection.'

Superstition and folklore have been woven into the history of mirror-glass for thousands of years; from the great myth of Narcissus to the popular belief that seven years' bad luck will result from breaking a mirror. These convictions persist. In some parts of Europe it is believed that breaking a mirror leads to unfaithfulness and lost virginity and in areas of the west of England mirrors are covered during storms.

Mirrors have powerful associations with death, the devil and good as well as bad fortune. The custom of covering a mirror during an illness to prevent the soul from leaving the body is linked to primitive man's belief that his reflection was his soul. Likewise, following a death it was customary for mirrors to be covered until after the funeral, since it was believed that the soul only left the body after burial.

The mirror is traditionally thought to reflect the truth as in the tale of *Snow White*: 'Mirror mirror on the wall, who is the fairest of them all?' In some parts of Germany it is said that on New Years Eve or Easter morning you can see your future husband or wife in a mirror, while in others new mothers or women with young children are advised not to look into a mirror.

The word 'mirour' derived from the French, often referred to small, polished-metal, usually hand-held mirrors, and in rare cases mirrors made from crystal. The term 'crystalline glass' appears as early as 1448 in the inventory of René d'Anjou, while 'looking-glass', may have been used to distinguish polished metal from rock-crystal mirrors, and is first cited in 1626. The Privy Purse Expenses of Henri II of France for 1532 record payment 'to a Frenchman for certayne looking-glasses.' That both were in use at the same time can be seen from an inventory of the possessions of the Earl of Leicester, taken at Leicester House in 1588. 'Three great glasses one standing on a verie faire frame, with bears and ragged staves on the top, with steele glass in it, the other II of crystall, value £40.'

Steel mirrors were made from polished rocks such as iron pyrites and obsidian or 'speculum'. Speculum mirrors were made, not from steel, but a silvery-white alloy, composed of a number of metals including rose copper and tin. William Salmon wrote in *Polygraphice* in 1701

> 'The reason why these Metalic Glasses are called Steel Glasses, is not from their being made of steel, for there is no steel in them, but from the very great Hardness of their Temper and Composition, equalizing that of steel, their being extremely hard white, and not very brittle, and therefore the more easily polished, and made admirably fine.'

Despite Henri II of France on 13 February 1551 granting to Sieur Theseo Mutio and an Italian gentleman born in 'Boullogne', the exclusive grace and privilege of making or having made within ten years and in this Kingdom mirrors in the fashion of 'Venice', mirrors were generally composed of metal or rock-crystal. William Salmon gave a recipe for speculum in 1701, which he maintained was 'fit for flat Looking-glasses'. His recipe included 'Refined Rose copper 1b. iij: melt it, then add of fine Tin 1b ix: as soon as they are melted add red Tartar calcined xviij: White Arsenick vj: Nitre iij: keep these in a melting heat for 3 or 4 hours, that the salts may evaporate; then cast into the Moulds.' The pieces of speculum made from a different recipe, giving different ingredients but also from Salmon '. . . will be so hard as not to be touched with a File.' Once taken from the mould, the speculum was polished like mirror-glass and only needed cleaning, 'if those Glasses are sullied or made dull with the air or any thick Vapour, you must clear them by rubbing not with Woollen or Linen but with a piece of Deer or Goat's skin, wiping it in an oblique line'.

It seems that the first serious production of flat glass suitable for mirrors is not the claim of any one country or area. What does seem certain, however, is that the Venetians adopted and improved a technique that had been established in Northern Europe and that this tin-mercury process, developed during the fourteenth century was to dominate mirror-making for nearly four centuries.

The reflective surface, whether it be polished metal, rock-crystal or tin-mercury-backed glass, was a highly valued possession. It follows, therefore, that these valued objects needed protection and were framed, and in some cases completely enclosed, with all manner of materials. Today almost the exact reverse of this situation prevails, with the exception of examples where the original mirror-glass is extant, the value of a mirror lies mainly in the frame. So it is on these frames that this study concentrates, drawing upon examples from diverse sources and tracing their development over the period *c.* 1650–1900.

Mirror glass

It is almost certain that man first saw himself reflected in the surface of still water without knowing what it was that he saw. Once he realized, he began to consider more convenient ways of looking at himself. Exactly when and where glass was invented remains a mystery, however a story related by Pliny, A.D. 23–79, is still told today. It tells of a group of Phoenician sailors who, when voyaging from Egypt to Syria, camped on a sandy beach in Palestine at the mouth of the River Belus. They used blocks of natron from their cargo (a form of sodium carbonate used in those days for embalming the dead), to build a hearth on the beach upon which to cook their food. When the fire was hot, 'rivulets of a fluid suddenly flowed out'. Unfortunately this delightful story cannot be accepted because the fusion of natron and sand in fire does not produce glass.

In order to achieve a bright, sharp, undistorted image a smooth, flat surface with high reflectivity is required. These qualities were found in polished rocks such as obsidian that was used as mirrors by the ancient Mexicans as long ago as 4000 B.C. By 3000 B.C. gold, silver and bronze, as well as glassy rocks, were used as mirrors. The combination of two of these materials, bronze and silver, was achieved by both Oriental and European cultures. Polished metal mirrors, some overlaid with platinum or silver, especially those from the Orient, are the first recorded reflecting surfaces made for personal use. The majority of the examples that survive today are hand mirrors, the handles cast in bronze and decorated with ivory and precious stones. From the hand mirror, the Greeks developed the standing mirror and the folding mirror, both small in scale, and made from polished metal with slightly convex reflecting surfaces. They were often supported by a standing female figure, with the base, upon which the figure stood decorated with animals that were rich with symbolic meaning. The development of a folding mirror was the first creative move away from a simple, flat sheet of mirrored glass, and its reverse side provided enormous scope for decoration – mythological images, designs with symbolic connotations and figures of the gods as well as erotica were used. Archimedes, *c.* 287–212 B.C., the Greek mathematician, who also developed machines of war, is reputed to have set fire to the Roman fleet, which was attacking Syracuse, by using a mirror placed in a tower to deflect the rays of the sun.

The Romans continued the traditional Greek forms of mirror and made mirrors from tin mined at Brindisi, in Italy. Small mirrors became the prerequisite of every fashionable Roman woman; in a mural at Pompei, Cupid is represented holding a mirror for a woman who is arranging her hair. Pliny (the Roman writer born in the North of Italy who perished when Versuvius erupted), makes reference to glass mirrors spread on the underside with a layer of zinc. This is confirmed by similar references in the writings of Alexander of Aphrodisias and Antonias of Padua.

Glass-making expanded during the Roman Empire from its early origins in the Middle East, particularly the Levant. The mirrors mentioned by Roman writers may

Opposite English mirror, George II, *c.*1740, (see 120)

fig 1 An eighteenth-century English coal-fired glass-works

well have been examples of the glass-makers art, or mirrors made from rock crystal backed with a sheet of silver or lead. Glass-making spread from the inner Mediterranean to all corners of the Roman Empire, including Gaul, Britannia and Germania.

The basic composition of a batch of glass has changed very little; 75 per cent silica, usually sand, 10 per cent lime and 15 per cent sodium or potassium oxide, although the exact method of glass-making varies. After the break-up of the Roman Empire, glass-making in Europe was roughly divided into two main areas: The North, including Germany, Scandinavia, France, Belgium, England and Bohemia, and the South, mainly Italy. These divisions were based upon technical traditions. In the North, glass-making was concentrated in the forested areas and used local sands and the ashes of burnt vegetation for the flux. The flux, known as the 'salt', was used to make the sand fusible at a reasonable, lower temperature. In the South, the silica was obtained by crushing white pebbles from the river beds and the flux from burning seaweed. As late as 1701, William Salmon, in his *Polygraphice* notes that 'The Venetians and Italians make Glass in the Isle of Muran of a white flint which they have out of the River Ticinus, where there is a vast quantity of them: and they are found also in the River Arnus both above and below Florence.' Clay was required for the pots, sandstone for the furnaces and wood, coal or peat for fuel.

During the Middle Ages (very approximately A.D. 500 to 1500), little progress with the manufacture of mirrors was made in Europe; the majority were still made from polished metal. But whilst flat colourless glass was not really available before the fourteenth century, the production of domestic glass was developing fast. The history of glass and mirror glass reads like a modern novel; the story contains death and destruction, tales of spies and spying, of vanity, sin and great wealth of royalty, parliamentary petitions and litigation – all the elements of a good yarn. Threats of death were made to Venetian glass-makers who might have been tempted to leave their work-place to travel abroad and start a rival business. Even glass-makers' tools and fragments of glass were forbidden exports from Murano. Spies were used by rival glass houses to obtain new methods of glass-making. In 1754, Morten Waern, a Norwegian spy, was sent to England to find out the secrets of English glass-making and to persuade English glass-makers to work in Norway. Waern was captured and imprisoned in Newgate but not before he had sent samples of raw materials and finished pieces back to Norway. Leonardo da Vinci used mirror-writing for secrecy as well as a mirror to compare his work to a reflected image of the original subject.

Vanity may be behind this desire to disclose new glass-making techniques and so further the quest for the perfect mirror. The ivory case of a small sixteenth-century girdle mirror of Italian origin has the words 'Complain not of me, O Woman, for I return to you only what you give me' inscribed upon it. Indeed, a mirror in the hands of a woman has, since the beginning of Christianity, been considered a symbol of sin. Pope John XXII, during the fourteenth-century, affirmed that 'The Devil can conceal himself in a phial or a mirror.' Lucius Sennaca, the Roman philosopher, notes that full-length mirrors cost more than it takes to provide a General's daughter with a dowry. Royalty made gifts of hugely valuable mirrors; in 1666 Louis XIV presented the Electress of Brandenberg with a large mirror costing 4,800 livres. In 1751 the King of

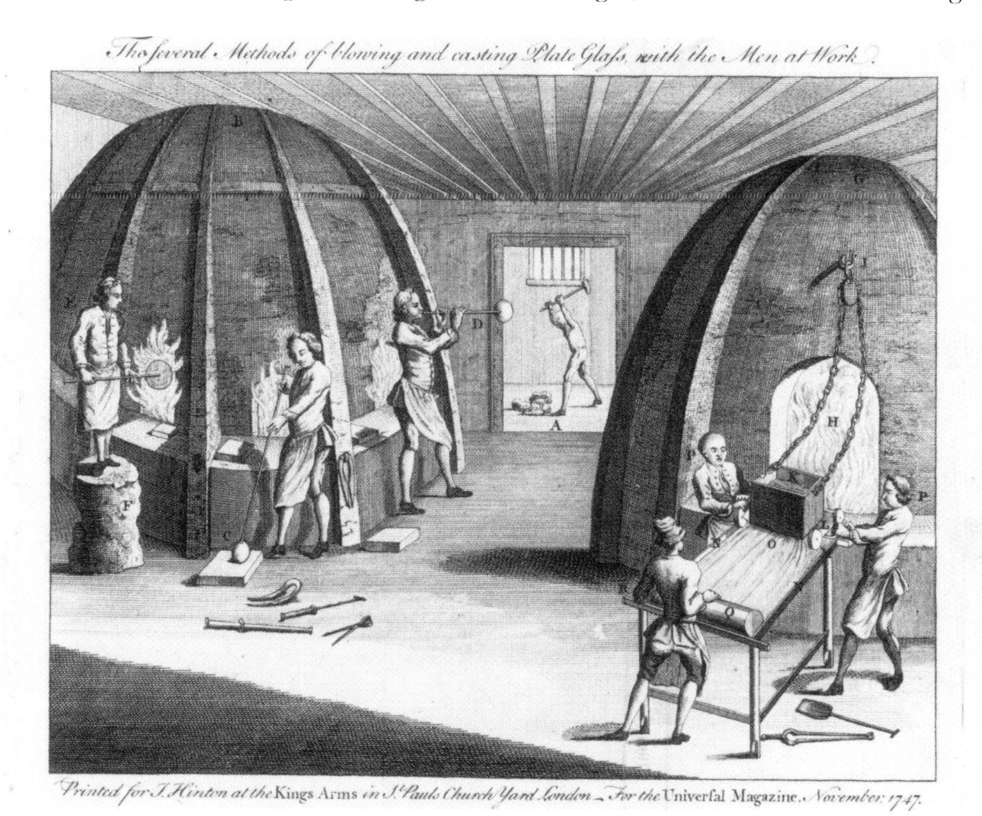

fig 2 Different methods employed for blowing and casting glass during the middle of the eighteenth century

Denmark was given several mirrors, made at the Saint Gobain manufactory, to the value of 24,576 livres. During the first half of the eighteenth century in England the Bear Garden Glassworks tried, through a petition to Parliament, to close a rival establishment. They failed but many violent accusations were made against their opponents. Death and destruction was due to the many conflagrations caused by the furnaces. The stories may be romantic but the production of glass was difficult and dangerous and required large numbers of highly skilled, as well as unskilled workers, many of whom were exposed to sometimes fatal injury. At the head of this dangerous enterprise would be the glass-house master, known in German as Hütten-Meister, in French Maitre-Verrier and in Italian as Padrone di Fornace. He would be responsible for the secrets of the ingredients and the quantities required. The duties of a glass-house master are detailed in a document of 1674, appointing one John Ludwig to a factory in Potsdam:

> 'He is to keep a watchful eye on the furnace and see that all that is necessary to bring and keep the furnaces and glass-house in good order is there: wood for fuel, clay (for pots), stone for the furnace, ash and the other materials, and take care nothing is missing as great trouble can ensue: he shall see to it that hard-working journeymen are retained and he shall keep them in order, also see that nobody sells and takes home his work of the week, but make sure that everyone each week gives what he has done to the glass-house clerk.'

The clerk, possibly the only other literate employee, was responsible for the accounts and for the general running of the business side of the enterprise. The smith was an important member of the team as he was responsible for making and maintaining the majority of the tools. Carpenters and wood-workers made moulds; large numbers of workers were required to collect and prepare fuel, stokers maintained the fires; all these in addition to the highly skilled men who were actually engaged in making glass.

fig 3 The tools used and the progressive state of the blown glass in the broad glass process

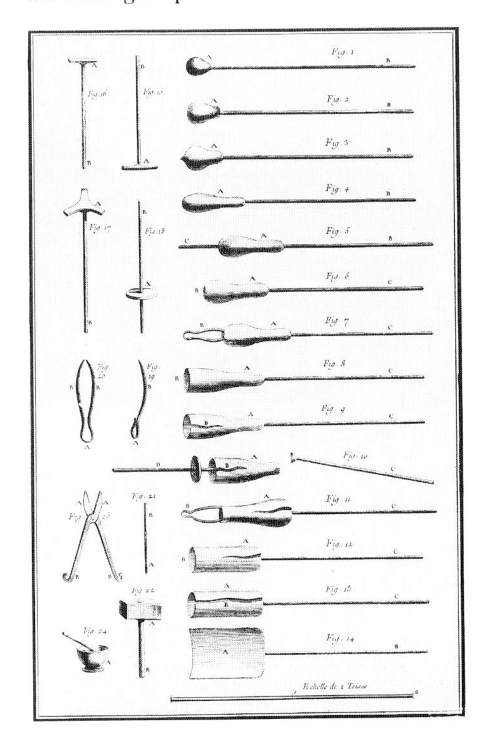

The makers of window glass and flat glass were considered to be the aristocrats among glass-makers. The formation of flat plates, suitable for mirrors, were made in two different ways; by the Lorraine or 'broad process' or by casting. The former process required the charging of the blowpipe with moulten glass and blowing a bubble which was then formed into a sausage shape, the ends cut off and the cylinder cut along its length and opened up flat. It was then placed in an annealing oven to cool. The drawback to this process was the small size of the plates that could be made. The glass bubble was rarely produced in the first attempt but returned to the furnace to retain the plasticity of the glass for further work. The size and clarity of the finished plates were matters of great competition between glassworks. By 1702 The Bear Garden Glassworks in London advertised plates of glass of up to 90 in 'Free from Veins and Foulness . . .'. Casting is just that; moulten glass is poured on to a flat metal surface with low sides the thickness of the finished plate. This process was invented by Bernard Perrot in Orléans in 1687. Some early flat glass, mainly used for windows (also using the broad glass method) was made by blowing a bubble that was cut at the end and by spinning the blowpipe quickly around on its own axis, making the bubble of glass open up in a flat disc or 'crown'. This crown glass was used for windows held in place by lead called 'leaded lights', with the crown in the centre of random panes. It was also used for the glass windows on the trunks of longcase clocks during the end of the seventeenth and early eighteenth centuries in Northern Europe, and called 'bulls-eyes' in England. The broad process was described in 1710 by Zacharias Conrad von Uffenbach after a visit to the Vauxhall Glass Works. He remarked that it is 'uncommonly hot work and the blowing very arduous', and continued:

> 'First they take out a great mass, which they repeatedly blow up in a circle and then again make red-hot; when it is large enough they take it to the so-called "pulpit" which is really a chair raised on several steps, below which a man stands with a pair of scissors and cuts the great bubble in pieces, then it is laid on a large sheet of iron, on which the glass is stretched. On this it is placed in the cooling oven and smoothed out with an iron resembling a scraper; then it is stood in an upright position and left for three days to cool. The panes are then sold to other people who cut and mount them, making mirrors of them, this is a special trade followed by many people in London.'

After the cooling process is complete, the glass is uneven at the edges and is far from smooth due to the contact of the hot glass with the air, the casting plate and the roller.

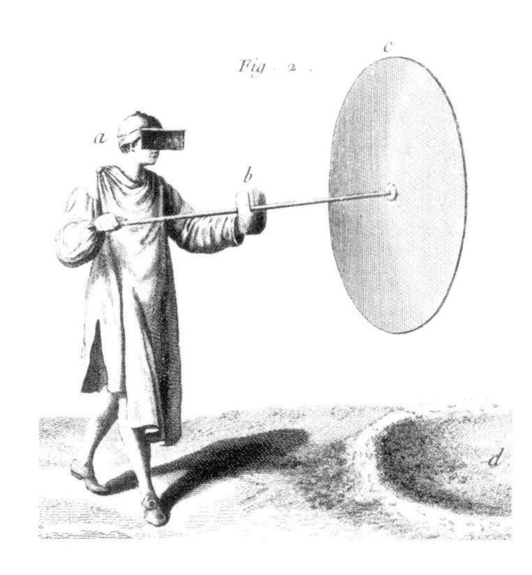

fig 4 A crown of glass being spun at the end of a blow pipe; after cooling it is laid on to a depression prepared in the sand

Dr Martin Lister, author of *A Journey to Paris* in the Year 1698, described the polishing process in a Parisian glass-works:

> 'There they are polished; which employs daily 600 Men and they hope in a little time to employ 1000 in several Galleries. In the lower [gallery] they grind the course Glass with a Sand Stone, the very same they pave the Streets in Paris; of which broken they have great heaps in the courts of the Work-Houses. This Stone is beat to Powder and

fig 5 Plate glass is removed from the annealing (cooling) oven

fig 6 Polishing broad glass with felt buffers at the ends of wooden ribs which are curved to create a constant pressure

fig 7 Silvering glass plates, the surface is covered with mercury and laid upon a sheet of tin foil, weighed down to remove excess mercury. Finally the plates are tilted and dried

> sifted through a fine Tamis. In the Upper Gallery, where they polish and give the last Hand, they work in 3 Rowes, and 2 Men at a Plate, with Ruddle and Powdered Haematites in Water. The Glasses are set fast in White Puttie, upon flat Tables of Stone, sawed thin for that purpose. The grinding the edges and Borders is very troublesome, and odious for the horrid grating noise it makes, and which cannot be endured to one that is not used to it: and yet by long custom these Fellows are so easie with it, that they Discuss together as nothing were. This is done below, and out of the way of the next.'

In the *Dictionarium Polygraphicum*, published in England in 1735, and probably compiled by John Barrow, the author describes the process:

> 'After looking-glasses have been ground they are to be polished, they still looking but something like slate. The polishing is performed in the following manner: the plate is laid down on a stone plac'd horizontally, and in a bed of plaister of Paris calcin'd and pulveris'd very fine and sifted; which being made into a sort of paste by water, and plaister'd up the edges of the plate, dries and hardens, and so keeps it immoveable; then the workmen fixing a strong bow of yew or some other tough wood to a board fixed up to the ceiling of the room, fixes also the other end into a hole made in a wooden parallopepid [rectangular block] of about four inches long, cover'd with a sort of coarse woollen cloth well drench'd with Tripoly tempered with water, works it with thin block and bow all over by strength of arm, till the plate has got a perfect politure.'

To turn a sheet of glass into a mirror it must be backed to make it reflect, a process known as silvering. The following is an extract taken from *The Art of Glass*, originally written by H. Blancourt, a Frenchman, and translated into English in 1699.

> 'The Glass is not perfected, till it be silvered, for without that, it is impossible it should distinctly show the opposite objects. . . . For this you must have a firm smooth Table, much greater than the Glass, whereon spread one or more Sheets of very fine Tin, let them be as thin as Paper and so prepared, as not to have any Rumple or Furrow, or Spot, else the Glass will be spoil'd. Over these sheets spread good Mercury, quite covering them with it, when the Mercury has soaked in well, place the Glass thereon, and it will stick to them; then turn it, and spread Sheets of paper on the filling; press it gently, smoothing and stroaking it with your Hands to take off the surplus Mercury; then dry it in the sun or by a soft Fire, and it will become perfect.'

England

The Romans brought the art of glass-making to England and once they had departed, the native English glass-making industry was gathered in the heavily wooded, south-eastern parts of the country, particularly in Surrey, Sussex and Kent. The output from these forest glass-makers was coloured or clear glass, some crude utensils and some flat glass for windows but unsuitable for mirror-making.

The documented history of English glass-making begins with Laurence Vitrearius from Normandy, who settled at Dyers Cross in about 1226 and made glass for Westminster Abbey *c.* 1240. By 1567 Jean Carré, now seen as the father of modern glass-making in England, had arrived from the Netherlands with other Protestants skilled in glass-making and obtained a licence to make glass. With the spread of the printed word during the Renaissance the demand for glass-makers and their secrets increased. Italy, particularly Venice, and the Low Countries produced the best glass in Europe at this time so it is not at all surprising that their skills were greatly sought after. One such glass-maker who settled in England was Giacomo Verzelini, a Venetian who came to London by way of Antwerp in 1571. Verzelini brought with him half a dozen Italian glass-makers and, encouraged by Queen Elizabeth I, opened a glass-works first in Crutched Friars and later in Broad Street in the City of London. But Elizabethan England was in the grip of a fuel crisis; there had been a rapid destruction of woodland caused by both the iron-smelters and the glass-makers which led to a Royal proclamation in 1615 prohibiting the use of wood fuel for glass-making. The degree to which wood was being used is illustrated by records of glass-making in Kent by John Lennard in about 1570. Between 7 June 1585 and 18 January 1586, 543 cords of wood were carried to the glass-house. (A cord of cut wood usually measured 128 cubic feet.) The Proclamation of 1615 not only forbade the use of wood for fuel but also prohibited the import of foreign glass. By 1620 the Venetian Ambassador, Girolamo Lando, wrote to the Doge and Senate confirming that the English Government had banned all imports of glass and added 'by this order they also mean to prohibit looking glasses of which they make a quantity here'.

The change from wood to coal fuel was the most significant occurrence to take place in the English glass-making industry during the early seventeenth century and gave England's glass industry a lead over the rest of Europe. As a result of using coal as a fuel for the furnaces, mirror plates were often disfigured by spots caused by the action of the coal fire on the lead flux used in the mixture. The difficulty in obtaining a pure plate is revealed in a letter from Lady Brilliana Harley, written in 1639 to her son Edward at Oxford:

> 'Dear Ned, if there be any good looking-glasses in Oxford, chuse me one aboute the biggnes of that I use to dress in, if you remember it, I put it to your choys, becuase I thinke you will chuse one, that will make a true answere to ones face.'

The monopoly for glass-making in England was rented to a group of nine businessmen for £1,000 per annum. One of these men was Sir Robert Mansell, a retired admiral, who by 1618 had bought out his partners and gained complete control of the industry, a monopoly which was to last until about 1640. During that time the glass-making industry was reorganized and glass-houses set up in many of the main coal-producing areas. Mansell received Government support for the suppression of all glass furnaces outside his control and he destroyed any that he found still working. Sir Robert is known to have had business links with Murano and it seems more than possible that he employed Venetians to produce mirror-glass in England. Part of his petition to Parliament reads:

'. . . and as concerning looking glasses Sir Robert Mansell hathe brought to such perfection, That he hathe chused our Natives to be fully instructed and taught therein, That the said glasses are now here made wch was never want to be in England beforetyme . . .'

Sir Robert Mansell's reign over the English glass industry came to an end in 1640 when Charles I was forced to summon Parliament for the first time in eleven years. Among the first decrees of this Parliament was to abolish the monopoly that Sir Robert had held for so long and that had meant such hardships to so many.

George Villiers, the second Duke of Buckingham, is another influential figure involved in seventeenth-century English glassmaking. Despite being described in a satirical poem of 1681 as '. . . chemist, fiddler, statesman and buffoon', he gathered glassmaking patents together, many belonging to others, and created a near monopoly. Perhaps the most famous of his enterprises was the Vauxhall Glass Works. The manager at Vauxhall was John Bellingham who had sold the Duke the secrets of mirror-glass making which he had acquired when working in both Haarlem and Amsterdam. John Evelyn, who had visited the glass-works, recorded in his diary for 19 September 1676, that he had seen '. . . looking-glasses far larger and better than any that come from Venice.' The term 'Vauxhall glass' is often used to describe any soft-coloured, shallow-bevelled, early eighteenth-century mirror plate, but there is no way of ascribing mirror plates to any particular glass-works. In 1664 the Worshipful Company of Glass-sellers and Looking-glass Makers was incorporated. In the same year importation was prohibited of 'Rough Glass-plates, or wrought into Looking-glass, spectacles, burning-glasses, Tubes or other Wrought glassplates', in an attempt to encourage domestic production and trade. By 1675 there were eighty-five members of the company including twenty mirror-glass grinders. There was a special reservation made in the Glass-sellers Charter of rights to one Thomas Tilson relating to 'christall glass and looking-glass plates'.

From early in the seventeenth century the raw materials of glass-making were dutyable. Barillia, the Spanish word for the ash required in glass-making, for example, was taxed in 1642 at the rate of £4 per 2 cwt barrel. In 1645 Oliver Cromwell 'ordered that an Excize of Twelve pence shall be laid upon every Twenty Shilling value of Glasse and Glasses of all sorts made within the Kingdom.' By 1695 'Fire glass and looking-glass plates' were dutyable at the rate of 20 per cent. It was not until 1698 and after numerous petitions from the Glass-Sellers Company that the duty was abolished.

The high cost of mirror glass made the owners of looking glasses careful and proud of them. The cost of replacement was such that old plates were often saved and re-silvered. Lady Verney wrote to her husband in 1648 to say that she had had the quicksilver renewed on a large mirror plate and the frame re-gilded. The mirrors in the Verney household (Claydon House, Buckinghamshire) must have been under some discussion as she also wrote 'here is a great looking glass . . . your sisters have threatened if they (the Steward and "Mrs Francis") would not lett them have itt to bring a troupe of horse to break down the walls where t'was.' By 1674 Lady Clayton, wife of the Warden of Merton College, Oxford bought a 'very large looking glass' at a cost of £10, but it was not large enough to see the whole of herself in, but only 'her ugly face and body to the middle'.

The size of mirror plates was the main point of competition between the glass factories. The Vauxhall Glass-Works advertised on 13 February 1700,

> 'large looking glass Plates, the like never made in England before, both for size and goodness, are now made at the old Glass House at Foxhall, known by the name of the Duke of Buckingham's House, where all persons may be furnished with rough plates from the smallest sizes to those of six foot in length, and proportionable breadth, at reasonable rates'.

Their great rival, the Bear Garden Glass-House at Southwick, were advertising two years later 'At the Bear Garden Glass-House are Looking Glass Plates, Blown from the smallest size upwards to 90 inches, with proportionable breadth, of lively colours, free from Veins and foulness, incident to large Plates that have been hitherto sold'. If one assumes that advertisements usually endeavour to give the best possible account of the merchandise then within two years, advances had permitted the Bear Garden Glass-works to increase the size of plates by some 30 in. The reference to 'free from Veins and foulness' would indicate that they had overcome the problems of coal firing reacting with the lead flux.

Competition between glass-houses was intense. In 1705 John Gumley, a prominent cabinet-maker entered into partnership with a group of merchants and set up a glass-house at Lambeth. The owners of the Bear Garden Glass-house attempted to obtain an order to close Gumley's factory. Heated exchanges followed until finally, in 1707, the Bill for the suppression of all new glass-houses was defeated. Gumley made a fortune from his business of glass-making and cabinet-making and his daughter married into the aristocracy.

The duty on glass, which was abolished in 1698, was reintroduced in 1745 at the rate of 9s 4d per cwt of ordinary glass and 2s 4d per cwt of green bottle glass. The difficulty in assessing the weight of materials, rather than the glass produced, required the attendance of an Excise officer at every glass-house. In 1784 each glass-house was licenced at the rate of £10 per annum. The considerable opposition to the duty led to the following notice in *The Gentleman's Magazine* in March 1746 'Saturday 29 Many of the glass-houses of which there are but 40 in the Kingdom have discontinued working'. Instead of the Government responding favourably to these protests they continued the tax and then doubled it in 1777 to raise funds for the war in America. In the *Plate Glass Book* by the 'Glass House Clerk', first published in 1757, a sheet of finished mirror measuring 60×42½ in cost £81. 17s excluding the retailer's profit. This price was made up as follows:

Cost of rough plate	£37. 10. 0
Excise duties	£18. 15. 0
Grinding	£ 7. 1 2. 8
Polishing	£ 7. 12. 8
Silvering	£ 7. 12. 8
Diamond-cutting	£ 2 . 14. 0

Compare this to figure of £450 for French mirror glass measuring 9 ft 6 in×5 ft 10 in, including the profit factor in Chippendale's workshop in 1775.

In 1773 a company (The British Cast Plate Glass Manufacturers), was formed to exploit the production of plate glass. Casting of plate glass had been practised in England before this date; as early as 1691 Robert Hooke and Christopher Dodsworth had been granted a licence 'to exercise and put in practice the new invention of casting plate glass, particularly looking-glass plates'. The *Dictionarium Polygraphicum* of 1735 states that 'the method of running and casting large looking glass plates has been considerably improv'd by our workmen in England . . . we cast all kinds of borders, mouldings etc.' John Bowles, who with John Dawson ran the Vauxhall Glass-Works throughout the eighteenth century with great success, gave evidence to the committee at the time of the incorporation of The Plate Glass Makers and said Vauxhall had experimented in casting but the apparatus had long since been destroyed. The majority of plate glass used in England at this time was being imported from Saint Gobain in Picardy where it was made by the casting method developed by Bernard Perrot in 1687 (see p. 23). Because the initial investment amounted to some £50,000 the proprietors sought incorporation by Act of Parliament to secure limited liability. Permission was granted, and The British Cast Plate Glass Manufactures was incorporated with works at Albion Place Southwark, London and at Ravenhead, St Helens Lancashire with production rights for twenty one years. The Company was given permission to raise a joint stock of £40,000 in £500 shares and to raise a further £20,000 if three quarters of the proprietors agreed. The Casting Hall at Ravenshead was the largest industrial building of the period, 113 yd long and 50 yd wide, when glass was first cast there in 1776.

The production of cast plate glass was under the control of Jean Baptiste François Graux de la Bruyère who was born at St Gobain in 1739. A local St Helens man, Richard Bright, wrote at the time:

> 'The great plate Glass manufactory which is to be established in this country is begun and they hope to be ready to work in about 28 months. There is in my opinion a very great danger of its not succeeding. They have but one man who knows any thing of the Secret. He is a foreigner, and if I am not misinformed the only proof they have of his ability is his own word. I wish they may not be deceived'.

In a description of Lord Bute's house at the time Lady Mary Cook wrote in her diary:

> 'Fine glasses there are only in one of the drawing-rooms, the rest are to be brought here, as soon as the new project for casting larger plates here than they do at Paris is brought to perfection.'

This new enterprise was beset with problems from the start. The French glass makers were not used to coal fuel which caused black drops of soot to fall into the pots; there was also a high proportion of waste to saleable glass, and the additional problems posed by the duty on glass. This tax had already been doubled in 1777 and was increased in 1781 by a further 5 per cent. The company operated at a loss; during the period 1780–83 income was only £40,000 and expenditure £44,000, of which a quarter was duty. The Parliamentary Committee set up to investigate the company advised that plate glass ought to be taxed on the weight of glass after it was squared and not on the weight of melted raw materials. In 1878 a tax of 1s $5\frac{1}{2}$d per sq ft was levied on imported French plate and English plate was taxed as suggested. Two years after production recommenced, in 1789 a Boulton and Watt steam engine was installed to drive the polishing machinery. By 1790 an agreement was reached with brothers George and Mathew Kemp of London, who 'possessed of a valuable Secret or Invention for making an constructing Mills and Machines for grinding and Polishing Plate Glass . . .' The process came into use in 1792 at the same time as Robert Sherbourne was appointed manager. The original capital had long since been used up, as well as a further £60,000 that had been raised in loans. In 1794 the twenty-one year old charter of incorporation expired, limited liability ended, and the creditors demanded their money. An application was made to the House of Commons for a renewed charter of incorporation. Although the bill was passed it did not reach the Statute Book and the business was sold to a Londoner, Thomas Oakes, for £105,000. He and the original proprietors continued as an unincorporated company until 1798 when a further bill was successful and the concern became The British Plate Glass Company. Robert Sherbourne introduced capped melting pots, which prevented furnace soot falling and spotting the glass. He also made considerable savings, controlled wastage and introduced the production of convex and concave mirror plates.

The company prospered and by 1801 was producing more than 7,000 plates a year, an output that encouraged the grateful directors to raise Sherbourne's salary to £1,000 per year by 1815. His successor was Frederick Fincham, the owner of a small glass works in Manchester. He introduced further economies and had reduced production costs 20 per cent by 1839 and increased production to 5,000 square ft of rough glass per week. By this time the company's Ravenhead Works was producing the most brilliant and hardest glass in England.

Competition came from The London and Manchester Plate Glass Company which, in 1855, claimed to be the largest in England. The increase in production was in part due to the repeal of the duty on glass in 1845 and a reduction in costs brought about by competition. A sheet of glass measuring 50×40 in, which in 1770 had cost over £60 could be bought for as little as 4 gns by 1865. Other small firms produced flat glass, one such was Chance Brothers in Smethwick. From 1848 until his death in 1884, the firm enjoyed the services of George Bontemps, a Frenchman and author of *Guide du Verrier* published in 1868. In 1861 the firm installed a Siemens Wanne tank furnace (see p. 26). Mirror-glass was also produced in London; there were two large firms engaged in the business, Charles Nosotti's in Oxford Street and George Sims in Aldersgate Street; the latter began silvering mirrors for the glass trade and is recorded as having silvered more than eleven acres of glass each year in the mid-1860s. Nosotti, from Milan, calling himself a carver and gilder, had settled in Westminster in 1831 and his firm was known as a 'looking glass and frame manufactory'. In addition to mirrors, the firm produced a wide range of furniture including a cabinet made for the Countess Waldegrave for Strawberry Hill and shown at the 1862 Exhibition.

Technological developments in grinding, smoothing and polishing came with the advance of the century and allowed English glass production to compete with those of Europe, especially German, French and Belgian. America, which had traditionally relied on Europe and England in particular, had started its own flat glass production and the loss of much of this market had a deep effect. The boom years declined with a further reduction of exports to America caused by the McKinley Tariff of 1890, prices fell 40 per cent between 1891 and 1893. The glass industry in England almost ceased, the only plate glass manufacturers to survive were Pilkington Brothers, a limited company since 1894 with share capital of £800,000. They were able to continue because they did not depend totally on the plate glass production for their profits. In 1901 Pilkington Brothers purchased the Ravenhead Works for £95,000.

France

Forests have in the past been a valuable resource for landowners; trees supplied the fundamental necessities of house-building and ship-building as well as fuel and indirectly provided a source of food and employment. The beechwood and oak forests of France were also ideally suitable for the production of glass, especially those forests in Eastern France and the forest of La Thiérache in particular.

Archaeological evidence shows extensive Roman glass-making in France, which continued after the decline of the Roman Empire. And despite the frivolous-sounding fact that in 1581 the French guild of mirror-makers joined with the guild of toy-makers, the production of glass and mirrors remained a major concern for the French.

In Lorraine, around the village of Darney, was an area that soon became a centre for the production of flat glass. There was timber in abundance, the finest sand, ferns that could be burnt to provide the 'salt' (flux) and it was well served by a developed road and river network for transport. The French glass-makers leased their land from the King who was represented by the Départment des Eaux et Forêts which was first established in 1319. The glass-makers paid the landlord a yearly rent or 'cens' in French, which allowed them to live, build houses and furnaces, cut timber and hunt.

It was in the forest of La Thiérache that Louis XIV installed his Manufacture Royale des Glaces in 1692 among the ruins of the old abbey at Saint Gobain. The original business on this site had been Abraham Thevant's 'Grande Glaces Compagnies' (founded in 1685), where mirror-glass was produced which was later ground and polished in Paris. The combined new glass-works was under the direction of François Plastier. Before the different companies were amalgamated into the Manufacture Royale des Glaces, the King had granted the privilege of glass-making to Nicolas du Noyer. Du Noyer employed two hundred workers at his glass-house in the Faubourg Saint-Antoine and allowed the King a discount of 30 per cent. Further towards the centre of France on the River Loire at Orléans the Duc Philipe of Orléans, the brother of Louis XIV, became interested in glass-making late in the seventeenth century. He patronized Jean Castello from the famous Altare family who, with his nephew Bernardo Perrotto, set up business in Orléans in 1662.

Bernard Perrot (as Perrotto became known in France), was responsible for the important invention of forming glass into panels by casting. He presented his idea to the newly founded Académie des Sciences on 2 April 1687, and in September 1688 the Académie awarded him the sole rights to the production of cast glass. In 1698 a visiting Englishman, Dr Martin Lister, recorded that:

> 'The Glass-house out of the Gate of St Antoine well deserves seeing: but I did lament the Fondery was no longer there, but removed to Cherborne in Normandy for cheapness of fuel. Tis certainly a most considerable addition to the Glass-making. For I saw here one Looking-glass foiled and finisht, 88 inches long, and 48 inches broad; and yet but one quarter of an inch thick. This I think could never be effected by the Blast of any Man; but I suppose to be run or cast upon sand as Lead is, which yet, I confess, the toughness of Glass Mettal makes very much against.'

The use of mirrors as lavish interior decoration was encouraged by Louis XIV and his Chief Minister, Jean-Baptiste Colbert who were eager to improve domestic French flat-glass production.

One of the earliest interiors using mirrors in France is the oval room at the Château des Maison built by François Mansart *c.* 1650. The fashion for incorporating mirrors into the interior included the addition of imported, often smaller, Venetian mirror-plates into the wall panelling above the fireplace. In 1697 a Swedish architect, Nicodemus Tessin the younger was advising Countess Piper on decorating her house in the latest French style:

> 'for the chimneypieces I would make them with mirrors . . . from top to bottom, that is the taste that prevails here and which is all the more justified since with two or four candles a room, on account of the reflection, is lighter and more cheerfull than another with twelve.'

To cover large areas of wall with mirror glass it ws necessary to use relatively small panels of glass which were abutted and held in place by studs with large heads overlapping at the corners. A contemporary explanation stated 'with panes of glass of such a size as the expenditure you have in mind will permit, all the panes being without bevelled edges, neatly juxtaposed so as to make as it were a single large glass'. It must have seemed incredible to people in the seventeenth century that one should be able to see the whole of oneself in a mirror. Lady Ciela Fiennes recorded in her diary after a visit to a house in Chippenham, Wiltshire seeing '4 pannells of glass in length and 3 in breadth set together in the Wainscoate' and noted that the effect 'shows one from top to toe.'

By 1672 France was capable of producing all the mirror-glass required for domestic use and imported mirrors were prohibited. Perrot's innovation now meant that it was possible to make finer, larger plates that were suitable for polishing and grinding, however, the Manufacture Royale des Glaces de France, directed by François Plastier and under the King's protection, also began the production of cast glass for mirrors in excess of 40 by 60 in and called 'grand glaces'. The result was that Perrot was denied his rights to glass production and was granted an annual pension of 1,000 livres.

It would be tempting to suppose that the King encouraged the flat glass production at the Manufacture Royale to supply the mirrors required for, perhaps, the greatest of all mirrored interiors, the Galerie des Glaces at Versailles. As the Manufacture Royale was not founded until 1688 in the Faubourg Saint-Germain, moving in 1692 to Saint Gobain, it cannot have made mirrors for the Galerie des Glaces which was modelled between 1678 and 1684.

France's prominence in the production of fine quality mirror glass of considerable size explains why many eighteenth-century English cabinet-makers looked to France for their supply. Thomas Chippendale was able to show Thomas Mouat, a friend of his partner James Rannie, who visited their cabinet-making premises in 1775: '3 mirrors of the vast size of 9½ feet long by 5 ft 10 inches broard from France, each of which sells for £450 str unframed.' Chippendale was contracted to deliver ten sheets of 'French plate glass in London silv'd and Ready to be put up' for Kenwood House in 1769 for a sum of £340. Another well known cabinet-maker John Linnell wrote in December 1770, that he had £600 worth of French glass at the Customs House awaiting payment of duty. By 1770 it has been estimated that between £60,000 and £100,000 worth of glass was being imported into England officially. There was a brisk trade in illicit imports including French furniture and fabrics as well as glass, many items brought in under the protection of the diplomatic bag. Parliament was petitioned in 1772 and again in 1773 and heard evidence against the well-known cabinet-maker John Cobb and others who were guilty of this malpractice. James Christie gave evidence to the committee in 1773 and said that he believed 'not one Third of the Quantity that is imported pays Duty; being in general smuggled; and a Kind of trading Company has been formed here for that Purpose'. The import of mirror glass to England was halted almost at once when Lord North, the English Chancellor, imposed a tax on imported glass in 1777. This tax, combined with the British Cast Plate Glass Manufacturers' attempts to produce plate glass that was cast in the same way as the French, greatly reduced the French flat glass production to a domestic market.

By about 1830 crown glass had been superseded by cylinder glass that was blown. This was possibly achieved by digging deeper pits with taller platforms, from which

fig 8 Flinging 'cannons' of glass in Belgium during the nineteenth century; pits of an increasing depth were dug to permit the creation of larger cannons

the blown glass could be flung to extend the cylinders. Belgian glass-workers had developed 'cannons' as they called the cylinders, to extend some 47 in by 1870. Val-Saint Lambert was set up as a glass-house in 1825. Situated a short distance outside Liege, it began with eleven glass blowers producing flat glass from two furnaces. Later, under the guidance of a French glass-maker Aime-Gabriel D'Aartigues, who brought resources and skill from his own factory at Voneche, the glass works flourished. In 1829 the enterprise employed a work-force of 400, by 1879 that number had risen to 2,800. Cast glass was still being made by the traditional methods at Saint Gobain and by 1804 they were producing sheets of 8×5½ ft and by 1899 huge sheets measuring 26½×13½ ft.

The production of glass was greatly assisted during the nineteenth century by the development, by 1860, of the Wanne, a tank furnace inside which the raw materials were fed in a continuous process and from which glass flowed constantly. It was developed by Hans Siemens from Dresden, the brother of Karl Wilhelm and Frederich Siemens who invented this gas heated system for founding steel. These large sheets of glass were, by about 1840, backed with the new method of silvering that had been developed by a German scientist Justus von Liebig. Prior to this date it had been necessary to hammer out a sheet of metal foil and fix it to the glass with mercury. Liebig's process allowed a thin film of real silver to be deposited on the glass (see p. 28). As a result, the nineteenth century in France saw, along with most European countries, an enormous increase in the use of mirror glass. Very large sheets were used as panelling in many ballrooms, while small mirrors were fitted into wardrobes and sideboards in salons and consoles, and pier tables were designed with mirrors both above and below them.

Germany

Germany and the German-speaking countries to the East of the Rhine were part of the split of glass-making traditions based on the need for fuel and a flux. The Northern European glass-makers relied upon the heavily forested areas for their fuel and used burnt ferns for their flux. The timber in these areas, usually coniferous, was cut into big logs and the cut wood stacked in rows around the glass-house with 'streets' running between them. It was forbidden for anyone to run about among the stacks with an open flame.

Glass-making in this part of Europe enjoys a long tradition probably reaching back to Roman times which had, in addition to glass-making, assisted the national economy by clearing the trees for agriculture. In these areas the landlord was probably a local prince from whom agreements were obtained. In Germany, a 'Zins', a yearly rent, was paid to the 'Landgraf', 'Herzog' or 'Kurfürst'. In 1564 the Duke of Saxony licenced one Hans Breitenbach to erect a glass-house in an isolated area of woodland to use up the 'alte nauhe Baüme' or rough old trees, for a period of ten years. With the spread of immigrant Venetian glass-makers towards the north, the forest glass industry was able to produce a better, purer product including window glass and probably mirror glass. One of the earliest glass-houses to be set up with Italian workmen was the glass-house at Innsbruck. The Archduke Ferdinand, 1520–95, was Regent of both Bohemia and of the Tyrol and lived in Innsbruck. The Hofglashütte at Innsbruck was the Duke's hobby. He gave free housing, food and fuel to Venetian glass-workers on condition that he should have priority over all of their production for his Schloss Ambras. Earlier, in the fourteenth century, the glass-makers of Nürnberg developed, and carefully guarded, a form of mirror made from a glass bubble that was cut and backed with polished metal or foil. These distinctive mirrors were also produced in Flanders and appear in the paintings of the period.

Some researchers credit Flemish glass-workers with the invention of the tin-mercury method of mirror making; a process that is reputed to have been passed on to the Italian glass-makers who perfected it. There seems little doubt that the fame of German and Flemish mirror-makers of the sixteenth century was widespread and their products ousted the necessity for mirrors made from polished metal. The numerous German States that had had their sovereignty guaranteed by the Peace of Westphalia in 1648 were to enjoy peace and stability for nearly 150 years. The life at the courts of these Kleinstaaten was centred around the Residenze, or ruler's palace, and in many states included the patronage of a glass-house. Frederick Wilhelm (1620–88), the Elector of Brandenberg, who was responsible for the great State of Prussia and its military might, started a glass-house near Potsdam at Drewitz in 1674. His interest in glass-making was such that he had his own furnace for the production of crystal and mirror glass. He also patronized Johann Kunckel (1630–1703), a scientist and glass-maker, the son of the glass-house master at Rendsburg in the north of Germany. He spent ten years at Drewitz developing ruby glass and working on various books on glass.

The great craftsmen of Germany, during the seventeenth century, produced highly decorative original frames for mirrors that employed many different materials. The gold and silversmiths of Augsburg produced lasting frames delicately worked in the finest of materials. The frame-makers of Dresden were famed for their work with amber; while ivory was employed in Munich, and glass, cut and shaped, was itself used by the Bohemians. These precious materials were used to protect what by then was a more usual, but which had only years before been a more valuable and highly prized commodity than any of them. Eighteenth century glass-makers produced mirror glass for the growing home market and may well have also imported larger plates from France and occasionally from Italy, when required. Germany, in common with most European countries during the eighteenth century, was slavish in its devotion to fashion, the Baroque and then the Rococo was followed by the Neo-Classical. All these styles required mirrors for use and effect, many of them were of considerable size for overmantels and pier walls. It is interesting that some that have retained their original mirror plates have needed two and sometimes three sheets of glass to achieve the height or width of the frame. There is no doubt that the French were able to produce large plates by the method of casting developed by Bernard Perrot in 1688, but the cost was very high. It may well be that the cost was a factor when German frames are fitted with two or more plates that were probably produced more cheaply by one of the numerous German 'spiegelfabriken' (glass factories). The Baroque and Rococo style, with swirling carved giltwood, was used both for mirror frames and for the panelling to rooms. The great palaces of Bavaria, built during the first half of the eighteenth century, were thought not to be complete unless they contained at least one mirrored room.

Inspired by the Galerie des Glaces at Versailles, a number of German palaces combined the effect of Chinese porcelain set against mirrored walls. The Charlottenburg, built in 1706, has walls covered with Chinese porcelain plates and vases displayed on brackets set into mirror-lined walls. During the nineteenth century, German glass-making was, like all others, to benefit from technical advances, but two German developments in particular were to have international benefits. The first was in 1835 when a scientist, Justus von Liebig, invented a new method of backing mirrors by depositing a thin film of real silver instead of, as before, laboriously hammering out sheet metal foil and fixing it to the glass with mercury, a process that was both time-consuming and very dangerous. It was not until 1857, however, that a Frenchman, François Petit-Jean, improved the process by means of the action of reducing agents such as formaldehyde or dextrose on aqueous solutions of silver. The second was the invention of the previously mentioned Wanne, or tank furnace. It was developed in 1860 by Hans Siemens for glass-making, from a furnace invented by his brothers, Karl Wilhelm and Friedrich for the founding of steel. The regenerative heating system worked on gas and assumed a very high temperature which could be closely controlled. By 1870 it was in common use throughout Europe for the production of flat glass.

Italy

Geographical divisions, based on technical traditions, divided Italy, and in particular Venice, from the rest of Europe after the break-up of the Roman Empire. Glass-making is known to have been carried out in Venice from the end of the tenth century, there is documentary evidence of glass-making from the thirteenth century and examples from the fifteenth century. By 1268 the 'fiolari' (makers of sheets of glass in Venice) had organized themselves into a guild with their own written rules. About a quarter of a century later the Grand Council of Venice had encouraged all Venetian glass-houses to move to the island of Murano where the risks of fire were reduced. The rules laid out by the Glass Maker Capitolare (a body set up by the Republic of Venice and the craftsmen to oversee the industry in 1271), limited working to seven months of the year – January to August – the remainder of the year was used to keep the accounts and carry out repairs. It also stated that the furnaces were to be fired with willow or alder and that two watches were to be kept every twenty-four hours. The Capitolare protected and organized the industry for more than five centuries, maintaining standards and upholding rules, as well as granting rights to the individual. One such right was granted in 1507 to the brothers Dal Gallo for the production of crystal glass mirrors 'cossa preciosa et singular', a method which they had invented.

Between 1450 and 1460 the glass-makers of Murano developed a colourless glass which they named 'cristallo'. The traditional method of making flat glass from cylinders of blown glass backed with metal foil was in use until the second half of the seventeenth century when the French developed a new casting process. The frames for these mirrors were made by 'specchieri' (mirror-makers) in Venice itself. Until the start of the second half of the seventeenth century Venetian mirror-glass had found its way, via Venice's trade links, to most European countries and was considered to be the best. The spread of technical knowledge to other countries by immigrant Italian glass-workers led to mirror-glass production in many of the countries that had for so long relied on Venetian exports. Glass-making in Venice during the eighteenth and nineteenth centuries turned to a domestic market which catered for the ruling and bourgeoise classes and satisfied the growing tourist trade. The inhabitants were content to live securely and pleasantly, in their palaces or villas, without having to risk their fortunes at sea as traders as they had done so successfully in the past. In the *Travels of a Frenchman in Italy, 1765–66*, there is a reference to the glass-houses of Murano, explaining how the houses were organized and describing the processes involved (see p. 257).

A market developed for glass, chandeliers and mirrors with intricate glass frames of fantasy as well as the particularly Italian fashion for engraved mirror glass. The short renaissance during the eighteenth century was brought about by Giuseppe Briati who developed the glass chandelier. The number of people in the glass-making industry had, by 1773, declined at Murano to 383, one-tenth of what it had been in its heyday. In 1806 all the guilds of Venice, including that of the glass-makers of Murano, were formally dissolved.

Scandinavia

There is authenticated evidence of glassmaking in Scandinavia from *c.* 1550. Remains of a cluster of forest glass-works have been found in Denmark around Vendsyssel in northern Jutland and Småland in Sweden. The Vendsyssel area is thought to have produced flat glass, probably for windows but not for mirrors. The manor house of Voergard, built by Lady Ingeborg Skeel between 1586 and 1591, was probably glazed from this glass-works and may even have been the reason why the enterprize was started. Småland was to become an important glass producing area with the foundation of the Kosta factory there in 1742. The industries of glass-making, iron smelting and potteries often worked together as in the case of Småland where they all relied on the same fuel as well as water (for power), and shared the need of outlets for their products. There was also a cross-fertilization of technical information.

By the seventeenth century Italian and German glass-makers had arrived in Scandinavia. The Germans came from the Hesse region, the Italians from Venice and other cities in north eastern Italy. Despite the tight controls (even threats of death), Venetian glass-makers travelled north through Europe, tempted by financial gain and adventure, as well as the prospect of working for new masters outside the restrictions of Venice and Murano. Glass, 'à la façon de venise' was very much in demand in Northern Europe by the wealthy, fashionable class, both for use and for display. Among the itinerant groups of glass makers of between two and six workers, some with wives and children, that arrived in Scandinavia was Giacomo Bernardini Scapitta. Scapitta was an Italian monk as well as a glass-maker who arrived in Sweden in 1676 by way of France, Holland and Germany. His fellow travellers included a Frenchman he had met in Amsterdam and a chemist's apprentice he met in Osnabrüch. The demand for glass-makers and their skills was such that he and his band were welcomed in

Stockholm and a glass-house was begun at Kungsholm. Two years later he was found to be a charlatan as well as dishonest and fled to England.

The factory that had been set up in Stockholm in 1640 by Melchior Jung was transferred by his son to Nystad (Savonlinna) in Finland. Finland was linked to Sweden by a political union that lasted from 1157 until 1809. The Nystad glass-works did not prosper and larger, successful enterprises were begun at Avik in 1748, Mariedal in 1779, Thorsnas in 1791, Nyby in 1783 and Notsjo in 1793. The increase in Scandinavia's affluence after 1666 is reflected in the general increase in glass production. After the Great Fire of London in 1666 the rebuilding of the City required vast quantities of timber which was supplied, in the main, by Norway and Sweden. Norway and Denmark were joined in 1397 and remained so until 1814; so it followed that Denmark prospered at the same time.

Iron ore as well as timber were exported from Scandinavia to England during the eighteenth and nineteenth centuries, both helping to fuel the vast growth in England's economy. Between 1741 and 1762 large glass-making factories were set up; Hurdals Verk, for the production of flat glass, was begun in 1755 and from 1760 until 1803 it was protected against competition by a ban on imports. The Kungsholm glass-house in Stockholm that Scapitta had been welcomed to, which was founded in 1676, mainly produced table glass rather than flat glass. While this factory finally closed in 1815, the first years of the nineteenth century saw the foundation of a new glass-works at Reijimyre in Ostergotland in 1810 and together with Kosta in Småland they led the field. During the middle years of the nineteenth century, however, workers from the factory at Kosta left in large numbers to set up in business for themselves. The manager of Kosta wrote in 1866 'it has become quite a mania among glassblowers to become their own employers.'

Flat glass production in Denmark was centred at Holmegaard in Seeland (founded in 1825), where they used local peat for fuel. The Hurdals Verk factory in Norway that was begun in 1735 for flat glass production, was reorganized after the end of the state monopoly in 1803 by the Burg Family and in 1888 a Siemens furnace was installed using a regenerative gas heating system. The Nuutajarvii (Notsjo) glassworks in Finland founded in 1793 was taken over by Adolf Torngren in 1849. In 1857 a group of Belgiums arrived to continue and eventually expand the flat glass production. Here too a Siemens Wanne furnace had been installed by 1876, which increased production and facilitated export to Russia.

Spain and Portugal

One of the main ingredients of glass is the 'salt' (flux) added to assist the melting process. Spanish 'Barilla' from Alicante gained a great reputation with European glass-makers, especially the Venetians. This alkali or flux was derived from the ashes of plants growing on the salt marshes.

James Howell wrote a letter dated 27 March 1621 describing how Barilla was made:

> 'I am now . . . come to Allicant the chief Rendezvous I aimed at in Spain, for I am to send hence a Commodity called Barrillia, to Sir Robert Mansel for making of Crystal Glass . . . This Barrillia is a

> strange kind of Vegetable, and it grows no where upon the Surface upon the Earth in that Perfection, as here: . . . It grows thus, It is around thick earthy Shrub that bears Berries like Barberries, betwixt blue and green; it lies close to the Ground and when it is ripe they dig it up by the Roots, and put it together in Cocks, where they leave it to dry many Days like Hay; then they make a Pit of a Fathon deep in the Earth, and with an Instrument like one of our Prongs, they take the Tuffs and put fire to them, and when the Flame comes to the Berries, they melt and disolve into an Azure Liquor and fall down into the Pit til it be full; then they dam it up, and some Days after they open it and find this Barrillia Juice turned to a blue Stone, so hard, that it is scarce malleable; it is sold at one hundred Crowns a Tun . . .'

Glass-making was probably brought to Spain by the Romans who also imported finished glass from their other colonies. In common with so many European countries Spain attracted itinerant glass-makers both from Northern Europe and from Venice. Glass factories were established in areas with suitable raw materials, a copious fuel supply and transportation for the finished products. It took time, however, for the Spanish to produce flat glass for windows and mirrors; during the early years of the eighteenth century a Catalan, Pedro Fronvila even developed an alternative method for making mirrors by pouring molten glass on to a brass table and polishing it with seventeen polishers. But it was not until 1728, when the Royal glass factory was founded that flat glass was produced in any quantity and quality. A Catalan glass worker named Ventura Sit started a glass works at San Ildefonso near the palace of La Granja. King Philip V and Queen Isobel Farnese encouraged Sit to produce larger plates of glass suitable for mirrors which were to be made only for the Royal palaces. In 1786 J. Townsend wrote in his *A Journey Through Spain* (covering the years 1786–7):

> 'The glass manufacturer is here carried to a degree of perfection unknown in England. The largest mirrors . . . are designed wholly for the Royal palaces, and for presents from the King. Yet, even for such purposes it is ill-placed, and proves a devouring monster in a country where provisions are dear, fewel scarce, and carriage exceedingly expensive.'

Flat glass production within the San Ildefonso glass works was under the control of John Dowling, an Irish engineer, who had invented a hydraulic polishing machine. During his travels in 1772–3, R. Twiss wrote in *Travels Through Portugal and Spain* of a visit to the factory in 1772:

> 'I called on Mr John Dowling, an Irishman . . . This Gentleman was so kind as to accompany me during my stay here. We first visited the Royal fabric for plate glass . . . These plates are not made for sale, but only for the King's use . . . Mr Dowling has likewise erected a machine which polishes 48 plates of glass at a time.'

In 1783 Dowling was imprisoned and so his association with the glass-works ends. Shortly after Dowling's departure the Marquis de Langle wrote in 1785 about the processes of glassmaking. Of the twenty annealing ovens he said:

> 'into which the glasses still red-hot are conveyed, where they remain

> hermetically enclosed for the space of fifteen to twenty-five days, until they gradually cool. All those that are cracked, or have any imperfections are cut for hand mirrors, window panes or glasses for carriages.'

After the cooling process the plates were ground by rubbing one plate against another using different types of sand as an abrasive. Finally, the lengthy polishing process required emery from a quarry near Toledo, the glass was rubbed by hand and the polishing finished by machine using a substance called *almagro*, a reddish earth. Despite attempts to use mechanical polishers and grinders it took one man approximately two months to grind a mirror and a further ten days for the polishing.

The Royal Glass Factory not only produced flat glass but table glass, engraved glass and chandeliers. Its fame spread throughout Europe and attracted many foreign workmen, many from France and some from as far away as Sweden. Throughout the reigns of Charles III (1759–88) and Charles IV (1788–1808), the glass works struggled to survive. The company had a retail shop in Madrid where the polished mirror-plates were finally quicksilvered and chandeliers assembled. The Madrid shop was found to be too expensive as the cost of any damage in transit from the factory had to be borne by the perfect pieces. A number of schemes were implemented to make the factory pay, including a decree in 1762 granting the exclusive rights to sell glass in Madrid and within twenty leagues around the factory. But attempts to sell the glass in America failed.

The nineteenth century began badly for Spain with the double abdication of Charles IV and his son Ferdinand in 1808. The victorious Napoleon Bonaparte installed Joseph Bonaparte on the throne and he reigned for the next five years. On 23 September 1809, the King made a public decree ending the royal patronage of the San Ildefonso glass factory. 'Desirous of opening new ways toward national prosperity' he offered the Real Fábrica de Cristales for sale. In 1814, when the rightful King Ferdinand VII resumed the throne the factory was reinstated. From 1829 and throughout the rest of the century the San Ildefonso factory experienced mixed fortunes once in private hands.

America

Glass-making was first begun in America as early as the autumn of 1608. The London Company erected a glass-house in Jamestown Virginia financed by a joint-stock company hoping to make large profits by exporting glass back into England. England was at this time in the middle of a dramatic fuel crisis as timber resources were being used up at a furious rate before the industry turned to coal-firing. A decree of 1623 in England, conferring the rights to make glass to Sir Robert Mansell, insisted that he could only use 'sea-coal', pit-coal or any other fuel whatsoever not being timber or wood'. As all the basic raw materials were available in the New World, including an abundance of timber for fuel, the London Company's venture seemed a sound one. By 1608 a glass furnace had begun in 'woods mere a myle from Iames Towne' but the enterprise failed in 1609 and by 1617 it had 'long since fallen into decay'.

In 1621 a second attempt was made to establish a glass-works in Jamestown. This time six Italian glass-makers were brought from Europe with the intention of making 'all manner of Beads and Glass', the beads were to be used to trade with the Red Indians. Despite widespread belief followed by archaeological activity, it seems that no beads were actually made at Jamestown. After careful planning and investment a series of disasters and mishaps led to the glass-house being abandoned in 1625. The demand for window glass and bottles was, in the main, satisfied by imports from England together with table glass and mirrors, despite several attempts to establish glass-houses in Salem in 1641 and New Amsterdam in 1645.

The first successful glass-house in America to have continuous production for more than a generation was founded by Caspar Wistar (1696–1752) in New Jersey in 1739. Wistar, a successful brass-button manufacturer, was an entrepreneur who had capital to invest. He imported four glass-makers from Rotterdam in 1738. The agreement with these men, Simon Kneismeir, Caspar Halter, John Martin Halter and Johan William Wentzell, was that they would share in the profits of the factory and pass on their skills to the men designated by Wistar. This, and other early glass factories like that of Henry William Stiegel (1739–85) from Cologne who had settled in Pennsylvania, were concerned with the production of window glass and bottles as a basic business with a sideline in rather crude attempts at making table glass to satisfy local demand. This production of table glass improved along with that of window glass, but it seems that mirror-glass continued to be imported together with the more elaborate table-ware throughout the eighteenth and into the nineteenth centuries.

There is, however, one candidate for the production of mirror-glass in America during the eighteenth century in John Frederick Amelung. Amelung, like Wistar and Stiegel, was a German, who, with capital of £10,000, began a glass-works near Fredrick, Maryland. He was producing window glass as well as green and 'white hollow ware' by 1787 with the assistance of the sixty-eight glassworkers he brought with him from Germany. In 1802 the Chelmsford Glass Works, a subsidiary of the Boston Crown Glass Manufactory, was established in Massachusetts for the production of broad or sheet glass made by the cylinder process. The manufacturing of this sheet glass into mirror plates would have been a relatively simple process having first achieved the smooth surface.

During the nineteenth century Pittsburg became one of the most important centres of glass production in America based on the coal industry and its strategic position on the confluence of three major rivers. A British visitor to Pittsburg in 1818 remarked that the town had a smoky appearance and referred to it as 'the Birmingham of America'. By 1893 America had eight plate-glass manufactories in full production, their growth encouraged by the imposition, in 1890, of the McKinley Tariff on imported glass.

Techniques

Carving and gilding

Men have toiled and died for gold; wars have been waged for it; it has inspired crimes of the deepest dye. 'To what dost thou not compel the minds of mortals, accursed greed for gold?' asked Virgil. Described in 1688 by Stalker & Parker as 'That darling-metal, which we foolish Mortals covet, nay almost adore, is certainly too pretious to be lavishly consumed, and unprofitably puff'd away.' On the other hand, the search for gold has been one of the great driving forces behind the spread of civilization. Since its first chance discovery, gold has been a measure of wealth, not only of individuals, but of religions and of nations.

The origin of the art of embellishing objects with gold leaf is lost in the mists of time. As early as 1700 B.C. it had been discovered that gold could be beaten into thin sheets and that the leaves of gold produced would adhere to a smooth plaster surface. Gold leaf was used by the Egyptians and the Phoenicians, and its use in ancient China is also documented.

Gold has many virtues. Not only is it one of the most valuable of all metals, but it is chemically inert and does not tarnish, giving it a long-lasting brilliance. Its malleability allows it to be beaten into leaves that are so thin that, when placed between two fingers, they dissolve into the pores of the skin. The average leaf produced today measures about 3⅜ sq in but it is approximately 1/250,000 of an inch (1 micron) thick.

fig 9 The four stages of gliding – draughtmanship – carving – gessoing – gliding

Since the Middle Ages, two distinct methods of overlaying wood with gold leaf have been used in Europe: water gilding and oil gilding. Oil gilding, the cheaper and simpler, was more durable and less vulnerable to dampness, but could not burnish and did not give the same lustre as water gilding. Cenino Cennini in his *Il libro dell'Arte* published in 1437, gives an account of the two methods of gilding. Over two centuries later, in 1688, Stalker and Parker in their *Treatise on Japanning and Varnishing* describe the processes showing the same basic principles being employed.

To produce gold leaf for use in gilding surfaces, gold ribbon was beaten or hammered by hand between layers of sheepskin or the intestines of an ox, called a '*cutch*' or 'gold beaters skin' and which is still used for the purpose. Special hammers and stone slabs were used to absorb the shocks that were transmitted to both the gold beaters and to the buildings. During the beating process it was necessary to remove all traces of moisture by periodically pressing with a hot iron. To prevent the gold from sticking to the cutch, a fine talc called brime was spread on the skins with a hare's foot, the process became known as briming.

The colour of the leaf depended on the quality of the gold used. The purest and most brilliant was 24-carat, but, as it was difficult to handle, 22-carat leaf was generally used, with 15-carat for the more ordinary work. Lesser quality leaf was liable to be affected by damp and had to be protected with a varnish.

Carving

Before the gilder can begin working on a frame, however, the carver must have completed his highly-skilled work. Unlike the majority of seventeenth-, eighteenth- and nineteenth-century craftsmen who produced furniture and frames, the carver's work was nearly always covered with layers of gesso, gilding or paint, nevertheless it was crucial that the basic frame was made to the highest standard. The majority of mirror frames were made from a soft, easily worked timber. The lime or European linden tree, with its close, even texture was ideal, particularly because it was knot-free it lent itself to the sharply delineating carving required, especially evident in the work of Grinling Gibbons (see [9]). Other great European carvers like Andrea Brustolon worked in boxwood and ebony while many a lesser name used cheaper indiginous timbers that were readily available.

From the paper or card design, the modern day carver works with a range of tools that have not changed since the examples in this book were first produced. The handles of the chisels and gouges were often made by the craftsmen themselves, from a range of timbers including fruit-woods and hardwoods. The transition from roughly-sawn timber to finished work is a long and highly skilled process.

During the second half of the nineteenth century, technical advances in industry led to the introduction of carving machines both in Europe and America for mass production. In 1747 *England, a General Description of All Trades*, recorded that 'Though Frame Making is certainely a Part of Joinery, yet making those for Pictures and looking glasses, Table and Slabs, especially the most curious sorts of them, in which usually there is a good deal of carving is a particular trade.' In the same year *The London Tradesman* stated that there is a 'class of carvers who do nothing else but carve frames for looking-glasses'.

fig 10 An eighteenth-century goldbeater's trade sign

fig 11 Carvers' tools have changed very little since the eighteenth century; now, as then, the handles of the tools are often carved by the craftsmen themselves

A lightness of touch and an element of fantasy found in the greatest mirror frames, can only be achieved by a skilled carver following an outstanding design. To enhance the required lightness, the carver will spend a good proportion of his time working on the reverse of the frame. By careful undercutting to reduce the depth of wood, an effect of great delicacy can be achieved. Since different elements of the frame are carved separately, the final stage of the carver's work is to assemble or 'join up' the frame.

Whichever gilding process was to be used (water or oil gilding), the carved wood was neither smooth nor hard enough to be a suitable ground for gold leaf and so the surface had to be prepared with gesso.

Gesso is still the normal ground for both water gilding and oil gilding. There are different types of gesso, depending on the method and effect required, but basically gesso is a preparation of ground chalk, slaked plaster of Paris or gypsum mixed into a paste with parchment glue, rabbit-skin glue, bone glue or pure gelatin. Cotton can be added to act as a reinforcer when the gesso is intended for work in high relief, sugar is an alternative, but it renders the gesso susceptible to damage by vermin. In liquid form, the gesso is coated on to the surface to be gilded, each layer is then allowed to dry, and the final surface is scraped and rubbed until smooth and hard. Examples do exist of looking-glass frames that were finished at the gesso stage and never intended for gilding.

Oil gilding

Oil gilding has one advantage over water gilding, in that it can be applied to a surface that has not been so laboriously prepared. Stalker and Parker recommend 'the scrapings from painter's pots and the cleansing or filth of their pencils, ground, mixed together and put in a canvas bag'. The liquid produced when the bag was squeezed could be used as a primer.

It is at this stage, when the gesso ground work has been prepared, that the two processes of oil gilding and water gilding differ completely. For oil gilding the 'mordant', or adhesive substance (used by Cennini and by Stalker and Parker), to overlay the prepared surface to receive the gold, was linseed oil. The oil had to be cooked for months in the sun until it hardened and became 'fat oil'. It was then mixed with white lead and verdigris, as recommended by Cennini, or with yellow ochre or raw sienna ground into linseed oil, according to Stalker and Parker. This substance was then brushed on to the prepared ground and allowed to dry for a day or so. Cennini recommends 'Test it with the palms of your hands; and when you find that one palm sticks to the other, it will be right'. Another test is to twist ones knuckles on the surface to obtain a squeak called a 'whistling tack'. The tacky surface was then ready for the gold, which was laid down and brushed into the work and polished with cotton wool or chamois leather.

Water gilding

Water gilding can only be laid on to a gesso ground. Bole, the material used to make the hammered gold leaf adhere to the gesso ground is a refined clay-like substance, often referred to as 'gilder's red clay' and consisting in the main of hydrous aluminium silicate. Originally called 'Armenian bole', it was mixed with a tempera of 'glair' (egg white and water mixed together), one of the oldest-known adhesives. In his treatise, Cennini recommends the use of garlic bulbs as a mordant for gold, 'Do not take small garlic bulbs, nor young ones; get them about half grown.' He then adds that this method has limited use and was unsuitable for damp churches. Bole has three functions: firstly, it helps to smooth out any irregularities on the gesso surface, secondly, it enhances the tone of the gilding; and thirdly, it conceals any areas that have escaped the gold leaf, or are exposed by burnishing. The bole is mixed with a binder, often parchment size, which is made from soaking scraps of parchment in water, then boiling them to form a tacky solution. It is generally made in three colours, red, blue and yellow, with varying shades of each. There are no rigid rules as to when each colour was used, in some cases they are used in combination. However, for looking-glass frames made during the early and middle eighteenth century in England, red bole was common, with yellow and grey used until the end of the century and predominantly a bluey-grey bole was used during the nineteenth century.

fig 12 The gold-leaf is lifted from the pad with the gilder's tip and laid on to a prepared surface

After applying a number of thin layers of bole, the surface is buffed with a dry linen cloth and the frame is ready for gilding. Before the gold leaf can be laid down, the surface is covered with cold water until 'flowing wet', but only small areas can be treated at a time as the surface dries out very quickly. The sheets of gold leaf are shaken from the book of rouged tissue, on to a chamois-leather covered pad. Held from beneath, the pad, stuffed with 'tow' or fibre of plat and measuring 10 by 14 in (according to Stalker & Parker) is protected from any draught by a high gallery of parchment pinned to the pad around three of its sides. The gold leaf is then blown flat on to the pad. A thin, badger-hair brush, called a 'gilders tip' is run through the gilder's hair to pick up a trace of oil from the scalp; the section of leaf is then cut into the required size, lifted from the pad with the '*tip*' and laid on to the prepared surface. Depending on the type of finish required, the leaf is then tamped into the carved areas and the highlights burnished. The areas of matt finish are gently polished with a pad. Burnishing requires great care; double gilding may often be used to create a truly rich finish. Thomas Chippendale (see p. 124) used two-coloured gold, with silvered details for some of the work he carried out for Edwin Lascelles at Harewood House in Yorkshire. The tool used for burnishing was originally a dog's tooth as well as various precious stones and hematite mounted on a stick bound with leather. Today the gilder uses an agate, fitted into a wooden handle, and prepared with various shaped heads as can be seen here; interestingly the tools and methods employed for gilding have changed little over the years.

fig 13 Like the carvers' tools, modern gilders' tools have changed very little since the eighteenth century

The process was described by Thomas Sheraton in his *Cabinet Directory*, 1803 (p. 227):

> 'In laying on the gold leaf, no water must be left under the gold, but it must be blown out, as much as the nature of the case will admit it of, or otherwise, when the cotton wool is applied to burnish it with, the gold will rub off. After this burnishing, proceed to a second layer or coat of gold as the first, which will cover all the defects of the first layer occasioned by the burnishing, and having waited till the second coat be dry, burnish as before; and if there be any defects of gold,

> such places must be repaired. Some recommend to have the work three times over, but twice will do as well, if carefully done.'

White gold is a combination of half silver and half gold and can be used as a substitute for silver leaf, but has a yellow tinge. Silvering is much cheaper than gilding but is subject to oxidization and tarnishes. The tendency of late-seventeenth-century craftsmen, who used silver leaf, to coat the surface with a varnish to prevent tarnish, tends to enhance the discolouration.

Veneering

The process of veneering consists of laying down sheets or pieces of veneer – cut wood – in to a solid carcass with glue.

Veneering was used as early as the eighteenth dynasty, *c.* 1567–1320 B.C., in ancient Egypt. Veneers made from imported timbers were cut approximately ¼in thick and fastened to the frame-work and carcass with wooden pegs, the peg-heads often adapted as ornaments. Examples exist of ebony, ivory, faience, glass and natural stone veneers. Howard Carter, the great Egyptologist, recorded a household chest, from the tomb of Tutankhamun at Thebes *c.* 1350 B.C. (Cairo Museum) that has panels veneered in a herringbone design, composed of 33,000 individual pieces of wood.

The use of veneer as opposed to solid wood suggests a need to economize with often imported and expensive timbers. Before the mechanization of the nineteenth century, all veneers were cut by hand saw, and a skilled operator could obtain six or eight veneers from one inch of wood. It is also thought possible that special workmen visited the cabinet-maker's workshop once or twice a year to transform into veneers timbers that had been especially reserved for the purpose. During the nineteenth century two types of machine were developed: the rotary cutting method which employed a broad knife to cut round the log producing a continuous paper thin veneer, almost without figuring, and the pendulum knife, a wide blade which swung in segments cutting a broad leaf of veneer with each sweep. The baulk of timber being cut was held in place with 'dogs' and the wood saturated with water before cutting to prevent the leaves of veneer from splitting. Each cut was supervised to ensure that the line of cleavage produced the maximum figure and any 'fade out' of the knife could be adjusted. This latter method produced a thicker cut veneer than the rotary process and with a better figure.

Timber can only be used for cutting into veneer if it is seasoned. Seasoning, removing the moisture from timber, begins the moment the tree is felled and can continue for up to seven years or more. Air drying can only successfully take place when the tree is planked and the boards stored out of the weather. Henry Bullock invented a machine in 1629 for cutting timber into plank form and then into veneers, another was invented in 1683 by John Booth and in 1703 George Sorold devized a horse or water-powered sawing machine. These developments for planking timber aided the drying process, allowing air to circulate between planks that were separated by lathes. However well seasoned timber is, it can be susceptible to swelling and warping if exposed to changes in atmosphere.

Not only is veneering economical, but it allows the cabinet-maker a greater choice of decorative features to work with. John Evelyn in his *Sylva*, first published in 1664, urged a greater use of cedar. 'It might be done with modest expense especially in some small proportions and in Faneering as they term it.' The figure in timber can be brought out by cutting wood so that various types of irregularities in the grain and variations in colour can be seen to the best advantage. Pieces of veneer cut in successive layers from the same log exhibit the same figuring, therefore, when laid together with their markings joined, they form a pleasing symmetrical pattern. There are numerous different cuts of veneer, each producing their own peculiarities, fiddleback and curl mahogany for example. Burrs or Burls are created by underdeveloped branches repeatedly cut back to form eyes, an effect also caused by abnormal growths often close to the bole of the tree. The eyes that form inside these excrescences are also thought to be made by presence of insects of bacteria. Birds-eye figure, which is similar, is limited to northern European Maple trees and is caused by a fungus. The 'plum pudding' effect, which is peculiar to West Indian mahogany, and highly prized as a veneer, is similar to birds-eye maple, but less tight in its patterning. Veneers, especially walnut of the late seventeenth and early eighteenth centuries, that are cut from timber in which branches have grown, often have areas that are not sound. These areas are usually cut away by the cabinet-maker and replaced with a patch using, as near a match as possible. These patches are often mistaken as restored or areas of poor repair, but in fact are usually original. John Evelyn, again in his *Sylva* recommends in the case of walnut: 'Timber about the Roots, which is admirable for fleck'd and chambletted work', and he adds, 'the older it is, the more estimable'.

Carcass wood and ground timbers are usually cheaper, local woods were often used for this purpose during the late seventeenth and early eighteenth century. Later in the nineteenth century imported woods were cheaper due to improved communications and were used for ground work.

Oyster cut veneers, that were so popular during the late seventeenth century in Germany and the Low Countries, are made by cutting across the grain of small branches, thereby showing the heartwood and growth rings and occasionally the lighter sapwood surrounding it. Intricate patterns were created using oysters that were themselves cut, laid in patterns, and surrounded by contrasting bandings.

To lay veneer both surfaces must be roughened; the underside of the sheet of veneer and the ground on which it will lie. This 'key' is done by a 'toothing plane' with a serrated edge. Both surfaces must be clean and free from grease or dirt before the coating of hot glue is applied. Headless veneer pins are used to locate and position the work and a 'caul' (a flat board) is then clamped to the bed, and pressure applied to the centre first to squeeze the excess glue to the outer edges. In place of the caul on curved surfaces, sandbags are used. The protecting layer of paper laid on the top of the work is removed when the glue has dried and the finishing process can begin.

During the second half of the seventeenth century, both the Dutch and Flemish became masters in the technique of veneering, stimulated by access to exotic woods from trade with the East. The great port of Antwerp became a focus for imported goods including lacquers, rare timbers and tortoiseshell. The impressive seventeenth-century Antwerp cabinets on stands that were veneered in tortoiseshell, moulded in ebony enriched with ivory and with gilt metal mounts, were the finest examples of the craft and enjoyed an international reputation. Complimentary frames were made for both paintings and looking-glasses veneered in tortoiseshell. The technique of ebony wave mouldings, a characteristic of Flemish work, was also used in conjunction with tortoiseshell or on its own for framing.

The art of veneering that was practised with such skill in Germany and the Low Countries spread to both France and England. It was introduced to France by Jean Macé who Marie de Medici had recalled from the Netherlands. Macé had worked in Middeburg, the capital city of the Province of Zeeland for two years *c.* 1620, before entering the service of the Queen-Regent when he was assigned a workshop in the Galleries de Louvre. The use of the technique of veneering marks the birth of *ébénisterie* in France, practised by *menuisiers en ébène*, a term later shortened to ebenisters or cabinet-makers.

England on the other hand had no guild system. The immigrant craftsmen who were attracted to England after the restoration of Charles II, and who brought their cabinet-making abilities with them, soon found their skills quickly assimilated by local craftsmen. John Evelyn in *An Account of Architects and Architecture*, published between 1696 and 1697 says about English craftsmen:

> '. . . For we daily find that when once they arrive to a thorough inspection and address in their Trades, they Paragon, if not Exceed even the most Exquisite of other countries, as one may see in the late Reformation and Improvement of our Lock-Smiths work, Joyners, Cabinet-makers and the like, who from very Vulgar and Pitiful Artists, are now come to Produce Works as Curious for the Filing, and admirable for their Dexterity in Contriving, as any we meet abroad'.

Lacquer and japanning

Lacquer

There can be little doubt that it was the naval supremacy of the English, Dutch, French and Portuguese that was responsible for the appearance in Europe of oriental wares during the second half of the seventeenth century. The earliest imports must surely have been objects made for an oriental domestic market that were bought as curiosities by ship's captains to be sold on their return as a means of supplementing their incomes. The great European Trading companies like the East India Company, founded in 1599, who were later to receive their charter from Charles II, the Dutch East India Company and the Compagnie des Indes of France, founded in 1664, were all quick to recognize the potential of a fashion that was to spread throughout Europe towards the end of the seventeenth century.

The close relations between the courts of Charles III and Louis XIV did much to stimulate the fashion. Louis XIV, who collected oriental works of art on a large scale, encouraged the production of quantities of furniture, *façon de Chine*. Workshops for the imitation of oriental lacquer called *laquage*, were started at the Gobelins factory in the 1680s.

The Dutch, who soon after 1602 obtained a monopoly of trade with Japan, are known to have sent items of furniture to China to be decorated. In *Collection of Voyages*,

1688, by Captain William Dampier, reference is made to the inferior quality of the oriental joiners in Tonkin, 'in laying the lac upon good fine joined work, they frequently spoil the joints, edges or corners of drawers or cabinets.' There has been a good deal of debate about the practice of sending items to the East to be decorated as very few, if any pieces extant today can be definitely identified. Towner, a Dutch Captain took with him on his second voyage 'an ingenious joyner' with a supply of deal boards 'to make fashionable commodities to be lacquered here.' Some Dutch japanning of the period is of a very high quality and design and it has been suggested that lacquer workers were imported from China and Japan to teach the local craftsman. In the seventeenth- and eighteenth-century Notarial archives of Amsterdam there are many references to 'lack-workers' or 'Japanish Verlakkers'.

Lacquer, known in China as early as the Shang-yin period, was highly prized for its colour and protective properties. Lac, the sap of the lacquer tree, *Rhus Vernicifena* is a greyish viscous fluid in its crude state, which is collected by the country peasants by tapping the tree to drain the fluid. The raw lac is then strained through linen and simmered over a fire. If left, it turns a blackish colour when exposed to the air.

There are three main types of wood decorated Chinese export lacquer – low relief, surface-painted and incised. Lacquer was also used as a finish for porcelain and metal. Only oriental patience could be responsible for lacquer composed of up to thirty-six coats, each needing to dry at a specified rate in order to produce a hard lustrous surface,

fig 14 An example of late seventeenth-early eighteenth-century Coromandel lacquer

described by Charles Lockyer, in an account of *The India Trade*, in 1711, as 'so shines a black that you may see your face in it.'

Chinese lacquer is said to have been made chiefly in the province of Honan, to the south-west of Peking, and carried by boats to the ports of the Coromandel coast, so giving rise to one of the names, Coromandel, that was given to lacquer when it was first imported to Europe. Japanese lacquer was nearly all imported by the Dutch from the small island of Deshima in Nagasaki harbour, and was generally confined to painted or raised surfaces of gold on a black ground that was known as *Takemakie*. It was preferred by some to the Chinese lacquer as it was of a higher quality. Bantam, the Dutch trading station in the Malay peninsular, gave its name to incised lacquer known as Bantam Work.

Ormolu-mounted Japanese lacquer panels were incorporated into many pieces of fine French furniture during the second half of the eighteenth century and towards the end of the century, by the Dutch.

The estimated quantity of original furniture imported to England during the four years preceeding 1700 was 244 cabinets, 6,582 tables and 55 tops for stands. These figures were supplied by the joiners to the English parliament when they became concerned that these imports were jeopardising their existence.

The trading companies sold their cargoes by auction to dealers in Indian goods. The word Indian was used to describe the wealth of merchandise being shipped from the East. An advertisement of 12 November 1709, from the *Daily Courant*, announces 'The Japan Company will sell all sorts of Lacquered Japan and China Ware at Garraway's Coffee House in Exchange Alley . . .' Another advertisement of 11 October 1708 is more detailed, 'To be sold by the Charon Company at the Marine Coffee House in Birchin Lane . . . Lacquer'd Tea Tables, Cabinets, Writing-desks, Chinaware and various sorts of goods . . .'

Looking-glass frames made from imported oriental lacquer are rare. Examples do exist, made towards the end of the seventeenth century, from reused Coromandel lacquer screens or panels. Convenient to ship, the six-, eight- or twelve-fold screens were popular not just for decoration, but were 'cut through', reduced and used in the form of veneers, the fact that the original scene was destroyed seemed of little consequence to the devotees of chinoiserie (cf. Wills, 1965, p. 66, fig. 6 for an example in the Victoria and Albert Museum).

A bill from Thos Rymell, dated 5 August 1694, for work carried out for Queen Mary II details . . . 'For cutting ye pannels out of foure screens . . . £2. 0. 0. . . . For cutting a large Japan chest and sliting . . . £1. 5. 0. For two birds of rite Japan and letting them into two tea tables . . . 12. 0. 0. . . .' The term 'right Japan' appears to mean that the lacquer was genuine oriental and not the European imitation.

Japanning

'That incomparable secret of Japan and China varnishes which hitherto have been reserved so choicely among the virtuosi', was John Evelyn's comment about imported lacquer (30 July 1682). However, so great was the craze for 'Indian wares', which were both expensive and scarce in England that firms and individuals began japanning – the European imitation of lacquer.

As the lac tree was not available in Europe, the substitute used was shellac varnish. It was made from the resin deposited on the branches of trees by the insect *Coccus lacck*. When dissolved in spirits of wine, the preparation was brushed on to the surface of the wood which had already been prepared with a mixture of whitening and size. The finished groundwork should, according to contemporary instructions, 'glissen and reflect your face like a mirror'. The raised designs were made with a paste of gum arabic and whitening, thickened with fine sawdust. The flat decoration was made with gold size or vermilion mixed with water and the finished article treated with a clear protective varnish. Later in the eighteenth century japanners favoured a mixture of issinglass and honey as a preparation for the wood, and watercolour instead of vermillion mixed with gum and water for the surfaces prior to the painting of the designs. In his *Handmaid to the Arts* published in 1758, Robert Dossie comments that 'this method will last as long as the Old Japan.'

The two types of lacquered furniture existed at the same time on the market although the imported furniture became more expensive after an import duty was imposed on East Indian goods. The widespread interest in 'Japan Wares', as both the imported and European work was called, led to the publication in 1688 of *A Treatise on Japanning and Varnishing*, by John Stalker and George Parker. They described their work as being 'a complete discovery of those arts.' Although much of their technical information has been obtained from the Dutch, they set out as their own original work, recipes for japanning, with over one hundred different patterns for Japan-work.

In an 'epistle to the reader and practitioner', Stalker and Parker wrote that 'the Nobility and Gentry might be completely furnished with whole setts of Japan-work . . . but now you may be stockt with entire Furniture, Tables, Stands, Boxes and Looking-glass frames.' They also draw their readers attention to the very different qualities of work both from Japan and England. They reported that they had seen some imported pieces which were 'mean and ordinary in Draught' although they admit that the ground work was 'pretty good'! Of poor quality English work they wrote,

> 'the Undertakers in this kind, they are very numerous . . . some of them have more confidences than skill and ingenuity and without modesty or blush impose upon the Gentry such stuff and trash, for Japan-work that wether tis a greater scandal to the name of the artificier.'

By 1695, a company called 'The Patentees for Lacquering after the Manner of Japan', advertised a sale by lottery between the 23 and 26 November of 'several parcels of fine Japan'd goods . . . cabinets, Scrutores, Tables, Stands, Looking-glasses, Tea Tables, Chimney-pieces, etc, being all fresh and new made.'

The professional japanner probably bought the carcass furniture including looking-glass frames from the cabinet-maker, decorated it and sold it on. One such japanner was Robert Jones at the Sign of the Japan Cabinet near King Edwards's Stairs in Wapping. The *Daily Courant* of 7 December 1720 advertised,

> '. . . a parcel of goods consisting of very fine Japan Cabinets, Desks and Book-cases, Chests-of-Drawers, Japan and Walnut, likewise plain Wainscoat and fine Japan trunks, Beaufets, Linen Cupboards, Looking-glasses and Sconces etc . . .'

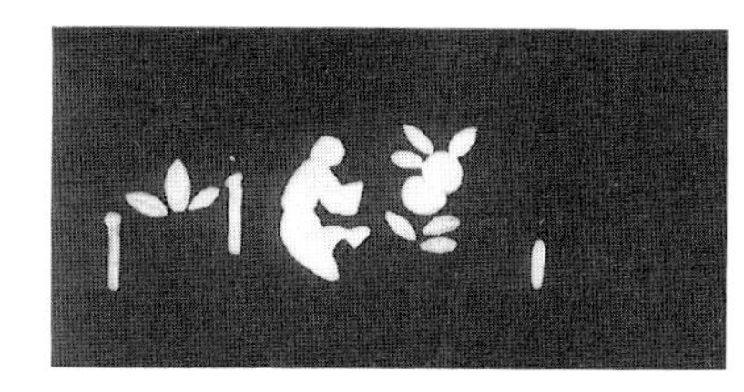

fig 15 This modern sample of japanned work shows the final stages of decoration on a prepared ground

The larger firms of cabinet-makers probably had a workshop devoted to japanning with a master japanner and several apprentices working on decorating newly made pieces as well as remaking imported wares purchased at auctions. There are many advertisements from the early years of the eighteenth century, when japanning was at its height, announcing sale of the stock in trade of cabinet-makers as well as japanners who for whatever reason had ceased business. One such is from the *Spectator* of 22 March 1711,

> 'At the Cabinet on Ludgate Hill still remains to be sold at very low rates, the following of Mr. Pistor, lately deceas'd, leaving all to be disposed of by Lady day-next, Three fine japan'd and 1 walnut cabinetts, 1 fine Walnut and 1 India Scrutore, 1 Wainscott desk and Bookcase on Drawers, 1 japan'd Tortoiseshell and 1 Black Plate case and three fine Princeswood Strong boxes, 1 Fine inlaid Copper-fram'd large Glass, Table and Stands; night India Japan'd large Glass, Table and Stands, 1 White Japan'd Glass and Table . . . 1 Japan'd Chimney Glass, some Japan'd Swing Glasses . . .'

There was a considerable trade in the export from England to both Spain and Portugal of japanned furniture, '*Gila Guerdy*' (Giles Grendy) in St John's Square, Clerkenwell is known to have been active in this trade amending designs for chairs and cabinets to suit foreign tastes. The extent of the export of furniture can be guaged from an account of a fire in August, 1731 in which 'he lost goods packed for exportation next morning' to the value of £1,000. The majority of this exported furniture was decorated on sealing wax red, detailed with gold chinoiserie figures and landscapes.

In France the earliest oriental lacquer was imported by way of Portugal and sold at the Foire de Saint Germain. As with the English, the French paid little regard to the scenes and patterns of the imported lacquers and treated them in a cavalier fashion, placing handles and mounts over areas of decoration. No examples exist of early seventeenth century French japanning although Les Sieurs Langlois, Père et fils were making *cabinets et paravents, façon de la Chine, d'une beauté singulierè* in 1691. Later between 1733 and 1740, the Duc de Bourbon was maintaining an atelier at Chantilly which produced japanned furniture that was so close to oriental lacquer that great connoisseurs were deceived by it. Lacquer and japanning continued to be a popular form of decoration throughout the reign of Louis XV and Louis XVI, but was used mainly for cabinet furniture rather than for mirror frames.

Despite the advantage the Dutch had over the rest of Europe, in being the first to trade with the Orient during the seventeenth century, they had a prodigious domestic market that demanded japanned wares. Dutch and Flemish japanning was of a better quality than that of England and may add credence to the theory that they imported oriental workers. The Spa near Aix-la-Chapelle, became the principal centre for japanning in Flanders and was the birth place of Gerard Dagly (1665–1714) who became famous in Germany as a japanner. Its products, known as *bois de Spa*, became popular throughout Europe. While the gaming rooms of Spa, also renowned, were decorated with gilt chinoiserie on a black ground.

Venice became the most famous Italian city for japanned oriental wares during the late seventeenth century. The carcass work would probably have been made from 'cirmolo', a white-ish pine from Cadore called 'Abete del Cadore', also known as custard-apple, and was generally favoured for its lightness and its ability to be shaped. This work then overlaid with many coats of gesso with (the 'Mobili laguna' and 'Venezia d'aqua' pieces from Venice receiving more layers than those of other regions). Each layer of gesso was polished and the last one decorated with raised work that was gilded and the other surfaces painted in tempera. The finished design was then painted over with 'Sandracca', a light straw-coloured varnish, made from shellac dissolved in spirit, which modified the tone of the colour according to how many coats the article was given. The production of fine japanned pieces was, in the main, reserved for the grand palaces and villas. A cheaper version was produced during the eighteenth century called 'arte povera'. Arte povera enjoyed great popularity amongst those who were unable to afford the genuine japanning, itself an imitation of the Oriental work, and its use spread to interior decoration, fashion and even to carnival masks, worn by the 'cicisbei' or galants. Pieces to be decorated in this way were painted a uniform ground colour and then decorated with prints, cut-out, and especially produced for the purpose by the Remondini firm of Bassano del Grappa and others. The prints were then coloured and gilded and the whole surface overlaid with varnish. Eighteenth-century Italian japanners formed a guild of *depentori*, a break away from the guild of painters of pictures called *pittori*. Italian japanning was also produced in Florence, Genoa and later in the eighteenth century, in Piedmont.

The production of japanned wares in Germany was centred in Berlin where craftsman Gerard Dagly had settled during the end of the seventeenth century. He had many students and imitators who were thought to have decorated the furniture at the Charlottenburg Palace. One of his followers, Martin Schnell, who worked for him from 1703 to 1709 and who was born in Dresden, returned there to produce designs for porcelain as well as japanned pieces. He was responsible for work at Schloss Pillnitz, the Japanische Palais, including an English-style bureau cabinet. Japanning was also carried out in Ausgburg and Hamburg. There are many famous German japanned rooms; Johann Jacob Saenger is known to have decorated a room in Schloss Ludwegsburg, the Residenz in Munich has a bedroom decorated with chinoiserie panels as does a room at the Schloss Nymphenburg, decorated by J. Hörringer in 1764.

Marquetry

Marquetry is the method of decorating the surface of furniture with geometric, foliate and arabesque patterns, classical motifs and other devices. Parquetry, on the other hand, is the use of solely geometric forms laid on to a carcass in a mosaic pattern. Inlay, another decorative form often confused with marquetry, consists of marking the outline of a pattern on the surface of the work to be decorated, cutting a line about $\frac{1}{8}$ in deep and fitting the wood pattern or line into it. This latter, crude decoration preceded the general use of veneer and marquetry and was popular in England using oak into which ash, bog oak, ebony, holly, poplar and, in rare cases, mother-of-pearl was set. Marquetry, as with veneering, was a skill practised by the Egyptians during the eighteenth dynasty (*c.* 1567–1320 B.C.), and examples exist in the Cairo Museum, particularly of chests from the tomb of Yuya and Tuyu.

During the course of the seventeenth century the Dutch and Flemish raised this sophisticated decoration to a high art form. As with veneering (see p. 38), their marquetry work was stimulated by access to exotic woods from their vast trading network in the East. The work of Pieter de Loose and Michael Verbeist, *c.* 1689, displaying elaborate designs of arabesques, vines and flowers, punctuated by figures and monkeys in engraved brass on a tortoiseshell ground, is perhaps the best example of this date.

Marquetry, or 'markatree' as it is often referred to in seventeenth-century English inventories, can be divided into two types: floral, and seaweed or arabesque (also known as endive marquetry). Methods of cutting these different types vary in detail; different coloured woods are required for floral marquetry, whereas in arabesque marquetry only one wood is used to contrast with the ground.

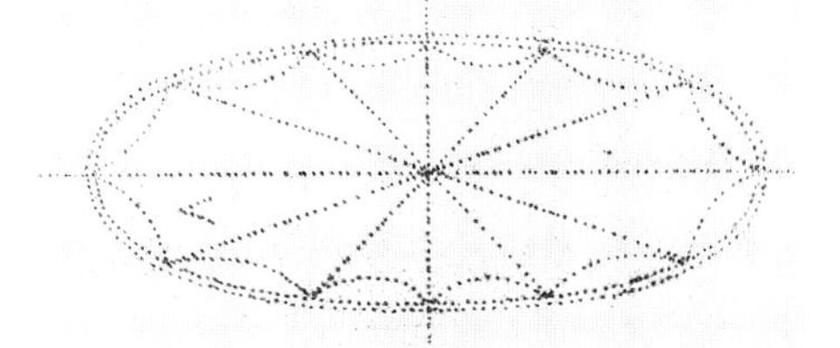

fig 16 The paper pattern used for a marquetry design after the bitumen powder or 'pounce' has been burnt on to the surface

Marquetry begins with a design being drawn on to paper – the master pattern – tiny holes are then 'pricked' through following the lines. Two patterns are required, one for the ground, the other for the inlaid design. Copies of the master pattern are made by placing it over a sheet of plain paper and sprinkling fine powder or 'pounce' of fine bitumen from a 'dolly' on to it. The pounce falls through the holes and can then be burnt into the paper beneath by placing it over heat. The jaws of the marquetry saw determine the size of panel to be cut, large panels, chest tops or door panels for example are made in two or four parts and joined by a wavy-cut line. The layers of veneer to be cut are piled together, as many as eight layers, each sandwiched by a protective layer of paper while the outsides are covered with waste wood to take the 'rag' of the saw. The design to be cut is then pasted on the top layer and the whole pile is securely gripped in the 'chops' of the 'donkey', the marquetry cutter's vice and bench.

The cutter, using a fine frame saw, cuts along the lines of the paper design and separates out the packets of veneers. As only one of the layers is required for each area of work, there are surplus pieces, to be used elsewhere, which confirms the view that few marquetry panels are unique. The next stage is to fit the selected pieces of light wood together to form the correct shape to fit the area cut in the ground, and assemble them on a sheet of glued paper. The assembled marquetry panel and the 'bed' or surface to be covered, must both be 'toothed' to give a key for the glue. The marquetry panel is then glued down and held in position by headless veneer pins and a 'caul'. The Caul is a piece of wood with a slightly curved surface which is placed down when it is hot and clamped in place. The heat from the caul penetrates the marquetry panel and softens the glue that has been allowed to dry slightly. As with veneering, pressure must first be applied to the centre to squeeze the excess glue to the outer edges. The caul is left in place for about thirty-six hours and the wood and glue allowed to harden for a week before the paper can be removed and the finishing process can begin.

Floral marquetry that was in vogue in North Europe during the end of the seventeenth century and early in the eighteenth century remained fashionable in Holland throughout the eighteenth century and saw a revival during the second half of the eighteenth century in most of Europe for cabinet work. Floral marquetry, which relies on a variation in colours and shades for its effect, employs several woods, some in their

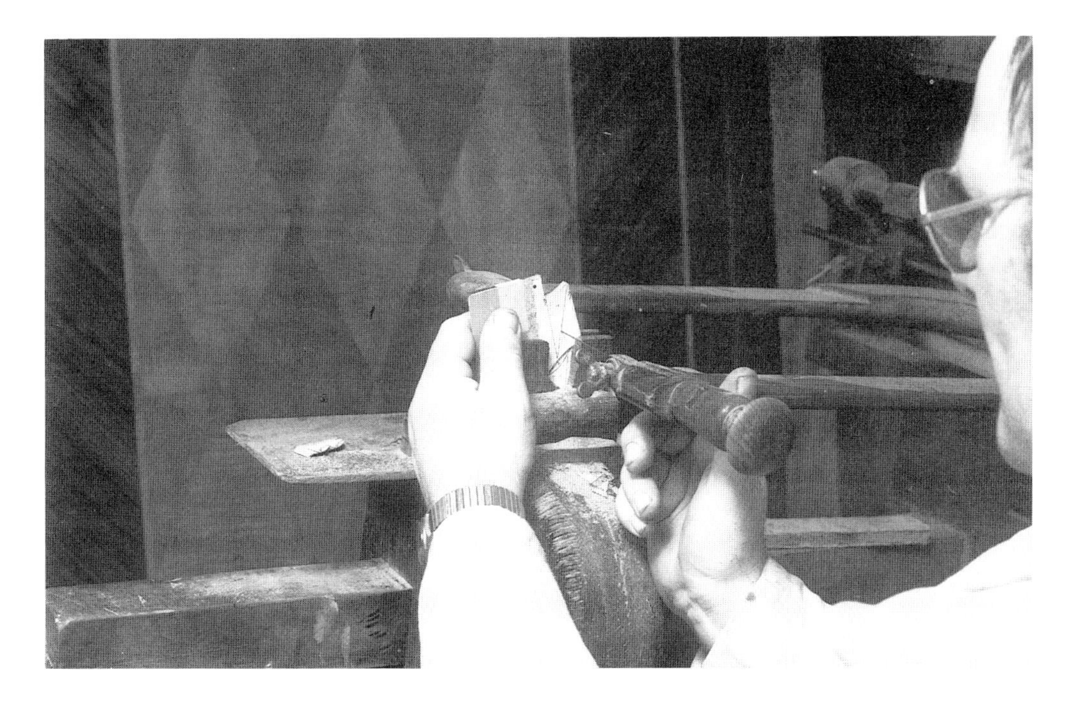

fig 17 A parcel of veneer being cut on a marquetry cutter's 'donkey'

natural state, others stained. John Evelyn in his *Sylva* (1664), mentions some of the different woods used in England.

> 'Berry for yellow, Holly for white, our inlayers use Fustic, Locust or Acacia, Brazille, Princes and Rosewood for yellow and reds, with several others brought from both Indies.'

The curiously named wood 'Fustic' was imported from tropical America and used both for its yellow colour and for its dye content. Thomas Sheraton wrote in 1803 that it was 'used in cabinet work about twenty years since; but it was found to turn by air and the heat of the sun to a dead, brownish hue, it was laid aside as unfit . . .'. The equally strange wood, 'Locust', was used for its yellow colour when seasoned and also known as Bois de Faux-Acacia or False Acacia. 'Brazille', mentioned by Evelyn, refers to Brazil Wood from both the Far East and from South America and favoured for its hardness and red markings.

Not all timber used for marquetry was imported, indigenous European woods used included laburnum, straight and figured walnut, mulberry, box, holly, sycamore and many more. Shading areas of inlay to create a two dimensional effect with leaves, flowers and areas of fan and paterae inlay, the latter later in the eighteenth century, was done with hot sand. Using boxwood or holly, both of which are light woods, the individual leaves and petals are taken between tweezers and run through hot silver-sand, which scorches the edges to grades of brown. Evelyn describes the process in *Sylva*:

> 'When they would imitate the natural turning of leaves in their curious compartments and bordures of flower work, they effect it by dipping the pieces so far into hot sand as they would have shadow.'

fig 18 The individual pieces of wood are laid into the prepared ground after shading

Boulle and inlaid metalwork

The Parisian André-Charles Boulle (1642–1732), or Buhl (his anglicized name), was a master cabinet-maker to the court of Louis XIV who perfected a process of veneering furniture using tortoiseshell, brass and occasionally, pewter. (Gerreit Jensen, who was of Flemish origin, is also known to have used metal for inlay but not in any quantity (see p. 65)). 'Boulle' furniture became fashionable throughout Europe, although it was more popular in France during the second half of the seventeenth century.

In 1672, Boulle took lodgings at the Louvre where French craftsmen, working under protection, were exempt from certain taxes, military services and strict guild rules. The *Manufacture Royale des Meubles de la Couronne* was controlled by the architect Charles Lebrun who designed a mirror bearing the King's arms and attracted other artists and craftsmen. One such man was Jean Bérain, a designer and contemporary of Boulle, who was responsible for some of Boulle's later designs for inlay. By the age of twenty-two, in 1664, he is recorded as renting a shop and studio next to the College of Reims, near the Abbey of St Geneviève, and later in 1673, two shops adjoining this establishment, to cater for his large and expanding business.

In common with many cabinet-makers and craftsmen of the seventeenth and eighteenth centuries, Boulle was no stranger to financial problems, debt and litigation. In 1684 he was sued by an innkeeper, François Begout, for non-payment of drink bought by Boulle for his workmen. Fifteen of those workmen sued him for their wages one year later. His financial situation had reached such a desperate state that by 1704 the King became involved, ordering a stay of proceedings for six months.

Boulle's technique of veneering surfaces with tortoiseshell and brass was time-consuming and elaborate. Tortoiseshell was in fact unsuitable and turtleshell was substituted, the best specimens found in the seas around Panama. The lengthy process of preparing the shell included boiling, moulding and polishing it, having first perhaps eaten the contents! Until recently the cutting process was thought to have been carried out on a sandwich of shell and brass glued together, following a scroll or arabesque pattern. Gillian Wilson's research, however (*Furniture History Society Journal* in 1972), suggests a slightly different method used by Boulle during the late seventeenth century. (The sandwich method was probably used during later revivals.) Cutting 'Boulle' from layers of shell and brass produces a number of identical panels in *première* and *contre-partie*. The marquetry cutter or *marqueteur* cuts the design in brass and the corresponding shell. When he has used the cut-out section, or *première*, he is left with the *contre-partie*. He is then able to veneer two identical panels in *première* and *contre-partie* for use on pairs of cabinets, commodes and stands. The most commonly-found Boulle furniture uses brass and red shell. The natural light brown shell is painted on the underside with a water-based paint before being laid down on the carcass. The brass, and in some cases, the pewter, were engraved after the veneering was complete. Boulle furniture was revived during the second half of the eighteenth century in France; Madame de Pompadour is recorded in 1753 as having bought Boulle furniture, eighteen years after the craftsman's death. This purchase may have been made from Boulle's son Charles-Joseph, who continued the workshops into the second half of the eighteenth century. English travellers who saw Boulle furniture particularly in France, but also elsewhere in Europe, returned to England with examples of the work. Lazane Duvaux, the fashionable Parisian *marchand-mercier* is known to have sold Boulle furniture to both Lord Bollingbroke and Lord Harvey between 1748 and 1758. Imitations of Boulle furniture do not appear in England before the early years of the nineteenth century. A Frenchman, Louis Le Gaigneur started a 'Buhl' factory at 19 Queen Street, Edgeware Road, *c.* 1815 and he supplied a writing table, inlaid with metal, to the Prince Regent for £250. Another firm, Town and Emanuel, of 103 New Bond Street described themselves on their trade label as, 'Manufacturers of Buhl Marqaeterie, Resner [sic] Furniture etc, of the finest and most superb designs of the time of Louis XIVth.'

fig 19 Ebony veneer and brass sheeting is cut to produce a 'Boulle-style' panel and paterae

The inlaid line decoration of the late-eighteenth century that employed stained box wood or sycamore, gave way early in the nineteenth century to inlaid brass. The brass lines used against imported timber, particularly rosewood, proved very popular. Sheet brass was cut into thin lines using a gauge made by the cabinet-maker for the purpose. Individual motifs including anthemions, flowerheads, palmettes etc. were stamped from sheets of brass, Thomas Sheraton in his *Cabinet Dictionary* (p. 95) (see p. 143), recommended brass borders, beading and stringing, he wrote that they

> 'are now much in use on English furniture and look very handsome in black, rose and other dark woods, the French far exceed this country in the brass work adapted for cabinet work.'

When the Bourbon monarchy was restored to France in 1814 after the Napoleonic war, English visitors began to visit Paris again. The fashionable French styles of furniture, particularly the Empire, found favour amongst the English. Beau Brummell, confidante to the Prince Regent and fashionable rake is known to have collected French furniture. When he fled from his debtors to France in 1816, the Christie's sale catalogue of his furniture from 12 Chapel Street, Park Lane included, 'a pier table of Buhl manufacture, the drawer and legs of tortoiseshell inlaid with arabesques of brass work and enriched with masks and mouldings of or-molu, a statuary slab at top!'

Inlaying with brass is only really practical on flat surfaces and is mainly confined to the frames of dressing-glasses, pier-glasses and cheval-mirrors. These rectangular forms lent themselves to single or double brass inlaid lines punctuated at the corners by inlaid brass flowerheads or squared paterae, often on an ebony ground. Cast metal mounts that had been so popular in France throughout the eighteenth century became generally fashionable. The French and English treatment of cast mounts is different. English mounts are rarely gilded brass or bronze (i.e. ormolu), but are lacquered brass. The columnar and pilaster sides to early nineteenth-century Northern European wall mirrors often have ormolu or gilt-metal mounts. Thomas Sheraton felt that French craftsmen depended on 'their superior brass-work', and expressed the view that:

> 'if our noblemen and gentry would contribute as much to the encouragement of a national brass foundry, as they do to some other institutions of less consequence, we might have as elegant brass-work for cabinets cast in London, as they have in Paris!'

Needlework

The use of needlework and stumpwork as decoration for mirror frames is mainly confined to England during the seventeenth century and to the Stuart period in particular. A relatively large number of examples exist today, thanks in part to the high regard in which these mirrors have always been held and to the use, in some cases, of glazing to protect the panels of needlework.

Caskets and boxes as well as looking glass frames were decorated with stumpwork and in rare cases incorporating beadwork. The earliest surviving English beadwork dates from the Stuart period and relies on small coloured beads sewn on to a linen canvas ground, some mounted on wire to create free-standing flowers and foliage for effect.

The inventory of Charles I's possessions sold after his execution describes 'a large looking glass sett in a frame of needlework embroydered with 3 faculties and the 7 liberal sciences', as well as a standing mirror 'set with silver gilt and embroidered with a woman in the foot.' The latter sold for £21, a relatively high price due in part to the previous ownership or, more likely, to the fact that it was decorated with needlework.

Inspiration for the designs for needlework frames were taken from pattern books with titles such as *The History of Four-footed Beasts and Serpents, whereunto is now added the Theater of Insects* (1658) and a *Booke of Flowers, Fruits, Beasts, Birds and Flies* by Peter Stern, published in 1658. Stern was able to advertise some twelve years later over five hundred engraved prints in sheet form ranging from portraits of the kings and queens, the seasons, senses, continents as well as natural history subjects and figures from the Old Testament. It has been suggested that some of the flowers, fruit and animals were

fig 20 An unfinished panel of seventeenth-century English needlework showing examples of commonly used symbolic motifs

representative, for example, strawberries for purity, carnations for love, moths for the transitoriness of human life, snails laziness, rabbits lust, silk-worms industry and bees hard work and order. The oak tree, oak leaves and acorns were particularly associated with Charles II who hid in an oak tree after the Battle of Worcester. Houses and castles were often incorporated and mica (talc) was used to heighten reality for the windows, lakes and streams.

Papier mâché, composition and carton-pierre

Papier Mâché

The majority of mirror frames made in Europe during the seventeenth, eighteenth and nineteenth centuries were made from wood, or used wood as a basis. Many and various forms of decoration were used, often carving as well as inlaying with other woods or metals and overlaying with gold leaf, lacquer and paint.

Papier mâché was certainly used as a substitute for wooden pictures frames in England as early as 1672. The Hon. Robert Bogle's essay entitled 'Of Mans' Great Ignorance of the Uses of Natural Things' (1672), refers to the suitability of papier mâché for 'Frames of Pictures and Diverse pieces of Embossed Work and other Curios Movables.'

Literally meaning chewed or mashed paper, papier mâché was known in the East long before its introduction to Europe, and the name appears originally not to have been French, despite the use of French words. It is probably that French emigré workers of the eighteenth century took the English word chew, which translated becomes *mâcher*, and developed the phrase papier mâché which is certainly a more attractive one to chewed paper. In France the product is known as *papier moulé*, or moulded paper.

The Chinese are known to have used moulded paper, toughened and decorated with lacquer for helmets and in 1910 in Manchuria's Kwantung Territory, pot lids of a similar composition were discovered and placed as Han Dynasty, *c*. A.D. 206. The use of pulped paper and pasteboard all depended on the Chinese invention of paper early in the second century A.D. The route that took papier mâché from China to Europe was via Persia, Damascus and by 1100, Morocco. During the tenth century it spread into Spain, France and Germany. The Italians learned the technique from the Orient via their extensive trade through the port of Venice.

The manufacture of papier mâché required a special preparation of paper mixed with glue, chalk and sometimes sand, to be mixed together into a fibrous pulp. This composition was then put into a heavily oiled or greased wood or plaster mould, allowed to settle and dry, and finally stoved. The result was a substance that was so hard it could be filed, sawn and planed.

An alternative method was to build up layers of paper pasted also using a mould. Robert Dossie, in the *Handmaid to the Arts*, 1758 (Vol. II, p. 361), suggests 'a paste of a thin consistance, made by boiling flour and water for a long time, and adding afterwards about two ounces of common size to a pound of the paste.' By 1763, one Peter Babel of Long Acre, near James Street, 'Designer and Modellier', announced himself 'one of the finest improvers of Papier mâché Ornaments for . . . Picture Frames etc' and refers to papier mâché as '. . . an invention of modern date imported by us from France and brought to great perfection.'

A similar material to papier mâché called 'fibrous slab' was developed around the third quarter of the eighteenth century by William Wilton. Slab was made from plaster and vegetable matter, hay, straw, nettles, treebark etc. Wilton established his first factory at Charing Cross and later in Edward Street, Cavendish Square and employed a number of French émigrés to make moulded ornaments for mirrors and chimney pieces. There is an account of a conversation between Mr Trigg, a fruiterer of Covent Garden, and Mrs Nollekens, wife of the sculptor, in which they discuss two old French women who lived at 27 James Street and who chewed paper for the manufacture of papier mâché, (John Thomas Smith in his 1828 biography of Nollekens.)

An improved composition of ground rags, glue, flour and water was patented in 1786 by Obadiah Westwood of Birmingham. The patent specification states that it could be used for 'Making Tea and other Trays, Card Pans, Caddies, Dressing Boxes, Bottle Stands, Ink Stands, Frames on Pictures and Looking Glasses. In 1772, Henry Clay of 19 Newhall Street, Birmingham, patented a process for making a tough, heat and moisture resistant material, capable of being oven-japanned to obtain an oriental lacquer-like surface. Mainly used for the manufacture of small objects, it was made from sheets of paper, with a porous texture, saturated with a mixture of flour and glue placed in moulds that were slightly larger than the object being produced. The strength and durability was achieved by glueing up to ten layers of paper together and drying them at 100 degrees F. between each addition. Dr Johnson, the diarist, visited Clay's factory in 1774 and recorded that 'the paper they use is smooth and whited brown'. In 1781, Sylas Neville also visited Clay's factory and noted in his diary, 'Stopt at Clay's, a very singular manufactory of baked paper which when varnished and polished has all the appearances of the fine wood Japan with the addition of figures after the antique, particularly the Etruscan.' Henry Clay employed over six hundred people at his Birmingham factory by 1802 when he retired, and he was a man notorious for his ostentation and conceit.

From the middle of the nineteenth century, technical developments allowed for a denser paper mâché to be made. It was steamed in the presses to be moulded into furniture without a framework. Typical Victorian decoration of gilt scrollwork was highlighted with inlaid shell depicting house windows, flowers, waterfalls and moonlight, as well as foil-backed cut glass. Two kinds of shells were used, an oyster-like shell of greenish tint and the giant sea snail. George Souter is credited with inventing pearl decoration in 1825 while he was working for Jennens and Bettridge. Good quality examples of paper mâché were often signed. Jennens and Bettridge impressed pieces with their name *c.* 1830 and from 1840 it was surmounted by a crown and 'Makers to The Queen'. Other firms who marked their products were Loveridge, Ilidge, F. Walton and Co. and Perry and Morton.

There are scarcely any contemporary references to papier mâché mirror frames, perhaps one reason for this may be that observers failed to recognize them as such. The *Reading Mercury and Oxford Gazette*, for December 1768, carried an advertisement for an auction sale of Hall Grove, Bagshott, Surrey, which included 'Pier and other Glasses in Papier Machee Frames.' Reference to papier mâché used for architectural decoration do exist. Mrs Delany, writing to her sister, Mrs Anne Dewes, on 17 December 1749, during a visit to London. '. . . I took a chair to do business; went in the first place to Mr Dufours, the famous man for paper ornament like stucco, bespoke a rose for the top of her Grace of Portland's dressing room.' Dufour's trade card describes him as 'Dufour, CARVER & GILDER, original maker of papier mâché at the Golden Head in Berwick Street, Soho, London'. Mrs Delaney wrote to her sister from Bulstrode where she was staying with the Duchess of Portland on the 21 December 1753 (four years after the ceiling rose was purchased from Dufour). 'We are all in disorder at present, the Duchess's dressing room all unfurnished to have a papier mâchée ceiling put up', she described the room as 'filled with scaffolds, and the ceiling ornamenting with papier mâchée.'

During the mid-eighteenth century, France exported large quantities of papier mâché boxes to Germany. This trade led to Fredrich The Great establishing a pulped paper factory in Berlin in 1765. Earlier Fredrich had employed the famous *vernisseur*, Jean Alexandre Martin to work on his palace Sanssouci during the 1740s. In Dresden, Martin Schnell, who was taught by the best-known japanner in Germany, Gerard Dagly, produced furniture of outstanding quality. Another German who produced pulped paper ware was Stobwasser, who established a factory in 1763 under the auspices of the Duke of Brunswick, and was famous for his signed snuff and tobacco boxes.

The American pulped paper industry was already established by 1771. The *New York General Advertiser* of that year recorded that John Keating had the first paper factory where he sold waste paper and made paper and pasteboard. Earlier in 1769, a carver and gilder from London named Marshall was making 'paper ornaments for ceiling and staircases in the present mode'. Although there appear to be no contemporary references to frames being made from pulped paper in the United States, the substance was in use. George Washington ordered papier mâché for the ceilings of the room at Mount Vernon from his London factory. His wife Martha also ordered curtains for two windows 'with papier mâché cornish to them, or cornish covered with cloth.'

By the mid-nineteenth century in America there were small papier mâché factories in North West Connecticut. The Litchfield Manufacturing Company founded in either 1849 or 1850 was located on the banks of the Bantam River. The company imported English japanners from Wolverhampton and Oxford to teach the local people the arts of japanning and painting. The Litchfield Manufacturing Company specialized in papier mâché clock cases and was later, in 1854, to merge with the Terry Clock Company under the guidance of P.T. Barnam, a major shareholder.

Composition

Said to have been invented by a Swiss clergyman named Liardet. Composition or 'compo' as it has become known, is a mixture of whiting, resin and size, heated and mixed together. The substance had a plastic consistency which allowed it to be moulded and shaped into motifs, which, when dry, were glued or pinned down. It was favoured by Robert Adam and others from the middle of the eighteenth century in England. Adam used this quick method of production and entrusted the carving of wooden moulds of his own design to George Jackson who later founded a factory for making 'architectural embellishments' in Rathbone Place, London. Used in conjunction with wire, it was moulded into sprays of flowers, leaves and wheat ears, as well as swags and garlands. When it was painted, decorated or gilded, it proved indiscernible from the carved wood decorative features. Perhaps it was the relatively low wages and living standards that allowed wood carvers, particularly in Italy, to continue producing large quantities of carved wood mirror and picture frames during the nineteenth century. Further North in France and England, composition had become more commonplace. As early as 1813, T. Martin, author of *The Circle of Mechanical Arts*, referred to 'a noticeable decline in craftsmanship. There are only eleven master carvers in London and almost six hundred journeymen, though at one time there were six hundred, carving in wood has long been in the background as a branch of the art!'

Unlike carved wood, which required each decorative feature and motif to be individually worked by a skilled carver, compo could be produced and moulded by a relatively unskilled workforce. Rarely used by itself, composition frames that were made during the nineteenth and early twentieth century were compo sections laid on to a wooden base or wire supports. Frames made using compo tend to be heavier than those made in wood or papier mâché and as the material ages, there is a tendency for it to crack. This may be caused by further drying out of the composition or more likely, the continued movement of the carcass-wood as it settles or the wire supports.

Not particularly favoured by looking-glass and picture frame makers during the second half of the eighteenth century, but in use for decorative architectural motifs, was lead and pewter, particularly for mirrored rooms and as fireplace decoration. Gilded lead devices were used by Robert Adam to cover the joins in the plain and decorated mirror-plates lining the walls of the Glass Drawing Room at Northumber-

fig 21 Samples of decorative motifs and mouldings made from composition using eighteenth-century moulds

land House (1770–74). The jambs and lintels of Adam period fire surrounds were enriched with moulded lead or pewter motifs. Pinned or glued to the pine or softwood fire surrounds, they were usually painted to harmonize with the interior scheme. Since they were used in this context there is reason to suppose that this method was also used to decorate mirrors.

Despite the popularity of composition combined with wood for mirror frames during the nineteenth century, papier mâché was the height of fashion for small moveable objects. By the time Henry Clay retired in 1802, he had been appointed Japanner in Ordinary to George III and The Prince of Wales. He had already supplied a set of console-tables as well as a sedan chair to Queen Charlotte. The lightweight material had made it possible for the chair men to reach higher speeds than with the wood and leather-covered models. Clay's Birmingham factory changed hands again in 1816 and was bought by Jennens and Bettridge. The firm of Jennens and Bettridge, with showrooms at 6 Hallam Street, West Belgrave Square, were to become 'Paper Tray Makers to His Majesty King George IV. They were later to receive the Royal warrant from Queen Victoria. The huge success of this firm led to an increase in the number of makers in the Birmingham area. By the year 1830, some thirty or more manufacturers making papier mâché wares.

Whilst composition continued to be used into the twentieth century, the papier mâché industry declined. The newly invented electroplating process that could produce objects more quickly and cheaply, fired the market's demand for cheaper goods.

Carton pierre

The firm of George Jackson and Sons not only made composition but also became the principal manufacturer of carton pierre. First introduced by the Parisian M. Miziène, carton pierre represented an improvement upon papier mâché, although it also was paper based. The process involved the reduction of paper pulp to a fine state, followed by the addition of glue and whiting. As with composition the substance was rolled out, cut into small pieces, and pressed by hand into oiled moulds. Similar moulds were used for composition and carton pierre, except that plaster moulds could only be used for the latter. Drying was encouraged to take place in a warm room, the hollow areas in the carton pierre having been filled with dry plaster or saw dust. The finished work is lighter than composition but less strong, despite the recommendation in one recipe to use the paper in which oranges were wrapped for 'strong work'! Examples of carton pierre can be seen in the principal apartment of the Tuileries, in the Louvre and at the Palais Royal.

The modern day restoration of carved wood mirror frames usually entails regilding. In order to regild a frame (see p. 36) it is necessary to strip all the old gilt and gesso down to the carved soft-wood surface. The acid used to strip a wood frame would render a carton-pierre frame into a sludge at the bottom of the tank. Regilding on small areas of restoration can be undertaken but since it does not follow the pattern of work in the workshop, it is unpopular.

Filigree or curled paper decorations

The term filigree is derived from the latin words *filum* and *granum* meaning line and grain. Early forms of filigree work were done with precious metals, usually silver and gold, but when this became too expensive papyrus and tree bark was used and later parchment and paper, coloured with gilt edges and decorated with coloured metal threads and beads. The tightly curled rolls of paper were worked into often very complex patterns incorporating shells and beads. Rare examples do exist of needlework, stumpwork and filigree all used together for a looking glass frame (cf. Ralph Edwards, 1954, p. 317 fig. 1 from the collection of the Late Viscount Leverhulme).

Filigree work was used in England as early as the fifteenth and sixteenth centuries for decorating the figures of saints and relics but its use diminished after the Reformation. During the middle years of the seventeenth century it was revived as a recreation for ladies to embellish mirror-frame panels, travelling-dressing boxes and later tea caddies.

In 1791 George III's third daughter, Princess Elizabeth, was supplied by a Charles Elliott with fifteen ounces of different filigree paper, one ounce of gold paper to decorate a box especially made for the purpose. *The New Ladies Magazine* of 1786 describes it thus:

> 'A Profusion of Neat, elegant patterns and models of ingenuity and delicacy suitable for tea caddies, toilets, chimney pieces, screens, frames, cabinets, picture ornaments etc. The art affords an amusement to the female mind capable of the most pleasing and extensive variety; it may be readily acquired and pursued at a very triffling expense.'

Verre églomisé

fig 22 An example of an incomplete *verre églomisé* panel illustrating how the gold-leaf is removed to allow the background glass to be painted

Verre églomisé is the process of decorating the underside of glass and backing it with metal foil, usually gold or silver leaf against a black, green or red ground. The name derives from a Frenchman, Jean-Baptiste Glomy (d. 1786), who lived in Paris at the junction of the rues de Bourbons and Sainte-Cloude. An art dealer, auctioneer and collector, Glomy is also known to have contributed to the first *Catalogue Raisonné* of Rembrandt's etchings published in Paris by Gersaint in 1751 and in London the following year. He devised this form of decoration for the underside of the protective glass of prints and drawings that he dealt in and collected. Later, during the nineteenth century, the process became known as *eglomisées* in France and *eglomizzati* in Italy.

The technique was not invented by Glomy; the Romans are known to have used this form of decoration from the fragments that have survived imbedded in the mortar on the walls of catacombs. Revived in Italy during the fourteenth century, its use spread to other European countries where it was mainly used to decorate religious artefacts and later secular pieces. Details of the process were recorded in *Il Libro dell'arte* written by Cenino Cennini in Padua during the late fourteenth century. According to Cennini's method the piece of glass that was to be decorated was coated on one side with glair [white of egg mixed with water] on to which was placed a sheet of gold leaf. When this had dried, the pattern was carefully inscribed with a fine needle, the background scraped away and then overpainted with a colour to show off the gold decoration. *Verre églomisé* panels with a metal foil backing are incorporated into the Vyvyan Psalter now in the Victoria and Albert Museum, on which the designs of flowers and fruit are drawn from Geoffrey Whitney's *Choice of Emblems* (1586).

Surviving examples of English mirror frames decorated with *verre églomisé* fall into two main periods. During the late seventeenth and early eighteenth centuries the border glasses, particularly of pier glasses with divided mirror plates, were decorated with *verre églomisé*. This was achieved by cutting narrow strips of glass into suitable lengths and shaping them to follow the line of the main plate. The *Dictionarium Polygraphicum* of 1735 (Vol. 1, p. 114) (see also p. 17), described the process:

> 'some fine impress cut in paper was applied to the piece of glass to be decorated which had been varnished. When the varnish was dry, the paper was moistened on the blank side leaving the 'lines of the picture perfect and distinct on the varnish side of the glass . . .'

The colours used were described as 'an additional and improving beauty.' The pieces of glass were then butted together and the join disguised by small giltwood mouldings or delicate gilt parchment leaves, the latter often decorated with black lines. *Verre eglomisés* border glasses were further enriched with panels of pierced and carved giltwood as well as narrow plates of engraved brass. (Cf. Wills, 1965, pp. 68–9.)

Verre églomisé designs used on border glass decoration during the end of the seventeenth and the beginning of the eighteenth centuries, show a strong French influence particularly redolent of designs by Jean Bérain (see p. 180). Such utilization of similar designs in both countries can make the identification of English and French looking glasses difficult. An advertisement in *The London Gazette* of 9 May 1691, explained that glass painting 'is continued at Mr. Winches a Glas Painter in Bread Street near Cheapside, where any gentleman may be accomodated in any anneal'd Draughtes or Effigies whatever'.

An interesting announcement appeared in *The Daily Courant*, 24 August 1727:

> 'Stolen out of the Shop of Benjamin Goodison, Cabinet Maker, at the Golden Spread-Eagle in Long Acre, on or about the 5th day of this present August, a large old fashioned Glass Sconce, in a Glass Frame, and a Green Ground, the Bottom Border of the Frame is Wanting: This is to give notice that if any Person shall bring the said glass, or give any account of it to the said Benjamin Goodison, shall receive three Guineas Reward.'

Between 1727 and 1767, Goodison supplied a large quantity of furniture to Royal Palaces. Goodison supplied new furniture for the apartments of Fredrich, Prince of Wales, including 'three glass sconces in carved gilt frames, with two wrought arms each.' In fact in his will he stated that The Prince of Wales was 'indebted unto me in a considerable sum of money!.' The advertisement reveals some interesting facts. The use of the term 'old fashioned', in 1727 would indicate that *verre eglomisé* was 'out' by that date. 'Gold Flowers painted on the Glass Frame' would indicate that it was decorated with *verre eglomisé* using the less common green ground. That 'the Bottom Border of the Frame is Wanting', may well indicate that this old fashioned mirror had been sent to Goodison by its owner for repair or to have the plates reframed more fashionably. The value of the reward of three Guineas can be judged from a bill from the reign of Queen Anne (1702–14) from Phillip Arbunot, Cabinet Maker.

> 'For a present from her Majestie to the Emperor of Morocco. For Two Large Scones with double Branches, finely gilded, being three foot deep, scaloped, diamond cut and engraved embollished with crimson and gold Mosaic work with flowers on the boydes of the Glasses etc £12. 7. 0.

It is amusing to note that the piece is referred to as a sconce which would indicate that a pair of candle-arms was fitted to the base, however the advertisement warns 'the Bottom Border of the Frame is Wanting!.'

As decoration for looking-glass frames, the process saw a revival during the early nineteenth century, not as a continuous narrow border to the main mirror-plate, but as a panel above it. Whereas a hundred years before the fashionable form of decoration would have been formal strapwork, Regency taste tended towards panels of chinoiserie, classical scenes or a trelliswork or coloured ground, floral arrangement and complete rural or naval scenes. After the death of George Washington in 1799, some American mirrors of this design were decorated with mourning scenes, one at the Henry Francis du Pont Winterthur Museum, with a classical urn bearing a bust of George Washington raised on a plinth with an inscription giving the full date of his death as 14 December 1799, aged 68 years.

As Director of the Haarlem Academy of Design from 1775, Leendert Overbeck of Haarlem (*c.* 1752–1815), was a tapestry designer and ornamentalist, thought to have revived the use of *verre eglomisé* in pictures.

England

In 1663 a pamphlet was published called *England's Interests and Improvement.*

> 'The French', it stated, 'had introduced new modes and new tastes and set us all agog, and having increased among us considerable trades, witness the vast multitude of broad and narrow silk-weavers, makers of looking-glasses, paper friezes and gilded leather.'

During the seventeenth century the production of English looking-glass frames as well as mirror-plates was greatly influenced by Europe. As early as 1618, Sir Robert Mansell was employing imported Venetian workmen to manufacture looking-glasses in England. Later in the century, Huguenots fleeing religious persecution brought their design skills as well as their considerable woodworking abilities to England, which enriched the production of looking-glass frames and furniture-making in general.

Inspite of this, English glass-production during this century had a restricted output of small, often poor quality, mirror-plates. The alternative, imported Venetian mirror glass, which was of a higher quality, was an expensive commodity whose ownership was limited to a very few. Because of this, the value and rarity of mirrors meant that their safekeeping was of great importance to their owners, many of whom were women. The majority of gentlewomen were skilled in the art of needlework and stumpwork, and during their considerable leisure-time they worked cushions, handkerchiefs, tablecloths and many items for use in the household or by the family. It was only logical, therefore, that they decorated the frames of their looking-glasses with needlework.

In 1660, restoration of the monarchy provided scope for a new subject to be celebrated in their needlework designs. Embroidered looking-glass frames of this period are often worked with representations of the King and Queen, as well as other emblems, including symbols of piety, status, as well as motifs representing the aspirations, hopes and expectations of both the embroidresses and their families (see p. 50).

Once complete, needlework for the frame, sewn either in panels or as a complete piece of work, was laid down on a background of oak or deal, which was then framed or, occasionally, glazed. The framed looking-glasses were themselves enclosed by wooden cases to protect the delicate silk-ground needlework and the glass from dirt and damage when not in use, or when travelling. The case, usually made of oak, had hinged doors at the front allowing the mirror to be used without removing it from its box. The panels of needlework that make up the looking-glass frame, often within tortoiseshell inner and outer mouldings and in some rare cases japanned frames, would have been given to professional cabinet-makers or framers for making up. A note exists inside a box worked by Hannah Smith in which she records that her needlework was sent to London from Oxford for this purpose, '. . . I was almost 12 years of age; when I made the end of my cabinet; at Oxford; and my cabinet was made up in the year of 1656 at London.'

1 Charles II, *c.*1660, an embroidered and enclosed mirror
11in (28cm) (see colour illustration on p. 97)

2 Charles II, *c.*1660, beadwork
23½in (60cm) (see colour illustration on p. 98)

In this example [1] the doors of the mirror are worked with figures representing the senses of smell and hearing. The majority of needlework, beadwork and rolled-paper frames were used for dressing-glasses and were fitted with a hinged strut at the back for support. As protection, and for decoration, the frames were also sometimes draped with fabric or even covered when not in use.

Intricate figures, including representations of Faith and Hope are shown in the corners of this frame [2]. Worked on a white ground, the coloured beadwork is outlined with tape. (Cf. Hackenbrock, 1960, fig. 225; Seligman and Hughes, 1926, pl. 73b; Wills, 1965, p. 65.)

Each of these panels of needlework [3] is individually framed with decorated mouldings. Another example of Flemish influence at this time was the popular use of tortoiseshell for the frames of needlework mirrors. The theme of the Restoration which chair-makers used to such good effect on the top rails of chairs of the period is echoed again here, [4] but instead of the more conventional crown, the putti are shown supporting a basket of flowers and fruit representing Hope, above a cartouche. (Cf. Edwards, 1954, p. 313 for a similar example at the Victoria & Albert Museum; Wills, 1965, p. 65 for an example with a coat of arms painted on the cartouche; Symonds, *The Antique Collector*, Nov.–Dec. 1948, fig. 9.)

Examples of mirrors from this period were not only gilded but also decorated with white gold or silver leaf and any putti figures were picked out in flesh tones. Since Silver leaf was less resistant to atmospheric conditions than gold it was often varnished for protection. Over the years the varnish has 'turned', giving a yellow-colour to the silvering. An alternative suggestion is that yellow varnish was intentionally applied to give the effect of gold leaf which was more expensive. The difference between the two finishes would have been difficult to distinguish in the dimly-lit interiors of the period.

The cushion-moulded and crested frame [**4**] was to prove a versatile design for carved wood, gilded and silvered frames, as well as veneered and marquetry frames, and it was used throughout the closing years of the seventeenth century. A variation on this form, which may originally have been a crested picture frame, has probably been redecorated [**5**]. Another mirror [**7**] has a spread eagle cresting which could well have symbolized power and victory to the original owner. The insertion of a later mirror-plate and a certain crudeness of construction may indicate that the frame has been reduced in size.

Continuing the Restoration theme, this oval mirror has a sunflower incorporated in the carving [**8**], possibly alluding to the sunflower motif, also used by Van Dyck, as a symbol of unswerving devotion to Charles I. Oval wall mirrors of this date are uncommon which may suggest the difficulty of cutting oval mirror-plates, or indicate that the frame was originally made for a painting. The cartouche may have been left blank to accommodate a painted coat of arms.

Grinling Gibbons (1648–1721) is perhaps the most famous of all English carvers. He was born in Rotterdam and is thought to have trained in the workshop of the sculptor, Arthur Quellinus (see p. *222*). Gibbons came to England in 1667 aged nineteen and was discovered by John Evelyn the diarist who, on 18 January 1671 described in his diary how he found the young man in a 'Solitary thatched house' near Deptford. At the time Gibbons was working on a reproduction in wood of a crucifixion by Tintoretto. Evelyn described the frame, 'there being nothing in Nature so tender and delicate as the flowers and festoons about it, and yet the work was very strong.' Gibbons and his contemporaries carved in an airy, light style, depicting flowers, fruit, vegetables and festoons, betraying also the influence of European designers such as Quellinus from Antwerp. A number of different timbers had the qualities required to create this effect required by Gibbons, and yet be strong enough to withstand handling. Lime or pearwood was used for work at Petworth House, Sussex, and 'a table of walnut tree curiously veined and varnished standing on a frame of lime-tree . . .' was recorded in an inventory of Wootton House in Surrey. Carved in the manner of Gibbons, this mirror [**9**] (and the following two, [**10 and 11**]) displays all the features of lightness and detail that are associated with his work (the backboard added later for stability). While there is no certainty that he worked on this frame, it can only be ascribed to the school of Gibbons, it is, however, carved with pea pods which are thought to be his signature. The portrait of Henry VIII after Holbein at Petworth House is framed in limewood carved by Gibbons between 1689 and 1692, at which time he was also working on the library at Trinity College, Cambridge, which was described by Horace Walpole as, 'the most superb monument to Grinling Gibbons' skill.'

3 Charles II, *c.*1660, an easel mirror with needlework decoration
31½in (80cm)

4 Charles II, *c.*1685, carved giltwood
54in (137cm)

5 Charles II, *c.*1680, carved and painted softwood
33in (84cm) (see colour illustration on p. 99)

6 Charles II, *c.*1680, carved giltwood
40in (102cm)

7 Charles II, *c.*1685, pierced and carved giltwood
25in (63cm)

8 Charles II, *c.*1670, carved giltwood
28in (71cm)

9 Charles II, *c.*1680, carved limewood, in the manner of Grinling Gibbons
71in (180cm)

10 Charles II, *c.*1680, carved walnut, in the manner of Grinling Gibbons
33in (84cm)

11 Charles II, *c.*1680, carved giltwood in the manner of Grinling Gibbons
27in (69cm)

12 Charles II, *c.*1680, carved and pierced parcel gilt and walnut
24in (59cm)

13 Charles II, *c.*1680, possibly Dutch, carved silvered wood, the cartouche with later arms
38in (96cm)

14 Charles II, *c.*1680, possibly Dutch limewood, in the manner of Grinling Gibbons
78in (198cm)

15 Charles II, *c.*1680, silver mounted
60in (152.5cm)

16 William and Mary, *c.*1690, curled paperwork
23in (58cm)

17 William III, *c.*1700 white japanned and curled paperwork
50in (127cm)

18 James II, *c.*1685, walnut and marquetry
31in (79cm) (see colour illustration on p. 100)

19 William and Mary, *c.*1690, seaweed marquetry in walnut
41in (104cm) (see colour illustration on p. 100)

20 William and Mary, *c.*1695, oyster-veneered olive wood and marquetry
47in (121cm)

This silver-mounted, ebonized frame [**15**] shows an English interpretation of a style of mirror decoration that was first fashionable in Italy early in the century. John Evelyn noticed, in 1644 on a visit to Genoa, what he described as tables of 'massy silver'. These silver tables were usually made of wood overlaid with silver, ensuite with a mirror and candle-stands, all similarly decorated.

'A silver table and frame all layed with silver' were recorded among the possessions of Charles I and sold in 1650 by order of The Council of State for £120. The monogram here is possibly that of Robert (Rich), twenty-sixth Earl of Warwick who succeeded to the title on 24 August 1673. He married, on 8 April 1641, Elizabeth, daughter of Sir Arthur Ingram of Temple Newsam, County York, he married again, before April 1668, his first cousin once removed, and second daughter of Edward, Second Earl of Manchester. He was buried on 16 April 1675. A similar frame is in the King's Bedroom at Knole Park, Kent. The latter is part of a set in ebony with applied plaques of embossed silver, hallmarked 1680, to which is attached the monogram of the Countess of Dorset and her second husband, Henry Powle, Master of the Rolls. There is also a second set at Knole entirely covered in silver. Another, formerly at Osterly Park, was of French origin, the mounts being struck with a Paris mark. There are also two English tables covered with silver at Windsor Castle and a top alone at Chatsworth. (Cf. Hayward, *Apollo*, 1958, vol. 671, pp. 71, 124, 155, 200; Scheurleer, 1966, p. 141.) Ensuite with a matching ebonized table made during the nineteenth century in the seventeenth-century style, this authentic seventeenth-century frame [**15**] is overlaid with repoussé silver mounts. A table of 'ebony garnished with silver' is recorded in a 1679 inventory of the property of Elizabeth, Countess of Dysart, (before she became Duchess of Lauderdale in 1672) at Ham House in Surrey.

Rolled paperwork was a pastime, described in 1786 as 'The art that affords amusement to the female mind capable of the most pleasing and extensive variety' (see p. 56). This example [**16**] is composed of panels of rolled paperwork and has been overlaid with later, possibly early nineteenth-century, paper prints. These might have been applied to cover damage, which would be unusual, as the panels are glazed, or used in some way to 'update' the mirror during the Regency period. The art of rolled paper decoration enjoyed a revival towards the end of the eighteenth century especially for tea caddies and small box decoration. This frame could well have been brought back into focus some 130 years after it was first made. (Cf. Schiffer, 1983, p. 27 for a frame displaying rolled paper decoration, described as 'quill work'.)

The publication in 1688 of a *Treatise on Japanning and Varnishing* by John Stalker and George Parker, popularized the art of japanning among the same leisured group that was already pursuing the arts of rolling paper, filigree work, shellwork and needlework.

The frame [**17**] including the pierced cresting, is decorated with japanned chinoiserie figures and landscapes on a white-ground in the then new fashion for all things oriental. In the centre of the cresting are the Sambrooke arms, the mirror frame being the work of Rachel Sambrooke who married into the Burne family in 1700.

Of typical late-seventeenth-century Flemish influence, with a cushion frame headed by a shaped crest, missing the pierced edging, this mirror frame [**18**] is decorated with panels of seaweed marquetry in the manner of Gerreit Jensen. The cresting is inlaid with pewter and copper Prince of Wales feathers and inscribed 'Ich Dien', (although it has been suggested that the feather motif may not be original). Jensen was active between 1680 and 1715, supplying furniture to the royal households from the reign of Charles II to the end of the reign of Queen Anne. His anglicized name, Gerrard Johnson, appears in many royal household accounts; in 1680 he is recorded as supplying 'a cabinet and frame tablestands and glass', sent as presents to the Emperor of Morocco by Charles II. Royal accounts also record two pieces at Windsor Castle, supplied during the reign of William III and described as being enriched with fine or arabesque marquetry. A 1697 inventory of furniture at Kensington Palace records tables, looking-glasses and stands with inlaid metal which were 'bespoke by the Queen and came in after her death from Mr Johnson.' The building accounts for the royal palaces during the reign of William and Mary indicate that Jensen held the monopoly of supplying the fixed mirrors for the chimney pieces and for the window-piers. A bill of 1699 for Hampton Court mentions 'a panel of glass 13 feet long with a glass in it of 52 inches with a crown and cypher in glass and other ornaments.' He was referred to as 'cabinet-maker and glass-seller' when he was re-appointed cabinet-maker to the crown in 1689.

21 William and Mary, *c.*1690 oyster-veneered walnut
32in (81cm)

Also in the manner of Gerreit Jensen the frame [**19**] is decorated with continuous, rather than panelled marquetry as in the previous example. (Cf. Edwards, 1964, p. 352 for a similar example from the Percival Griffiths Collection; see also Symonds, 1929, p. 70 for the identical mirror.) Both the next two mirrors [**20 and 21**] are decorated with olive-wood, oyster-cut veneers. The first example [**20**] is a more elaborate and features panels of marquetry inset around the frame in the same general pattern as the embossed silver inlay. It is also likely that these two mirrors would originally have had crestings. These detachable crestings that are so often missing, were usually fixed on to the top of the frame with thin pieces of wood, either pinned to the frame, or fitted into iron brackets. Evidence of this construction is obvious from the back of the frame and can determine whether there was originally a cresting. Not only were these detachable crestings liable to have become separated and accidentally lost, they were also possibly discarded when they warped. Looking-glass and picture frames of this period were often hung high on the wall with the top edge set at some distance out from the wall. As a result, the single, shaped deal board upon which the veneer was laid to form the cresting often curved and warped, thus preventing the frame from being hung flat against the wall as a later fashion dictated and possibly explaining why the crestings were purposely discarded.

The Revocation of the Edict of Nantes in 1685, which had up until then protected Huguenots in France, brought Protestant refugees to Holland and England. Among those affected was a young man whose later designs, were to influence both countries. Daniel Marot (1663–1752) was born in Paris, the son of Jean Marot, a designer and engraver. The young Marot studied under Pierre Le Pautre and worked in the atelier of André-Charles Boulle. Following the Revocation, he fled to Holland and entered the service of William, Prince of Orange, (before the Prince's accession to the English throne), and later styled himself *Architecte du Roi de la Grande Bretagne*. Whilst in Holland he published, *c.* 1695, a set of engraving in his own style of the current French taste, entitled *Nouvelle cheminées à panneaux de glace à la marcène de France*. These designs show mirrors built into the overhanging form of Dutch chimney pieces. He also published, around this time, another volume of chimney-piece designs, *Nouvaux Lievre de Chiminées à la Hollondoise*. Marot's influence on the decorative arts was considerable, due in part, to the availability of a large number of his engraved designs, the first collected edition of which appeared in 1702. The extent of Marot's influence on the designs of English looking-glass frames towards the end of the century is revealed in this example [**22**]. (Cf. Ward-Jackson, 1958, pl. 7 for designs by Marot in the Victorian and Albert Museum.)

The fashion for the square form of looking-glass had begun to give way to the taller, pier-glasses, a taste encouraged by the improvement in mirror-glass making. The Duke of Buckingham had developed his glass-making company at Vauxhall *c.* 1662, under the managment of John Bellingham, who had sold his employer secrets of the glass making process that he had acquired when working in Holland. John Evelyn wrote of a visit to Vauxhall in his diary on 19 September 1676 where he saw 'looking glasses far larger and better than any that came from Venice'. In order to achieve this saught-after height, a pier-glass [**23**] is composed of divided plates, joined together often with the join of the two plates bevelled. (Formerly in the collection of Maxwell Joseph). The cushion moulded frame is decorated with carved, silvered leaves on an ebonized ground, reminiscent of ebony frames overlaid with silver-mounts. The cresting has graduated from a solid board with a veneered surface and minimal piercing, to a fully pierced and richly carved feature. Improvement in the skills of the glass maker and grinder, (the latter was also responsible for the bevelling) led to glass being used as a frame in itself [**24**]. Here the narrow border-glasses were shaped to follow the main plate, bevelled, and abutted, the join disguised with gilded leaves decorated with black lines. (Formerly at Madingly, University of Cambridge.) These advances in glass cutting allowed the hitherto straight top edge of the plate to be arched and as a result the cresting could be carved to follow the arch down to the shoulders of the mirror, as illustrated by the broken arch top mirror [**26**], where the curved form is accentuated by the addition of carved decoration. (Formerly in the collection of the Dukes of Leeds, Hornby Castle.) Red and gold *verre églomisé*, (see p. 56) decorate the border glasses and cresting of this looking-glass [**27**]. These linear, arabesque designs show a strong French influence, particularly those of Jean Bérain (1638–1711). (The tapestry reflected in the mirror is a Brussels Gothic tapestry of a court scene *c.* 1520, which once hung opposite this looking-glass in the Gallery at Tyninghame, East Lothian, Scotland, the home of the Earl of Haddington until the contents of the house were sold at auction in 1987.) Similar pier-glasses with *verre églomisé* border-glasses can be found at Penshurst Place, Kent. (Cf. Marquoid and Edwards, 1954, p. 322; Wills, 1964, p. 68 fig II; and for another without a cresting, from the collection of Colonel Way, Lenygon, 1914, p. 210, fig. 313.)

Unlike the majority of English cabinet and looking-glass makers who are not mentioned outside references to their names in accounts, John Gumley is different. Gumley, (fl. 1694–1729) made a fortune, he owned Gumley House in Isleworth and his daughter, Anna Maria, married William Pulteney, Earl of Bath. She was described as a 'vixen' and an 'enobled doxy'; a poem of 1717 calls for a mirror to reflect the truth:

> 'Could the sire, renowned in glass, produce
> One faithful mirror for his daughter's use'

22 William and Mary, *c.*1690, carved giltwood
51½in (131cm)

23 William and Mary, *c.*1690, silvered on an ebonized ground
71in (180cm)

24 William III, *c.*1695, one of a pair, carved giltwood pier-glass
90in (229cm)

25 William III, *c.*1695, giltwood pier-glass, cresting possibly not original
68in (173cm)

26 William III, *c.*1695, carved giltwood pier-glass
100in (254cm)

27 William III, *c.*1700, *verre églomisé* and giltwood
69½in (177cm)

28 William III, *c.*1700, carved giltwood pier-glass
78in (198cm)

29 William III, *c.*1700, carved giltwood pier-glass
92in (234cm)

30 William III, *c.*1700, carved giltwood pier-glass (far left)
97½in (247cm)

31 William III, *c.*1700, carved giltwood pier-glass (left)
107in (271cm)

32 William III, *c.*1700, carved giltwood pier-glass (above)
77in (196cm)

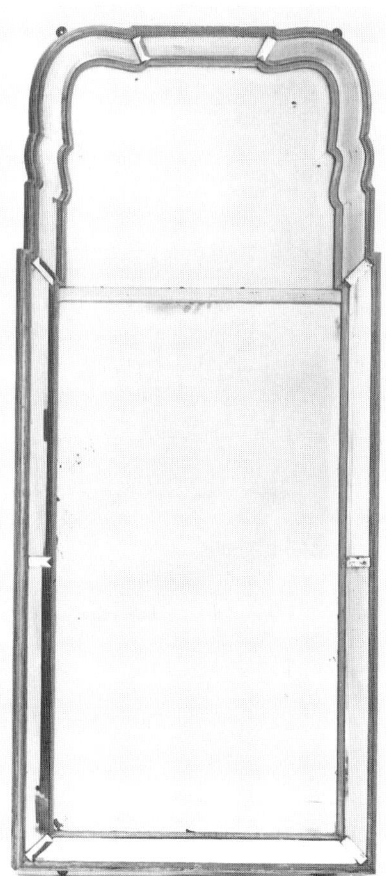

33 Queen Anne, *c.*1705, giltwood with mirror border glasses (far left)
70½in (179cm)

34 Queen Anne, *c.*1705, carved giltwood pier-glass with mirror borders (left)
68in (173cm)

John Gumley set up a glass-house at Lambeth in 1705 and was immediately involved in a court case with a rival firm, The Bear Garden Glass-works, Bank Side, Southwark. He was successful in this case, but in the exchange of hostilities The Bear Garden maintained that Gumley was 'no true inventor' and that he 'still sells glass in his shop in the Strand and the rest of his partners are merchants and tradesmen in the city, and none of them ever bred up in the Art or Mystry of making glass'. A mirror with border-glasses at Hampton Court Palace has 'Gumley' carved on the gilt slip that divides the glass panels on one pilaster, and another with an inscription, 'John Gumley 1703', scratched on the lower part of the mirror is at Chatsworth, Derbyshire.

Sir Richard Stede printed a description of 'Mr Gumley's Glass Gallery over the New Exchange' in his periodical *The Lover* on 13 March 1715:

> 'A place where people may go and be very well entertained, whether they have or not a good taste.' He concludes by saying that 'We have arrived at such perfection in this ware, of which I am speaking, that it is not in the power of any Potentate in Europe to have so beautiful a mirror as he may purchase here for a trifle.'

Gumley was in partnership with a cabinet-maker called James Moore, (active between 1694 and his death in 1726) who specialized in making gesso furniture. He was particuarly known for gesso tables, some of which he inscribed his name upon. The firm of Moore and Gumley supplied furniture which included mirrors and sconces as well as gesso tables. Lord Bristol's diary for 1710, records, 'To Mr James Moore . . . in full for the bill for glass piers, sconces etc £33.10*s*'. (See also mirrors [**50 and 51**])

35 Queen Anne, *c.*1705, silvered wood and mirror bordered pier-glass 61in (155cm)

John Gumley died in 1729, three years after his partner James Moore. The retail side of his business, conducted in the Strand, was continued by his mother. His second son, John, was left his share in the business of 'Richard Hughes and Co., Plate Glass Manufacturers, Vauxhall'.

By the end of the seventeenth century it was possible to make glass-plates of considerable size. *The Post Man* for that year reported that Vauxhall offered for sale 'large looking-glass plates, the like never made in England before', which were, 'six foot in length and proportionate breadth'. Despite The Bear Garden losing their case against Gumley, they went on to advertise 90 in plates 'of lively colour, free from bladders, veins and foulness incident to the large plates hitherto sold'.

Frames developed alongside this improvement in glass-making. The use of crests is continued in this example [**28**] using mirror-plate engraved with the arms of two families (Codrington and Calley) at the time of a marriage. (Records show the glass was made for Oliver Calley of Burdrop Wiltshire, baptised April 1672, who married Isabella, daughter of Robert Codrington of Codrington, Gloucestershire, and who died in 1715. (Formerly at Burdrop Park, Wiltshire and in the collection of Gerald Hochschild, Paris.)

The following group of mirrors bear similarities in the general effect created by the shape of the frames. One frame [**33**] has bevelled border-glasses and repeats the shape of the carved wood frame [**32**]. (Formerly in the collection of Sir Michael Duff, Bt. Vaynol Hall.) Echoing the same shape, this mirror [**34**] is more elaborately decorated with straight pilasters flanking the main plate, surmounted by carved gilt-wood capitals and bevelled glass for the fluting. (Cf. Wills, 1965, p. 74, fig. 22 for a frame by Gumley

37 William III, *c.*1690, overmantel mirror with mirror border-glasses mounted with dark blue glass paterae
30½in (77cm)

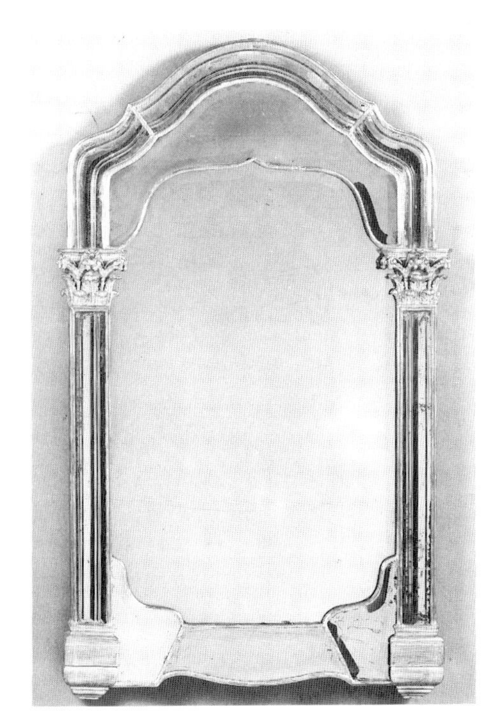

36 Queen Anne, *c.*1705, carved giltwood
48in (122cm)

38 Queen Anne, *c.*1705, overmantel mirror with mirror border-glasses
24in (61cm)

with similar border-glasses and corinthian pilasters, in the Royal Collection at Hampton Court Palace.) A comparable use of pilasters in this example [**36**] creates an affect particularly favoured by Gumley. (Formerly in the collection of the Duchess of Argyll.)

A specialized carver and gilder active during the end of the seventeenth century and the beginning of the eighteenth centuries was John Pelletier. Pelletier, probably of French origin, appears in 1690 in the Royal accounts, his bill giving details of carved and gilt frames for tables, stands, screens and mirrors. Both the design and carving of his work are of high quality and reveal a strong French influence in the *torchères* and table, which are at Hampton Court Palace.

During the seventeenth century the fashion for looking-glasses fitted into the Wainscot panelling above the chimney-piece was superseded by the overmantel mirror. A late seventeenth-century example of an overmantel mirror [**37**] has three main plates and wave cut border-glasses overlaid with blue and clear glass leaves and *fleur de lys*. (Cf. Wills, 1965, p. 73 for a mirror at Chatsworth supplied by Gumley in 1703 with similar clasps to the border-glasses). The main plates of another example [**38**] are overlapped and the edge of the flanking plates is scalloped to distract the eye from the join, drawing it to the engraved flowers at each side of the plate. (Cf. Wills, 1965, p. 70, fig. 14; Schiffer, 1983, p. 63, fig. 123.) The familiar William and Mary form of looking-glass, with a cushion moulded frame and shaped cresting is echoed in this Queen Anne frame [**39**]. The crest is no longer a separate piece but has become part of the gessoed and gilded frame. The heavily distressed mirror-plate in this example is certainly the original as it is shallow-bevelled to follow the shape of the frame. Descriptions of the early method of silvering make no mention of fixing the backing or protecting it in any way and here dampness has presumably been absorbed from the atmosphere and perhaps the wall, and starting at the edges, it has wiped the tin from the glass. To the purist, there is no doubt that the original mirror-plate enhances the value of the looking-glass, many however, have been replaced. To replace an original plate for one's personal taste is acceptable provided the original plate is very carefully preserved and the replacement is suitable for the frame. It is possible to have the plate resilvered, but this can only be done by a specialist using great care and ought only to be undertaken after careful consideration and expert advice. The bevelling of this original plate [**40**] follows the shape of the simple moulded frame but here the distressing is more regular due to the construction of the back boards of the mirror which has contained the distressing and prevented the outer edges from being affected. The base of this frame is fitted with a pair of brass candle-holders which can be moved in their sockets. The addition of candle-arms, mainly to the smaller type of early-eighteenth-century mirror, allowed much needed light to be reflected in the mirror-plate, thereby doubling the amount of candlepower. (Cf. Wills, 1965, p. 78, fig. 31.)

Bevelling or 'diamond-cutting', as it was called in the seventeenth and eighteenth centuries, is described in *Art of Glass*, by A. Blancourt, published in 1699. 'The Diamond-Cut is done by grinding the crystal on drift sand and Water, as much as you think convenient.' The plate in this example [**42**] is also distressed, more heavily towards the lower edge, graduating upwards in its effect, but, as with a previous mirror

39 Queen Anne, *c.*1710, carved giltwood
34½in (88cm)

40 Queen Anne, *c.*1710, one of a pair, giltwood mirror
29in (74cm)

41 Queen Anne, *c.*1710, giltwood and gesso
26in (66cm)

42 Queen Anne, *c.*1710, carved giltwood
40in (101cm)

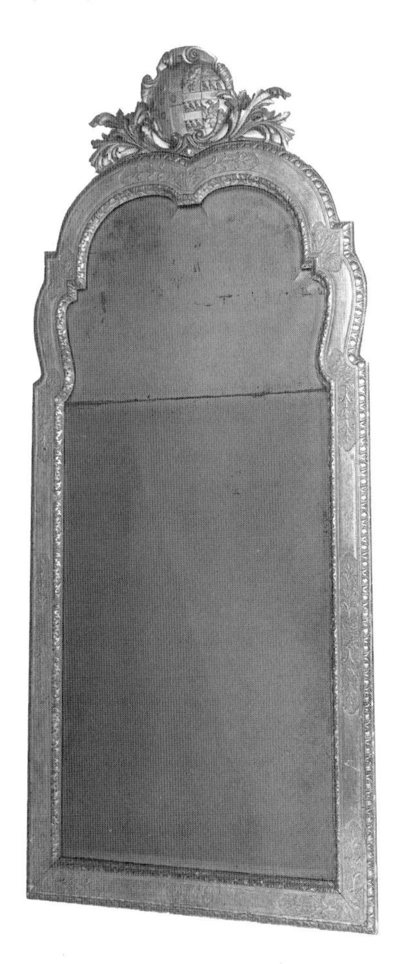

43 George I, *c.*1720, carved giltwood pier glass in the manner of Gumley and Moore
80in (203cm)

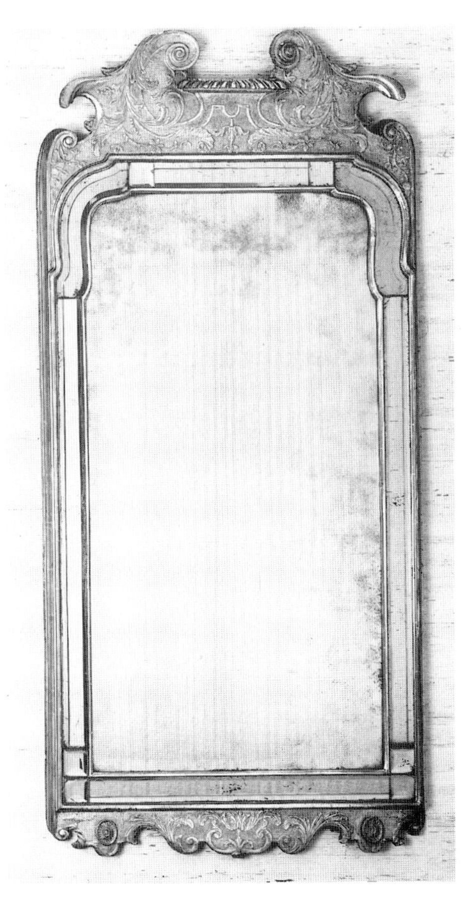

44 George I, *c.*1720, one of a pair, carved gilt gesso, formerly with a cartouche and a pair of candle-arms
54in (137cm)

[40] it is contained at the sides. Glass candle-arms are a rare feature, many have been broken and replaced with brass ones. The sockets for glass arms are usually larger than those made to take brass arms (see 42). Here the crest has moved away from the earlier, solid arched shape and now forms the central feature of the top of the mirror, flanked by scrolls that in later frames develop into the fullness of a swan neck and then into an architectural cornice. This pier-glass [43] has a basic William and Mary period shaped frame which is no longer cushion moulded but flat. The panels of leaf and scrolled decoration on a punched ground are placed in a similar pattern to the silver panels used during the late seventeenth century. The original bevelled plates are in two parts to achieve the necessary height and the join is bevelled on both plates. Family arms again form the cresting and suggest the celebration of a marriage uniting two families. (Formerly at Stowe House, Buckinghamshire.) In the next example [44] an apron has now developed to complement the cresting; this apron is fitted with a pair of oval Adam-style paterae, probably added later in the century, *c.* 1770, when the candle-arms might have been lost. The scrolled cresting with the gadrooned shelf would have been centred by a cartouche or similar decorative device. As in previous mirrors [34–36] the main plate is bordered with bevelled or diamond cut border-glasses following the overall shape.

Large mirror-plates in carved giltwood frames were costly items of furnishing which, despite their fragility, have survived in surprisingly large numbers. Unlike chairs and cabinet furniture that have suffered relatively heavy, every-day use, mirrors that were fixed to the wall and prized both for their decorative qualities as well as for the value of the plates, have been preserved. Many have been redecorated, some have had the mirror-plates replaced, a few have been altered and a great number have been copied at various times. This is a simple but none the less effective looking-glass in walnut veneer [45]. Walnut continued to be, until the 1730s, the predominant English cabinet-timber as well as mirror frame timber. Here a bevelled mirror-plate [45] is framed with cross-grained walnut veneer with a cross-grained moulding on the outer edge, laid on a deal carcass. This simple form of rectangular mirror was also used for toilet-glasses as well as, in rare cases, for bureaux, which were raised on cabriole legs and doubled as desks and dressing tables.

As a development from the plain frame [45], carved and gilded moulding now comprises the entire frame [46]. One of a pair, this mirror was probably made for the pier-walls of a smaller room. Pier-walls, the space between the windows which in small rooms was limited, confined the decoration to the crest, while the base of the frame would have rested on the chair rail. (Formerly in the collection of Sir Peter Norton Griffiths.)

The fact that they were a pair, as well as the arrangements of the plates, indicates that this example [47] is also a pier-mirror. In this case the striking simplicity of the frame makes it difficult to date, but the plain gilt moulding points towards an intention to fill a pair of pier-walls in an unpretentious Queen Anne interior.

The ornate nature of the skilful diamond cutting on the border-glasses and cresting scrolls here, [48] necessitates a relatively simple frame, yet it still brings together a number of developments in design and craft. Glass candle-arms were fitted and when reflected in the cutting on the apron, the candles must have produced a fine effect

45 Queen Anne, *c.*1710, moulded, cross-grained walnut
36in (91cm)

46 Queen Anne, *c.*1710, one of a pair, carved giltwood
53in (135cm)

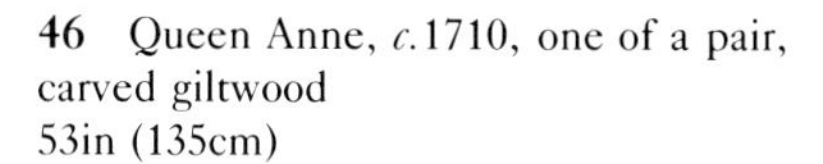

while increasing the light. Despite allusions to an earlier period, suggested by the strapwork motif used on the cresting, the crest is pierced and under-cut to give a lightness of effect. (Cf. Edwards, 1964, p. 363, fig. 5, for a mirror of similar outline made for Erthig, Denbighshire, and supplied by James Moore, Wills, 1965, p. 76, fig. 27.)

A relatively simple gilt gesso moulded frame this example, [**50**] has outset sections at each side and is centred by an acanthus-leaf plume. The cresting has a wealth of decoration including eagle heads grasping swags of flowers. This aquiline feature, possibly emblematic of power, is not uncommon and is found on tables as well as mirrors. Both mirrors [**50 and 51**] feature eagles and are in the manner of Moore and Gumley, the frames bearing a strong resemblance to that of a mirror in the Untermeyer Collection. James Moore who flourished between 1708 and 1726, was in partnership with John Gumley (see p. 71) and supplied mirrors to Erthig in Denbighshire, a house owned by John Mellor. There are accounts of purchases receipted by James Moore between 1722 and 1726, 'a fine large sconce silver framed', is in the accounts for 1723. (Cf. Hackenbrock, 1958, pl. 137; Gilbert and Beard, 1986, pp. 57–8; Edwards and Jourdain, 1955, p. 137, figs 35 and 36, and a pair of mirrors from the Benjamin Sonnenberg Collection, sold at Sotheby's, New York, 9 June 1979, lot 1647.)

While these frames [**51 and 53**] are similar in style to those designed by Moore and Gumley, the distinctive top frame decorations of the earlier example, [**51**] are in a manner often associated with John Belchair of St Pauls Church Yard. The double outsets on the sides of this frame are echoed in the second example [**53**] by the carved

47 Queen Anne, *c.*1710, one of a pair, giltwood pier-glass
74in (188cm)

48 George I, *c.*1720, giltwood with mirror borders, in the manner of James Moore
67in (170cm)

49 George I, *c.*1720, giltwood pier-glass
60in (152cm)

50 George I, *c.*1720, carved giltwood
58in (147cm)

51 George I, *c.*1725, carved gesso and giltwood, in the manner of Moore and Gumley
65in (165cm)

52 George I, *c.*1720, carved giltwood and gesso
69in (175cm)

53 George I, *c.*1720, carved giltwood and gesso
46in (117cm)

54 Geroge I, *c.*1720, carved giltwood and gesso
51in (130cm)

55 George I, *c.*1720 carved giltwood
48in (122cm)

56 George I, *c.*1715, walnut and gilt sconce
28in (71cm)

57 George I, *c.*1715, one of a pair, carved giltwood with candle-arms
44in (112cm) (see colour illustration on p. 101)

58 George I, *c.*1720, carved giltwood and gesso
47½in (120cm)

59 George I, *c.*1715, giltwood overmantel mirror with painting attributed to Francesco Solimena
63in (160cm)

60 George I, *c.*1725, gilt-gesso
46½in (118cm)

applied scrolls beneath a tight, but almost fully evolved, swan-neck cresting and a more vigourously developed apron. (Together with 52, formerly in the collection of Countess Mona Bismark,.) The eagle-head motif here, [**55**] is similar to those mentioned previously, [**50 and 51**], but in this case the eagle is holding ears of corn, possibly representing abundance, a combination of symbols which would have given a powerful message to the onlooker of a rich landowner able to provide amply for his family and friends.

Sconces were made in pairs or sets of four and six to give extra light. On this sconce [**56**] with a cross-grained walnut and parcel-gilt frame, the early style of cresting is balanced by an apron fitted with a candle-holder.

One of a pair of mirrors [**57**], has a fully developed swan neck cresting, in this case centred by a plumed mask, while [**58**] shows a variation of the swan neck treatment in a pierced form. The central, rather weak plume, has a band of balls as a collar which may have had some significance for the original owner. The candle-holder reserves on the apron of this example are covered with carved giltwood paterae, either to hide the marks of missing candle-arms, or originally put there to be replaced with candle-arms if the buyer wished.

Surmounted by a painting attributed to Francesco Solimena (1657–1747), this overmantel mirror [**59**] is flanked by female busts above candle-holders and would have rested on a mantel-shelf. Here the candle-holders have oval backplates that are now cast in brass and decorated with an edge moulding and the scrolling-arms decorated with masks, similar to those at the side of the frame, their gilt lacquer finish was an attempt to imitate ormolu. (Formerly in the collection of the Earl of Haddingham, Tyninghame, East Lothian.)

At the sale of William Stanhope's house in Albemarle Street in 1733, 'a chimney glass of three large plates 51 ins by 30(?) ins in a gilt Frame and a Top for a Picture', was included. Flanked by the eagle-head motif, in this case with classical husks in their beaks, the crest of this mirror [**61**] has a plume of acanthus leaves resting on an unusual lambrequin, an earlier feature often used by Marot (see p. 225).

With a full compliment of features and retaining the original gilding, this example [**62**] has swan neck cresting carved with egg-and-dart mouldings, the handling of which indicates an early use of a motif that enjoy popularity throughout the middle of the eighteenth century. Egg and dart is also used here [**63**] but the flatness in the treatment of the frame suggests an Irish origin, and if this is the case, would place the mirror ten to fifteen years later.

Both pier-glasses [**64 and 65**] are over 5 ft high, composed of divided plates to achieve maximum height, the latter [**65**] has the added feature of an engraved top plate while its frame has an asymmetrically-carved shell on the apron hinting of the Rococo style to follow. This element, combined with the pierced cresting, points to the mirror being an *avant-garde* or a later provincial example based on a 1730s frame.

Throughout the eighteenth and nineteenth centuries it was commonplace to 'update' cabinet furniture by changing the handles on drawers and in some cases replacing the feet. A typical example of this would be a William and Mary walnut chest of drawers with drop handles and bun feet. A decade or so into the reign of George I, (*c.* 1724), this chest would have seemed old fashioned. A simple and relatively cheap

61 George I, *c.*1725, carved giltwood and gesso
44½in (114cm)

62 George II, *c.*1730, carved giltwood with candle-arms
40in (102cm)

63 George II, *c.*1730, carved giltwood
47in (120cm)

64 George II, *c.*1730, one of a pair, giltwood pier-glass (left)
61½in (156cm)

65 George II, *c.*1730, one of a pair, giltwood pier-glass, restored, and with later additions
63½in (160cm)

66 George II, *c.*1730, giltwood overmantel, with mirror border-glasses (extensive additions to a Queen Anne frame).
57in (145cm)

67 George II, *c.*1730, carved giltwood and gesso
50in (127cm)

68 George II, *c.*1735, walnut and parcel-gilt
47in (119cm)

method of 'updating', without having an expensive new chest made, was to change the bun feet for bracket feet and the drop handles for swan neck handles with engraved backplates. Although examples are rare, similar 'updating' occurred with looking-glasses as shown here [66]. Basically a Queen Anne period frame of *c.* 1710 this example has mirrored border-glasses bevelled on both sides and the joins of the abutted plates are disguised with gilded paper leaves. The outer frame, together with the coat of arms centring the cresting and the sides carved with fruit, leaves and scrolls have all been added, *c.* 1730, thus effectively updating the frame by fifteen to twenty years.

Parcel-gilding, where veneered or solid wood furniture was embellished with areas of water or oil gilding, was fashionable in England *c.* 1730. The main part of this parcel-gilt walnut looking-glass frame [68] is veneered with burr-walnut, which displays the light burrs found in walnut that has been pollarded, the cresting however is veneered with straight grained walnut which was cheaper.

In 1715, a year after George I, Elector of Hanover ascended the throne, the English translation of Andrea Palladio's *Four Books of Architecture (I Quatror Libri)* was published. For half a century English taste was dominated by the revival of this Italian Renaissance artist's work, encouraged primarily by Colin Campbell and Lord Burlington. In 1727, Palladianism received a further stimulant when William Kent published the designs of Inigo Jones (1573–1652), once architect to the Jacobean court. Inigo Jones had first introduced Palladio's classically inspired buildings – their interiors, doorways and overmantels – to England, but it was not fully taken up until the early eighteenth century. William Kent (1684–1748), a Yorkshireman from a modest background, was fortunate enough to have been sent to Italy in 1709 to study paintings, having been apprenticed to his father, a coach painter in Hull. Whilst in Italy he met Lord Burlington as well as other rich and influential young English aristocrats, many of whom were to commission him later. He returned to England in 1719 and worked as a decorative painter at Kensington Palace, at Houghton and at Holkham Hall in Norfolk. The latter was built by Thomas Coke, later the First Earl of Leicester, (one of the people he had met in Italy, and with whom he returned there in 1714, 1716 and 1717 to purchase paintings and sculpture).

For the houses on which he worked, Kent designed furniture and interiors as unified schemes. Horace Walpole described Kent's work as 'audacious, splendid, sumptuous and of finished technique, and as these qualities were in demand, Kent was supreme in his own generation.' His designs for furniture included mouldings that were large in scale as well as masks and figures with lavish use of acanthus. Kent used mirrors *en suite* with pier-tables of an architectural symmetry that balanced with other features in the unified scheme. The design of this frame [**69**] is influenced by William Kent, especially in the mask motif. (Cf. Edwards, 1964, p. 363, fig. 40 for a similar mask on a mirror at Ragley Hall, Warwickshire.)

The typical forms of George II period gilt-gesso looking-glass frames with variations on decorative designs are illustrated with the following group of mirrors [**69–74**]. (74 was formerly in the collection of Sir Michael Duff, Bt. Viynol Hall.) Altered by the addition of the French cresting taken from an earlier mirror, and by removing the apron, this frame [**75**] is, nevertheless, of a typical outline.

'Three glass sconces in carved and gilt frames, with two wrought arms each, for The Prince of Wales' were made by Benjamin Goodison for Hampton Court. These royal mirrors, designed for the Prince's apartments are very similar to this example [**76**] except that they have crestings centred by a Prince of Wales plume. Goodison also supplied a mirror for the Prince's apartment's at St James's Palace between 1729 and 1733, 'a large pier-glass in a tabernacle frame gilt – £50'. (Cf. Edwards and Jourdain, 1955, p. 103, figs 39 and 40.)

Benjamin Goodison flourished between 1727 and 1767 at the Golden Spread Eagle, Long Acre, and supplied a large quantity of both mahogany and walnut, as well as giltwood furniture, to the royal palaces. His boldly designed furniture was enriched with large, simple ornaments – shells flanked by opposing acanthus scrolls and plumed masks are particularly associated with his work. Supplied at the same time as the mirrors for Hampton Court were gilt stands, 'carved term fashion' with female heads supporting Ionic capitals and standing on four acanthus leaf-carved scrolled feet. He also worked for Sarah, Duchess of Marlborough, for whom he bid at an auction for a house in Dover Street, securing it for £1,915 and received £21 from her 'for buying it so

69 George II, *c.*1735, carved giltwood and gesso
73in (185cm)

70 George II, *c.*1735, carved giltwood and gesso
58in (147cm)

71 George II, *c.*1735, carved giltwood
75in (191cm)

72 George II, *c.*1735, carved giltwood, with later apron (left)
67in (170cm) (see colour illustration on p. 102)

73 George II, *c.*1735, one of a pair, carved giltwood, with possibly a later apron
57½in (146cm)

73a George II, *c.*1735, carved giltwood, possibly provincial with later cresting
48in (121cm)

74 George II, *c.*1735, carved giltwood
65in (165cm) (see colour illustration on p. 102)

75 George II, *c.*1735, carved giltwood pier-glass with alterations
72in (183cm)

76 George II, *c.*1735, carved giltwood, in the manner of Benjamin Goodison
51in (129cm)

77 George II, *c.*1735, carved giltwood
69in (175cm)

78 George II, *c.*1735, carved giltwood overmantel mirror
width 61in (155cm)

extremely cheap'. He provided chimney- and pier-glasses as well as several marble-topped walnut tables for the house which the Duchess gave, completely furnished, to her grand-daughter, Isabella, Duchess of Manchester. He supplied for Goodwood House, Sussex, *c.* 1740, a set of three carved and gilt mirrors, with the cypher of the Duke of Richmond incised on the glass. The frame, with a female head carved on the pediment and a bearded mask on the apron, displays typical features favoured by Goodison.

In his will, dated 29 May 1765, Benjamin Goodison left half his fortune, some £8,000, plus two parcels of land to his 'dear son Benjamin Goodison'. He also mentions that the Prince was 'indebted unto me in a considerable sum of money'. Goodison was succeeded by his nephew, Benjamin Parran in 1767. An interesting insight into the provenance of this giltwood mirror [**77**] is provided by the inscription written on a label attached to the back: 'Bought to Taymouth Castle from the Marquis of Bradaldene's apartments at Holyrood Palace, 16 May 1860'. The overmantel mirror with typical gilt gesso decoration [**78**] has a similar pattern of frame to the upright mirrors of the period. Upright and pier-mirrors of the early eighteenth century far outnumber the overmantels. This in itself is not surprising because there are many more pier-walls and suitable spaces for upright mirrors in a room, whereas there is usually only one chimney-piece over which to place an overmantel mirror. Their rarity, however, could also be explained by the fashion of hanging a painting over the chimney-piece.

Here, [**79**] a giltwood pier glass has the cresting centred by a cartouche which was left blank for the owner to emblazen his crest upon. The area of frame between the inner and outer mouldings has been sanded to give a textured surface. This effect was achieved by sprinkling sand on to the last coat of gesso and allowing it to dry before it was gilded over in the same way as the remainder of the frame.

Made of burr-walnut and parcel-gilt, the area around the apron of this frame [**80**] may have been altered. Due to the limited height of the frame it is unlikely to have been a pier-glass, designed to rest upon an *en suite* or similarly veneered console-table, unless it was made for a room with a low ceiling. The oval form of this mirror-plate [**81**] was popular at this time. While heavily carved egg-and-dart moulding flanked by skilfully carved ribbon-tied oak leaves and acorns held at each side of the frame by swirling acanthus leaves, heralded the approach of the Rococo influence, which was within fifteen years to supersede the architectural form of frame. (Formerly in the collection of Hon. Mrs Nellie Ionides.) (Cf. Wills, 1965, p. 85, fig. 59.) Veneered with red or Virginia walnut imported from America, it is possible that this walnut and parcel-gilt frame [**82**] orginally had both a swan neck pediment and an apron. During the sixteenth, seventeenth and eighteenth centuries walnut was cultivated in Italy, Germany, France and in some parts of England. The timber was held in such high regard in parts of Germany that no young farmer was permitted to marry until he could prove that he had planted a specified number of walnut trees. The Bergstas, an area between Heidelberg and Darmstadt was subject to ancient laws; the borderers were obliged to plant and care for the walnut trees that were planted beside the roads, so that 'a man may ride for many miles about the country under a continual arbour, or close walk, the traveller both refreshed with the fruit and the shade.' England relied

79 George II, *c.*1735, carved giltwood pier-glass, cartouche replaced
73½in (187cm)

80 George II, *c.*1735, burr walnut and parcel-gilt with a possibly re-shaped apron
43in (110cm)

81 George II, *c.*1735, carved giltwood with the arms of the Earls of Manchester
70in (178cm)

82 George II, *c.*1735, red walnut and parcel-gilt with alterations
43in (109cm)

83 George II, *c.*1735, one of a pair, carved giltwood altered or with missing apron
51in (129cm)

84 George II, *c.*1735, carved giltwood
51in (129cm)

84a George II, *c.*1735, carved giltwood with sanded border decorated with real sea shells
69in (175cm)

85 George II, *c.*1730, carved giltwood
57in (145cm)

86 George II, *c.*1740, carved giltwood with alterations
53in (135cm)

87 George II, *c.*1740, carved wood and gilt-gesso
78in (198cm)

88 George II, *c.*1740, carved giltwood overmantel
width 47in (120cm)

on the continent and America for its supply of walnut (the latter supply more often used as solid wood rather than as a veneer) since English walnut was scarce.

As early as 1706, John Evelyn's statement highlights this point: 'were this timber in greater plenty among us, we should have far better utensils of all sorts for our houses, as chairs, stools, bedsteads, tables, wainscott, cabinets etc, what universal use the French make of the timber of this sole tree, for domestic affairs, may be seen in every room both of poor and rich'. Both England and the continent continued to use walnut until the advent of mahogany. Although it might at first appear to be an overmantel mirror, there is a strong possibility that this mirror [**88**] was originally a picture frame converted into a looking-glass by the addition of a mirror-plate. Had it been an overmantel mirror it would have had a pediment at the top with a carved panel between it and the frame, or the pediment, fixed on to a straight edge, rather than in this case, where it is inset. The large numbers of walnut and parcel-gilt mirrors with incised decoration, with or without this distinctive gilded bird crest, [**91**], have appeared on the American market over the years, possibly indicating that this style is American in origin. Alternatively, this form, with its particular decoration, may have been fashionable with American collectors and exported from England in large numbers during the early years of this century. The majority of looking-glass frames and overmantel mirrors of this date were decorated with gilt-gesso or veneered with walnut and parcel-gilded, some painted to match the wainscoting of the room.

The wainscoting above the chimney piece of which this pine-framed overmantel, may have formed a part, was the work of the joiner [**94**]. In 1632, a document was drawn up to settle disputes between the carpenters and joiners. The situation had become so bad that the carpenters company had imprisoned a number of joiners for interfering in the carpenters' work. The lists that were drawn up divided the work and mentioned 'all sorts of wainscott and sealing of Houses' under the joiners work, as well as 'all carved works either raised or cut through or sunk in with the ground taken out being wrought and cut with carving tools without the use of planes'. The timber used for wainscotting depended on the amount of money the owner of the house wanted to spend. Oak was often used as well as walnut and cedar, while deal and fir were usually painted. John Evelyn recorded in his diary in 1677 after a visit to Euston Hall, Suffolk: 'The waintscott, being of fir and painted does not please me as well as Spanish oak without paint'. It seems probable that this overmantel originally would have been painted and was stripped and wax-polished during the twentieth century. This walnut-veneered and parcel-gilt mirror [**100**] illustrates a form of looking-glass frame that continued to be made throughout the reign of George I (1714–27), and into the reign of George II (1727–60). The demand for such mirrors, however, was inevitably limited to the wealthy, devotees of fashion, and local craftsmen continued to produce furniture in the provinces in styles that had long since been overtaken. The majority of frames of this date rely on a certain amount of parcel-gilding to highlight decorative features. Since this frame, [**101**] has no gilding, only carefully made crossgrained walnut scrolls for decoration, it could have been made in the provinces.

Crossgraining is a skill used to great advantage by cabinet-makers during the period when walnut was extensively used, and requires patience and skill to prepare the small pieces of timber required. The sections of crossgraining that surround the inner carved

89 George II, *c.*1740, carved giltwood and gesso
51in (129cm)

90 George II, *c.*1740, burr walnut and parcel-gilt
58in (147cm)

91 George II, *c.*1740, carved walnut and parcel-gilt
82in (208cm)

92 George II, *c.*1740, walnut and parcel-gilt
49in (124cm)

93 George II, *c.*1740, carved giltwood, with possibly a restored apron (pediment and cresting missing)
60in (152cm)

94 George II, *c.*1745, pine overmantel mirror
width 58in (147cm)

95 George II, *c.*1740, carved giltwood, with later brass candle-arms and missing apron
53in (135cm)

96 George II, *c.*1740, walnut and parcel-gilt
60in (152cm)

97 George II, *c.*1740, walnut and parcel-gilt
56in (142cm)

98 George II, *c.*1735, walnut and parcel-gilt with brass candle-arms
54in (137cm)

99 George II, *c.*1740, walnut and parcel-gilt
45in (115cm)

100 George II, *c.*1730, walnut and parcel-gilt
41in (104cm)

giltwood slip frame are clearly illustrated in this example [**102**]. This same inner frame now starts to be shaped [**104**], moving away from the regular straight lines of just a few years before. (The lower left scroll is missing in this example.) There is also a greater richness of parcel-gilt decoration, which again signposts the approaching Rococo style). Overmantel mirrors with paintings such as this example [**106**] are uncommon, although they evade the knotty problem of whether to place a mirror or painting over the mantel. In this case the painting, from the studio of John Wootton, is in an Italianate style, (oil on canvas). The scrolls to each side of the base of this frame, [**106**] have lost either their flowerhead-carved paterae or candle-arms. Here the use of black paint [**107a**] may be an example of 'blacking' gilded furniture at the death of a member of a family or monarch. (Cf. Schiffer, 1983, p. 93, fig. 204.) The following group of mirrors [**108** to **110**] are examples of the use of mahogany and parcel-gilt. (The poor proportions of the first frame [**108**] suggests it is probably a provincial example.)

Mahogany is a native of Central America, the northern part of South America and the islands of the West Indies. Given its name in 1760 by Nicholas Jacquin of Leyden, it was later changed to '*Swietenia Mahogani*' to include all the mahoganies. The mahogany tree grows to an immense size, often attaining 150 ft and some 10–12 ft in diameter at the bole. During the nineteenth century gangs of between twenty and fifty men were required to fell the trees; working under a 'Captain' they used the services of a 'huntsman' who climbed the tallest tree to locate the next one to be felled. A platform was built to a height of 10–15 ft above the ground for the 'axeman ' to work from. Paths were cleared through the dense forest to remove the dressed logs to the nearest river. Moving the logs was done at night, because of the intense heat, by teams of oxen managed by two drivers. The logs were marked by the owners with their initials and left to wait for the flood tide to float them to the sea. The logging gangs followed the timber downstream in flat-bottomed canoes, or 'pitpans', preventing log jams and guiding them towards a boom formed at the mouth of the river. The logs were then formed into rafts and floated to the wharf for further dressing and shipment.

Mahogany was known in England as early as 1671 when it was listed in John Ogilby's *America*. It is mentioned in advertisements, accounts and bills of lading *c.* 1720 and is first recorded in royal accounts *c.* 1724 when Moore and Gumley (see p. 71) supplied 'mahogany supping table and two mahogany dessert tables'. By 1743 large enough quantities of mahogany had begun to arrive from Jamaica for Catesby to write in his *Natural History*: 'The excellence of this wood for all domestick uses is now sufficiently known in England'. Early imports were from Santo Domingo, a Spanish settlement, and produced timber of a very hard texture of a dark colour with a straight grain. Later, *c.* 1750, Cuban mahogany was imported; it was less hard but was prized by cabinet-makers for its 'curl' and other fine markings. The third type of mahogany came from Honduras in Central America during the second half of the eighteenth century. This was a lighter timber with a more open grain. Thomas Sheraton (see p. 143) in his *Cabinet Dictionary* of 1803 states that is was 'the principal kind of mahogany in use among cabinetmakers'. Unlike so many cabinet woods then in use, mahogany heartwood had the quality of repelling worm, as reported *c.* 1830 by *The Cabinetmaker's Assistant:*

101 George II, *c.*1740, walnut veneered
54in (137cm)

102 George II, *c.*1740, walnut and parcel-gilt
41in (104cm)

103 George II, *c.*1735, walnut and parcel-gilt
48in (122cm)

104 George II, *c.*1740, walnut and parcel-gilt
(lower left scroll missing)
53in (135cm)

105 George II, *c.*1740, walnut and parcel-gilt
$47\frac{1}{2}$in (121cm)

106 George II, *c.*1740, carved giltwood overmantel mirror with painting in the manner of John Wootton
68in (173cm) (see colour illustration on p. 103)

107 George II, *c.*1745, walnut and parcel-gilt
48½in (123cm)

107a George II, *c.*1740, black-painted and parcel-gilt
61in (155cm)

108 George II, *c.*1745, mahogany and parcel-gilt
37in (94cm)

109 George II, *c.*1745, mahogany and parcel-gilt
44½in (113cm)

110 George II, *c.*1745, mahogany and parcel-gilt with altered cresting
63in (160cm)

111 George II, *c.*1745, carved giltwood
60in (152cm)

'mahogany, of all kinds, possesses another valuable property, namely durability; and in this respect it is equal, if not superior to, any other wood with which we are acquainted. Although, while in the tree, it is subject to the ravages of various insects, we have never seen nor heard of any instance, in which, after being manufactured, it has suffered from this cause. It cannot be reckoned an exception to this statement, that when planted in their clamps or veneers on any of our home-grown hardwoods which fall speedily to decay, it should be perforated by the insects which destroy them; for we never find it attacked when detached from other woods.'

It has been suggested that the top of this oval moulded frame, scrolling leaves [**111**] have been added at a later date, which may explain why the stylised shell cresting is partly obscured.

The next group of frames [**112–116**] can be attributed to Mathias Lock. The first of these, [**112**] uses scrolls headed by masks, a distinctive feature of Lock frames and, together with the treatment of the cresting, also points to a Lock design. The Hinton House mirror was designed by Lock *c.* 1743, the drawing for which (in the Victoria and Albert Museum) is inscribed 'a large Sconce for the Tapestry Room' as well as bearing a note of its cost in time, 138 days, and money; Lock notes the total cost of the frame as being £36–5s, of which £34–10s was for the carving. (Cf. Wills, 1965, p. 86, figs 60 and 61; see also Schiffer, 1983, p. 169, figs 169 and 171 where the mirror is shown with a console-table; Hayward, The Connoisseur, Dec 1960, vol. CXLVI pp. 284–86.)

Mathias Lock flourished between 1740 and 1769. Very little is known about this carver and designer who pioneered the introduction of the English Rococo. Aged about fourteen he was apprenticed to Richard Goldsaddle, a carver in St-Martins-in-the-Fields in 1724. He married Mary Lee at St Paul's, Covent Garden, in July 1734. With his collaborator, H. Copeland, Lock monpolized the field of cabinet-making for more than a decade before the publication of Chippendale's *Director*. Lock's earliest known work is his *Six Sconces*, published in 1744. In 1746 his addess is given as Nottingham Court, Castle Street, near Long Acre, later, in 1752, it is 'near ye Swan, Tottenham Court Road'. It has been suggested that Lock worked for Thomas Chippendale between 1752 and 1768, (the years Chippendale's publications appeared). During 1769, two new works by Lock were published: *New Book of Pier Frames* and *New Book of Foliage*. An interesting but slightly old-fashioned frame for its date, *c.* 1755, the creation of this mirror [**117**] possibly coincides with a time when Lock could have been working for Thomas Chippendale (1752–68). The frame is of a 1730s architectural form with the exception of the term figures to each side – a much favoured Lock feature. (Cf. Ward-Jackson, 1958, pl. 116 for a drawing by Chippendale of *c.* 1750 with similar frieze and panel. The use of figures and the eagle, however, are clearly based on an anonymous drawing of *c.* 1740 reproduced *op. cit.* pl. 26.)

Frames of this design [**118**] (carved mahogany and parcel-gilt with a ho-ho bird cresting), were popular in America at this time; some were made in Britain for export, others were made by craftsmen who had set up in East Coast towns, particularly Philadelphia.

John Vardy, who died in 1765, was an architect and Clerk of the Works at Whitehall

112 George II, *c.*1745, carved giltwood pier-glass in the manner of Mathias Lock
63in (160cm)

113 George II, *c.*1745, one of a pair, carved giltwood in the manner of Mathias Lock
82in (208cm)

114 George II, *c.*1745, carved giltwood in the manner of Mathias Lock
78in (198cm)

115 George II, *c.*1745, carved giltwood in the manner of Mathias Lock
50in (127cm)

116 George II, *c.*1745, carved giltwood overmantel mirror in the manner of Mathias Lock
77in (196cm)

117 George II, *c.*1755, carved and painted parcel-gilt in the manner of Thomas Chippendale
95in (242cm) (see colour illustration on p. 104)

5

18

19

57

72

74

106

117

125

126

149

154

173

118 George II, *c.*1750, carved mahogany and parcel-gilt
51in (130cm)

119 George II, *c.*1740, one of a pair, walnut and parcel-gilt
37in (93cm)

120 George II, *c.*1740, carved giltwood
60in (153cm)

121 George II, *c.*1750, carved giltwood with mirror borders in the manner of John Vardy
78in (198cm)

122 George II, *c.*1750, carved giltwood
78in (198cm)

123 George II, *c.*1750, carved giltwood
50in (127cm)

124 George II, *c.*1750, carved giltwood
37in (94cm)

125 George II, *c.*1750, one of a pair, carved and painted giltwood
63in (160cm) (see colour illustration on p. 105)

126 George II, *c.*1750, carved giltwood and gesso
66in (168cm) (see colour illustration on p. 106)

127 George II, *c.*1750, one of a pair, carved giltwood
106in (269cm)

128 George II, *c.*1750, carved giltwood pier-glass (left)
69½in (176cm)

129 George II, *c.*1750, carved giltwood
65in (165cm)

and St James's *c.* 1749. He was closely associated with William Kent and published *Some Designs of Mr Inigo Jones and Mr William Kent* in 1744. One of Vardy's drawings, (the Royal Institute of British Architects) shows a pair of carved and gilt side-tables and pier-glasses designed for the third or fourth Duke of Bolton and intended for Hackwood, Basingstoke, Hampshire, where they remain. This giltwood frame with mirror borders [**121**] is similar in design. (Cf. Ward-Jackson, 1958, pl. 42 and fig. 43.) A relatively simple frame [**124**] has a reeded flowerhead-carved moulding. It has been suggested that the asymmetrical apron of scrolls and leaves is of a later date. This may well be another of those instances where a picture frame, hence the crest, has been converted into a looking-glass.

We have become so used to the regilding of mirror frames that one is inclined to forget that many frames were painted in white or in colours to match an interior decoration, or, as in this case [**125**], painted and highlighted with gilt. The prominent use of a basket of flowers as a feature is probably just decorative, but it can be read as the attribute of the goddess Pomona and of taste, with additional connotations of charity. A good example of a 1750s frame [**126**] has both asymmetrical as well as symmetrical decorative features. Symmetrical elements are the oak trees growing up both sides of the frame, possibly symbolic of the Tree of Life which issue from a pair of cornucopiae, or horns of plenty, from which the earth's abundance flows. The orgin of these symbols is probably to be found in the ancient belief that power and fertility resided in goats' or bulls' horn.

The following mirror [**127**] is one of a pair with an interesting provenance. They were formerly at a house called Stanwick Park, designed by Decimus Burton, which was demolished in 1923. The pair is also illustrated in the Duke of Northumberland's archives as being in the collection at Alnwick Castle, Northumberland, and were recently removed from Syon House, Middlesex. The joins in these three mirror-plates [**130**] have been disguised by overlaying them with fruit and leaves carved in wood; in the early eighteenth century the joins were abutted and bevelled. By this date, the necessary skills were there to make a piece of glass large enough to fill this frame, indeed glass of much larger proportion was being used for pier-glasses. A partial explanation for the use of three plates could be the tax that was imposed on glass in 1745 by the then Chancellor of the Exchequer, Henry, Lord Pelham. A duty was imposed of 9s 4d on each hundred weight of ordinary glass and 2s 4d on green bottle glass. The effect of this could have been the greater re-use of existing plates upon which no tax had been levied. This imposing mirror [**132**] again in the manner of Mathias Lock (see 112–116) was clearly intended to complement the other furnishings of a fine and probably important mid-eighteenth-century house. (Cf. Ward–Jackson, pl. 67, for a frame with similar features.) This relatively plain oval frame [**138**] with a gadrooned inner moulding surrounded by pierced foliage dates from between 1750 and 1755 is complete in itself. The scrolled and leaf-carved cresting might have been added five or ten years afterwards to 'up-date' the frame or very much later in an attempt to make the frame more valuable. Whilst this basic frame [**141**] is also complete in itself, it has been suggested that it was made into an overmantel mirror, using the top section of a larger pier-glass. Had this been the case, the decoration on the other side of the base of the frame would have had to have been reduced to create a

130 George II, *c.*1750, carved giltwood overmantel mirror
width 53in (135cm)

131 George II, *c.*1750, carved giltwood
72in (183cm)

132 George II, *c.*1750, carved giltwood in the manner of Mathias Lock
101in (256cm)

133 George II, *c.*1750, carved giltwood
50in (127cm)

134 George II, *c.*1750, one of a pair, carved giltwood
33in (84cm)

135 George II, *c.* 1755, carved giltwood
55in (140cm)

136 George II, *c.*1755, carved giltwood
overmantel mirror
width 51½in (131cm)

137 George II, *c.*1755, carved giltwood
55in (140cm)

138 George II, *c.*1755, one of a pair, carved giltwood
48in (122cm)

139 George II, *c.*1755, carved giltwood
58in (147cm)

140 George II, *c.*1755, carved giltwood
43in (109cm)

141 George II, *c.*1755, carved giltwood
overmantel mirror
width 53in (135cm)

142 George II, *c.*1755, one of a pair, carved giltwood
41in (104cm)

143 George II, *c.*1755, one of a pair, carved giltwood
45in (114cm)

144 George II, *c.*1755, carved giltwood
45½in (116cm)

145 George II, *c.*1755, carved giltwood pier-glass in the manner of Thomas Johnson
70in (178cm)

146 George II, *c.*1755, carved giltwood pier-glass
78in (198cm)

147 George II, *c.*1755, carved giltwood pier-glass
91in (231cm)

148 George II, *c.*1755, carved giltwood
92in (234cm)

149 George II, *c.*1755, carved giltwood (above) 59in (150cm) (see colour illustration on p. 107)

150 George II, *c.*1755, one of a pair, carved giltwood possibly originally with candle-arms.
74in (108cm)

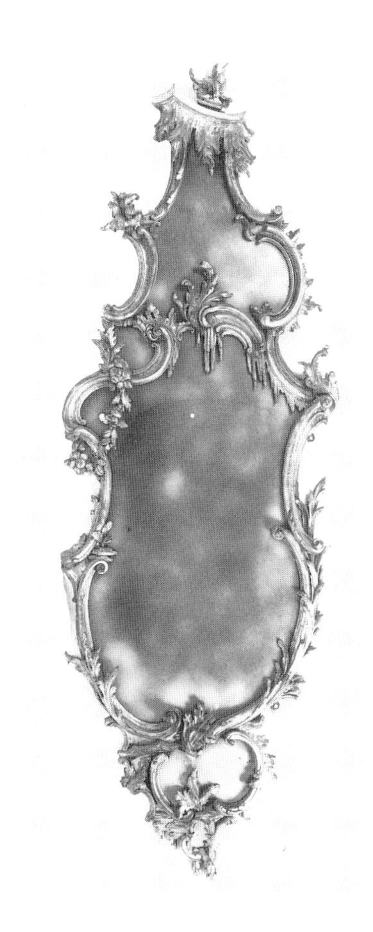

straight edge and consequently would have been out of proportion with the rest of the frame. The following mirrors [**142 and 143**] both of which are in pairs, share a number of common features, for example similarly positioned acanthus-leaf crestings), and may have come from the same workshop. Typical decorative details of this period are included in this mirror [**144**]: the trees flanking the mirror-plate; the swan centring the apron; the ho-ho bird cresting, as well as the pilasters at each side and the icicles or waterfalls below the C-scrolls and rocks. These features re-occur, mixed with other chinoiserie details, scrolls and acanthus leaves. Another pier-glass, [**145**] is in the manner of Thomas Johnson, whose name appears in Mortimer's *Universal Director* for 1763 where he is described as a 'Carver, Teacher of Drawing and Modelling and Author of a Book of Designs for Chimneypieces and Other Ornaments; and of several Other Pieces'. Johnson was an active Mason and was Clerk of the Charlotte Street Chapel, Pimlico, as well as Tyler and Janitor to several other Lodges. From his address at Queens Street, near Seven Dials, he produced his first book of designs, *Twelve Girandoles* in 1755. Later, between 1756 and 1758, he had moved to The Golden Boy, in Grafton Street from where he produced a larger work *One Hundred and Fifty New Designs*. The book, published monthly in parts, included frames, candle-stands, candelabra, tables and lanterns. The book was dedicated to Lord Blakeney, who, as William Blakeney, had been Lietenant-Governor of Minorca between 1748 and 1756. Lord Blackeney was Grand President of the Antigallican Association, founded in London in 1745 with the aim 'to extend the commerce of England and discourage the introduction of French modes and oppose the importation of French commodities.' Johnson described himself as 'a truly anti-gallic spirit'. In such a climate, it must have been difficult for artists and craftsmen to come to terms with such an obviously French style as the rococo. But a novel published in 1757 argued 'Far be it from me to so condem my countrymen for adopting any Invention in Arts or Sciences, which owes its Birth to the fertile Genius of our bitterest Enemies – No – let us endeavour at raising ourselves to an equal, if not superior Pitch of Excellence in every Science and Profession to all the Nations of the Globe'. Johnson's style is perhaps best described by Edwards and Jourdain in *Georgian Cabinet Makers*: 'Johnson's fancy is bizarre, and in a search for liveliness and novelty he has recourse to realistic human and animal forms, which are introduced with no regard to congruity.' He did, however, claim that his drawings 'may be performed with modifications' or 'sleight' as Thomas Chippendale refers to it.' This Anglicized French style took a hold nevertheless as exemplified here, [**147**], where a later Rococo outer frame was added to 'update' the old-fashioned possibly early eighteenth-century inner frame.

Although not directly attributed to William and John Linnell, the basket of flowers [**149**] is a recurring feature of their designs. (Cf. Hayward and Kirkham, 1980, pl. 187 and pl. 188, which reproduces a design in the Victoria and Albert Museum and the mirror taken from it which was made for Sir Monoux Cope at Bramshill, Hampshire; (Hayward, 1969, vol. V, figs 75, 140, 142 and 149 for illustrations of several designs by John Linnell with similar features to this example.) The chinoiserie latticework decoration of another frame [**154**] is also reminiscent of the furniture designed by Linnell for the State Bedchamber at Badminton House, Gloucestershire. (Cf. Coleridge, 1968, fig. 122, for a pair of pier-glasses of similar inspiration attributed to Ince

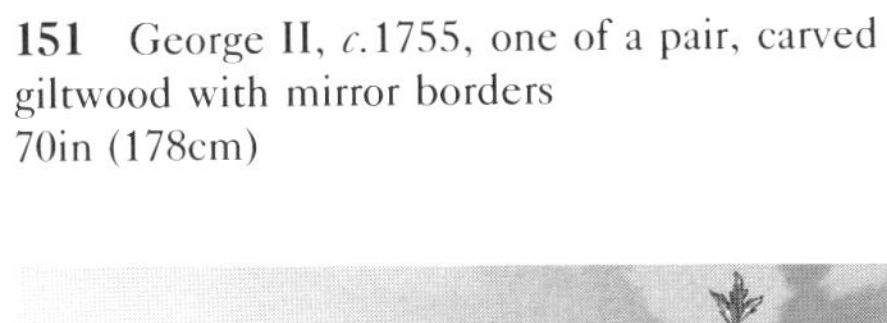
151 George II, *c.*1755, one of a pair, carved giltwood with mirror borders
70in (178cm)

152 George II, *c.*1760, carved giltwood
42in (106cm)

153 George II, *c.*1760, carved giltwood
58in (147cm)

154 George II, *c.*1760, carved giltwood and painted overmantel mirror in the manner of John Linnell
width 75in (191cm) (see colour illustration on p. 108)

155 George II, *c.*1755, carved giltwood overmantel mirror
62in (158cm)

156 George II, *c.*1755, carved giltwood pier-glass with mirror border glasses
81in (206cm)

157 George II, *c.*1755, carved giltwood, possibly Irish
79in (201cm)

and Mayhew; Schiffer. 1983, p. 112, fig. 258 for an illustration of an overmantel mirror in the Victoria and Albert Museum; *Apollo*, 1939, vol. 29, pp. 130–31.) This glass [**156**] combines the Chinese, Gothic and Rococo and reflects the designs of William Linnell. (Formerly in the collection of Jessi Woolworth Donahue.) (Cf. Hayward and Kirkham, 1980, p. 105, fig. 202, for a design in the Victoria and Albert Museum; Ward-Jackson, 1958, pl. 131, for a design by Edwards and Darley, of similar form.)

Matthew Darly, (*fl.* 1744–80) seems to have begun his career in 1741 as an engraver of satirical prints. He later worked for Chippendale, with whom he seems to have shared a house, as well as for Ince and Mayhew. He styled himself 'The Political Designer of Pots, Pans and Pipkins', calling himself 'Professor and Teacher of Ornament'. With George Edwards (1694–1773), an eminent ornithologist and book illustrator, he published, in 1754, *A New Book of Chinese Designs, Calculated to Improve the Present Taste.* This is an example in the manner of William and John Linnell [**160**]. (Cf. Hayward and Kirkham, 1980, fig. 188 for an identical mirror ordered by Sir Monoux Cope between 1755 and 1760; Edwards and Jourdain, 1955, fig. 132, for another pier-mirror formerly at Bramshill). The Linnells, William and his son John, flourished in business between 1730 and 1796, first as carvers and later as general furniture makers of high repute. William Linnell, the son of a yeoman from Hemel Hempstead in Hertfordshire, was apprenticed in 1717 to Michael Savage in London for a fee of £10, and completed his apprenticeship in 1724. He later married Mary Butler, the daughter of Samual Butler, a London coachmaker, and their son John was born in 1729. By 1729 William had become a senior member of the Joiner's Company, having first obtained his freedom and become a member of the Livery, a mark of considerable social prestige at the time. The family, by now there were six, lived in Long Acre, the main furniture-making area in London. The eldest son, John, appears not to have been formally apprenticed, but probably trained under his father. John was described as 'an excellent carver in wood' in a list of members of St Martin's Lane Academy, founded in 1735 by William Hogarth, and again as a 'carver' when he entered the Livery of the Joiner's Company in 1781. Father and son worked together from new premises at 28 Berkley Square, until William's death in 1763, by which time the business had expanded and included among their customers many influential members of English society. A complete inventory of the contents of 28 Berkley Square was made after William's death and was advertised to be sold by auction in May 1763. The stock in-trade included 'magnificient large pier and other glasses, elegant carved termes, brackets and girandoles'. John Linnell, then aged thirty-four, took over the family firm in 1763, employing between forty and fifty people. He was a talented painter, and used his skills to create designs for individual pieces as well as for interior design. There are nine hundred of his drawings for frames of all kinds, including overmantles and girandoles, many finished in watercolour, some with measurements, names of clients and prices charged in code, all preserved in the Victoria and Albert Museum.

This mirror [**161**] can also be attributed to John Linnell from the drawings of Linnell that were traced by James Chance. (Cf. Hayward and Kirkham, 1980, p. 82, pl. 159 for a tracing in the Victoria and Albert Museum, by James Chance (1882), of a drawing by John Linnell in which there is a design for a mirror with similarities to this example.) James Chance and his brother Edward came by the original drawings through the Richmond family into which Julia Tatham, daughter of the designer G.H. Tatham, who was the nephew of Thomas Tatham, a relation of John Linnell, married. Edward Chance described Linnell's drawings in 1882 as a 'valuable thick folio volume of original designs and drawings' which 'established him (John Linnell to have been of great ability.'

Two mirrors [**162 and 163**] have similarities with the previous two examples and it is likely that they were either made to a design of Linnell, or carved by a competent craftsman of the period who was influenced by Linnell's style.

Bearing the label 'Made for Constable Burton in 1762', the next mirror [**163**] may be from a design by Timothy Lightoller, a carver architect of great skill who worked for William Constable (1721–91) between the years 1757 and 1767. Ivan Hall, describes Lightoller as having 'the knack of persistance, and the astuteness to take advantage of other designs by tailoring them to a potential patron's aesthetic and financial requirements.'

Based on a design by William Jones from *The Gentlemen's or Builders' Companion of 1739* this carved and giltwood pier-glass is attributed to Francis and John Booker

158 George II, *c.*1755, gilt *carton-pierre*
72in (183cm)

159 George II, *c.*1755, carved and painted wood
54in (137cm)

160 George II, *c.*1755, carved giltwood and *carton-pierre* pier-glass in the manner of William and John Linnell
94½in (240cm)

161 George II, *c.*1760, carved giltwood attributed to John Linnell
56in (142cm)

162 George III, *c.*1760, carved giltwood
60in (153cm)

163 George III, *c.*1760, carved giltwood
45in (115cm)

[**164**]. (Cf. Wills, 1965, p. 84, fig. 53 for an identical mirror and fig. 52 for another attributed to the Booker family; Ward-Jackson, 1958, pl. 24, for a frame with similar pediment supported by classical columns designed by Williams Jones in 1739.) The Booker family are thought to have settled in Ireland during the Restoration and to have come originally from Nottinghamshire. John Booker, father of Francis and John described as 'Looking Glass Merchant', was married to Sarah Shaw in January *c.* 1711. The Essex Bridge address on their trade card, is first mentioned in 1728 when John the father, became a churchwarden of the parish of St John. The two sons took over their father's business in about 1750, after his death in January of that year. By 1761 they are listed in Peter Wilson's *Dublin Directory*, as 'glass grinders' and as 'sellers' until 1772. (Cf. Fitzgerald, 1971.) Reference is also made to William Jones: '*The Gentlemen's or Builders' Companion* containing a variety of useful designs for doors, gateways, peers, pavillions, temples, chimney-pieces, slab-tables, pier-glasses or tabernacle frames, ceiling pieces, etc.' The book was first sold in Dublin by Robert Owen on Skinners Row for 12s. It is quite possible therefore that this [**164**] was the design for this and other frames attributed to the Bookers. A pair of pier-glasses in this distinctly architectural form bearing the trade label of John and Francis Booker were formerly at Charleville, Enniskerry, Ireland and another was from Newtown Park House, Blackrock, Ireland, with an unlabelled example from Malahide Castle County, Dublin, Ireland.

Although of a regular form, this frame [**166**] has been cleverly designed with asymmetrical elements, so while an initial impression is given of balanced formality no two features are repeated – for example, compare the long scrolls at the top corners of the frame and the acanthus leaves on the outside edges. A contrasting frame [**167**] is of a similar size, and appearance, but relies on complete symmetry. Combining three elements of design that range in date over a period of ten to fifteen years, the cresting on this frame [**168**], is centred by an empty cartouche with a rocaille carved frame, and the bottom of the inner moulded frame is decorated with unpierced foliage. The heaviness of these two areas of decoration would indicate an early treatment of the Rococo of *c.* 1750. The lightly-drawn scrolling around an outer frame, decorated with naturalistically-carved acanthus leaves, is typical of the middle period of the Rococo taste for giltwood mirrors of *c.* 1760. The final and latest decorative feature of the period is the use on the crest of the crossed-palm boughs supporting the open cartouche. The boldly carved flowerheads flanking the main plate covering the joins in the border-glasses were a popular feature with cabinet-makers of the period, especially when used in conjunction with carved ribbons for mouldings. (Formerly in the collection of Viscount Cornwallis, Ashurst Park, Kent.) Despite the damaged area on the left of this frame, [**171**], it conveys a feeling of symmetry, yet the cresting and apron are asymmetrical, but cleverly designed to balance. Here the cresting is particularly successful – the small bird is carefully balanced by the urn with a pointed lid that is, in part, supported by the long C-scroll upon which the bird is perched. The tree centres the cresting and acts as the axis to the rest of the decoration.

In his preface to the third edition of *The Gentleman and Cabinet-Makers' Director*, Thomas Chippendale notes for plate CLXX 'A Table and Pierglass'. 'A skilful carver may, in the execution of this and the following designs, give full scope to his capacity.'

164 Irish Georgian, *c.*1755, carved giltwood pier-glass with mirror borders, attributed to Francis and John Booker of Dublin
75in (190cm)

164a Irish Georgian, *c.*1755, carved giltwood overmantel in the manner of Francis and John Booker of Dublin
width 79in (201cm)

165 George II, *c.*1755, carved giltwood pier-glass in the manner of Francis and John Booker of Dublin
64in (163cm)

166 George III, *c.*1765, carved giltwood
71in (180cm)

167 George III, *c.*1760, carved giltwood
58in (147cm)

168 George I, *c*.1755, carved giltwood pier-glass
70in (178cm)

169 George II, *c*.1755, one of a pair, carved giltwood
width 42in (107cm)

170 George III, *c*.1760, carved giltwood overmantel mirror
width 56in (143cm)

171 George III, *c*.1760, carved giltwood
50in (127cm)

171a George III, *c.*1760,
carved giltwood
60in (152.5cm)

172 George III, *c.*1760, a pair of carved
giltwood pier-glasses
60in (152cm)

The following plate CLXXI, 'a pier glass frame' shows similarities to this pair of pier-glasses [**172**] with the exception of the top of the frame.

The name Chippendale is associated with a vast amount of furniture made during the middle years of the eighteenth century, including cabinet and seat furniture, as well as carved and gilded mirrors and sconces. The plain fact is that almost none of what is described as Chippendale was made by him or taken from his designs. Thomas Chippendale was born at Otley in Yorkshire in 1718, the son of John Chippendale, a joiner. He is certain to have received practical experience from his father and grand-father, both of whom were joiners or carpenters. There is little information about the early life of Chippendale until he was twenty nine and married in London to a Catherine Redshaw of St Martin-in-the-Fields. No firm record of his artistic training survives; it has been suggested that he attended St Martin's Lane Academy, established in 1732, or that he attended a professional drawing teacher. A candidate for this post is Matthew Darly, a versatile ornamentalist whose card offered 'Drawing Taught on Evenings', and who took over the tenancy of Chippendale's house in Northumberland Court and possibly shared that house for a short time.

In 1754 Chippendale produced *The Gentlemen and Cabinet-Makers' Director* with 147 signed plates of designs, 98 of which were engraved by Darly. The publication of the *Director* was an attempt to attract commissions and increase business for his new St

a

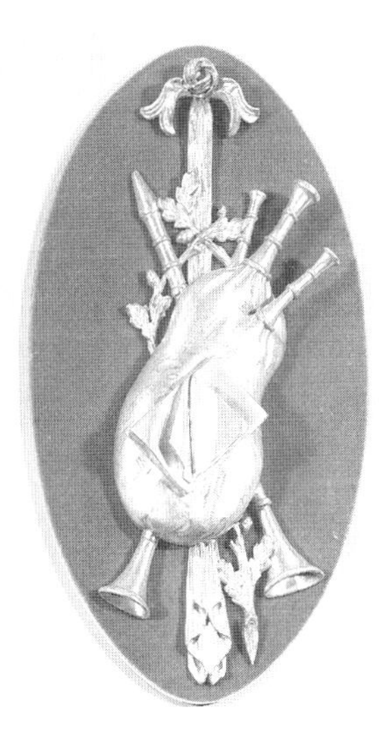

b

d

c

e

173 George III, *c.*1760, a pair, carved giltwood overmantel mirror with the elements of the mirror shown separately a–e
74in (188cm) (see colour illustration on p. 108)

f

Martin's Lane premises. A large number of copies of the book found their way into country house libraries as well as into the workshop of many provincial and other London cabinet-makers. The first edition was followed in 1756 by a second and in 1759 with a third, all of which spread his designs to a wide audience and may explain why his name should have become so much better remembered than almost any other in the field.

This remarkable giltwood overmantel mirror [**173**] is a combiation of approximately seven different mirrors and a pair of wall appliques. Such an unusual compilation is in some way explained by its Irish provenance, but there is no clue as to the date of the amalgamation. The elements – two single and a pair of girandole-shaped frames – may have been united during the eighteenth or nineteenth centuries. Here a central girandole or applique is composed of a rustic scene carved in the manner of Thomas Johnson, while the top three frames are united by a pair of musical trophy appliques, the combined frames supported by a triple-plate overmantel mirror.

Originally from the very top of the overmantel mirror, [**173a**] this girandole has been copied to form a pair and has had the candle-arms fitted at a later date. The pair of appliques [**173b**] that flanked the girandole [**173a**] have been restored and mounted on to velvet backboards. Original girandoles [**173c**] that were used to complete the upper part flanking the appliques. A close-up photograph taken of the compilation overmantel [**173d**] which clearly shows the centre, formed of an asymmetrical girandole. In the centre is a milkmaid milking a goat before a rustic cottage. This pair of giltwood wall appliques [**173e**] are fitted with shelves for porcelain. The final element is the triple plate overmantel mirror upon which the compilation is based.

Both [**176**] and [**177**] are made of carton-pierre, a substance similar to papier mâché (see p. 51) which, when painted or gilded can be mistaken for carved and gilded wood, but which commands a far lower price at auction because it is difficult to restore, a factor which also explains why so few examples exist today.

Made of carved wood this well drawn frame [**179**] has the unusual addition of smaller mirrored glasses fitted to the cresting and below the ho-ho birds, although the right-hand side glass is missing. While the mirror plates are intact in the next example [**180**] – a basic early-eighteenth-century form of inner frame incorporating two plates – one of the mirrors is engraved in an old fashioned way and may be an example of re-used mirror glass of *c.* 1710.

It is uncommon to find wall mirror frames of this date [**187**] made in mahogany. Because most entertaining took place at night when the rooms were lit with candles, the gilded surfaces of looking-glass frames, girandoles, tables and chairs gave a richer impression than polished timbers. This frame may have been a special order, perhaps for a gentleman's study or an estate office, where gilded wood might have been inappropriate, however, the decorative features at the bottom corners are unusual and could even have masonic relevance. (Formerly in the collection of Judge Irwin Untermeyer, New York.) (Cf. Hackenbrock, 1958, pl. 146, fig. 176.)

'Graining', the process of painting wood with the colour and figure of another, was normally carried out in order to give softwood the appearance of a more costly timber, usually walnut or mahogany. In this case, [**188**] a carved softwood frame has been treated to simulate another softwood – pine. Whether of original eighteenth or later

174 George III, *c.*1760, one of a pair, carved giltwood girandole with candle-arms
30in (76cm) (see colour illustration on p. 169)

175 George III, *c.*1760, carved giltwood
24in (61cm)

176 George III, *c.*1765, gilt *carton-pierre*
47in (120cm)

177 George III, *c.*1760, gilt *carton-pierre* (left)
43in (109cm)

178 George III, *c.*1760, one of a pair, carved giltwood
66in (168cm)

179 George III, *c.*1760, carved giltwood
57in (145cm)

180 George III, *c.*1760, carved giltwood
71in (180cm)

181 George III, *c.*1760, carved giltwood
66½in (169cm)

182 George III, *c.*1765, carved giltwood
52½in (133cm)

183 George III, *c.*1765, one of a pair, carved giltwood
62in (157cm)

184 George III, *c.*1765, carved giltwood
47in (120cm)

185 George III, *c.*1765, carved giltwood
42in (107cm)

nineteenth-century origin, this rather extraordinary decoration can only have been done for the sake of colour. The original surface of the freshly carved frame would have had darker contrasted areas which, perhaps, looked too new and did not suit the interior decoration. (Formerly in the collection of the Earl of Haddingham, Tyninghame, East Lothian.) Painting and graining furniture was first used in England towards the end of the sixteenth century for the imitation of oak. In 1664, the painter John Baptist van Ersell received instructions from John Cosin, Bishop of Durham, for work in the chapel at Bishop Auckland 'to paint the chairs and desks the colour of the new wainscot in a walnut tree colour'. During the late eighteenth century imitation wainscot became popular. The effect was achieved by giving the paint work a complete coat of brownish oil which was then scratched over with bone combs of varying degrees of coarseness, exposing the ground work in grainy lines. Later, when it was dry, the surface was given a coat of varnish. The same process was used for this frame and if the decoration is nineteenth century, it may well have been worked over the original painted, or more likely gilded, surface, in adherence to an interior decorative scheme.

This frame [**189**] was adapted from a design by Thomas Johnson, a carver and designer of furniture. The same design was also the inspiration for a pair of pier-glasses supplied by George Cole to Paul Methuen for Corsham Court, Wiltshire, and carved by Johnson. Cole is known to have been paid substantial sums of money for work carried out at Corsham between 1761 and 1763. (Cf. Johnson, 1758, p. 10, republished in *One Hundred and Fifty New Designs* in 1761, p. 55 left; Edwards, 1964, p. 368; Hayward, 1964, pp. 36–37; Kimball and Donnell, Metropolitan Museum Studies II, November 1929, p. 44, figs 9 and 10; Bracket, 1927, pl. XLIV; Coleridge, 1968, pp. 184–5. pls 104 and 105.)

Many of the decorative elements here [**190**] were also drawn from Thomas Johnson's designs published in 1758, which included a number of girandoles. The unusual use of female heads with acanthus-leaf head-dresses as cresting on this pair of girandoles are similar to the designs on pls 48 and 145 from *Twelve Girandoles*, published in 1755. (Cf. Hayward 1964, no. 123; See also Coleridge, 1968, pl. 310, where this pair of girandoles [**190a**] are illustrated.)

A common combination of decorative elements used by popular designers during the middle years of the century, can be seen on this frame [**191**] including ho-ho birds which, in this case, are set on the frame almost to align with the cresting. A slightly different approach [**196**] achieves a lightness of design and gives an uncluttered appearance – an effect created either by the hand of a provincial carver or due to an intentional move away from such abundant use of decoration. Another example of the receding use of ornamentation is shown on one of a pair of pier-glasses [**198**] where the majority of the carved decoration has been concentrated at the top and base of the frame. This noticeable reduction in decoration indicated a move towards the Neo-classical period, away from the lavish Rococo frames of the 1750s and early 1760s. Neo-classical husks trailing from and towards Rococo scrolls [**199**] are a clear sign of things to come. (Formerly in the collection of Lord Newland, Grosvenor Square.)

The following group of mirror frames [**200 to 209**] are examples of the crossed bough form of frame. Such frames were thus not the work of any particular period or

186 George III, *c.*1765, carved giltwood overmantel mirror
width 63in (160cm)

187 George III, *c.*1765, carved mahogany
34in (86cm)

188 George III, *c.*1765, carved wood painted to simulate pinewood
66in (168cm)

189 George III, *c.*1765, one of a pair, carved giltwood pier-glass after a design by Thomas Johnson (left)
77in (196cm)

190 George III, *c.*1760, a pair of carved giltwood girandoles
49½in (126cm)

190a George III, *c.*1765, one of a pair, carved giltwood girandoles in the manner of Thomas Chippendale
33in (84cm)

191 George III, *c.*1760, carved giltwood
66in (168cm)

192 George III, *c.*1765, carved giltwood overmantel mirror
width 45in (114cm)

193 George III, *c.*1765, a pair, carved giltwood
40in (102cm)

194 George III, *c.*1765, carved giltwood
52in (132cm)

195 George III, *c.*1765, carved giltwood
overmantel mirror
width 54in (136cm)

196 George III, *c.*1765, carved giltwood
50in (128cm)

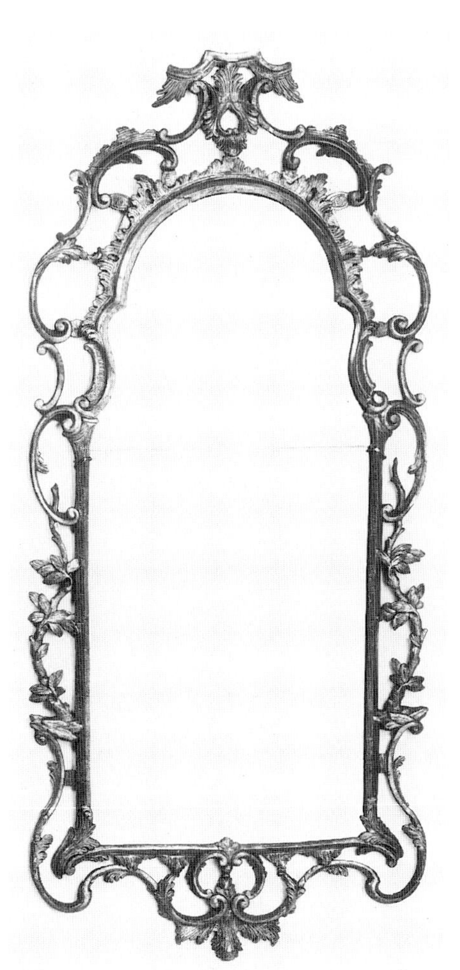

197 George III, *c.*1765, one of a pair, carved giltwood pier-glasses
64½in (164cm)

198 George III, *c.*1765, one of a pair, carved giltwood pier-glasses with mirror border glasses
72in (183cm)

200 George III, *c.*1765, carved giltwood
40in (102cm)

201 George III, *c.*1765, carved giltwood
48in (122cm)

199 George III, *c.*1770, carved giltwood
31½in (80cm)

202 George III, *c.*1760, carved giltwood with mirror border glasses
123in (312cm)

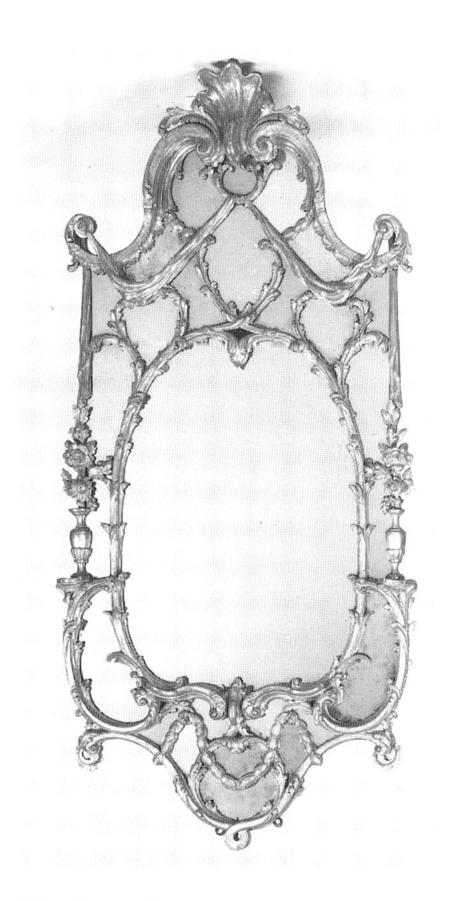

203 George III, *c.*1765, one of a pair, carved giltwood
60in (153cm)

204 George III, *c.*1760, carved giltwood
44in (112cm)

205 George III, *c.*1765, carved giltwood
48in (122cm)

206 George III, *c.*1765, carved giltwood
40in (102cm)

207 George III, *c.*1765, one of a pair, carved giltwood
37in (94cm)

208 George III, *c.*1765, one of a pair, carved giltwood
58in (148cm)

209 George III, *c.*1765, carved giltwood
56in (142cm)

210 George III, *c.*1770, carved giltwood
55in (140cm)

designer, the designs span an approximate ten- to fifteen-year period. (Examples of original designs incorporating the crossed bough feature are illustrated in Ward-Jackson, 1958, pl. 208, for an original design incorporating the crossed bough feature dated 1768, by Robert Adam; Ince and Mayhew, *Universal System of Household Furniture*, 1759–62, pl. LXXVII, for frames for convex or concave glasses; Hayward, 1964, pl. II, for designs published in 1758 for oval mirrors and Johnson *A New Book of Ornaments* for a design dated 1760 for an oval mirror (pl. 7 from Wheal reprint). See also designs by Linnell which feature the form; Hayward and Kirkham, 1980, p. 84, fig. 163 for a design for a sconce in pen and ink and watercolour of *c.* 1760–65; *op. cit.* 115, fig. 220, for a design for the side of a room, showing a pier-glass over a commode and chest of drawers *op. cit.* pp. 101–2, figs 195 and 196, for two further drawings by Linnell.)

Continuing the rationalization of decorative style, this early Neo-classical mirror [**210**] has a Graeco-Roman motif – an anthemion – as the cresting. Further examples of typical Neo-classical features, combined with Rococo scrolls and acanthus-leaf sprays, are also found here, [**211**], for example the classical urn, ribbon-tied husks and the oval-moulded and fluted patera at the base of the frame. In comparison this frame [**213**], seems 'under-nourished'. Originally its sides and base might well have had more decorations applied, alternatively the extant decoration might have been an additional feature which was later attached to the simple oval frame.

In partnership with Samual Beckwith of Long Acre, William France was employed by the first Lord Mansfield, the Great Chief Justice, for work at his houses – Kenwood, (in Hamstead) and at another in Bloomsbury Square between 1768–71. Despite the fact that France was responsible for almost all of the furniture supplied to Kenwood House, including 'mirrors in recesses' in the library, Thomas Chippendale was paid £340 for supplying 'French plate glass'. Dated 14 June 1769, from London the bill was divided thus:

'Two plates, 74 by 44 ins at £69.10 ea	£139.00
Four dos, 74 by 26 ins at £35.00 each	£140.00
Four dos, 74 by 13 ins at £15.00 ea	£340.00
The above dimensions are in English measures	
P. Thos. Chippendale.'	

It is interesting that English glass-makers could also have supplied the mirror glass. The supply from France was by no means a sure thing as this order was not delivered on time. The glass was to have been supplied within three months, in fact Lord Mansfield paid France a first installment of £170 on the understanding that it would be returned if Chippendale failed to deliver. The glass was finally delivered when Thomas Chippendale, Jr and William France signed a receipt for the second installment on 27 January 1770. The mirrors have remained in the library at Kenwood as has some of the other original furniture supplied by France. The furniture from Kenwood indicated by France's bills includes a list of articles 'performed from Mr Adam's designs' and which includes 'two very rich frames for Tables with eight legs to each, richly carved ornaments under the rails finished in a masterly manner'. Included on that list are the mirrors in the library

> 'For two frames to the plates of glass in the two Recesses to Mr Adam's drawing with upright pillars and angular do, all enriched with the most Delicate Antique ornaments and Arches of light ornaments issuing from the pillars and with a frieze at the top of the whole and bottom ornaments supported from the Base for the centre of each plate with Basso Relief, and all ornaments curiously worked and the whole gilt in burnished gold and plate Brass behind all the centre ornaments to keep square . . . £149.8s'.

France, it would seem, was conservative in his work and his frames have a good deal of the mid-eighteenth-century style about them rather than the Adam designs of the period. One of a pair, this mirror, [**217**] is almost identical to frames made by France for Sir Lawrence Dundas, now at Aske Hall, Yorkshire. (Cf. *Apollo*, September 1967, p. 217.) An undated note of Sir Lawrence's expenditure for furnishings for Aske Hall and Moor Park for the years 1771–72 in his own hand, records a total of £9,300, of which £2,000 was paid to France. The same note also records 'Glass from Paris' to the value of £1,500. For the London House, Sir Lawrence called upon the services of Robert Adam to enhance the interior. Lady Shelburn reported in her diary a visit to Lady Dundas in 1768:

> 'I had pleasure in seeing a house, which I had so much admired, and improved so much as possible. The Great Room is now hung with red damask, and with a few large and capital pictures, with very noble glasses between the piers . . .'

In 1774 he was referred to as 'the late William France', but the firm of France and Beckwith continued to be employed by the Crown until early in the nineteenth century. France had succeeded William Vile as cabinet-maker to the Crown in 1764. Three main elements are combined in this fine frame [**219**]; it is both a picture frame for an eighteenth-century Dutch school painting and overmantel-mirror, as well as a display piece. Of chimney-pieces, Chippendale observed that a skilled carver may 'give full scope to his capacity in the execution of these designs'. The design for this frame incorporates small brackets specifically devised for the display of Chinese export porcelain a highly-prized commodity at the time. Royal accounts for 1766 record the purchase of 'a chimney glass' for the Queen's closet at St James's from John Bradburn, in which the frame is described as 'gilt in burnished gold with 46 brackets for China with rich festoons of flowers, a crown on the top'.

Many of the mirror frames illustrated in this section are in some way influenced by the work of Robert Adam, (1728–92), and may have been made as part of unified schemes. Adam and his brother James (1732–94) were responsible for the shift away from the Rococo style during the later eighteenth century. While Robert's designs were in the main intended for a relatively small and exclusive group of wealthy landowners, tailored for both their London and country residences, the force of his influence was such that it penetrated the vernacular and thus spread the taste for Neo-classical style to a greater public, including the increasing number of cabinet-makers. Adam believed, importantly, that the subjects of decoration and furnishing were both within the province of the architect. The illustrious architect Sir John Soane paid tribute to Adam in a lecture delivered in 1812:

211 George III, *c.*1770, carved giltwood
70½in (179cm)

212 George III, *c.*1770, carved giltwood
42in (104cm)

214 George III, *c.*1770, carved giltwood pier glass
80in (184cm)

213 George III, *c.*1780, carved giltwood
42in (107cm)

215 George III, *c.*1770, carved giltwood (left)
64in (162cm)

216 George III, *c.*1770, one of a pair, giltwood
39in (100cm) (see colour illustration on p. 169)

217 George III, *c.*1770, one of a pair, carved giltwood, with gilt-metal candle-arms, attributed to William France
78in (198cm)

218 George III, *c.*1770, a pair of carved giltwood girandoles in the manner of William France
Each 31½in (80cm)

219 George III, *c.*1775, carved giltwood overmantel mirror with eighteenth-century Dutch school oil painting
89in (226cm)

220 George III, *c.*1775, carved giltwood
64in (163cm)

221 George III, *c.*1775, carved giltwood
46in (117cm)

> 'The light and elegant ornaments, the varied compartments in the ceilings of Mr Adam, imitated from the Ancient Works in the Baths and Villas of the Romans, were soon applied in designs for chairs, tables, carpets and in every other species of furniture. To Mr Adam's taste in the ornament of his buildings and furniture we stand indebted, inasmuch as manufacturers of every kind felt, as it were, the electric power of this revolution in art.'

Adam trained under his architect father, William Adam (1669–1748), in Edinburgh. He studied in Rome between 1754–58 where he came into contact with other Neo-classical artists for example Giovanni Piranesi and Charles–Louis Clérisseau. During his time travelling in Italy he prepared a vast repertory of drawings of classical architecture and motifs which later he was to draw upon. On his return to England in 1758 he began practising in London and many of the aristocracy were attracted to his style of work, including Lord Coventry of Bowood, Wiltshire, Lord Shelbourne of Kedleston, Derby, Robert Child at Osterley, Middlesex and the Duke of Northumberland at Syon House, Middlesex. Many of the designs for these wealthy clients were reproduced in *Works in Architecture* which Robert and his brother began publishing in parts in 1773. His work at Osterley Park in one of the drawing rooms was described by Horace Walpole as 'worthy of Eve before the Fall.'

Adam's designs touched not only architecture, furniture and furnishing but small details of the interiors of a room such as door furniture and fire irons which accompanied his chimney-pieces. Adam used a number of different cabinet-makers to execute his designs, (as with the Library at Kenwood when William France was used), these included Chippendale, indeed Christopher Gilbert in his work on Chippendale comments '. . . Adam's contribution to Chippendale's success cannot be lightly set aside,' and continues, 'Adam apparently regarded him [Chippendale] as the most accomplished exponent of Neo-Classical furniture in London and, when expedient, trusted him to equip his most elegant interiors with decorum.'

Matthew Darly published several sets of designs in the Neo-classical style, including *A Complete Body of Architecture* in 1773, and *A New Book* of *Ornaments in the Present (Antique) Taste* in 1772. This mirror [**220**] closely resembles a design by Darly (Cf. Ward-Jackson, 1958, pl. 258). This pair of neo-classical mirrors in the Louis XVI taste [**222**] were from Wycliffe Hall, Yorkshire, where they were listed in the inventory as having come originally from Norfolk House, St James's Square, London. (Cf. Ward-Jackson, 1958, pl. 247, for a mirror of similar design by John Linnell but with a cresting and candle-arms.) The traditional oval Adam shape of frame is repeated in the oval paterae punctuating the border-glasses [**227**]. (Formerly in the collection of Lord Greville.) (Cf. Musgrave, 1966, fig. 154, for a similar example.) Another example, [**231**], appears to be an Adam period girandole but may well be an 'improved' piece. A number of features lead to this conclusion: the basic function of a girandole is to reflect light, in this case only the top few inches of a fresh pair of candles could ever be reflected in the mirror glass; the proportions of both the dolphins and the urn are wrong, they are out of scale and seem to have been an afterthought. The original frame with gadrooned and pip moulding may have originally had the sprays of leaves at the

222 George III, *c.*1780, one of a pair, carved giltwood
135in (343cm)

222a George III, *c.*1780, carved giltwood
49in (124cm)

223 George III, *c.*1775, carved giltwood
55in (140cm)

224 George III, *c.*1775, *carton-pierre*
47in (120cm)

225 George III, *c.*1775, carved giltwood
75in (190cm)

226 George III, *c.*1775, carved giltwood girandole
36in (91cm)

227 George III, *c.*1775, one of a pair, carved giltwood
66in (168cm)

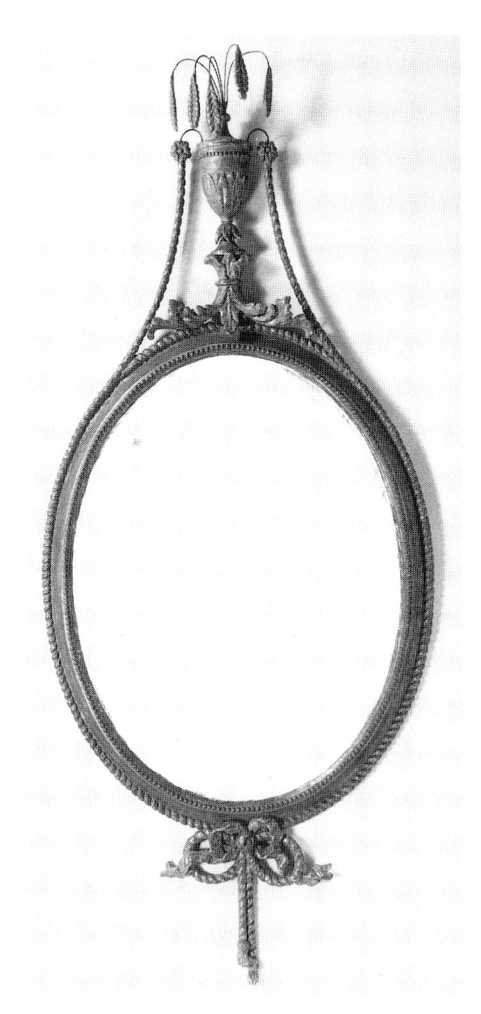

228 George III, *c.*1775, carved giltwood, wire and composition
49in (124cm)

229 George III, *c.*1775, carved giltwood, wire and composition
46in (117cm)

230 George III, *c.*1780, one of a pair of carved giltwood, wire and composition girandoles
43in (109cm) (see colour illustration on p. 169)

231 George III, *c.*1785, carved giltwood, composition and wire girandole (far left)
38in (97cm)

232 George III, *c.*1780, one of a pair of carved giltwood, wire and composition girandoles
39in (99cm)

top and the base, but the rest of the decoration has been added to make the frame more valuable.

George Hepplewhite, whose name has become a household word, is one of the most shadowy figures connected with the subject. He was apprenticed to the firm of Gillows of Lancaster and later moved to London where, by 1760, he was established as a cabinet-maker in Redcross Street, St Giles's, Cripplegate. While little information about him is available; a certain amount of conjecture points to the possibility that his firm thrived by supplying designs for cabinet-makers, but without being involved in the actual manufacture of furniture. Despite the association of his name with a period of English furniture, in particular shield-back dining chairs, no pieces of furniture can be authenticated by bills or documents. He died in 1786 and his widow Alice continued the business as 'A. Hepplewhite and Co.'. Two years later she published *The Cabinet-Maker and Upholsterer's Guide*, a volume of some 300 designs that proved so successful that new editions were published in 1789 and 1794. The Success of the *Guide* was far-reaching and popularized the Neo-classical style in America, although it

233 George III, *c.*1780, carved giltwood 58in (148cm)

234 George III, *c.*1780, carved giltwood $64\frac{1}{2}$in (164cm)

was by this date, on the wane in England. Despite the claim in the *Guide* to have 'followed the latest or most prevailing fashion only . . .' the work was criticized by Sheraton: 'if we compare some of the designs, particularly of chairs with the newest taste, we shall find that this work has already caught the decline, and perhaps in a little time will suddenly die in the disorder.'

Thomas Sheraton (1751–1806), is another of the great names of English furniture. Born in Stockton-on-Tees in the County of Durham, his early life is almost as much of a mystery as that of Hepplewhite, although he is known to have been a competent draughtsman at an early age and to have been responsible for an engraving of Stockton High Street *c.* 1785. In about 1790, Sheraton came to London and is recorded as having lived at various addresses over the next fifteen years, including 4 Hart Street, Grosvenor Square in 1791, 41 Davies Street, Grosvenor Square between 1793 and 1795, 106 Wardour Street, Soho, from 1795 and, until his death, 8 Broad Street, Golden Square. An interesting insight into his life is recorded by Adam Black in his memoires written when Black briefly worked for Sheraton:

> 'He lived in an obscure street, his house half shop, half dwelling-house, and looked himself like a worn-out Methodist minister with threadbare black coat. I took tea with them one afternoon. There was a cup and saucer for the host, and another for his wife, and a little porringer for their daughter. The wife's cup and saucer were given to me, and she had to put up with another little porringer. My host seemed a good man, with some talent. He had been a cabinet-maker, was now author and publisher, teaching drawing and I believe, occasional preacher. I was with him for about a week, engaged in most wretched work, writing a few articles, and trying to put his shop in order, working among dirt and bugs for which I was renumerated with half a guinea. Miserable as the pay was, I was half ashamed to take it from the poor man.'

Sheraton published *The Cabinet-Maker and Upholsterer's Drawing Book* in three parts with the *Appendix . . . and an Accompaniment to the . . . Drawing Book* issued between 1791 and 1794. Other published works included the *Cabinet Dictionary* in 1803, which contained explanations of all the terms used in the furniture-making trade, and the *Cabinet-Maker, Upholsterer and General Artists Encyclopaedia* in 1805, published the year before his death. An obituary notice in the *Gentlemen's Magazine* for November of that year gives the following account: 'In Broad Street, Soho, after a few days illness of a phrenitis: ages 55, Mr. Thomas Sheraton . . .'. It continues,

> 'He was a very honest, well disposed man of an acute and enterprising disposition, but like many other self-taught authors, showing the want of a regular education in his writings. He has left his family it is feared in distressed circumstances.'

This mirrored wall applique [**232**] is made from carved wood, and wire-supported elements made of composition, some of which are missing. (Cf. Musgrave, 1966, pl. 162, for a girandole of similar form.)

In the designs for furniture at Kenwood House, made by Adam in 1774, there is a frame with similar elements to this mirror [**233**]. (Cf. Ward-Jackson, 1966, pl. 229.) A

235 George III, *c.*1785, one of a pair of carved giltwood pier glasses with glass borders
83in (101cm) (see colour illustration on p. 170)

236 George III, *c.*1790, one of a pair, carved giltwood with mirror borders in the manner of George Hepplewhite
$34\frac{1}{2}$in (196cm) (see colour illustration on p. 171)

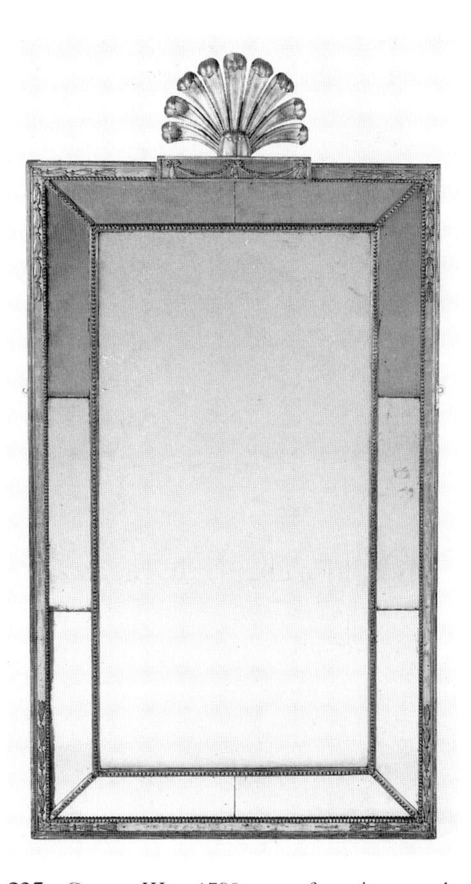

237 George III, *c.*1790, one of a pair, carved giltwood with an inner glass border altered cresting
65in (165cm)

238 George III, *c.*1790, carved giltwood overmantel mirror with glass border
width 63in (160cm) (see colour illustration on p. 172)

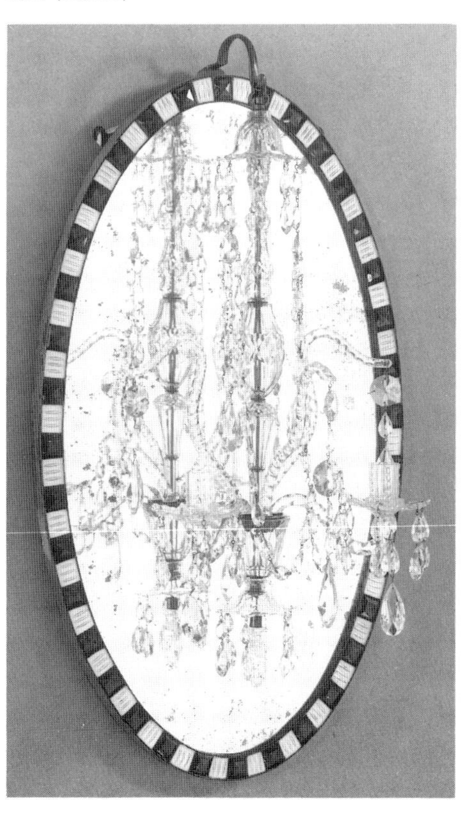

239 Irish Georgian, *c.*1790, a girandole with clear and coloured glass stud border
$35\frac{1}{2}$in (90cm)

traditional Neo-classical pier-glass with a divided central plate, the next example, [**236**] has the joins in the border glasses disguised by paterae and leaves. (Cf. Hepplewhite, *The Cabinet Maker and Upholsterer's Guide* for two similar designs for mirrors.)

Of less restrained nature, [**239**], this is one of a group of apparently uniquely Irish mirrors, whose novelty lies in the addition of a hanging chandelier in front and in the composition of the frames themselves, encrusted as they are with 'jewels'. Made of rectangular, facetted glass, the 'jewels' are silvered on the reverse and laid side-by-side, dark blue 'jewels' are normally arranged to alternate with white, the latter sometimes grooved on the back, and these groves or flutes then gilded. Outlining the frame and holding the 'jewels in place is a continuous copper bezel. Some frames have only an unbroken band of 'jewels', while others have coloured borders of amber, green and purple, often thought to be of a later date. Mirrors incorporating these colours were still being made in Dublin in recent years. The chandeliers are suspended from brass fixings at the top of the frame that are screwed into the backboard of the mirror. The lights are built around a central rod with hollow arms radiating out beneath drop-hung coronas from a bowl punctuated by S-shaped arms hung with chains and drops.

Ireland had a rich glass-making tradition in well-known centres like Cork and Waterford, but only for a domestic market as the Excise Act of 1745 prohibited the export of Irish glass. After the repeal of the act, however, the Irish glass industry received a considerable boost from a wider market. A number of glass-makers moved to Ireland to take advantage of the new business, including J.D. Aykboum, a London glass manufacturer of German origin, who eventually conducted his business from a warehouse in Grafton Street, Dublin. Of this group of typically Irish mirrors, one alone is recorded, signed on the back by John Aykboum. Further examples of this Irish group [**240–243**] reveal, as on this frame, [**240**] the original bracket support for the hanging cut-glass light. (Cf. Schiffer, 1983, p. 187, fig. 485 for a mirror frame with cut glass attachments from The Victoria and Albert Museum; Wills, 1965, p. 127, fig. 157), and another pair, [**241**], where the brackets have been converted into candle-arms and sockets fitted. One of two almost identical mirrors [**242**] has a frame composed of plain cut-glass prism studs or 'jewels' rather than the more traditional blue and white. A continuation of the clear and blue 'jewelled' Irish mirror is here, [**243**], combined with the predominant, English Regency feature of ball-decorated moulding. The traditional English mirror of this period would have been fitted with a convex glass, probably within an ebonized moulded-wood slip frame. This example has plain glass rather than convex because of its oval shape could have had a hanging cut-glass light as with the earlier examples, but there is no sign of any fixing from the front to suggest this.

The 'Regency' period is, in strictly historical terms, the years between 1811 and the accession of George IV in 1820. Over the years, it has come to mean a style of English furniture that begins *c.* 1800 and continues well into the reign of George IV and is a more acceptable term than 'English Empire'. The French version was to reach its zenith under Napoleon and was adapted by the countries that formed the Napoleonic Empire, Holland, Italy, Spain; Germany and Sweden also embraced the style.

The first signs of the Regency style in England can be seen as early as 1791 with the publication of Sheraton's *The Cabinet-Maker and Upholsterer's Drawing Book* and his

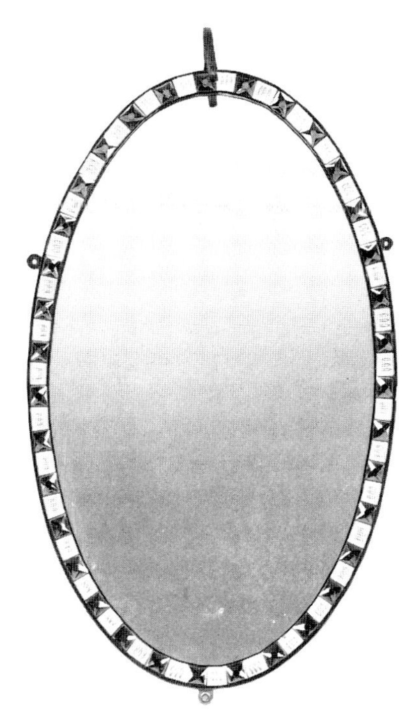

240 Irish Georgian *c.*1790, one of a pair, with mirror borders and coloured glass studs 28½in (72cm)

241 Irish Georgian, *c.*1790, a pair, with coloured glass studs
23in (59cm)

242 Irish Georgian, *c.*1790, plain cut-glass prism studs
24½in (62cm)

243 Irish Georgian, *c.*1820, one of a pair, coloured and clear glass moulded borders
43½in (111cm)

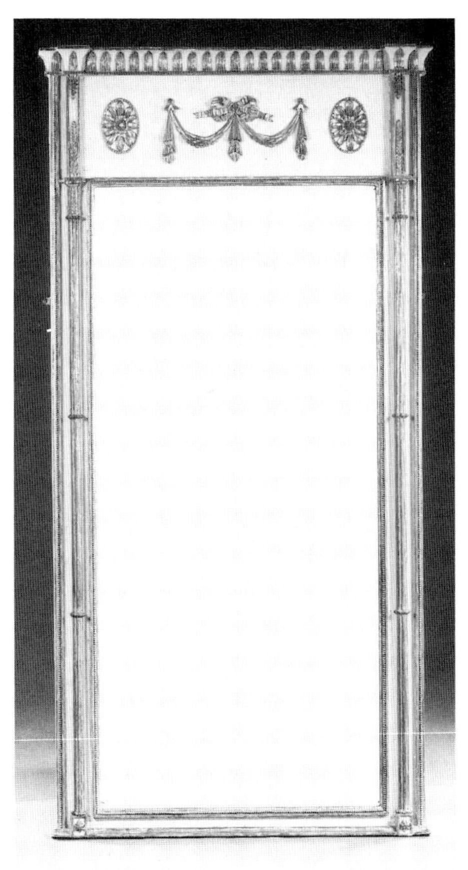

244 George III, *c.*1805, one of a pair, giltwood and painted
77in (196cm)

244a George III, *c.*1805, carved giltwood and composition overmantel
34in (86cm)

245 George III, *c.*1800, painted and composition pier-glass
46in (117cm)

248 George III, *c.*1805, carved wood and *verre églomisé*
46½in (118cm)

246 George III, *c.*1810, carved giltwood wit canvas painted panel
88½in (225cm)

249 George III, *c.*1805, carved giltwood and *verre églomisé*
38in (98cm)

247 George III, *c.*1800, carved giltwood
54in (137cm)

250 George III, *c.*1810, giltwood and ebonized
22½in (57cm)

Cabinet Dictionary in 1803. The Regency period was subject to rapid changes in emphasis and design, many pieces of furniture were described in the *New Circle of the Mechanical Arts, 1819* 'daily falling into disuse while others were introduced which, for a time, are considered indispensably necessary for our comfort'.

George Hepplewhite, in his *Cabinet Maker and Upholsterers Guide* wrote that pier-glasses '. . . should be made nearly to fill the pier and nearly touching the table beneath it'. At nearly 77×42 in this example [**244**], would seem to fit his requirements. The decoration of this pair has been renewed in parcel-gilt and white paint which may well repeat the original decoration. Favourite Adam-period features – the oval flowerhead paterae and ribbon-tied festoon – dictate the classical effect of the crestings. Of similar outline to [**244**], with column sides supporting a moulded top above a decorated panel, in this case, however, the mirror-glass is oval [**245**]. The same style of leaf decoration is used on both frames at the top moulding, but the paterae on the oval frame [**245**] is developing away from the oval, Adam form and becoming round. The decoration has been changed to simulate marble but may be original on the columns and top moulding.

The classical origins of the Regency taste are clearly represented in these frieze panels which are painted on canvas [**246**]. The leafy corbels flanking the frieze resemble the leaves on the two previous examples. With bead moulding, fluting and gadrooning, this oval frame [**247**] could be argued to be complete in itself without the cresting, implying that the eagle cresting and leaf-carved base decoration, which are indeed similar to those used on later convex mirror frames, were added later. If, however, this example (and there are others like it) is not an 'improved' frame, it probably represents a transition in style.

Around this date a form of decoration called *verre églomisé* (see p. 56) became popular both in England and America. (Examples have come from New York City, Albany, New York and Massachusetts, while Edward Lothrop of Boston and John Doggett of Roxbury are recorded as makers.) Predominantly used for the panels above mirror-plates [**248**], the subjects depicted in *verre églomisé* panels, and backpainting varied from rural and pastoral scenes to great sea battles, geometric designs, garlands of flowers and fruit, groups of classical motifs and, in the case of one American mirror in the Henry Francis du Pont Winterthur Museum in America, a mourning tribute to George Washington who died in 1799. Others were decorated with panels of glass, reverse-decorated with coloured engravings. The overall style of these frames is continued here [**249**]; the *verre églomisé* panel combines a geometric pattern and a classical muse. In his *Dictionary* (1803), Thomas Sheraton devotes much space to 'Back Painting' and to 'mezzotinto back prints'; he observes that direct painting may be performed on glass and without a print, by persons skilled in drawing and painting on paper or canvas.

Described by Sheraton as an 'agreeable effect', a convex mirror plate, here in a circular frame [**250**] gave an amusing, distorting effect which was to prove very fashionable over a twenty or thirty-year period. In his *Cabinet Dictionary* of 1803, Thomas Sheraton wrote under the heading of Mirror: 'as an article of furnishing, a mirror is a circular convex glass in a gilt frame, now become universally in fashion, and considered both as a useful and ornamental piece of furniture'. The process of making convex mirrors was not new to this age. Examples are illustrated in early manuscripts and paintings, perhaps the best known is the portrait of Giovanni Arnolfini and Giovanna Cenami painted by Jan Van Eyck in 1434, (National Gallery, London). They were made in Nuremburg, Germany, during the fifteenth and in France during the eighteenth century. It is possible that it was convex glass imported from France that Ince and Mayhew referred to in their engraved *Universal System of Household Furniture* (1759–62), 'Eight Designs of Frames for Convex or Concave Glasses which have a very pretty Effect in a well furnish'd Room'. Early convex glass, to judge from illustrations was made by the blown method as they give the impression of being the half a bubble of blown glass cut when the glass was still moulten. Great skill must have been needed to handle such a delicate shape of glass through the blowing, cutting and silvering processes. It seems feasible that, by the mid-eighteenth century the French had invented a method of making these glasses in a mould. The great upsurge of popularity in England of these amusing mirrors coincides with the effect of the French Revolution, *c.* 1795, leading to a reduced number of imports, which boosted the manufacture of convex plates at the Ravenhead works of The British Cast Plate Glass Manufacturers. This overmantel mirror [**251**] was probably made for a bedroom or small sitting-room rather than a drawing-room. (Formerly in the collection of the Earl of Haddingham, Tyninghame, East Lothian.) Examples do exist of overmantel mirrors that combine flat and convex glasses. (Cf. Edwards, 1964, p. 378, fig. 80.) In two parts, this circular frame [**252**] shows the inner, usually standard, ebonized slip frame which is often reeded and contained within a giltwood moulded frame. Later examples display varying degrees of decoration. The eagle cresting is a predominant form of decoration on Regency convex mirror frames. A symbol of victory and power, the eagle

251 Regency, *c.*1815, carved giltwood overmantel mirror with ebonized slip moulding width 66in (168cm)

252 George III, *c.*1810, carved giltwood
diameter 54in (137cm)

252a George III, *c.*1810, carved wood and composition
45in (115cm)

253 George III, *c.*1810, giltwood and ebonized
38in (97cm)

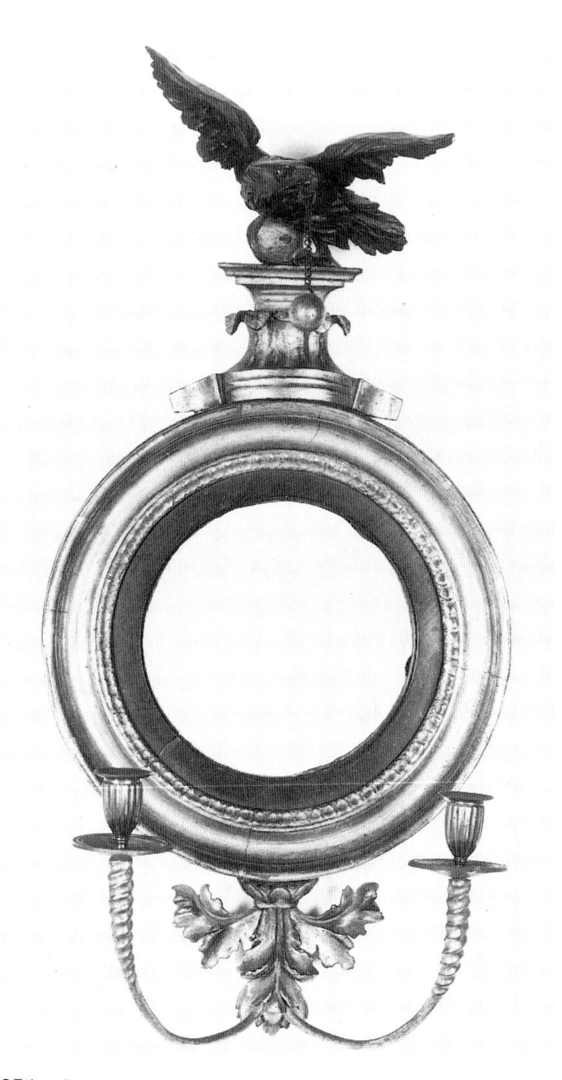

254 George III, *c.*1810, giltwood with ebonized cresting and moulded slip frame
25in (65cm)

is often represented on Regency convex mirror frames grasping a chain in its mouth. The chain is usually attached to a single gilt ball or a double chain to two balls. The origin of this is thought to lie in the tactic of firing chained cannon balls from battle ships in order to demast the enemy. They are also reputed to be useful for keeping flies away from the glass where they often leave deposits.

In this case the convex glass within a plain moulded frame has cresting and apron decoration in an Eygptian style [**253**]. Interest in Egyptian decorative motifs in France was aroused by Bonaparte's expedition to Syria and Egypt in 1798–1801 and, in England by Nelson's victory at the Battle of the Nile in 1798. Many archaeologists and travellers had led the way in the exploration of Eygpt during the late eighteenth century but it was the publication in 1802 of Denon's *Voyages dans la Basse et Haute Egypte* that created a following in both France and England, and by 1806 it was described in a *Collection of Architectural Designs for Mansions* as the 'present prevailing fashion'. Thomas Hope was perhaps the best known English proponent of Egyptian style. Hope was the descendant of a family of merchants who had fled their native Holland in fear of a French invasion. He had spent eight years in the study of architectural remains in Greece, Turkey, Asia Minor, Syria and Eygpt. It was at his London house in Duchess Street and at his country house at Deepdene, Dorking that Hope created classical interiors as a setting for his collection of Egyptian and Roman sculpture. Hope published his *Household Furniture* in 1807, for which he made the majority of the drawings. George Dance, (whose austere architecture was influential) visited Hope's London house in 1804 and described it as an 'amusement'; his designs were criticized (*The Edinburgh Review*, July 1807) as being 'too bulky, massive and ponderous to be commodious for general use' and as an 'assemblage of square timber and massive brass as weigh down the floor and crush out the walls of an ordinary London house'. Despite this criticism, Egyptian taste became the vogue and found favour in all forms of furniture and decoration to the extent that a contemporary literary work refers to a particular library as 'all covered with hieroglyphs and swarming with furniture crocodiles and sphinxes'. Hope had great difficulty in finding craftsmen able or willing to follow his designs. After 'most laborious search', he found Bogaert, a wood carver who had originally come from the Low Countries. Pier-glasses with classically decorated friezes were used by Hope to extend the perspective of rooms, and overmantel mirrors with divided plates, often flanked by term figures, added to the atmosphere.

The designs of George Bullock, who died in 1818, relied, for much of his decorative influence on the revival of the styles of the Frenchman André-Charles Boulle.

After the fall of Napoleon, the English were once again travelling to France where they were influenced by the French Empire Style. By 1835, when Henry Whitaker published his *Designs of Cabinet and Upholstered Furniture*, the heavier carved leaf scrolls, that featured in Victorian decoration, could be seen emerging. Sea creatures are not an uncommon form of decoration on mirror frames and furniture during the Regency period and probably continue the association with England's naval supremacy. Included here, [**263**] is the sea-horse, or hippocampus the fabulous marine creature with the fore-parts of a horse and the hind-parts of a fish that drew Neptune's chariot; another reference to the sea god is the dolphin. Despite the style of

255 George III, *c.*1810, giltwood and ebonized
54in (137cm)

256 George III, *c.*1810, carved giltwood and ebonized girandole
50in (127cm)

257 George III, *c.*1810, giltwood and ebonized
44in (112cm)

258 George III, *c.*1810, carved giltwood ebonized
48½in (123cm)

259 George III, *c.*1815, carved giltwood and ebonized
40½in (103cm)

260 George III, *c.*1810, carved giltwood and ebonized
59in (148cm)

261 George III, *c.*1810, carved giltwood and ebonized
56½in (144cm)

262 George III, *c.*1810, carved giltwood
46in (117cm)

263 Regency, *c.*1815, carved giltwood and ebonized girandole
53in (130cm)

264 Regency, *c.*1815, carved giltwood and ebonized
38in (127cm)

265 Regency, *c.*1815, giltwood, ebonized and cut-glass
40in (102cm)

266 Regency, *c.*1815, carved giltwood and ebonized
55in (140cm)

267 Regency, *c.*1820, giltwood overmantel with gilt-metal mounts and ebonized borders
width 53in (135cm)

this mirror being so closely associated with the early nineteenth century its popularity persisted and the style continued to be made and reproduced later in the century. (Cf. Joy, 1977, p. 384, for a design for a Regency style convex looking glass in a catalogue produced in 1881; Bracket, 1927, pp. 203–4 for a suite of furniture with dolphin supports; Collard, 1985, p. 197 for a frame with a sea-horse cresting.) A basically traditional form of Regency convex mirror [**266**] has, however, two unusual features: The cresting is centred by an acanthus-leaf scroll and placed above is a typical 'Brighton Pavilion' decorative device – a dragon – both of which are asymmetrical and uncommon at this period. The concave moulded frame in this example [**268**] is now filled with a continuous giltwood tube punctuated with lotus leaf clasps rather than the earlier gilt balls; while using deer as a cresting device [**270**] is relatively uncommon. (Cf. Schiffer, 1983, p. 227, fig. 602 for a frame decorated with a deer flanked by dolphins.)

By the turn of the century, the majority of designers had turned away from earlier styles and regarded the Baroque and Rococo either as 'French' or coming via France, the enemy they had so recently defeated. The nineteenth century in England, nevertheless saw a revival of styles that led to a muddled and eclectic period, particularly that of the Victorian era, a factor that hinders accurate dating. For example, this George II style frame [**271**] was made some seventy years after George II died. The result is a combination of the style of the 1750s with a 'roundness' of the early nineteenth century. (Formerly in the collection of the Earl of Haddingham, Tyninghame, East Lothian.) Of typical George III design this frame [**272**] was at first thought to date from 1765; it is, however, one of a group that was perhaps made to

268 Regency, *c.*1820, carved giltwood and ebonized
33in (84cm)

269 Regency, *c.*1820, one of a pair, carved giltwood and ebonized
59in (150cm)

270 William IV, *c.*1830, giltwood and composition
$45\frac{1}{2}$in (116cm)

271 William IV, *c.*1830, carved giltwood in the rococo style
56in (142cm)

272 William IV, *c.*1830, one of a pair, carved giltwood in the rococo style
66in (168cm)

272a William IV, *c.*1830, carved wood and composition in what the French call the Troubadour style.
68in (173cm)

supplement an existing eighteenth-century interior or purely as a copy of an earlier style. Indeed there are a number of nineteenth century frames that were made as copies to harmonize with eighteenth-century interiors. One example is the overmantel mirror in the Swan Drawing Room at Welbeck Abbey, Nottinghamshire, thought to have been supplied by George Sinclair during the first third of this century. Sinclair of the Sinclair Galleries, Shaftesbury Avenue is known to have started his career by 'removing, altering and reconstructing the fine old marble chimney pieces of the old mansions', and to have been patronized by the Cavendish-Bentinck family, the owners of Welbeck Abbey until 1879. Whilst many of the elements of the Welbeck mirror derive from eighteenth-century designs, their execution is machine-like and precise. Another example of nineteenth-century Rococo revival is the group of pier-glasses at Crichel House in Dorset. The three pier-glasses in the Long Drawing Room have been described by Christopher Gilbert as 'spectacular Victorian translations of Chippendale's designs'.

This mirror [**272a**] is an example of the so called 'Troubadour Style' – the French version of the Gothic revival style. Its use became wide-spread after the Restoration, fuelled by the writings of Châteaubriant and the novels of Sir Walter Scott. Due to the flamboyance of the ecclesiastical details which were typically used on both furniture and the applied arts, Troubadour was also called 'Cathedral Style'. By 1835, however, the fashion had given way to the Renaissance and other revivals of the eighteenth century.

This nineteenth-century interest in the style of the mid-eighteenth century was fuelled by various reprints of designs of the great eighteenth-century designers. Between 1830 and 1860 John Weale of 59 High Holborn compiled a number of volumes of designs, including, to name but two, *Chippendale's Designs for Sconces, Chimney and Looking-Glass, Frames, in the Old French Style*, and *Old English and French Ornament by Chippendale, Johnson, Inigo Jones, Lock and others*, the last running into three editions published in 1835, 1846 and 1858. Another influential publisher was M. Taylor of 1 Wellington Street, Strand, who in 1841 published *A Collection of Ornamental Designs applicable to Furniture, Frames and the Decoration of Rooms in the Style of Louis XIV*, under the name of Mathias Lock.

Trade in antique as well as reproduction furniture during the nineteenth century was very active. During the 1830s and 1840s firms like Wilkinsons of Oxford Street, as well as Nixon and Son of Great Portland Street, dealt in and sold antiques and reproductions. Copies were therefore made throughout most of the middle years of the century and if taken directly from the original drawing books, now prove difficult to detect having aged some hundred and forty years. Another early-nineteenth-century 'revival' mirror [**273**] this time the frame was quite clearly made to receive the pair of oil paintings above the mirror-plate. Both paintings are examples of the 'Chinese School', *c.* 1830 and therefore date this frame accurately.

Throughout the nineteenth century, the '*cheval-glass*' [**274**] was highly popular. (Cf. Joy 1977, p. 389.) The term 'cheval', implies a French origin, however, the word for a mirror of this type in France is 'Psyche' (see p. 205). Cheval – horse – with four legs may be a clue to the name, but then the majority of furniture has four legs. Richard Brown, 'an architect and professor of perspective' whose *Rudiments of Drawing Cabinet*

Detail

273 Early nineteenth century, giltwood overmantel in the Chippendale style surmounted by Chinese school paintings 48in (122cm)

273a Victoria, *c.*1840, gothic style, carved giltwood overmantel mirror 80in (203cm)

274 Victoria, *c.*1840, mahogany cheval mirror 68in (173cm) in the Elizabethan style

and Upholstery Furniture was published in 1820, wrote of the cheval mirror, 'a cheval glass could have the figure of Narcissus to show our folly in being too much in love with our own persons'. Another example [**275**] is in mahogany, the most common cabinet timber of the period, and would have matched the rest of the bedroom furniture. The development of these mirrors coincided with the production of larger and cheaper sheets of mirror-glass and with a period of great interest in both ladies' and gentlemen's fashion. The combination of wood and composition [**276**] is not a nineteenth-century development. Robert Adam used both for looking-glass frames and for applied decoration. Composition proved ideal for mirror frames, it was used in

275 Victoria, *c.*1840, mahogany cheval mirror
70in (178cm)

276 Victoria, *c.*1845, one of a pair, giltwood and composition pier-glass
72in (183cm)

moulds to duplicate the most intricate of designs without the need to employ a carver each time. (See p. 54).

Advances in industrial technology during the century and the development of alloys of metal are responsible for this gilded frame [**277**]. The new middle class's demand for a larger range of cheaper goods was satisfied by factory-made objects like this toilet-mirror.

This large overmantel [**278**] in the Gothic and Rococo style centred by a carved giltwood ducal coronet left the visitor in no doubt of the rank of their host. (Cf. Joy, pp. 391–93 for drawings published between 1850 and 1880 of similar pier-glasses and pier-tables.) Made of carved wood and composition, this example, [**281**], (one of a pair of overmantel mirrors) was probably made to go above a pair of fireplaces at each end of a large Victorian salon.

From *c.* 1835 onwards, factory-made furniture satisfied a large and increasingly wealthy middle class. Throughout the nineteenth century there was a revival of interest in the styles of earlier periods. The 'old French' combination Rococo style was

277 Victoria, *c.*1840, gilt-metal toilet-mirror
25in (64cm)

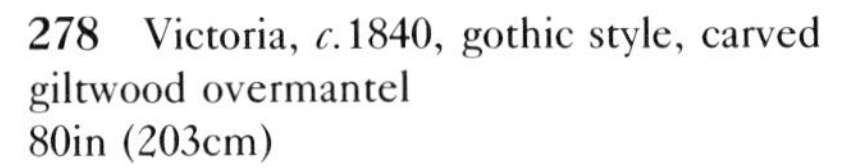

278 Victoria, *c.*1840, gothic style, carved giltwood overmantel
80in (203cm)

279 Victoria, *c.*1850, carved giltwood
39½in (100cm)

280 Victoria, *c.*1850, one of a pair, carved giltwood pier-glass with matching table
101in (257cm)

281 Victoria, *c.*1850, one of a pair, giltwood and plaster overmantel
96in (244cm)

popular for looking-glass frames, which were almost mass-produced using composition. From 1835, the building of the Palace of Westminster in an Elizabethan style did much to popularize the fashion for Tudor, Jacobean and Stuart styles, as did the publication in 1836 of Henry Shaw's *Ancient Furniture*. The Great Exhibition of 1851 encouraged designers, craftsmen and many factories to show off self-confidence in their products to an admiring world. Items in wood, metal, china, pottery, composition papier-mâché and many more materials vied to win prestige. Unlike so many mirror frames of this period that relied on composition for the decorative detail, this circular example [**282**] is made entirely out of carved wood and is fitted with a convex mirror-plate more typical of the early years of the century. Also carved, this frame [**283**] is decorated with naturalistically painted mulberry leaves. (Early specimens of mulberry trees were planted in England by James I in 1609 in both St James's and Greenwich parks.)

282 Victoria, *c.*1850, carved wood with convex glass
29in (74cm) diameter

A number of names emerge from this period: Lorenzo Booth was a lithographic draughtsman and designer of 15 Coleman Street, London who published the *Exhibition Book of Original Design for Furniture*, subtitled *The Original Design Book for Decorative Furniture* in 1864. His book contained nearly 300 designs and an essay on decorative furniture in which he was critical of the furniture exhibited in 1851 and 1862. He also included the following prophetic remark: 'No future historian will be able to identify mid-nineteenth century styles with anything except what we have borrowed or imitated, or positively copied from our predecessors'. This walnut and parcel-gilt mirror [**285**] is in the manner of Booth. (Cf. Joy, 1977, p. 380 for a design for a pier-glass of similar form, published by Booth in 1864.)

Another figure at this time was Alfred Stevens 1817–75, an English painter, sculptor and designer, who originally designed this mirror [**288**]. (Cf. Cooper, 1976, p. 44; The Catalogue of the Drawing Collection of the the Royal Institute of British Architects, 1975; *Country Life*, 12 May 1928, *The Connoisseur*, September 1975, and Calvin, *The Dictionary of British architects 1600–1840*, 1978, pp. 856 7.) Stevens had studied in Italy where he developed a lasting passion for High Renaissance art. His greatest work was the interior of Dorchester House, built for R.S. Holford by Louis Vulliamy (1791–1871), son of the famous clock-maker. R.S. Holford was a millionaire patron of the architect and he commissioned Stevens on the recommendation of the critic John Morris Moore in 1859. Work in the house included Stevens' designs for metalwork, especially cast iron stoves and fireplaces, decorated profusely with figures, foliage and architectural motifs in the Renaissance style and made by Henry E. Hoole & Co. of Sheffield. Stevens also worked on the painted ceilings but died in 1875 before the work was completed; Dorchester House was demolished in 1929.

Charles Hancock from Cheltenham made this large, wrought-iron girandole mirror [**293**] ornamented with floral design, consisting largely of three-dimensional roses, lilies and passion flowers, it is reminiscent of Letheren's work *c.* 1887. While there is no evidence to support the theory that Hancock studied under Letheren, there is no doubt that he was influenced by his work. By 1903, Hancock was making all kinds of ironwork and obtained the commission for the Royal Gates to Hyde Park, which were designed by the Office of Works and removed in 1959. This example of his work [**293**] is now in the Cheltenham Museum.

283 Victoria, *c.*1850, carved and painted pier-glass
69in (175cm)

284 Victoria, *c.*1860, gilt-metal girandole
40in (102cm)

285 Victoria, *c.*1865, walnut and parcel-gilt
39in (99cm)

286 Victoria, *c.*1870, one of a pair, giltwood and composition pier-glass
83in (211cm)

287 Victoria, *c.*1870, engraved brass easel toilet-mirror in the manner of Thomas Cole
36in (92cm)

288 Victoria, *c.*1870, walnut and parcel-gilt, designed by Alfred Stevens
70in (178cm)

289 Victoria, *c.*1870, satinwood and rosewood overmantel in Adam revival style 76½in (195cm)

290 Victoria, *c.*1870, oak, ceramic and mirrored hall stand by Gillow and Co. 87in (221cm)

291 Victoria, *c.*1865, oak dressing mirror in the manner of Charles Bevan 36in (91cm)

292 Victoria, *c.*1870, carved oak and inlaid overmantel 75in (190cm)

293 Edward VII, *c.*1910, wrought-iron, by C.W. Hancock of Cheltenham
40in (102cm)

294 Victoria, *c.*1880, mahogany in the style of William Kent
66in (168cm)

295 Victoria, *c.*1880–90, carved giltwood pier-glass
96in (244cm)

296 Victoria, *c.*1880–1900, carved walnut in the Charles II style
26½in (67cm)

297 Victoria, *c.*1900, inlaid with walnut and ebony in the style of William and Mary
44in (112cm)

298 Victoria, *c.*1890, one of a set of four, carved wood and composition wall light's (right)
39in (99cm)

299 Victoria, *c.*1890, one of a pair, carved giltwood and composition
60½in (154cm)

300 Victoria, *c.*1890, carved giltwood overmantel mirror in the rococo style
65in (165cm)

301 Victoria, *c.*1900, carved giltwood overmantel mirror in the rococo style
52in (132cm)

302 Victoria, *c.*1890, one of a pair, giltwood and composition pier-glasses
71in (180cm)

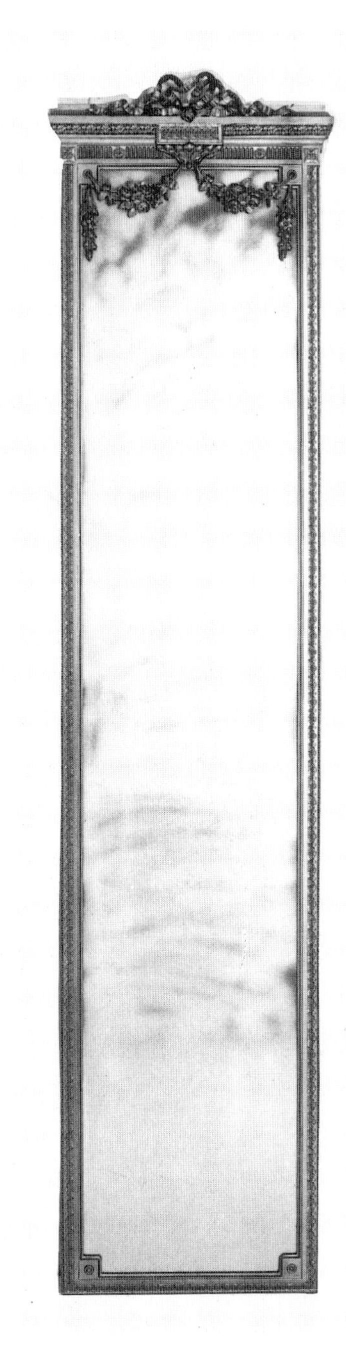

303 Victoria, *c.*1900, one of a pair, giltwood and gesso pier-glass in the Louis XVI style
98in (249cm)

304 Victoria, *c.*1900, one of a pair, carved giltwood and composition pier-glasses in the Adam style
72½in (184cm)

305 Victoria, *c.*1900, hammered copper, Art Nouveau
21½in (55cm)

306 Victoria, *c.*1900, pewter dressing-mirror by Fattorini and Sons
19in (49cm)

307 Victoria, *c.*1900, carved wood and painted, Art Nouveau (left)
26in (66cm)

308 Edward VII, *c.*1901, silver and shagreen by Liberty and Co. maker's mark Birmingham
7in (17cm)

309 Edward VII, *c.*1910, walnut and parcel-gilt overmantel in the style of George II
width 54½in (138cm)

310 Edward VII, *c.*1910, walnut and parcel-gilt in the style of George II
59in (150cm)

311 Victoria, *c.*1900, carved giltwood in the style of George II
44in (112cm)

312 Victoria, *c.*1900, carved giltwood in the rococo style
width 70in (178cm)

313 Victoria, *c.*1900, carved giltwood in the rococo style (right)
67in (170cm)

174

230

216

235

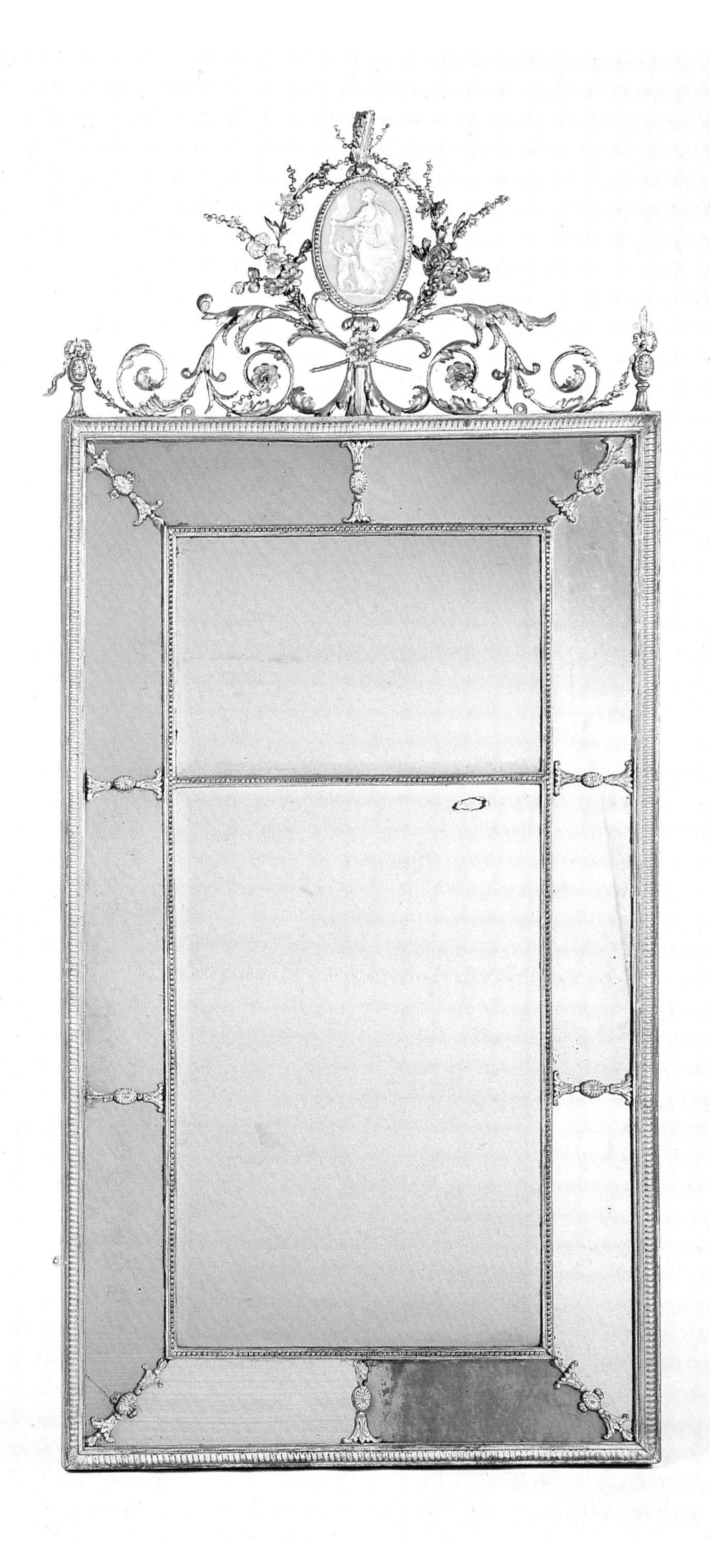

236

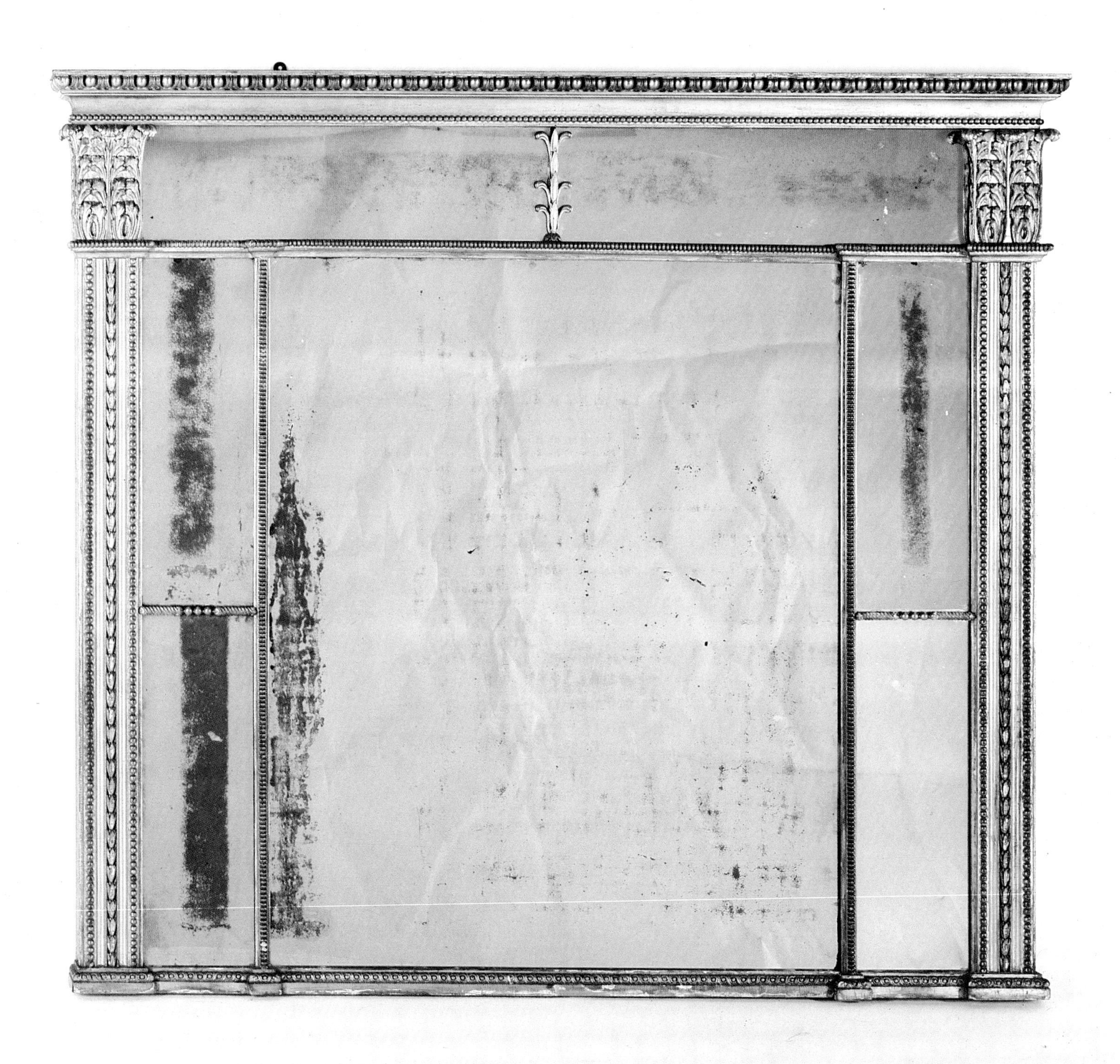

238

325

427

435

During the nineteenth century the French influence on English interior furnishings began with the restoration of the French monarchy, following the defeat of Napolean, and continued until late in the century. The revival of a taste for eighteenth-century designs in England encompassed many of the French periods and was called 'The Louis Quatorze Taste', and later 'Louis style' for anything remotely French. Dating from the end of that period of interest, this 'Louis style' frame [**295**] was still popular enough for James Shoolbred & Company to feature it in their catalogue. (Cf. Joy, 1977, p. 153.)

The firm of Shoolbred, alongside Heals and Maples, had the largest shops in the Tottenham Court Road, (the former is no longer in business). Shoolbreds had a cabinet factory with specialist workshops for upholstery, bedding, carpets etc., and became one of London's first great department stores; they received the Royal Warrant during the 1880s. In 1880 another catalogue was issued, by C & R Light: '*Cabinet Furniture Designs and Catalogue of Cabinet and Upholstey Furniture, Looking Glasses etc.*, and was distributed to retail shops in every part of the country to order from. Charles and Richard Light were cabinet-makers and looking-glass manufacturers of Curtain Road, Shoreditch, (one of the most famous nineteenth-century furniture making areas in London). Theirs was one of the largest wholesale furniture firms in the country, producing furniture for the lower end of the market from their new factory in Great Eastern Steet which opened in 1898. Designs by C & R Light were used for the following two mirrors [**298 and 299**]. (Cf. Joy, 1977, p. 384 for a similar design published by C & R Light *c.* 1881, and Joy, 1977, p. 386 for an almost identical design published by C & R Light in 1881.)

The original design for this frame [**300**] was published in Mathias Lock's *A New Book of Ornament for Looking Glass Frames, Chimney Pieces* . . . later published by John Wheal in a *Collection of Ornamental Designs Chiefly after Chippendale*, published in 1834. (Cf. Gilbert, 1978, pp. 224–5 for an identical example and drawing.)

The term Art Nouveau is thought to have originated with the opening of a shop of that name in Paris in 1895 (see p. 217). The inspiration for the style, of which this frame [**305**] is an example, came from nature, in the waving forms and sinuous curves of plants and in the flowing shapes of waves and flames. The style spread throughout Europe to America, and in spite of its French name, England played a leading role in the movement. Liberty, who sold this frame [**308**] were founded in Regent Street in 1875 by Arthur L. Liberty. The company began as an 'Oriental Warehouse' selling imported goods from the Far East as well as fashionable Moorish wares from Egypt. Their Art Nouveau furniture was distinguished for its high quality and became known, particularly abroad as the 'Liberty Style'. The success of the style in Europe prompted J.P. White to write in 1901, of 'that school of modern British designers which, as yet little known to the British public, has excited so much interest and met with so much flattering imitation from Continental artists.'

This George II style overmantel mirror [**309**] is in a form of frame that did not exist *c.* 1730, and is therefore a creation of the imagination. It is technically correct in being veneered with walnut and decorated with water gilded leaves, mouldings and scrolls, but the shape is wrong. Some of the 'reproduction' mirrors [**314 and 315**] of this

314 Edward VII, *c.*1910, carved giltwood in the Queen Anne style
41in (105cm)

315 Edward VII, *c.*1910, carved giltwood in the Queen Anne style
36in (91.5cm)

century are easy to detect, as they do not achieve the original line, proportion or decorative details.

As mentioned previously, (see **[271–273]** it becomes more difficult to detect frames that have been taken from eighteenth-century designs and are carved by master carvers skilled in the art. Further adding to the difficulty in the detection of fakes or copies, is the modern practice of regilding. Regilding becomes necessary when the gesso beneath the gilt has been disturbed by damp, heat or damage and has caused flaking to the gilt surface thus possibly discouraging potential buyers, compounding this is the tendency to replace old glass for similar reasons. The result means one is faced with a completely new-looking frame. The careful and considerate restorer, however, will do all he can to preserve the 'old surface' to both the front and particularly the back of the frame, if regilding.

France

Jean-Baptiste Colbert (1619–83), born in Reims, entered the service of Cardinal Mazarin and after his death became the Chief Minister to Louis XIV. Colbert was to prove himself more than able, not just as Controller-General with a talent for finance and tax reform, but as a guardian and reformer of the Arts. In 1664 he was appointed *Surintendant des Bâtiments du Roi*. By 1667 the Hôtel of the Gobelins brothers was raised to the status of *Manufacture Royale des Meubles de la Couronne des Gobelins*, and made responsible for furnishing the royal palaces and developing a national style. Colbert appointed the painter and designer Charles Lebrun (1619–90), already chief painter to the King, to be the first director of the *Manufacture Royale* in 1663. Lebrun, who had studied in Rome between 1642–6, recognized the valuable contributions that could be made by Flemish and Italian craftsmen. These talents combined with the excellence of French metalwork, in both gold and bronze, and the skills of the *ébénistes*, produced tapestries, metalwork and furniture unrivalled in Europe.

Phillippe, duc d'Orléans, the King's brother, took an active interest in the glass industry in France. He patronized Jean Castello from Altare who, with his nephew Bernard Perrot, set up a glass-works in Orléans. It was Perrot's invention in 1688 for casting glass that made it possible to produce panels of greater size and clarity than by the old method of blowing glass (see p. 14). A new Royal factory was set up in 1688 in the Faubourg Saint-Germain and in 1693 the production was transferred to the village of Saint Gobain. There, on the fringe of the forest of La Thiénacle, the *Manufacture Royale des Glaces de France* had the sole rights to all cast mirrors above the size of 40 in (102 cm) (or *60 pouces*) and was to become the most important supplier of mirror-glass in Europe. The relatively small mirror-plate [316], which clearly shows signs of its age, reflects the influence felt in France from foreign craftsmen and frame-makers. This pierced, leaf-carved style of frame can also be found in Holland and in England during the second half of the seventeenth century. The design of the cresting makes a clear statement of allegiance to the Crown, while other symbols carved around the frame, include a pair of birds and a pair of dogs. This frame was later converted into a toilet-glass by the addition of a rear-mounted strut. Smaller mirror-plates (those not made at the *Manufacture Royale des Glaces* and under 40 in (102 cm) in size were legally produced at rural glass-works by the blown method [**317**]. Being thinner and more fragile, the plates were difficult to handle and demanded great skill from the glass-cutter since they often broke at the finishing or cutting stages. Here the carefully-shaped arched top is accentuated by carved cresting.

Lead frames provided an ideally smooth surface upon which to lie sheets of 22 carat gold leaf. Usually the lead was cast in sections and fitted around the glass and on to a wooden backboard (in this case [**318**], the backboard has been replaced) a complicated process which probably necessitated a run of frames being cast from the same

316 Louis XIV, *c.*1680–90, carved giltwood
21½in (55cm)

317 Louis XIV, *c.*1685–90, carved giltwood
30½in (77cm)

318 Louis XIV, *c.*1700, etched glass and gilt lead
71in (180cm)

319 Louis XIV, *c.*1700, brass inlay and tortoiseshell toilet-mirror in the manner of Boulle
26in (66cm)

320 Louis XIV, *c.*1700, brass inlay and tortoiseshell toilet-mirror in the manner of Boulle
23in (58cm)

320a Reverse of **320**

moulds. Here the etching to the border glasses that surround the main divided plate is in a similiar strapwork design to the work of Bérain.

Jean Bérain (1637–1711), was an architect and ornamental designer, and one of the creators of the Louis XIV style. After settling in Paris in *c.* 1644, he followed his father, a Lorraine gunsmith, and published designs for the decoration of small arms and locks. In 1674 he became *Dessinateur de la Chambre et du Cabinet du Roi*, which entailed designing for royal festivities, ballets and operas. Three years later he became the royal garden designer and was granted lodgings in the Louvre. His commissions included a desk for the Cabinet des Médailles at Versailles in 1684 and a throne for the Salle d'Audience in 1687, as well as designs for a vast range of other works: clocks, tables and even a carriage for the King of Sweden in 1696. In addition, he was granted the exclusive right to exploit the production of imitation rock-crystal, which he claimed to have invented in 1699. In 1711 he published a collection of some 300 engravings of his designs, only 47 of which were by his own hand however, the others were by his engravers, Jean and Pierre Le Pautre and Daniel Marot (see p. 226). Bérain's daughter was married to Jacques Thuret the royal clockmaker and her godfather was the great Lebrun himself.

Toilet-glasses or dressing-glasses [**319 and 320**] were designed to rest upon a table supported by a strut at the back. The attention paid to dress and make-up meant that these mirrors were highly regarded and may well have been transported in especially made cases. (It has been suggested that the adjustable toilet-Glass was a French invention since they first appear in early seventeenth-century French domestic interiors as in *La Vue*, an engraving of *c.* 1630 by Abraham Bosse.) Both glasses are framed with metal and tortoiseshell in the manner of Boulle. André-Charles Boulle (1642–1732) was born in Paris, the son of a carpenter. By the 1660s he was well established and described himself as an architect, mosaicist, engraver and bronze-worker, having already been elected as a painter to the *Académie de Saint-Luc*. In 1672 he became *Ebéniste du Roi* on the recommendation of Colbert, who recommended him to the King as the most skilful furniture-maker in Paris. From workshops in the Louvre he made furniture for the Palace of Versailles, including his, subsequently destroyed, masterpiece for the Dauphin's Grand Cabinet produced between 1681 and 1683. He is known to have worked for members of the Court as well as for wealthy commoners including the financier and art-collector Pierre Crozat. He collaborated with Lebrun and more particularly with Jean Bérain whose designs he used for his marquetry. (Cf. Frégnac, 1975, fig. 8, p. 211; Watson, 1956, pl. 81). Designs in brass and tortoiseshell on the front and back of this example [**320** and **320a**] are typical of Bérain's work (see p. 48). Also typical of Bérain's rather whimsical style are the linear arabesques, grotesques and scrolls worked in *verre églomisé*, which adorn the border-glasses of this central mirror-plate [**321**], to which complementary cresting may originally have been added. (Cf. Frégnac, 1975, fig. 6, p. 211.)

Measuring well over double the regulation size, this *grande glace*, [**322**] may well have been produced at the Manufacture Royale des Glaces. The central plate is framed with blue-ground *verre églomisé* decoration, again in a Bérainesque manner. The random white marks on the main plate are where the foil backing has been damaged, possibly through careless handling. (Cf. Frégnac, 1975, fig. 6, p. 211; Roche, 1985, fig. 64, p. 45.) In this example, [**324**] the central mirror-plate is surrounded by angled strips of border-glass within carved giltwood mouldings. The double angled border-glasses could more easily have been cut as one, but dividing and canting the glass in this manner would have produced a dazzling effect when reflecting candlelight. There are many examples of this type of mirror that have lost their crestings; larger crestings were turned into separate mirrors while others were simply lost. Intact in this case, the cresting is decorated with a quiver of arrows crossing a flaming torch, bound together with a ribbon. Both these symbols represent love in some way, the arrows, often accompanied by a bow, are the attributes of Cupid and the putti; the torch, or flambeau, represents the fire of love. Such a clear use of symbols could well indicate that this was a love-token or a wedding gift, in either case a generous one. (Cf. Roche, 1985, figs 59 and 60, p. 40.)

This pair of richly-carved giltwood mirrors is very much in keeping with the majesty of the age [**325**]. They may well have been made *en suite* with a pair of console-tables and the room punctuated with carved giltwood torchères. Although the inner moulded frames are basically quite simple, they are surrounded by a wealth of ornament, incorporating numerous decorative motifs derived from classical antiquity. Importantly, a shift of emphasis is revealed by these frames in the general lightening of the Baroque style, a change in taste which has been signalled by the King himself in 1698 in a recommendation to his architect Mansard: 'Il faut qu'il y ait de la jeunesse mêlée dans ce que l'on fera' ('A touch of youthfulness must be blended into what you are about to do').

'Trumeau' was originally the French term which signified the interior wall between two windows. By the late seventeenth century it was the name given to the mirror or pier-glass hung on this wall, and later still, in the mid-eighteenth century, it also meant the overmantel mirror. The inner moulded form in this example [**326**] is very similar to the previous illustration, as is the mask. In addition there is more than a passing reference to love in the panel above, with the ribbon-tied quiver and flambeau (see also [**324**]). Sometimes the cresting becomes an integral part of the frame and seems not to have been an afterthought [**327**]. In this case it is decorated with a jubilant god and goddess dancing upon the clouds, flanked by Power and Victory in the form of a pair of eagles. It has been suggested that this frame was made in the region of Aix-en-Provence.

An earlier form of cresting used in this provincial carved giltwood mirror can give the appearance of having been added later [**328**]. An interesting contrast developes between the relative heaviness of the frame and the lighter, freer carving of the cresting which incorporates a drape or lambrequin as a support for a vase of flowers. The flowers represent hope while the drape was a favourite element exploited both by Bérain and Marot.

An example of poorly matched, replacement plate-glass is shown in this, one of a pair, pier-glass [**329**]. It is possible that these plates are indeed eighteenth-century, but the colour is uneven and they are unlikely originally to have been part of this frame. The expense of mirror-plate also dictated the common European practice of achieving the height required by using divided plates. There was also a brisk trade in re-silvering and re-shaping old mirror glass, before fitting it into more fashionable

321 Louis XIV, *c.*1700, carved giltwood with *verre églomisé* borders
46in (116cm)

322 Louis XIV, *c.*1700, gilt bronze with blue *verre églomisé* borders
102½in (260cm)

323 Louis XIV, *c.*1700, carved giltwood with mirror borders
82in (209cm)

324 Louis XIV, *c.*1700, carved giltwood with mirror borders
79½in (202cm)

325 Louis XIV, *c.*1700, one of a pair, carved giltwood with mirror borders
76in (193cm) (see colour illustration on p. 173)

326 Louis XIV, *c.*1710, carved wood and parcel-gilt
97in (246cm)

327 Louis XIV, *c.*1710, carved giltwood and gesso
79in (201cm)

328 Louis XIV, *c.*1710, carved giltwood
59in (150cm)

329 Louis XIV, *c.*1710, carved giltwood pier-glass
86in (219cm)

330 Louis XIV, *c.*1700–10, carved giltwood
54in (140cm)

331 Louis XIV, *c.*1710, Southern France, one of a pair, carved giltwood
29in (74cm)

332 Louis XIV, *c.*1700–10, carved giltwood with mirror borders
68in (173cm)

333 Louis XIV, *c.*1710, carved giltwood with mirror borders
50½in (128.5cm)

334 Régence, *c.*1715–20, carved giltwood with mirror borders
72½in (184cm)

335 Régence, *c.*1720, carved giltwood with mirror borders
77in (195cm)

336 Régence, *c.*1720, carved giltwood
54in (137cm)

337 Régence, *c.*1720, carved giltwood with mirror borders
65½in (166cm)

frames. Reference to the use of two or more mirror plates within one frame can be found in an inventory made in 1734 on the death of the painter Noël Nicholas Coypel. In the cloister of Saint-Germain l'Auxerrois, the inventory described 'A pier-glass of three mirrors between the windows, one single mirror on the chimney-piece, another of two mirrors set in a gilded frame'. Another inventory of 1779 of the furniture and effects of his Serene Highness Monseigneur Le Prince de Condé at the Palais de Bourbon and in its furniture store mentions, in the apartment of Madame La Duchesse Bourbon, 'above the mantelpiece and above the console opposite, two mirrors, each in three sections . . . Two pier-glasses of three sections each between the four windows . . . Eight mirrors, each divided into three sections, on the eight leaves of the four doors . . . and many others.' The unusual treatment of the mirror-glass in this oval frame may appear out of place [**330**]. Filling a frame with more than one piece of mirror-glass is not unusual; this book has many examples of the need to assemble cheaper, smaller plates, to create the height for pier- or tall-mirrors. The problems are none the less acute with a large oval as in this case. The casting process of glass-making produced rectangular plates which were quite suitable for straight-edged frames, but cutting the glass introduced an additional risk and cost. Here then is a less risky and cheaper method of glazing an oval and one which had already been used for lining the walls of the Galerie des Glaces (1679–84) at Versailles.

By contrast, this unusual early eighteenth-century mirror, possibly from southern France is strongly influenced by Italian designs, and may well retain the original gilding and mirror plate [**331**]. Each side of the frame is decorated with cunningly carved masks and with a vase of flowers as a cresting.

Many examples of traditional carved giltwood mirrors from this period exist, [**332–335**] some of which have distinguished carved features, including lambrequins and trailling foliage, baskets, of flowers, sea creatures and shells.

The diverse styles of the late seventeenth century and early Louis XV period are occasionally bridged by frames that incorporate elements from both of the periods. A moulded frame with richly carved panels and corner clasps is a form often used for picture frames during the middle years of the eighteenth century, the designs on the cresting of this example [**336**] retain the strapwork motifs favoured by Bérain and Marot.

The earlier form of Régence frame with its plain inner mouldings and outline border-glasses has, in this example, been extended to include an integral arch, instead of a separate cresting, and outscrolled corners with short feet at either side of the base [**337**]. Filled with flowers and foliage, the cornucopia at each side of the mirror are an interesting addition due to their association with concepts of plenty. (Cf. Frégnac, 1975, fig. 7, p. 211; De Ricci, 1929, p. 207.) Although this mirror is of a traditional shape for the period – rectangular with border glasses and a cresting – the decorative scheme of the frame has a wealth of symbolism [**338**]. Whether imbued with meaning for the original owner, or merely a convenient and popular form of decoration, the symbols include a pair of baskets filled with flowers, a pair of crossed quivers and flambeau, musical instruments, winged female figures or angels and a dominant male bust of a warrior as the centre of the cresting.

338 Régence, *c.*1725, carved giltwood with mirror borders
74in (188cm)

339 Régence, *c.*1725, carved giltwood with mirror borders
78in (198cm)

340 Régence, *c.*1720, carved giltwood and gesso overmantel mirror
width 55in (140cm)

341 Louis XV, *c.*1730, carved giltwood with mirror borders
75in (191cm)

342 Louis XV, *c.*1730, carved giltwood with mirror borders
71in (181cm)

343 Louis XV, *c.*1730–35, carved giltwood with mirror borders
69in (175cm)

344 Louis XV, *c.*1730, carved giltwood with mirror borders
83½in (212cm)

345 Louis XV, *c.*1730–35, carved giltwood with mirror borders
77in (196cm)

346 Louis XV, *c.*1750, carved giltwood with mirror borders
70in (178cm)

During the early eighteenth century, the architect De Cotte introduced a pair of fireplaces surmounted by overmantel mirrors as the main feature of one of his interiors. Robert De Cotte (1656—1735) was born in Paris, the son and grandson of architects. Early in his career he worked for Jules Hardouin-Mansart, *Premier Architecte du Roi*, and in 1682 he married Hardouin-Mansart's daughter. He gave up his early work as a building contractor to concentrate on architecture and assisted with the completion of the Château de Marly, becoming a member of the Academie d'Architecture. In 1709, after travelling in Italy, he took over the post of *Premier Architecte* from Hardouin-Mansart. Assisted by such men as Pierre Le Pautre and François Vasse, De Cotte presided over the transition of style from Baroque to Rococo, his influence spreading as far as Germany and Spain. Jacques-François Blondel (1705–74), the architect, wrote after a visit to the Hôtel Mazarin: 'as if by magic, the mirrors repeat and seem to multiply into infinity all ornaments and architectural features. The use of mirrors above fireplaces was alluded to in a letter of 22 March 1697 from Paris when the Secretary to the Swedish Ambassador, Daniel Conström, suggested how the new Royal Palace in Stockholm should be arranged in the latest French fashion:

> 'as for the chimneys, I would make them with mirrors from top to bottom, that is the present fashion, and rightly so, for, by reflection, a room with two or four candles is brighter and gayer than another with twelve.'

The development of the form of the frame from earlier periods, when the cresting was a separate element and the base line of the frame was straight, to the later integration of the cresting as part of the outline, and the evolution of short leaf- or scroll-carved feet from the base line, is easily seen in some transitional frames [**343**]. Later still the corners are given even more prominence and become richly-carved features.

Here the scrolls at the base are still present with rocaille feet, but the shoulders of the frame have been absorbed into the outline and the cresting no longer appears as if an after-thought or separate entity. Papier-mâché was also being used for frames at this time (see p. 51). A combination of wood and papier-mâché, this unusual example, [**347**] betrays a strong Dutch influence, while the inner flat-moulded frame is typical of earlier frames veneered with Walnut.

The majority of the illustrations from the Régence period up to, and after the neo-classical period combine elements of, or are wholly in the Rococo style. Rococo is a delicately light and elegant decorative style which succeeded the Baroque. The word 'Rococo', like so many designations of style, began as a term of ridicule, but was first used as an art-historical term, *c.* 1840. Closely associated, the term *rocaille*, meaning rockwork and shellwork, was devised in the seventeenth century to describe the decorations used in grottoes and artificial caves which were encrusted with decorative rock and shells. The style began to emerge in France during the closing years of the seventeenth century in the asymmetrical designs of Pierre Le Pautre and in the figuring of bizarre silks woven at Lyon; this early phase was confined to France and coincided with the Régence style.

One French designer whose influence was felt more strongly outside France was Juste-Aurèle Meissonnier (1695–1750). Born in Turin, he was the son of a provincial

347 Louis XV, *c.*1730, carved wood and papier-mâché pier-glass
65in (165cm)

348 Louis XV, *c.*1735, carved giltwood pier-glass
73in (185cm)

349 Louis XV, *c.*1730, carved giltwood
65in (165cm)

350 Louis XV, *c.*1735, carved giltwood
97in (245cm) (see colour illustration on p. 174)

351 Louis XV, *c.*1735, carved giltwood
87½in (222cm)

352 Louis XV, *c.*1740, carved giltwood
57in (145cm)

353 Louis XV, *c.*1740, carved giltwood
66in (168cm)

354 Louis XV, *c.*1740, carved giltwood
39½in (100cm)

355 Louis XV, *c.*1740, carved giltwood
72in (183cm)

goldsmith and sculptor. By 1720 he had arrived in Paris and in 1725 he succeeded Bérain as *Architecte Dessinateur de la Chambre et du Cabinet du Roi*. Very little of his work survives apart from his *Oeuvre* containing 118 engravings, a later edition was published in 1750. That his work was less popular in France than abroad is possibly explained by his difficult personality, since he was said to be 'présomptueux et mégalomane'.

Of moulded, carved and gilded wood, this may originally have been a picture frame [**350**]. At the centre of the unusual cresting is an eye placed within a triangle, representing God the Father and the Trinity, the latter borrowed from Renaissance imagery. The winged figures at each side may be messengers of God supporting a crown, the emblem of sovereignty both divine and secular.

Complementing the fashion for placing mirrors above the fireplace was the use of mirrors to disguise the unused opening during the summer months. In conjunction with this innovation was the use of painted panels, often still-lives and *trompe-l'oeil* subjects. Alexis Loir, goldsmith to Louis XIV, who died in 1713, had in his apartment in the rue des Bernardins, 'a large picture painted on canvas representing a forest, which serves as a firescreen to the chimney-piece in the vestibule'. Mirrors that had been fitted into grooves fulfilled the same function. When the English economist, Arthur Young, wrote in his *Travels in France and Italy* (covering the years 1787–89), of a visit on 14 June 1787 to the house of Jean du Barry brother of the Comtesse, in the Place Saint-Germain in Toulouse: 'Here I remarked a contrivance which has a pleasing effect, that of a looking-glass before the chimney instead of the various screens used in England; it slides backwards and forwards into the walls of the room'. Although not by his hand, many of the features commonly found in Meissonnier's work, including C-scrolls, shell motifs and acanthus leaves have been incorporated into the design of this frame [**351**]. By contrast the next frame, [**352**] could well be a provincial piece of work, since it lacks any real vitality, movement and quality.

There is very little knowledge of Parisian wood-carvers of the eighteenth century. Around the date, however, when this frame [**354**], which may originally have been a picture frame, was made, one of the principal carvers was François Roumier. Roumier was born at Corbigny and is recorded as working as a wood-carver from 1701. He styled himself *Sculpteur du Roi* and worked for the Crown at Versailles, Marly and Fontainebleau. His *Livre de Plusieurs Coins de Bordures* (1724), contained seven plates of designs with corner scrolls, light, lively borders and strapwork in an early Rococo style. His next published work was dedicated to Robert de Cotte, the architect, and contained eight plates of trophies which Roumier had carved for the choir of the Jacobin church. In 1750, two years after his death, his *Livres de Plusieurs Pieds de Tables ou de Cabinets* was published.

A French picture frame from this period dispells a commonly held assumption that most cabinet antiques rise steadily in value. Measuring 130×90 in (330.2×228.6 cm) and in carved giltwood, the frame was offered at auction in London on 20 July 1916 and was purchased by the frame-maker and dealer, Buck, of Baker Street London for £525. It was later included in an exhibition of picture frames in Paris in 1931. The frame was again offered at auction after Buck's retirement in May 1962 and was sold for £252. It is fairly commonplace to find mirrors which have been reduced in height. The proportions of such frames seem unbalanced and top-heavy [**355**], although in reduc-

356 Louis XV, *c.*1740, carved giltwood 36½in (93cm)

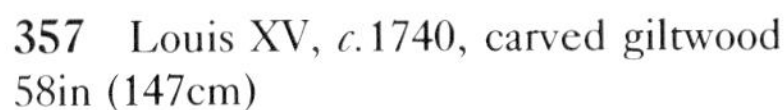

357 Louis XV, *c.*1740, carved giltwood
58in (147cm)

358 Louis XV, *c.*1740, carved giltwood
88in (221cm)

ing a frame of this kind it is a relatively easy exercise to shorten both ends of the side mouldings.

Perhaps to comprehend its large size, this *grande glace* features an extravagantly decorated frame while unusual mirrored cresting incorporates trailing flowers [**358**]. As Pierre Verlet writes in his book *French Furniture and Interior Decorations of the 18th Century* 'one meets flowers everywhere in eighteenth-century decorative schemes – carved, painted, chiselled, woven and embroidered – as though they were the mark of the time'. The flowers in this example are combined with a carved griffin, the fabulous monster with the head, wings and claws of an eagle and the body and hind-quarters of a lion.

Compare this [**359**] and the next five illustrations, which form part of a distinctive group of mid-eighteenth century mirrors. Centred with ribbon-tied symbols of learning the crest could well indicate that the mirror was originally intended for a library. This symbolism can be reinforced if one believes that each side of the frame is decorated with a carving of the tree of knowledge. (Cf. Frégnac, 1975, fig. 1, p. 212.) Similar carving at each side of another frame [**360**] but, in this case of a vine bearing grapes, combined with the basket of flowers in the cresting, might suggest that this frame was intended for a dining room, a theory that could equally well apply to a similarly-carved

359 Louis XV, *c.*1740–50, carved giltwood with mirror border glasses
63in (160cm)

360 Louis XV, *c.*1750, carved giltwood with mirror borders
46½in (117cm)

361 Louis XV, *c.*1765, provincial, carved giltwood (right)
51in (130cm)

363 Louis XV, *c*.1760, carved giltwood
105in (267cm)

364 Louis XV, *c*.1750, carved giltwood and gesso
75in (191cm)

362 Louis XV, *c*.1765, provincial, carved giltwood with mirror borders
70in (178cm)

365 Louis XV, *c.*1750, provincial, carved giltwood
47½in (121cm)

366 Louis XV, *c.*1750, carved giltwood
57in (145cm)

367 Louis XV, *c.*1750, carved giltwood
73in (185cm)

368 Louis XV, *c.*1750, carved giltwood and gesso
77in (196cm)

369 Louis XV, *c.*1750, carved giltwood
64in (163cm)

370 Louis XV, *c.*1750, carved giltwood
37in (94cm)

but inferior frame [361] that was probably made in the provinces. The eighteenth-century preoccupation with floral decoration is evident in another member of this group [362] which has vases of flowers at the top and base as well as flowers at each side.

There is no doubt that at this date mirror-glass of sufficient size was available to fit such a large frame but it would have been more expensive; two plates were often fitted for this reason [363]. Fruiting vines carved at each side of another frame [367] symbolize autumn, Plenty and Bacchus. The value of such a mirror can be gauged by a pier-glass of similar size measuring 41 in high by 35 in wide (including border-glasses) valued in 1771 at what is equivalent of approximately £4,000 today. The following group of mid-eighteenth-century mirrors display similar details of design and decoration. Ribbon-tied husks trailing down from the cresting point towards a period of transition [372]. A trumeau mirror [373], intended for the wall between the windows, (see p. 181) is decorated unusually with holly and berries and backed by a green-painted board; the divided plate has been subjected to damp at some time and the abutted edges have suffered as a result. It is interesting to note that the majority of English frames surrounding divided plates of this date usually had carved wood decoration to conceal the joint. Many picture frames are offered as mirrors and can be effective as such. This Louis XV giltwood picture frame is typical of the period [376]. Until recently the value of converted picture frames has been lower than frames intended to take mirror-plates, however the recent interest has caused a rise in the value of picture frames used for their original purpose.

The use of musical instruments to decorate mirror frames clearly indicates that the frame originally would have been intended for a music-room or at least made for a lover of music [377]. The inventory taken in 1779 of the music room at the Palais de Bourbon included two harps, a large harpsicord in a green-painted case, a chair for the harpsichord, two drums with green taffeta covers, a music-stand made from wild cherry as well as two mirrors. Although no mention is made of the decoration on either of these mirrors, it is entirely possible that they were carved with musical instruments.

Arguably one of France's most original contributions to the arts, the Rococo was subject to criticism from the early 1730s. By 1737 Blondel described it as a 'ridiculous jumble of shells, dragons, reeds, palm-trees and plants which is the be-all and end-all of modern interior decoration'. Provoking such criticism as this it is perhaps surprising that it lasted as long as it did and exerted such widespread influence, even outside France. The Rococo was to be replaced by Neo-classicism, a change that began *c.* 1750 but wasn't fully implemented until the 1770s. The metamorphosis was therefore gradual, and for some, like the Marquis Marigny who instructed the architect Jacques-Germain Soufflot, 'I do not want any of those modern chicory-leaves, nor do I want any of that classical austerity; I seek a happy medium' – a little confusing. Some late eighteenth-century frames are clearly more Neo-classical than Rococo but since they have elements of both, can be described as transitional.

In general Neo-classical frames are rectangular with square corners; gone are the soft curves and rounded angles. This transitional example is strictly rectangular in shape but has vestiges of rococo leaf-carved scrolls evident at the lower corners and amongst the cresting [378]. A more typical and familiar Neo-classical form of rectangular frame

371 Louis XV, *c.*1740–50, carved giltwood
70in (178cm)

372 Louis XV, *c.*1760–5, carved giltwood
86½in (220cm)

373 Louis XV, *c.*1750, carved giltwood and painted pier-glass
77in (196cm)

374 Louis XV, *c.*1750, giltwood and painted pier-glass
65in (165cm)

375 Louis XV, *c.*1750–60, carved giltwood
47½in (120cm)

376 Louis XV, *c.*1750, carved giltwood picture frame
31in (79cm)

377 Louis XV, *c.*1760, carved giltwood
55in (140cm)

378 Louis XV/XVI Transitional, *c.*1770, carved giltwood
76in (193cm)

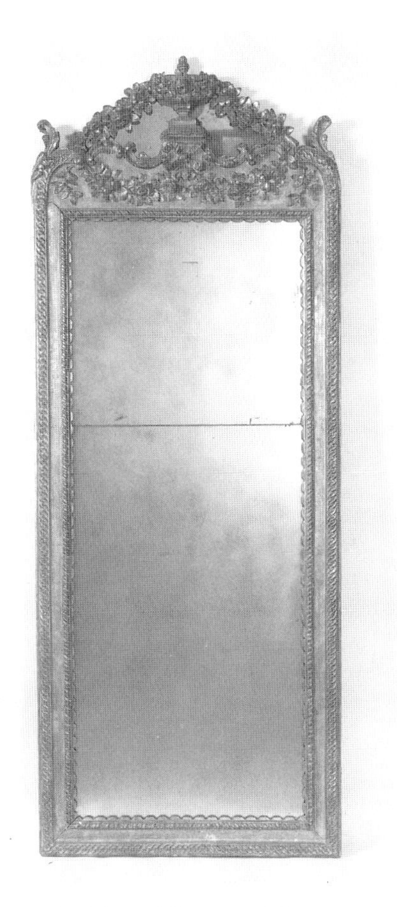

379 Louis XVI, *c.*1775, carved giltwood pier-glass
84in (213cm)

380 Louis XVI, *c.*1775, carved giltwood
91½in (233cm)

381 Louis XVI, *c.*1775, carved wood and painted with matching console-table
36½in (93cm)

382 Louis XVI, *c.*1775, one of a pair, carved giltwood
54in (137cm)

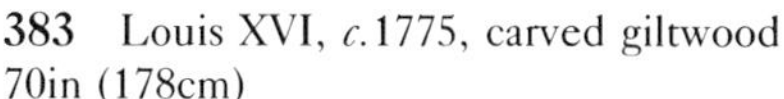

383 Louis XVI, *c.*1775, carved giltwood
70in (178cm)

384 Louis XVI, *c.*1780, carved giltwood
62½in (159cm)

has outset paterae-carved corners [**380**]. Such treatment of the corners is also found on case furniture and chairs, of this date (the latter often having this feature at the top of the legs), and was by no means the trade mark of one particular designer, but used by many, for example by Delafosse. (See Eriksen, 1974, pl 438).

Jean-Charles Delafosse (1734–91), architect and designer, was the son of a wine merchant living in the rue du Roi-de-Sicile. He was apprenticed to the carver Jean-Baptiste Poulet who was *Directeur Garde* at the Académie de Saint-Luc, however he seems not to have completed his apprenticeship. By 1767 he styled himself 'architect and teacher of drawing' while in 1775 he was 'assistant professor of geometry and perspective' at the Académie de Saint-Luc. In 1781 he became a member of the Académie de Bordeaux. In 1768 Delafosse published *Nouvelle Iconologie Historique* at a cost of 48 livres, which included some 111 designs, many of which he had completed some years before. Delafosse designed several houses in Paris from 1776 and also published *Mémoire pour une boucherie et tuerie générale*, proposing a general abattoir on an island in the Seine. By 1773 he had issued 258 plates, and by 1785 another 120 were completed. Each set of six plates cost 1 livre 6 sous. The gilder and print dealer Jean-Félix Watin, through whom it was possible to purchase the designs, offered to simplify them if the cost of the finished article was not to be prohibitively high! One of a pair of transitional mirrors which features the familiar Neo-classical rectangular frame with the addition of a breakfront section at the top and base is overlaid with Classical and Rococo elements, the latter including the acanthus-leaf scrolls [**382**]. The cresting of

385 Louis XVI, *c.*1780, carved giltwood
49½in (126cm)

386 Louis XVI, *c.*1775, carved giltwood
60in (152cm)

387 Louis XVI, *c.*1780, carved giltwood
90½in (230cm)

388 Louis XVI, *c.*1780, carved giltwood
53in (34.6cm)

389 Louis XVI, *c.*1780, carved giltwood
76in (193cm)

390 Louis XVI, *c.*1780, carved giltwood
pier-glass
65in (165cm)

this relatively simple frame, [**383**], is centred by a pair of winged cherub masks (presumably denoting the wind) surrounded by clouds and flanked by garlands of flowers.

Many provincial examples of Louis XVI mirrors lack any real quality, either in terms of design or execution [**385**]. Evidently this frame has been regilded in recent years and the gilder has been lavish with the use of valuable 22 carat gold leaf, since the leaves of gold have been overlapped thereby giving the effect of double gilding. As a result, paler lines in the gilding can be seen around the frame. When the effect is intentional, the process is called double gilding. Although little documentation exists concerning frame-makers of eighteenth-century France, some carvers, also known as sculptors, are recorded. One such was Honoré Guibert (1720–91), who was born in Avignon and who married a sister of the painter Vernet in 1744. It was Vernet who recommended him, while he was still living in Avignon, to carve the frames for six of Vernet's views of French harbours. In 1763 he became a *Maître Sculpteur* in the Parisian Guild and a member of the Académie de Saint-Luc. He is known to have worked for the Court, producing mostly picture frames and *boiseries* to his own designs. Carved around a rectangular moulded frame [**386**], this guilloche pattern is a common decorative device and was used by Guibert on panelling in the Salon de Compagnie at the Petit Trianon at Versailles. (Cf. Eriksen, 1974, pls 66 and 67). He also worked there on the opera house (1768–69) to designs by Gabriel.

This moulded frame has a cresting celebrating the Victory of Love [**389**]. The central hatchment is filled with a heart entwined with leaves and flowers within an oval frame, overlaying either a flambeau or quiver of arrows, all of which is surmounted by a crown of laurel leaves forming a crest. Probably made outside Paris in one of the regional centres of mirror frame-making, possibly near the border with Italy, this pier-glass consequently reveals a strong Italian influence [**390**]. Originally, this painted and parcel-gilt trumeau or overmantel mirror [**391**] would have been part of the *boiserie* or wood panelling of a room. Above the rectangular mirror-plate a painted *scène gallante* depicts a young couple admiring a caged bird. Because the caged bird is possibly an allegory of spring, the rest of the *boiserie* may well have included painted scenes prepresenting the other seasons.

The term 'ormolu' is generally reserved for eighteenth-century and later metal objects gilded by the mercury gilding process [**393**]. (Formerly in the collection of the Marquis de Piron.) Perhaps the most outstanding craftsman specializing in chased and gilded metalwork at this period was Gouthière.

Pierre Gouthière (1732–1812/14), became a Maître Doreur in 1758 having perfected, if not invented, a variation of the mercury gilding process whereby parts of a gilt-bronze object could be given a matt finish to contrast with the burnished areas. He became well known in 1770 when he worked for Madame du Barry at the Pavillon de Louveçiennes. His other patrons failed him financially and by the outset of the Revolution he was in complete ruin and died in poverty. Like the earlier example [**391**] this painted and parcel-gilt mirror [**395**] (one of a pair) originally would have been incorporated into the *boiseries* of a room. The *menuisiers* (specialist carvers responsible for this type of work), relied on oak or walnut as their basic material. In some cases pine or mahogany as well as limewood were used where intricate, applied

391 Louis XVI, *c.*1780, parcel gilt and painted overmantel (above left)
65in (165cm)

392 Louis XVI, *c.*1785, carved giltwood
65in (165cm)

393 Louis XVI, *c.*1785, ormolu
15½in (39cm)

394 Louis XVI, *c.*1785, provincial, carved and painted
86in (218cm)

395 Louis XVI, *c.*1785, one of a pair, parcel-gilt and painted
84in (213cm)

396 Directoire, *c.*1795, mahogany, gilt-bronze and inlaid brass cheval-mirror
77½in (197cm)

397 Empire, *c.*1805, mahogany and gilt bronze cheval-mirror
65in (165cm)

398 Empire *c.*1808, ormolu-mounted burr elm dressing table
64in (162cm) overall height

carvings figured in the design. By the reign of Louis XVI the overall use of gilding had been superceded by a predominance of painted decoration for *boiserie*. Paint was used in some cases to simulate rare woods like *bois de rose* (tulipwood) and mahogany, as both were imported and expensive, but more commonly plain colours were used, as in this example, which is pale green.

A good specimen of the Empire style is this mahogany and metal-mounted 'cheval' mirror, made between 1795–99 [**396**]. (Cf. Dumonthier, 1923, pl 28). This simplification of the Louis XVI style emerged before the Revolution and continued into the Empire period. Its relative austerity was probably due more to economic necessity than aesthetic preference, as the country had been nearly bankrupted by war and revolution. There are two common names, both French, given to this style of mirror in Europe: the 'cheval' mirror in Britain, and the 'Psyché' in France. There seems to be no logical reason why the British should use the word 'cheval' to describe this type of mirror other than for its direct translation into 'horse' and, by extension, for its four legs. The use of a French word to describe a relatively new type of mirror may be partially explained by the fact that French art was so highly esteemed by the British who travelled extensively in that country, and therefore anything fashionable could be given a French name. 'Psyché', however, is just as obscure. The mythological story of Cupid and Psyche was told by Lucius Apuleius (second century A.D.), in *The Golden Ass*. Psyche was a maiden who was so beautiful that Cupid, who had been sent by the jealous goddess Venus to arouse Psyche's love in some worthless being, fell in love with her himself. He took her to his palace where he only visited her after dark, forbidding her to set eyes on him. Psyche was both fearful and curious about Cupid's appearance and one night took a lamp to gaze on him as he slept. Unfortunately she spilled some hot oil on him and he awoke and Cupid left his palace, abandoning Psyche to wander the earth in search of her lover and performing impossible tasks set by Venus in the hope of winning Cupid back. Finally Jupiter took pity on her and she was carried to Mount Olympus by Mercury where she was reunited with Cupid. Perhaps the French word, Psyche, was used to associate the beauty of Psyche with that of the image reflected in this type of mirror, or, more likely it refers to Psyche's curiosity to see her lover, an idea compounded by the fact that Psyché mirrors feature candle-arms to illuminate the reflection. The inner arched frame of this Empire psyché mirror is veneered with the vigorously figured mahogany, particularly popular during this period in France [**397**].

The great furniture-makers of the Empire period, such as Georges Jacob who had been trained during the previous period, formed a bridge between the Louis XVI style and the Empire. From a Burgundian peasant background, Georges Jacob (1739–1814), became a *Maître Menuisier* in 1765, first working in the Rococo and then graduating to the Louis XVI style. He was one of the first furniture-makers to exploit the attributes of high quality mahogany without using gilt for his early chairs. He also planed away the inner angle of the chair frames beneath the seat to give lightness without forfeiting strength and he was also responsible for introducing the sabre leg and lyre-back into France. But, like Gouthière, the Revolution nearly ruined him – the Comte d'Artois alone owed him 85,000 livres – but he was helped by the artist, J.-L. David, who introduced him to Percier and Fontaine who subsequently designed the furniture Jacob made for the *Comité du Salut Public*. He handed over his business to his sons Georges-Jacob II (1768–1803) and François-Honoré-Georges (1770–1841), who began to stamp their work 'Jacob Frères'. In 1803, after the death of Georges Jacob II, François-Honoré-Georges assumed the name Jacob Desmalter and went back into business with his father under the name *Jacob Desmalter et Cie*. From a large, almost industrial-sized workshop, the firm made some of the best Empire furniture, rich with applied gilt-bronze ornament in the Antique style, again often to the designs of Percier and Fontaine. Their most famous client was the Empress Josephine and much of the furniture made for her is still at Malmaison. A wooden panel on the reverse of this mirror [**398**] bears the inscription 'Napoléon I, Empereur des Français à sa belle-soeur la reine de Westphalie, Paris 1808'. A virtually identical *table de toilette* fitted with later ormolu candle-arms was delivered by the dealer A.T. Baudouin to the Empress for use in her bedchamber at the Grand Trianon in 1809, where it is still conserved. (Cf. de Grouër, 1985, fig. 153, p. 191.)

This unadorned example of a cheval-mirror [**399**] was made at a time when British

399 Empire, *c.*1810, burr elm cheval-mirror
81½in (207cm)

400 Empire, *c.*1810, ormolu-mounted mahogany cheval-mirror
76½in (194cm)

401 Empire, *c.*1810, ormolu-mounted mahogany cheval-mirror
76½in (194cm)

402 Empire, *c.*1810, bronze and ormolu toilet-mirror
26in (66cm)

403 Louis XVIII, *c.*1820, mahogany travelling dressing-mirror with brass candle-arms
25½in (65cm)

406 Charles X, *c.*1825–30, engraved and gilt bronze Palais Royal miniature dressing-table
12in (30cm)

404 Louis XVIII, *c.*1820, one of a pair, mahogany pier-glass and matching console-table (left)
67½in (171cm)

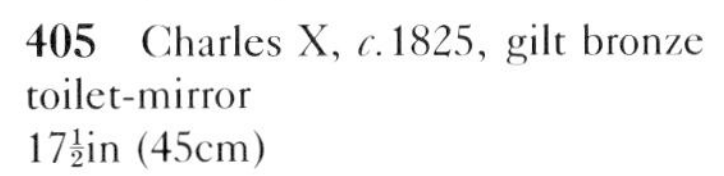

405 Charles X, *c.*1825, gilt bronze toilet-mirror
17¾in (45cm)

407 Louis Philippe, *c.*1830–35, gilt metal toilet-mirror
28in (72cm) (see colour illustration on p. 188)

blockades were preventing the importation of exotic timber. As a result burr-elm, an indigenous timber in plentiful supply, has been used as the veneer.

A typical feature of Empire period mirrors is the use of decorative gilt-metal mounts cast by highly-skilled metal workers. This heavily-decorated, traditional cheval-mirror [**401**] is typical of the Empire style, encrusted as it is with details produced by a *fondeur-doreur* (Cf. Dumonthier, 1923, pl. 35.). Pierre-Phillipe Thomire was the outstandng *fondeur-doreur* of the Empire period. Like so many of his generation, Thomire began working in the Louis XVI style. He assisted with the decoration of the Coronation coach of Louis XVI in 1776 and supplied mounts for furniture by Beneman, Scwerdfeger and Weisweiler, as well as clock cases for the Sèvres Porcelain Factory. During the Revolution he manufactured arms but returned to decorative bronze work to become *Ciseleur de l'Empereur*. The level of skill attained by the French metal-workers during this period is displayed by the high quality of the work on this dressing or toilet-glass [**402**]. From the female figures at each side of the glass, to the lion-paw feet, the piece has strong Classical associations. Even the support for the mirror is in the form of a bow, an allusion to Cupid. This unusual travelling dressing-glass [**403**] retains traces of a brass label which reads: *(MIR)ROIR A (V)OLTES/LB/BREVETTE SGDG*. The downswept supports are fitted with a pair of candle-arms which are detachable for travelling. Such extravagant use of mirror-glass [**404**], gives some indication of how much cheaper it had become to produce flat glass. Designed to be placed above a console-table with a Belgian marble-top, the mirrored lower back panel almost certainly would have reflected one of a pair of handsome objects thus enhancing the decorative scheme of the room and accentuating the lavish use of mirror-glass. The flat, veneered surfaces of the frame to this pier glass also show the rich, vigorously grained timber that was so popular at this time.

Some forty or fifty years after the original cheval glass had been introduced, this popular form of mirror was still being produced. In this *c.* 1840 example [**408**], the brass lion-paw feet appear to be English and could well have been added to the scrolling feet of the mahogany supports.

Louis Philippe, the son of the duc d'Orléans, returned to France from exile in England and became King in 1830, and there followed a period of nearly twenty years' stability, peace and prosperity. This fine quality example of cast gilt bronze or brass asymmetrical frame is in the mid-eighteenth-century Rococo style. The mirrored cresting is surmounted possibly by clouds and a stylized shell and sunrays, reflecting the glory of the age. Calamander-wood, indigenous to Sri-Lanka and Southern India was used in this ormulu-mounted cheval-mirror [**412**]. A predominantly black timber with irregular streaks, it clearly lends itself to contrasting metal mounts and the brass inlay. Calamander-wood was not, however, generally used in Europe before the end of the eighteenth century but a century later, by 1875 the Englishman, Thomas Laslett, remarked of it in his *Timber and Timber Trees*: 'now getting scarce; it is one of the most valuable ornamental woods of Ceylon and South India'. This frame was made just after the marriage of Napoleon III to Eugénie de Montijo in 1853, an event that revived the monarchy as arbiter of fashion. Simply because the Empress took great delight in anything to do with Marie-Antoinette and refurnished her apartments in the Louis XVI style, she began the Europe-wide revival of the style.

408 Louis Philippe, *c.*1840, rosewood and bronze cheval-mirror
70in (178cm)

409 Second Republic, *c.* 1850 gilt bronze with maker's mark 'EB'
40½ (103cm)

411 Second Republic, *c.*1850, one of a pair, giltwood and gesso
88in (224cm)

410 Louis Philippe, *c.*1845, carved giltwood
72in (183cm)

412 Napoleon III, *c.*1855, ormolu-mounted calamander-wood cheval-mirror
81½in (207cm)

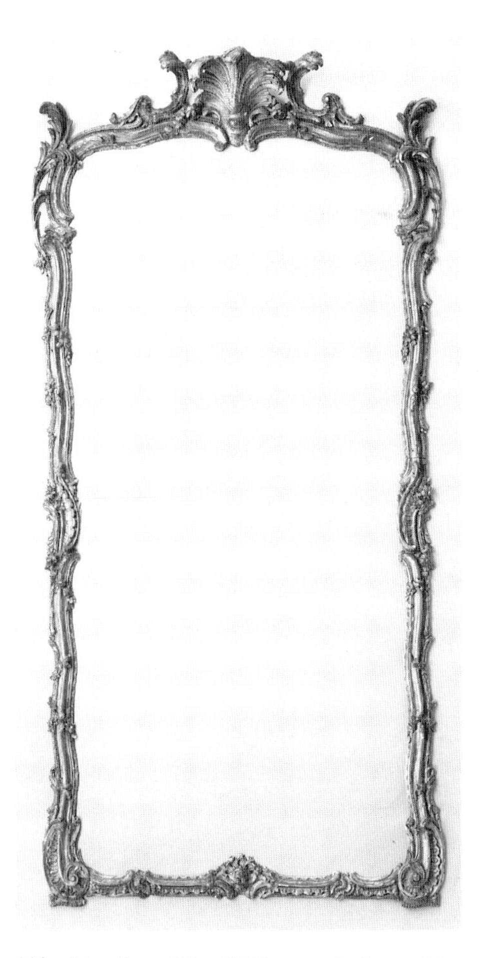

413 Napoleon III, *c.*1855, carved giltwood in the style of Louis XV
107in (272cm)

414 Napolean III, *c.* 1855, carved giltwood with mirror border glasses
82in (208cm)

415 Napoleon III, *c.*1860, one of a pair, Dieppe ivory mirror
33½in (85cm)

416 Napoleon III, *c.*1860, one of a pair Dieppe ivory mirror
41in (104cm)

417 Napoleon III, *c.*1860, one of a pair, carved giltwood and gesso pier-mirror and matching console-table
98in (249cm)

418 Napoleon III, *c.*1860, one of a pair, tortoiseshell and brass toilet-mirror in the manner of Boulle
26in (67cm)

Frames such as this Louis XV revival example in carved giltwood [**413**] along with other Louis XV revival pieces, were produced not just for a domestic market but also for export, mainly to England. By the 1880s large factories were producing furniture and the Paris furniture industry employed approximately 17,000 workmen. Of these the carvers, the élite, were paid between 90 centimes and 1 franc 5 centimes per hour. Compared to an ordinary cabinet-maker earning between 40 and 80 centimes per day this was a good wage, but not compared with the head cabinet-maker to the Crown workshops who was earning nearly 400 francs per week on a fixed salary, rather than the usual casual or piece-work basis.

The following mirrors are both in the same style and differ only in shape and decoration; one is carved with the monogram of Mary Queen of Scots, helmetted coats of arms, dolphins, cherubs, eagles and a heart [**415**]. The other has similar armorials and features but includes the motto 'Monjoye St Denys' [**416**]. Composed of carved and engraved ivory, both mirrors originate from Dieppe, where there was a strong ivory-carving tradition; for instance, David le Marchand (1674–1726), who also worked in England, spent some time working there. During the second half of the nineteenth century, the ivory workers of this thriving French port did not confine themselves to the production of mirrors, although they predominate, but they made a range of furniture decorated in this way. (Cf. Payne, 1981, p. 141, figs 350–2.) Very little else is recorded about the nineteenth century Dieppe ivory industry, except that the craftsmen produced a wide range of usually small, carved objects for the growing tourist trade. The frames and the majority of the furniture produced was 'veneered' with leaves of carved ivory that were pinned to a wooden carcass.

The pair to this Boulle-style toilet-mirror is decorated in *première-partie*, while this illustrated example [**418**] is in *contre-partie* (see p. 48). The shape is a pure revival of the Louis XIV period of *c.* 1700 (see 319). Another Louis XIV revival mirror, [**420**] contains two sheets of glass. Of necessity, an early eighteenth-century frame of this size would have required both plates (although the size of mirror glass was less limited by this date) in the revival mirror, however, the divided plates contribute to its authenticity. (The top plate is now missing.) Both the inner and outer frames of this overmantel mirror [**422**] are carved with vine leaves and grapes. Such Bacchanalian decorations suggest this frame was made for a dining room.

This gilt-bronze frame decorated with panels of 'Boulle' work is punctuated with 'Sèvres-type' portrait medallions [**423**]. Although the Sèvres factory did supply porcelain for furniture, it was unlikely to have been responsible for these panels. The factory was declared state property in 1793; seven years later Alexandre Brongniant (1770–1847) was appointed director and rejuvenated the factory which was extensively patronized by Napoleon. In 1848 the factory was reorganized again and in 1876 it was moved to new premises near Saint-Cloud.

While the Empress Eugénie promoted the Louis XVI Revival style, to such an extent that her entire suite at Saint-Cloud was decorated in this revival style, she did soften and make the style more comfortable by utilizing the plushness of contemporary upholstery.

During the second half of the nineteenth century, furniture, including mirrors, as well as industrial and agricultural exhibits, jewellery, statuary and all kinds of products

419 Napoleon III, *c.*1860, brass with mirror borders
59in (150cm)

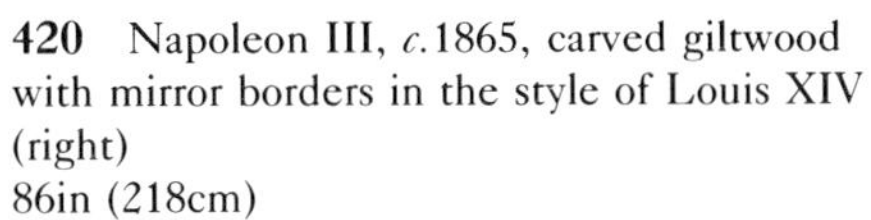

420 Napoleon III, *c.*1865, carved giltwood with mirror borders in the style of Louis XIV (right)
86in (218cm)

421 Napoleon III, *c.*1865, carved giltwood in the style of Louis XV
68in (173cm)

422 Napoleon III, *c.*1860, carved giltwood overmantel in the style of Louis XV
84½in (215cm)

423 Napoleon III, *c.*1865, gilt-bronze and 'Sèvres' mounted pier-glass in the manner of Boulle
96in (244cm)

424 Napoleon III, *c.*1865, carved giltwood mirror in the style of Louis XVI
41½in (105cm)

425 Third Republic, *c.*1890, one of a pair, carved giltwood with mirror borders in the Louis XIV style
64in (163cm)

426 Third Republic, *c.*1890, carved giltwood mirror with mirror borders in the style of Louis XIV
70in (178cm)

427 Napoleon III, *c.*1870, ormolu- and porcelain-mounted
47in (120cm) (see illustration on p. 175)

428 Napolean III, *c.*1870, ormolu-mounted tortoiseshell and brass toilet-mirror in the manner of Boulle
30¼in (77cm)

429 Third Republic, *c.*1890, carved giltwood in the style of Louis XVI
80½in (204cm)

were manufactured and exhibited as examples of the country's 'great achievements' both to impress other nations and to encourage trade. France was the first, in 1797, to hold an industrial exhibition in the courtyard of the Louvre. The 1851 Crystal Palace Exhibition in London was the first international exhibition which led to a number of Expositions Universelles in Paris, beginning in 1855, the most famous of which was the 1889 Exposition when the Eiffel Tower was opened as part of the exhibition. For just such display, this example [**427**], is a rich creation in gilt-metal, porcelain and enamelled glass which combines a number of French skills.

Boulle-style decoration remained popular in France from the reign of Louis XIV, with a lapse only during the Napoleonic era, until the present time. The richness of detail, the contrasts in colour and in many cases the quality of the work, as exemplified on this toilet-glass [**428**], has been appreciated by almost every collecting generation both in France and in England as well as further afield. The continuing popularity of the decoration was enhanced by an almost direct family link from André-Charles Boulle (see p. 48), until well into the second half of the nineteenth century. Boulle's son, Charles-Joseph, continued the workshops for the period following his father's death in 1732 to the second half of the eighteenth century. The Boulle workshops were responsible for training Etienne Levasseur (1721–98). Levasseur, who was received Maître in 1767, specialized in repairing and copying Boulle furniture. He was

430 Third Republic, *c.*1890, gilt-bronze toilet-mirror with candle-arms
23½in (60cm)

431 Third Republic, *c.*1890, carved giltwood in the style of Louis XVI
69in (175cm)

432 Third Republic, *c.*1890, carved and giltwood with mirror borders in the style of Louis XVI
61in (155cm)

433 Third Republic, *c.*1890, carved giltwood with mirror borders in the style of Louis XVI
88in (224cm)

434 Third Republic, *c.*1890, gilt-metal frame with convex plate
diameter 25in (63cm)

435 Third Republic, *c.*1890, gilt-bronze-mounted kingwood and purpleheart-veneered cheval-mirror
72in (183cm) (see colour illustration on p. 176)

436 Third Republic, *c.*1890, carved giltwood in the style of Louis XVI
58in (147cm)

437 Third Republic, *c.*1900, gilt-metal
33in (84cm)

438 Third Republic, *c.*1900, carved giltwood in the Régence style
89in (226cm)

439 Art Nouveau, *c.*1900, carved wood
42in (106cm)

also one of the first French *ébénistes* (see p. 40) to use mahogany, often inlaid with brass. He continued working throughout the reign of Louis XVI and was succeeded by his son Pierre-Etienne and his grandson, known as Levasseur Jeune, who worked into the Louis-Philippe period. The continued fashion for Boulle furniture during the nineteenth century was fuelled by the development of machines that facilitated the cutting of brass and tortoiseshell. This mechanization meant that small workshops were able to purchase ready-made sections of Boulle and veneer them on to carcass-work of their own manufacture.

This large giltwood mirror in the Louis XVI style was made *en suite* with a console-table together the two pieces measured nearly 10 ft high by nearly 5 ft wide, with the mirror's straight lower edge resting upon the marble top of the console-table [**429**]. Originally the home of such a piece would have been an elegant salon which was probably furnished from disparate periods. The fashion for furnishing in a single, revival style was diminishing, replaced by the taste for a hectic mixture of handmade as well as machine-made pieces from different periods. The inclusion of machine-made pieces was not just a matter of money 'but an undoubted feeling of pride in the achievements of production'. (Cf. Payne, 1985.) This gradual rejection of the strict requirement to furnish each room with pieces designed in a style corresponding to its surroundings is reflected in this giltwood frame, [**432**]. Predominantly in the Louis

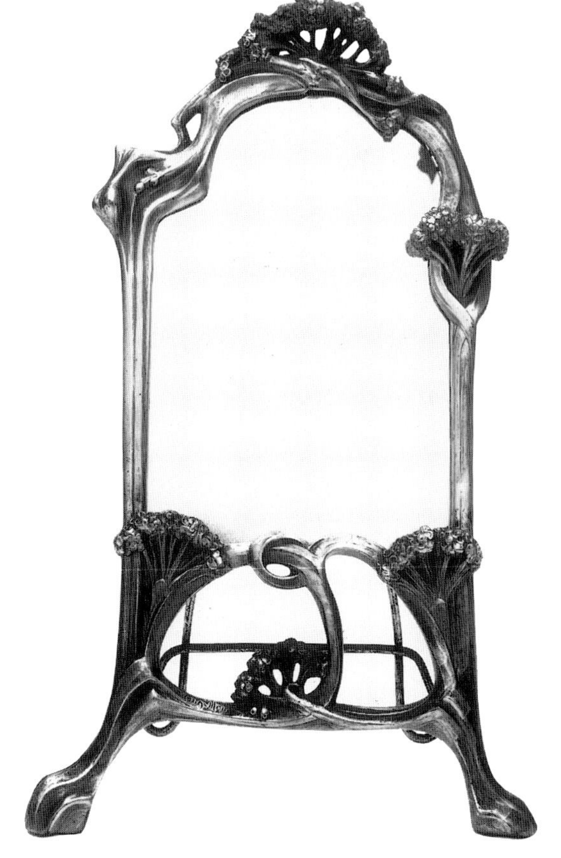

440 Art Nouveau, *c.*1900, bronze, by Charpentier
21in (55cm)

441 Art Nouveau, *c.*1900, gilt-bronze by Auguste Moreau (far right)
18in (46cm)

XVI style, it includes, however, acanthus-leaf-carved scrolls to each side accompanied by canted border glasses, all of which is surmounted by a Louis XVI style swagged cresting.

Around this time the 'suite' for furnishing, living rooms, dining rooms and bedrooms was gaining popularity, encouraged by the distribution of furniture catalogues, usually published by big shops and department stores. This gilt-bronze-mounted, kingwood and purpleheart-wood veneered cheval-mirror [**435**] forms part of a bedroom suite, consisting of a pair of bedside cupboards, a double bed with *Vernis Martin* decorated panels, a wardrobe, and a dressing table and stool. The last three mirrors of this section [**439 to 441**] are excellent examples of the new decorative style which originated in the 1880s and reached the height of popularity *c.* 1900. Its name, Art Nouveau, derived from the name of a Parisian shop owned by the Hamburg dealer Samuel Bing. Having moved to Paris in 1871, Bing visited the Far East in 1875. He opened a shop *La Porte Chinoise* for the sale of oriental, especially Japanese, goods and in 1893 he travelled to New York. Later in 1895 he opened a shop in the rue de Provence in Paris and called it *L'Art Nouveau*. His shop became a show-case for all manner of objects, furniture, paintings, glass and ceramics.

Alexandre Charpentier (1856–1909) was a sculptor and furniture designer who was inspired by the English Arts and Crafts movement led by William Morris. Cast in the form of a female bather [**440**], the frame overlaid the mirror-glass, making it almost more of a sculpture with mirror-glass backing and signed with a monogram. Again adhering to the sinuous lines of the Art Nouveau movement, this frame [**441**], was made and signed by Auguste Moreau. Eventually this movement which placed such a premium on originality and craftsmanship and which was in many respects a non-revivalist style became an unlamented casualty of the 1914–18 war.

Germany and Northern Europe

Although a great deal of Germany's furniture was scattered and lost during the European and world wars from the seventeenth to the twentieth century German and Northern European furniture remains an extraordinarily diverse subject which covers a vast range of styles, each drawing something from its own area as well as from those countries that border it. Examples of this stylistic the exchange abound, pieces made in the South of Germany are often indistinguishable from Italian examples and may even have been made by Italian craftsmen working in Germany. In the North, trade with the Baltic states, as well as with Holland and England, produced examples that could be ascribed to both those countries, especially those pieces made from imported timbers, found only in Scandinavia. In addition the influence of French style was most certainly felt in Germany, indeed many eighteenth-century Germans, like so many English, regarded France as the fountainhead of artistic taste.

The new social order that emerged after the Thirty Years War (1618–48), strengthened the fortunes of the aristocracy, who, as a result, required a more sophisticated approach to the planning of their palaces and houses. Joseph Furttenbach (1591–1667) from Ulm, published *Architectura Privata* between 1640–1 in which he gave details and plans of his own house. His plans were for an arrangement whereby all rooms were accessible from a central hall with doors leading from room to room. The number and size of these rooms depended on the rank and wealth of the owner and each room had a specific function; ante-room, salon, cabinet etc. Furnishings therefore were required to suit each of these rooms.

442 North Europe, dated 1632, carved oak and polychrome, attributed Crispin van de Passe II
31in (79cm)

Towards the end of the seventeenth century the South of Germany, especially Munich, grew closer to Italy with the marriage of the Prince Elector of Bavaria, Ferdinand Maria, to a Princess from the House of Savoy. This frame may well have ben made for a picture, but is now fitted with a mirror plate [**442**]. It can be attributed to Crispin van de Passe II (1593–*c.* 1670). (Cf. Jervis, 1974, pl. 307 and p. 41.) De Passe was born in Cologne the eldest son of the engraver, draughtsman and painter, Crispin de Passe I (1570–1637), from Zeeland. The young De Passe was trained by his father and published the vast majority of the Plates for *Hortus Floridus* in 1614, some of which were copied by Thomas Johnson in 1730 (see p. 116). From about 1617 to 1630 De Passe was in Paris where he went to teach painting and to work as an engraver on the recommendation of Prince Maurice of Orange. In 1621 he published in Utrecht, *Oficina Arcularia* . . ., an accomplished furniture pattern book. He was influenced by Hans Vredeman de Vries' *Differents Pourtraicts de Menuiserie* and his 1621 edition of *Oficina* contains two plates taken from Vredeman. In around 1639 De Passe moved from Utrecht via Rotterdam to Amsterdam where he published a second edition of

442a Five designs for cartouches from *Oficina Arcularia* . . . (1621, Utrecht) by Crispin van de Passe II.

442b Design for a cartouche, plate 42 from *Neues Zierakenbuch* . . . (*c.*1645, Frankfurt) by Friedrich Unteutsch.

Oficina; a third edition was published in Paris in 1651. By 1645, however, he was in a lunatic asylum in Delft and is thought to have died there *c.* 1670. Stylistic details on this mirror frame [**442**], have much in common with those shown in De Passe's designs for five cartouches in a plate taken from *Oficina Acularia* . . . [**442a**] and with a cartouche designed by Friedrich Unteutsch from his *Neues Zieratenbuch* . . . [**442b**]. (See also [**458a**].)

Usually carved in ebony, this type of Flemish wave moulding decoration, is fairly common for both mirrors and picture frames during the second half of the seventeenth century [**443**]. Strong trade links with the East were responsible for the appearance of this highly-prized, pure black ebony in Europe. Much later in 1853, *The Cabinet Makers Assistant* (published in England), records nine different types of ebony being imported at that time, the best from Mauritius and East India: '. . . The Mauritius ebony, when first cut, is usually quite sound, and with a view to preservation, it is immersed in water for many months; and when taken out, the two ends are secured from splitting by iron rings and wedges . . . It is sold from £16 to £20 per ton.' Later, *bois d'ébène* became a most highly valued timber for French furniture, favoured by the most outstanding

443 Flanders, *c.*1650, wave moulded ebony
44½in (113cm)

444 Flanders or France, *c.*1650, carved ebony
52½in (133cm)

445 Flanders, *c.*1650, tortoiseshell and ebony with mirrored cresting
38½in (98cm)

446 Flanders, *c.*1680, carved pine
48in (122cm) (see colour illustration on p. 237)

447 Holland, *c.*1660, polychrome glass and ebony
51in (130cm)

448 Holland, *c.*1660, gilt-metal repoussé
58in (147cm)

449 Flanders, *c.*1680, carved giltwood, wave moulded ebony and gilt-metal
40½in (103cm)

450 Holland, *c.* 1680, ebony and gilt-metal repoussé
42in (106cm)

451 Flanders, *c.*1685, velvet backed gilt-metal repoussé
55in (140cm)

452 Flanders, *c.*1685, walnut marquetry
39½in (100cm)

453 Holland, *c.*1690, gilt-metal repoussé
37in (94cm)

454 Flanders, *c.*1690, carved giltwood, possibly originally a picture frame
66in (167cm)

455 Flanders, *c.*1690, carved giltwood
63in (152cm)

Menuisiers. Ebony wave mouldings are combined here with tortoiseshell veneer [**445**]. Antwerp enjoyed an international reputation during the seventeenth century as a centre for the production of fine veneered and decorated furniture (see p. 38). The main demand was for fine cabinets, veneered in tortoiseshell with ebony mouldings and painted drawer-fronts, often depicting scenes from the Old and New Testaments. While the most popular veneer was red tortoiseshell backed with coloured foil, which contrasted with the black ebony. Such richness of ornamentation is revealed in the next carved frame [**446**]. Originally intended for a painting, the symbolism of the carved elements of the frame could well have had some relevance to that painting or to the aspirations of the original owner.

Artus Quellinus or Quellien (1609–88) is often associated with the Dutch Baroque. He was born in Antwerp and trained as a sculptor. In about 1634 he travelled to Italy where he would have been influenced by the great Italian Baroque sculptors and designers. He returned to Antwerp in 1639 and by 1650 he had begun work on the new Town Hall in Amsterdam.

Typical of the work produced in the Lowlands at this time, this relatively small frame [**447**] was probably intended to be used in a family room, since the decorative panels are of an intimate and domestic nature, illustrating scenes from the parable of the prodigal son.

An early example of the gilt-metal work that is particular to Flanders, [**448**] the gauge brass sheeting of this frame is pierced and embossed with patterns – scrolls, fruit, flowers and all matter of decorative motifs popular during the second half of the seventeenth century. Another example of this type of decoration is shown here, [**449**], combined with carved gilt-wood and ebony wave mouldings. (This style of frame found favour again during the nineteenth century and many examples date from that period).

Dutch and Flemish craftsmen were also renowned for marquetry cutting, as shown on this frame [**452**] (see p. 45). This love of decoration is similarly revealed in the intricate carving on three more frames [**454, 455, 456 and 458**] so typical of the seventeenth century (456 may, however be Scandinavian (cf. Wallin vol I, p. 190 fig. 338)). Possibly by Pieter de Loose, of Antwerp, the work on the second example, is reminiscent of the carving of Grinling Gibbons, a contemporary in England, taught by Artus Quellinus. Carved with a pair of billing birds, the cresting on this frame, [**456**] was possibly made in celebration of a marriage. (Cf. Schmitz, 1923, pl. 179.) From late in the century, the carving on this frame [**458**] incorporates grotesque masks similar to the 'Knorpelwork' or auricular design of Friedrich Unteutsch (*c.* 1600–70). (Cf. Jervis, 1974, pl. 367.) Born in Berlin, the son of a master-gunner, Unteutsch travelled for nine years before settling in Frankfurt in 1628. He became a master cabinet-maker in 1631 and was appointed 'Stadtschreiner' in 1635. His *Neues Zieratenbuch* . . ., *c.* 1645 was published in Frankfurt in two parts and contained nearly eighty designs for furniture and carved wood ornament, the elements on one of which, [**458a**] bear strong similarities to those on this frame, [**458**]. (See also 442b.)

456 Scandinavia or Germany *c.*1690, carved, parcel-gilt and painted, with engraved mirror panels
62½in (158cm)

The strength of the stylistic influence exerted upon Germany by her neighbours is clearly shown in mirrors from this period. Possibly from the south of Germany, this is a baroque frame [**460**] that again reflects the artistic impact of Italy and the great

457 Flanders, *c.*1690–1700, carved giltwood with mirror panel borders
58½in (149cm) (see colour illustration on p. 238)

458 Germany, *c.*1700, carved giltwood in the manner of Friedrich Unteutsch
74in (188cm) (see colour illustration on p. 239)

458a Design for a cartouche, plate 7 from *Zeues Zieratenbuch* . . ., (*c.*1645, Frankfurt) by Friedrich Unteutsch

459 Holland, *c.*1710, carved wood and polychrome overmantel mirror (left)
66in (168cm)

460 South Germany, *c.*1700, carved giltwood
38in (97cm)

461 Germany, *c.*1700, carved giltwood in the manner of Sebastian Deglar
78in (198cm) (see colour illustration on p. 240)

462 Flanders, *c.*1700, marquetry with engraved copper and pewter inlay on tortoiseshell
50in (128cm)

463 Flanders, *c.*1710, carved giltwood pier-glass
38½in (98cm)

464 Germany, *c.*1720, carved giltwood pier-glass (possibly reduced in height)
36in (91cm)

465 Holland, *c.*1730, carved giltwood
81in (206cm)

designer-sculptors. Forming the basis for the frame, scrolling acanthus leaves are incorporated with the flat, broad sweeping scrolls of the auricular designs of the 1650s. (Cf. Kreisel, 1968, vol. I pls 676 and 678 for similar mirrors in the Bamberg Residenz which, although more elaborately decorated, show a similar handling.)

In the following examples, [**463 and 464**] the frames show numerous similarities with both French and English mirrors of this period and were possibly made in the western part of Germany. (A frame of similar influence is at the Schloss Fasanerie bei Fulda, made in the Lohr near Frankfurt. (Cf. Kreisel, 1970, vol. II Pl. 217).) Both these frames have divided, possibly original, mirror plates which are abutted, but, unlike most English frames of this period the edges are not bevelled either at the join or around the sides.

Although this frame [**465**] is dated *c.* 1730 it still retains elements of the early design details of Daniel Marot (1663–1752). The cresting, in this example, formed of a plumed canopy with lambrequins, is a typical Marot device. Marot was born in Paris, the son of Jean Marot, and was the nephew of Pierre Golle, the Royal cabinet-maker. After the Revocation of the Edict of Nantes in 1685 Marot fled to Holland and entered the service of Prince William of Orange, later William III of England (1650–1702). His work in Holland as a designer and interior decorator included work for Prince William at his palace Het Loo between 1689 and 1702. His later works included the Huis Schuylenburch in the Hague *c.* 1715 and at Kasteel Duivenvoorde *c.* 1717 and as late as 1734 at Huis ten Bosch.

Venetian, especially Murano, glass-makers travelled during the late seventeenth and early eighteenth centuries despite restrictions, working at and developing glass-works. Entirely framed with glass this frame [**468**] has a highly Venetian flavour and could well be the result of itinerant workmanship in Germany or Silesia. Known in America as 'courting mirrors' this example [**469**] relates to a group of mirrors of similar outline, and usually with shaped crestings. In this case the use of tortoiseshell veneer would indicate a Dutch, possibly Antwerp, origin; it was certainly a form popular in Northern Europe late in the seventeenth and early in the eighteenth century. Painted glass panels decorated with chinoiserie figures beneath Marot-type canopies with lambrequin borders, point to the continuing early eighteenth-century interest in the Orient. Examples of 'courting mirrors' that still have their original wooden carrying boxes are recorded in the possession of American families. It seems unlikely, however, that these mirrors were made in America, they were probably brought over in especially-made cases from Northern Europe by Dutch or German imigrant families.

No discussion of German mirrors can ignore the Spiegelkabinett or Mirrored Room. Perhaps the inspiration for the development of the mirrored room in Germany lies in Lebrun's 1682 Galerie des Glaces at Versailles. The seventeen wall mirrors in the Galerie des Glaces were made by the cylinder process. Each complete mirror consists of twenty-one rectangular panes, 3 ft 6 in (107 mm) by 2 ft 6 in (762 mm) of approximately $\frac{1}{4}$ in (6 mm) thick glass with bevels. Visitors from Germany would have been impressed by such magnificence and encouraged to introduce the use of mirrors at home to create the same effect – the result was equally impressive. At Pommersfelden, Ferdinand Plitzner (1678–1724) (a cabinet-maker of Franconian origins who trained under Johann Metusch), created a panelled room of walnut and carved giltwood overlaid with brackets for Chinese export porcelain, with a mirrored ceiling. One of the most unusual mirrored interiors is at La Favorite, the summer residence built for Ludwigwilhelm Margrave of Baden-Baden at Rastatt, near Baden-Baden, designed by Rossi and Röhne and decorated by Pfleger and H.G. Stöhr. In this room, the Spiegelkabinett, the effect is created by regular and irregular panels of mirror glass, set both individually and in groups within moulded frames, on the walls and ceiling. Continuing this scheme, the walls of the Florentine room are decorated, not only with mirror but with panels of Florentine mosaic, lacquer, marble, alabaster and mother-of-pearl, while lozenge-shaped panels of mirror-glass are contained within lead frames and overlaid with portrait miniatures of philosophers, scholars and artists painted on ivory. The Palace of Charlottenburg boasts a gold mirrored gallery in the rococo style created by Georg Wenzeslaus von Knobelsdorff. Built as a hunting lodge for Electress Amalia (1734–39), the Amalienburg, in the park of Schloss Nymphenborg near Munich, contains a mirrored room.

François Curvilliés (1695–1768), although a Waloon, became the leading German Rococo architect and designer and creator of the Amalienburg Spiegelsalon. Large mirrors composed of rectangular panels, with glass strips overlaying the joints, are framed by a profusion of stucco decoration by J.B. Zimmermann. The whole effect is richly finished by Curvilliés' choice of silver-leaf against a white ground. Curvilliés, who had studied architecture in Paris under J.F. Blondel *c.* 1720–24, also designed the Spiegelkabinett and the Paradeschlafzimmer, State Bedroom, at the Munich Residence at Ludwigsburg (built in 1716 and designed by Johan Friedrich Nette). The Spiegelkabinett is lined with irregularly shaped plates of mirror glass (including circular), to reflect the candlelight, which are surrounded by the stuccowork of Antonio Giuseppe Bossi. Bossi was to become the court stuccoist at Würzburg in 1734 and later died insane in 1764. The Würzburg Residence has a Spiegelkabinett that combines the stuccowork of Bossi and the designs of Johann Wolfgang van der Auvera (1708–56). Auvera, a native of Würzburg, and the son of the court sculptor, was sent by the Prince Bishop to study in Vienna from 1730–6. After his return to Würzburg he designed the Spiegelkabinett *c.* 1744, the drawings for which are still at the Residenz. (Cf. Hinz, 1976, fig. 360.) Auvera was also responsible for pieces of furniture in the same room, notably the carved console-tables of sculptural form with *verre églomisé* tops, which are considered to be some of the finest examples of German Rococo furniture.

The German love of Spiegelkabinetts carried over into the nineteenth century. Louis II of Bavaria built himself a copy of the Galerie des Glaces at Versailles at his palace at Herrenchleimsee between 1870 and 1880 and he is reputed to have had the mirrored rooms of the Linderhof designed as an incentive to self-contemplation and escapism.

A full-length reflection of oneself or of a room in a mirror-lined wall seems only mildly interesting today, however, to those rich enough to contemplate the expense during the closing years of the seventeenth and the early years of the eighteenth century, it must have been an almost overwhelming delight and fascination.

One of a set of four large, carved giltwood mirrors or girandoles [**470**] this frame may very well have formed part of the decoration of a Spiegelkabinett or mirrored room.

466 Holland, *c.*1730, carved giltwood pier-glass
101in (256cm)

467 Germany, *c.*1735, carved giltwood
47½in (121cm)

469 Holland, *c.*1720, tortoiseshell, with painted border glasses
20in (51cm)

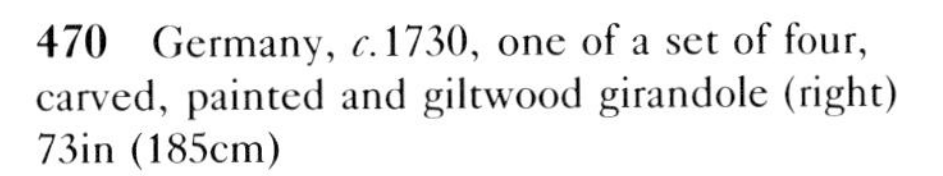

470 Germany, *c.*1730, one of a set of four, carved, painted and giltwood girandole (right)
73in (185cm)

468 South Germany, *c.*1720, with blue and clear border glasses
71in (180cm)

471 North Germany or Denmark, *c.*1735, walnut and parcel-gilt
40in (102cm)

472 Germany, *c.*1730, one of a pair, giltwood
89in (226cm)

473 Germany, *c.*1740, carved giltwood
32½in (82cm)

474 Germany, *c.*1740, carved giltwood
55in (140cm)

475 South Germany, *c.*1740, one of a pair, carved giltwood
27½in (70cm)

476 Germany, *c.*1745, carved giltwood
70in (178cm)

478 South Germany, *c.*1745, carved giltwood
65in (165cm)

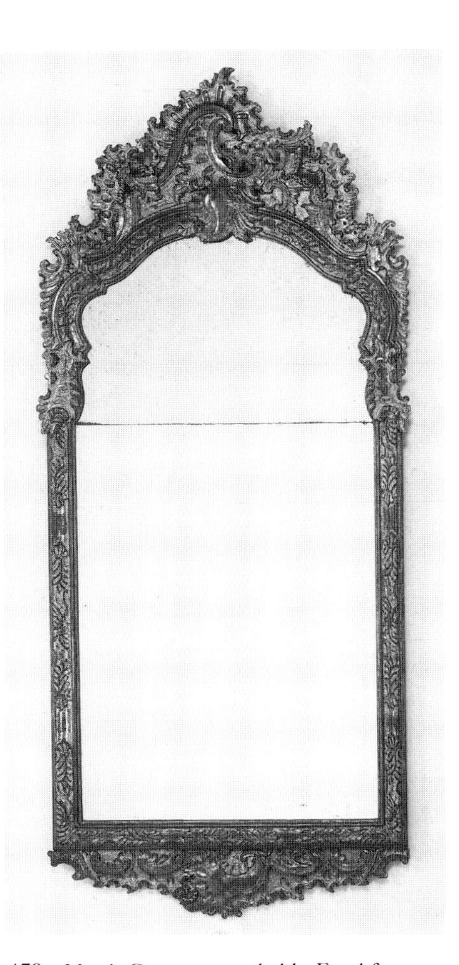

477 South Germany, possibly Ansbach
*c.*1745, carved giltwood
35½in (90cm)

479 North Germany, probably Frankfurt,
*c.*1750, carved giltwood
67in (170cm)

480 South Germany possibly
Ansbach–Bayreuth, *c.*1750, carved and painted
wood (left)
56in (142cm)

481 Germany, *c.*1750, carved and painted
wood (above)
75in (190cm)

482 Germany, *c.*1750, painted and parcel-gilt
58in (147cm)

Beneath the mirror plate the lower central panel bears evidence of the fixings for candle-branches, hence girandoles and while there is no proof in the photograph, the shaped frames around the central plate could have originally been fitted with mirrors.

This walnut and parcel-gilt frame is certainly from the North of Germany or even Denmark [**471**]. Very similar forms of mirror are found in England at this date, but it differs slightly in the gilt decoration that is overlaid on the walnut veneer. Such a hybrid style was the result of extensive trade between the Northern German and Baltic ports. Measuring nearly 7½ ft in height this fine pair of mirrors would originally have been intended for a palace or castle [**472**]. In many respects the carving is reminiscent of the work of Johann Michael Hoppenhaupt I (1685–1751) at the Schlossmuseum, Berlin. Hoppenhaupt I was a carver and sculptor from Mensburg and was the father of Johann Michael II (1709–69) (see p. 232) and Johann Christian Hoppenhaupt (1719–86); both brothers worked in Berlin and Potsdam for Frederich the Great.

A strong French influence which is evident in the elements of this provincial frame [**473**] would point to the frame having a west German origin. As we have seen before, however, many German designers and craftsmen travelled to France for training and guidance which would explain the persistence of this influence.

Also revealing the adoption of different stylistic traits, this unusual giltwood frame combines the heavy details of the baroque with, in places, the lightness of rococo decoration [**474**]. Two kneeling cherubs are carefully carved, giving the impression that they are supporting the mirror frame upon their shoulders, while two fantastic birds united by a swag, could well imply a marriage, especially since the birds are resting upon scrolls which are spilling fruit and grapes symbolic of plenty.

Possibly from Ansbach, the important Franconian centre for Rococo furniture, the mirror [**477**] retains its original decoration and mirror plate. Another example, from *c.* 1750, is illustrative of a transitional style with a formal, inner moulded frame which is enriched with an asymmetrical cresting and has an apron redolent of the Rococo period [**479**].

Ansbach was next in importance to Würzburg in the development of early German Rococo furniture. The Ansbach Residence was redecorated between 1736 and 1744 under the supervision of the Italian architect Leopold Retti and Paul Amadeus Biarelle. Biarelle (born in Liège) worked with his brother, Johann Adolph who executed designs by Curvilliés at Schloss Falkenlust near Cologne. From 1737 they both worked at Ansbach in collaboration with Johann Georg Worflein on console-tables and mirrors. Elsewhere, designers working in Bayreuth, formed another centre that was renowned for combining scrollwork and naturalistic Rococo decoration for mirror frames.

Friedrich the Great's sister, Wilhelmine, the wife of Margrave Friedrich, joined her husband in his enthusiasm for Rococo furniture. They encouraged designers, sculptors and carvers to furnish the results of their passion for building with grand console-tables and mirrors. As well as using gilded wood, the frame-makers of Bayreuth often covered their softwood mirror frames with painted decoration or with gesso stained to imitate other woods. This frame has a flat base section with an added moulding and was intended to rest upon a matching console-table [**483**]. The great overall height of the frame when combined with the height of the console-table, suggests that the single

483 South Germany, *c.*1750–60, carved giltwood
84in (214cm)

484 Potsdam, *c.*1750, carved giltwood
67in (170cm)

487 Germany, *c.*1750, carved giltwood
64½in (164cm)

485 North Germany, *c.*1750, one of a pair, parcel-gilt mahogany
51in (130cm)

486 Germany, *c.*1750, carved giltwood
60in (152cm)

piece of mirror-glass may not be the original but, as there are no signs of where the carving could have masked a join, it is likely that in this case a single, expensive, sheet of glass would have been fitted. Made in Potsdam, this mirror retains the original glass with bevelled edge [**484**]. (Cf. Freytak, 1978, fig. 59; Schmitz, 1923, Pl. 179.) Potsdam had enjoyed a long glass-making tradition as well as princely patronage. Friedrich Wilhelm, Elector of Brandenberg (1620–88), built himself a glass-house at the farm of Drewitz, near his favourite hunting lodge to the south-west of Potsdam in 1744. The glass-house obtained its fuel from the Elector's forests nearby and received immunity from outside competition and taxes. By 1685, after producing both table-glass and mirror-glass, he gave up his interests at Drewitz and built a glass-house on an island on the Hakendam for his protegé Johann Kunckel, the glass-maker and scientist.

One of a pair of parcel-gilt mahogany mirrors, the style of this frame [**485**] is, at this date, peculiar to Northern Germany and to Scandinavia. The outline design of this frame is more usually associated with an earlier date *c.* 1740, but frames of that date which were common to Northern Germany, Scandinavia and England, are often veneered with walnut rather than the mahogany in this case. This style of mirror continued to be made in Germany, long after its popularity had faded in England, and was made in the fashionable cabinet timber of the period – mahogany – enriched with applied giltwood rococo decoration, including the ubiquitous foliage and rocaille work. Here the swan-neck top is centred by a basket of flowers instead of the cartouche, eagle or shell of earlier periods. This pair of mirror-backed wall appliqués [**489**] are giltwood with the faces painted in flesh tones. Asymmetrical, the inner frames are balanced by surrounding brackets intended to display porcelain. Supporting a shelf, each bracket is carved with a different face surmounted by a hat. Centred at the base with an ormolu candle-arm holder (the arms now missing), this is one of a pair of well-carved mirrors or girandoles [**491**], which can be compared to the work of Nahl. (Cf. Kreisel, 1968, vol. II, fig. 718 for a mirror by August Nahl, *c.* 1750, at Schloss Fasanerie by Fulda, with a similar lightness of touch and a similar exotic bird.)

August Nahl (1710–85) was a leading German designer, carver and furniture-maker, well known for his rococo work. Born in Berlin, he was the son of a sculptor who worked under Schlüter. He trained in Paris and from 1736 in Strassburg where he worked on the Palais Rohan. In 1741 he returned to Berlin as *Directeur des Ornaments* under Knobelsdorf, where he developed his own light and vivacious interpretation of the French Rococo, based on his experience in France. Nahl was employed at Schloss Charlottenburg as well as Schloss Sans Souci in Potsdam, where he worked on the Music Room. In 1746 he fled to Strassburg and from there to Bern to escape from the insatiable Friedrich the Great. By 1755 he was in Kasel where he worked on the decorations at Schloss Wilhelmstahl between 1755 and 1773.

This frame [**492**] is in the manner of Johann Michael Hoppenhaupt II (1709–69). Hoppenhaupt II was trained by his father, who was a carver. He later worked in Dresden and Vienna before coming to Berlin in 1740 where he was made 'Kabinetts-bildhauer' at the Berlin schloss. He and his brother, Johann Christian, worked on carving, design and interior decoration both in Berlin and at Potsdam under the direction of Knobelsdorff and Nahl. Both brothers shared a predilection for naturalistic ornament in

488 South Germany, *c.*1750, carved giltwood
65in (165cm) (sse colour illustration on p. 240)

489 Germany, *c.*1750, a pair, carved, painted and parcel-gilt wall appliqués
45in (114cm)

the style of the garlands of flowers at each side of this frame. A similar use of this form of decoration is apparent in drawings by Hoppenhaupt at the Staatlich Kunst Bibliothek in Berlin. These drawings, of which there are seventy, were engraved by Johann Michael Meil between 1752 and 1755 and include designs for panelling, chimney-pieces, console-tables and mirrors, commodes, chairs, clocks, chandeliers as well as coaches and sedan chairs. The designs were influenced by Curvilliés and are full of asymmetry and invention, combined with a generous use of naturalistic ornament, as well as more fanciful Chinamen, putti and dragons. These designs certainly influenced Franz Habermann from Augsburg and Thomas Johnson from England (see p. 116). In 1755 Hoppenhaupt designed a pair of commodes, made by Schilansky the cabinet-maker for the Residenz at Ansbach for Sophie Dorothea, the Prussian queen mother. In the Treasury of the Residenz, Munich, is a toilet set composed of brushes, boxes, a silver-mounted torch designed by J.E. Heuglin, and enamelled panels, decorated with figures of classical heroes, painted in gold relief on a polychrome ground and attributed to the Fromery workshop, Berlin. These decorations, and those on a box with Heuglin mounts and an enamel lid attributed to Christian F. Herold, are reminiscent of those on this mirror [**494**], thus leading one to suppose that originally the mirror was part of a similar set.

Alexander Fromery, from Berlin, was a maker of enamel boxes. The porcelain painter, Christian Friedrich Herold, or Heroldt (*c.* 1700–79) seems to have begun working in Berlin for Fromery. Between 1725 and 1777 he worked at the Meissen porcelain factory as a painter and continued to decorate for Fromery. The inner flat frame of this mirror [**501**] is decorated with overlaid strapwork on a textured surface to increase definition.

Another important name is that of Matthias Funk (1697–1783), whose style is emulated

490 Germany, *c.*1750, carved giltwood
61½in (156cm)

491 South Germany, *c.*1750, one of a pair, carved giltwood girandole
51in (130cm)

492 Germany, *c.*1755, one of a pair, carved giltwood
84½in (214cm)

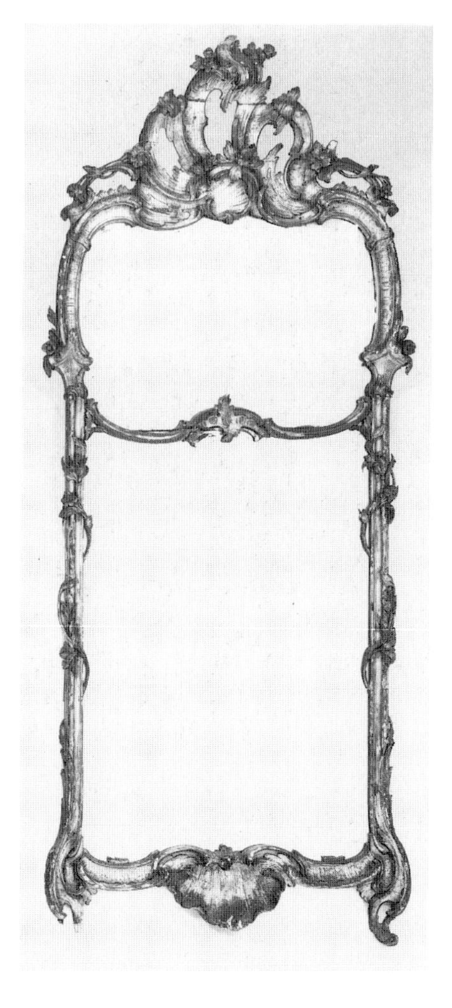

493 Germany, *c.*1755, carved giltwood
91in (231cm)

494 South Germany, *c.*1755, enamelled and gilt-metal toilet-mirror, gold relief, on a polychrome background
22in (56cm)

495 South Germany, *c.*1755, carved giltwood
104in (264cm)

496 Germany, *c.*1750–60, carved giltwood
20in (51cm)

498 South Germany, probably Bayreuth, *c.*1760, carved and painted
29½in (75cm)

497 Germany, *c.*1760, carved giltwood
51in (129cm)

499 Austria, *c.*1760, a pair, carved and gilt-bronze girandoles with enamelled candle-arms
Each 19in (49cm)

500 Austro-German, *c.*1760, carved giltwood, possibly originally containing a coat of arms
57in (145cm)

501 North Germany, *c.*1760, carved giltwood pier-glass
68in (173cm)

502 Germany or Switzerland, *c.*1765, one of a pair, carved giltwood pier-glass with matching console-table
overall height 102½in (260cm)

457

461

488

503

538

553 a & b

554

567

571

575

594

619

624

in this German or Swiss mirror and console-table [**502**]. Funk, the son of Johann Lorenz Funk, was probably of Swiss origin and had two younger brothers, Johann Friedrich (1706–75) and Daniel Beat Ludwig (1726–87). Their father came from Frankfurt to Switzerland in 1695. Matthias Funk developed an important cabinet-making workshop in Switzerland and employed journeymen from Germany and Sweden. His brother, Johann Friedrich, made and carved furniture particularly pier-glass frames and console-tables. (Cf. Kreisel, 1970, vol. II, fig. 1137 for a similar example in the Hotel Musique, Bern, by Johann Friedrich Funk; Ehret, 1986, fig. 25, p. 42.) This set [**503**] was originally made for the Estate of Imshausen, near Bibra in Hesse. A combination of three elements of eighteenth century designs is shown in this frame [**504**]. Cross-grained moulded walnut used for the inner frame is a freature more usually associated with the early part of the century, while the surrounding carved giltwood decoration embraces both the rococo and the neo-classical in the form of acanthus-leaf scrolls and garlands of husks.

Possibly from Northern Germany or Scandinavia, the overall design of this frame [**505**] is similar to mid-eighteenth-century English mirrors with the exception of the classical urn cresting. The neo-classical style never seems to have fully developed in Germany as it had in France and in England, particularly under its leading exponant, Robert Adam. As late as 1775, Johann Christian Fiedler, the court cabinet-maker to Friedrich the Great, was

503 Germany, *c.*1770, one of a pair, carved giltwood pier-glass with matching console-table
74in (188cm) (see colour illustration on p. 240)

504 Germany, *c.*1770, carved giltwood
43in (109cm)

505 North Germany or Scandinavia, *c.*1780, carved giltwood
68in (173cm)

506 Germany, *c.*1805, painted overmantel, highlighted with gilding
76in (193cm)

507 North Germany, *c.*1820, Biedermeier, fruitwood veneered with ebonized mouldings
40in (102cm)

508 North Germany, *c.*1820, Biedermeier, Karelian birch veneered cheval mirror
80in (152cm)

509 Germany, *c.*1820, Biedermeier, mahogany and parcel-gilt cheval mirror with brass candle-arms
66½in (169cm)

510 North Germany, *c.*1820, Biedermeier, fruitwood veneered dressing-mirror
69in (175cm)

511 North Germany, *c.*1820, Biedermeier, walnut and parcel-gilt
57in (145cm)

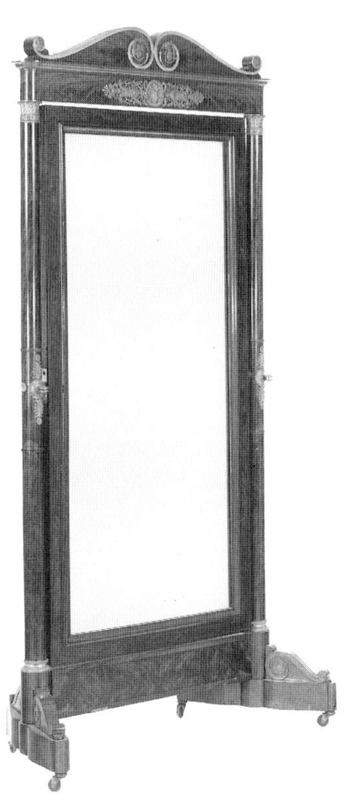

512 Germany or Low Countries, *c.*1810, mahogany and gilt-metal mounted cheval mirror
90in (230cm)

513 North Germany, *c.*1820, ormolu-mounted, parcel-gilt walnut and mahogany cheval mirror
86in (219cm)

514 Germany or Holland, *c.*1825, carved mahogany pier-glass
67in (170cm)

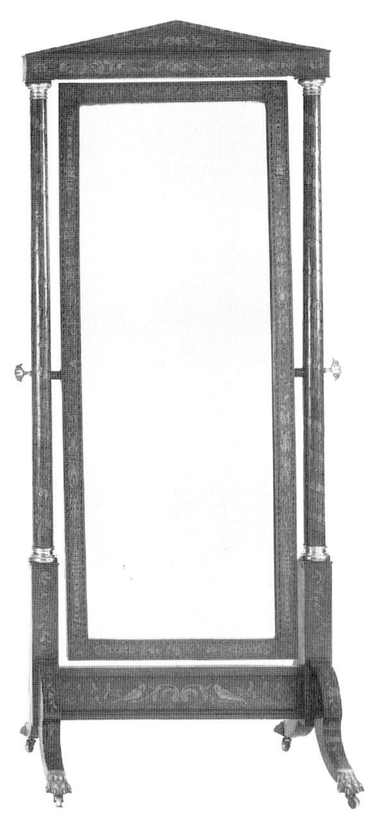

515 Holland, *c.*1830, mahogany and fruitwood marquetry cheval mirror
75in (190cm)

516 North Germany, *c.*1830, mahogany inlaid with stringing
93in (236cm)

517 Austro-German, *c.*1830, maple and amaranth cheval mirror with inlaid decoration
72in (183cm)

518 Germany or Holland, *c.*1830, mahogany cheval mirror with gilt-metal finials
72in (183cm)

519 Germany, *c.*1830 oyster laburnum veneered, giltwood and ormolu-mounted cheval mirror
84in (213cm)

still producing pieces in the full rococo style. Classical elements such as urn crestings and garlands of husks [**504**], as well as bead mouldings and paterae were incorporated into the Neo-classical style as ornamental features.

In Germany the Empire style that spread from France throughout Europe was relatively short-lived. Despite the great David Roentgen, who had done much to spread the Empire style with finely inlaid cabinet furniture, the style itself barely survived the last years of Imperial power. After the Napoleonic war, the building of new palaces came to a standstill and the middle-classes had become impoverished. From the aftermath of the war there developed a decorative style in Germany and Austria between 1815 and 1848 that came to be called Biedermeier. The term Biedermeier is a combination of the German adjective 'bieder', meaning plain, unpretentious and inoffensive and 'meier', one of the most common surnames in Germany, and was given to a character invented by Ludwig Eichrodt and Adolph Kussmaul in 1853. Under this fictional name they produced poems for the journal *Fliegende Blätter*, inspired by the unconscious humour in the poetry of Samuel Sauter (1766–1846). Biedermeier symbolized German bourgeoisie of the early nineteenth century and the name covered the period's decorative style for furniture as well as porcelain, glass and carpets etc. Solid, homely and comfortable-looking, the furniture especially has great 'gemütlich'; made in light-coloured woods, often outlined in contrasting ebony, and with limited ornamentation, the clean and simple lines of Biedermeier furniture have a modern appearance. The effect is illustrated here with this small mirror veneered in a typically light-coloured fruitwood with contrasting ebonized mouldings [**507**].

This form of dressing-glass [**508**] in which it is possible to see the full-length figure, was developed in England during the late eighteenth century. Its evolution was due to changing fashions and the availability of large pieces of less costly mirror-glass. This fashionable novelty was adopted in France, Germany and America. In this example, the frame is made of Scandinavian Karelian birchwood, which derives its name from the Finnish province where great quantities of the timber have been obtained. Birchwood's distinctive grain is produced by larvae attacking the timber and making cavities, which are filled with cells of a deep brown colour. Despite this mirror's august provenance (formerly in the collection of Robert von Hirsch) it is not of the highest standard since there is a possibility that the central mirror frame did not begin its life with the stand [**509**].

Throughout the eighteenth and into the nineteenth century, the designs shown on this Dutch marquetry frame [**515**] were to remain popular. By contrast the unusual decoration on this cheval mirror [**519**], is more often associated with the seventeenth century – relatively small, oyster-cut, laburnam veneer – in this case, however, supported by stylized cornucopia. By the mid-nineteenth century this mirror [**521**] would have been in the latest style. Shortly after the 'Second Rococo' style first appeared in Germany, from France, in the 1830s, it usurped the Biedermeier style and became the accepted norm for furniture design throughout Europe.

An example of the romantic, historical style of the second half of the century, this frame follows the form of late-seventeenth-century Flemish mirrors, complete with embossed metal and contrasting ebony mouldings [**522**].

The following six mirrors [**524 to 529**] are examples of German, probably Meissen porcelain-framed looking-glasses. Predominantly a product of the nineteenth century,

520 North Germany, *c.*1835, Biedermeier, fruitwood toilet-mirror.
24½in (62cm)

521 Germany, *c.*1840, carved giltwood
57in (145cm)

522 Holland, *c.*1850, ebonized and gilt-metal
49in (124cm)

523 Holland, *c.*1870, one of a pair, carved ebonized and parcel-gilt mirror in the seventeenth-century style
61in (155cm)

524 Dresden, *c.*1870–90, polychrome porcelain
53in (134cm)

525 Dresden, *c.*1890, porcelain
29in (74cm)

526 Dresden, *c.*1890, porcelain with wooden outer frame
diameter 26½in (67cm)

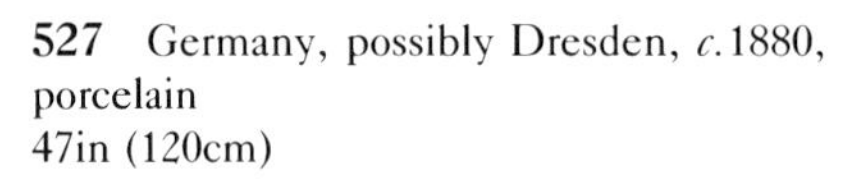

527 Germany, possibly Dresden, *c.*1880, porcelain
47in (120cm)

528 Dresden, *c.*1880, porcelain
39in (99cm)

529 Dresden, *c.*1890, porcelain girandole
26in (66cm)

530 Holland, *c.*1880, red tortoiseshell and ebony in the seventeenth-century Flemish style
23½in (60cm)

531 Germany, *c.*1880, silvered repoussé
64in (153cm)

534 Holland, *c.*1920, carved giltwood and painted overmantel mirror
79½in (202cm)

532 Germany, *c.*1890, carved giltwood pier-glass
85in (216cm)

533 Swiss (Berne) or Austrian, *c.*1880, carved pine hall stand incorporating a mirror
Overall height 83in (210cm)

Meissen porcelain mirror frames were associated with the rococo revival of the 1840s to 1890s. Frames made in this porcelain, also known as Dresden, were designed either to be wall-hanging or free-standing for dressing tables. Although delicately handled, the decoration of the frames tends towards fussiness, incorporating flowers and foliage, often painted in vivid colours and punctuated by putti in flesh tones, usually on a white ground. The famous underglaze blue cross swords mark (adapted from the royal arms), was first adopted in 1724 and is probably the most copied of all porcelain factory marks. In addition Meissen bears an impressed mark, usually numerals, which refers to the mould number according to an inventory started in 1763. Initials in underglaze blue are probably those of painters except in the case of 'A.R.' which stand for Augustus Rex and indicate that the pieces were intended for the royal collection.

The effect of this typical red tortoiseshell and ebony frame [**530**] is emulated today, although the results are often intended as picture frames. The foil or coloured backing of the tortoiseshell ranges from the more common red, to green and brown and, in some cases, yellow (see p. 40).

Copied from a late seventeenth-century original, this nineteenth century frame has a wood base completely covered with repoussé silver [**531**]. In complete contrast, this typically nineteenth-century Swiss or Austrian pine bear stand, fitted with a mirror [**533**], is a variation of a more commonly found hat and stick stand. Usually made in sections and from more than one piece of wood, a join can be seen in this case just above the large bear's face. Examples do exist fitted with barometers. (Cf. Payne, 1985, p. 367, figs 1091 and 1092 for examples without mirrors.)

In this final example the overmantel mirror [**534**] was originally made *en suite* with a fire surround, the latter is carved with leaves and flanked by winged griffins forming the jambs to each side.

Italy

During the closing years of the sixteenth century and into the seventeenth century – the Renaissance – a number of extremely wealthy families emerged in Italy. In Rome nepotistic Popes almost guaranteed their 'nephews' aristocratic positions; their villas: Borghese, Chigi, Panfilj and Barberini, were perhaps the grandest in Europe. The great port of Genoa with its trade links throughout the world produced many wealthy merchant families, while the Republic of Venice developed as a fashionable centre for the old and the newly-rich families like the Rezzonico, bankers who bought their way into the patriciate at some considerable expense. The competition between these families to create grander palaces and churches within a settled and active economy produced a perfect social climate for artistic endeavour and an ideal background for splendidly ostentatious decoration.

While Italian cabinet furniture is often criticized for the poor quality of its construction, its external effect is nevertheless, undiminished by the lack of attention to the unseen. Mirror frames, on the other hand, were carved from local timbers by a separate group of highly skilled Venetian craftsmen. The 'intagliadori' carvers, as opposed to the 'marangoni' cabinet-makers, used their experience as carvers, to work either on their own, or their patrons' designs, or on those supplied by designer-sculptors. One such designer was Filippo Parodi (1630–1702), who produced tables and frames of great style and elegance to fulfil his patrons' appetite for splendour. Commissions were normally for purely decorative furniture calculated to impress visitors to their palaces. Thus, galleries lined with Greek and Roman sculpture; set against frescoed walls and ceilings, were punctuated by large and impressively carved and gilded console-tables bearing vast inlaid marble tops. This taste for larger furniture with boldly-carved foliage often incorporating human figures of a sculptural form, reflects the Baroque desire for a total dramatic concept. Baroque taste had superceded the often eccentric Mannerist style of reversed and broken pediments and panels of strapwork relief (in itself a reaction to the classicism of the Renaissance). But whereas sixteenth- and early seventeenth-century Italian furniture had influenced the rest of Europe, late-seventeenth-century Italian furniture began in turn to be influenced by the French.

In *Travels of a Frenchman in Italy* written between 1765 and 1766, the Murano glass-houses are mentioned:

> 'The arts are cultivated more in Venice than in the rest of Italy. The glassware of Murano goes everywhere, only that of France is considered preferable. The only glass-house on the island of Murano is that of Giovanni Mota. They work only two days a week there, and the dozen or so workers employed are enough to blow 600 pieces of glass in a morning. The frit is made of ash from Spain and earth from Vicenza, baked in a separate oven for six hours, and this frit, placed in another crucible for seven or eight days, serves to make the glass.

535 Venice, *c.*1650, carved giltwood and painted
25in (63cm)

536 North Italy, second half seventeenth century, carved giltwood in the manner of Filippo Passarini
63in (160cm)

537 North Italy, *c.*1680, carved giltwood
53½in (136cm)

538 Venice, *c.*1680, gilt-bronze decorated with rock crystal, coloured glass and gemstones
31½in (80cm) (see colour illustration in p. 241)

539 Piedmont or Lombardy, *c.*1680, giltwood and ebonized walnut
58in (148cm)

540 Sicily, *c.*1685, carved giltwood
53½in (136cm)

They blow glass four and a half feet across each way, but usually it is only three feet at the most. After blowing the plate glass with great effort, they cut it and lay it on a stone, then with an iron shovel they put it at an inclined angle over the furnace to cool gradually. Silvering, or tinning, consists of laying on a perfectly smooth table of iron or marble a sheet of beaten tin the size of the glass. This tin is covered with a thin layer of mercury, and on top of this 'is laid the plate of glass, which has previously been polished with emery.'

Richly-carved foliate scrolls are interspersed with the heads of putti painted in flesh tones on this carved, gilt-wood frame [**535**]. (Cf. Morazzoni, 1945, fig. 9a.) Of similarly lively handling, this frame, inspired by the work of Passarini [**536**], has mirror-plate which may just replace the original, or, as was so often the case, may replace a painting. If this is the case, the figure almost hidden amongst the foliage could have had some significance for the painting.

Felippo Passarini, born in Rome in 1638, is well known for his exuberance of style. Many of his designs for clocks, tables, brackets, pulpits, beds and mirrors are contained in *Nuove Inventioni d'ornamenti d'architettura e d'intagli diversi utile ad Argentieri Intagliatori* (with colour plates), published in Rome on the year of his death, 1698.

His vigorous, and often theatrical designs favoured the use of scrolls, acanthus and military trophies in an often fantastic Baroque style (Cf. Palacios, 1984, vol. II p. 70, fig. 124, for a drawing by him inscribed 'Roma 1698'; Morazzoni, 1945, p. 19, fig. 3; Morazzoni, 1954, p. 63, Rosa, 1963, p. 81, fig. 196). Typical of the northern Italian school of carving, this example is in the style of grand frames especially carved to be placed above console-tables, *en suite* or in the same form [**537**] (Cf. Morazzoni, 1945, p. 18). More extravagant still, this rare mirror frame, [**538**] reflects the colourful elegance of Venetian art translated by the local craftsmens' skills into coloured glass, rock-crystal and hardstones. The high quality of the metal-work, casting and chasing, combined with the exquisite decoration places this frame in another category altogether. Indeed, although dated a little earlier, the artistry of this frame is comparable to the work of the designer sculptor Francesco Ladatte (*c*. 1706–87). Ladatte or Ladetti was a formidable sculptor in gilt-bronze; such was his ability in producing bronze mounts, candelabra, clock-cases and other objects, that he was appointed sculptor in bronze to the King in 1745. Born in Turin, he was only twelve when he went to Paris to be trained; there, at the age of twenty-three, he was awarded first prize for his sculpture by the Academy. Having worked in Rome for a while and again in Paris between 1737–43, when he became a member of the Academy and exhibited at the Salon, he returned to Turin in 1744. The treatment of the inner wave moulded frame [**539**] resembles a popular contemporary Flemish form of decoration for both looking-glass frames and picture frames. Made of ebonized, native walnut, these mouldings, however, confirm an Italian origin, since a Flemish frame of this quality would more likely have been made in ebony. Testimony to this Northern European influence is the record of foreign craftsmen working in Rome and Florence, including: Giacomo Herman (*c*. 1688) and Giovanni Falghero (or Falker, in German) both Germans, Giovanni Signist, a Swiss; and Leonardo Vander Winne, a Fleming. (Cf. Bacceschi, 1962, p. 22, fig. 124.)

541 Florence, late seventeenth or early eighteenth century, carved giltwood 78in (198cm)

542 North Italy, *c.*1700, carved giltwood 86½in (220cm)

A fine example of a seventeenth-century Florentine frame, [**541**] (formerly in the collection of the Earl of Haddingham, Tyninghame, East Lothian) precedes another Northern Italian frame [**542**], probably from Venice or Genoa. The latter bears cresting in the form of a shell centred by two mermaids carrying a Venus-like figure. Putti holding cannon to each side of the frame, continue the nautical association. The flamboyant handling of the carving is in the style of the great sculptor-carvers such as Maragliano and Parodi, both from Genoa. (Cf. Morazzoni, 1945, p. 20.)

Like the earlier example, [**538**], this frame demonstrates the art of the Venetian glass decorator [**543**] (formerly in the collection of Lord Greville). Each of the strips of border glass surrounding the central plate, engraved with an allegorical figure, is decorated with finely-worked emblems of war, surrounded by foliage. Whilst the form of this frame dates it towards the end of the seventeenth century, areas of the decoration on the strips of glass seem out of place and do not continue to the next piece, suggesting that the mirror has been 'made up' from the sections of another looking-glass.

The overall form of this cushion-moulded frame, [**544**] is in keeping with the late-seventeenth-century style of Northern European frames. This form, however, continued to be used in Italy and tended to be enriched by a scrolled cresting and carving to the sides, which suggests that this example may be a later frame that has had that carving removed. (Cf. Morazzoni, 1945, p. 956.) In accordance with the rest of Europe, Italy was also in the grip of an obsession with the Orient during the end of the seventeenth and the early years of the eighteenth century, as manifested by this frame [**545**]. Later, in 1720, Filippo Bonnani went so far as to write a treatise on lacquering and listed some ten different methods employed by English, French, German, Polish and Italian craftsmen. In eighteenth-century Venice, the words lacquer and lacquerer did not exist and there is no corresponding Italian word for the term 'japanning'. The word 'lacca' was used for both oriental lacquer and European imitations. It is generally thought that the interest in lacquer and japanning began in the second half of the seventeenth century, influenced by the Portuguese and Dutch trade with the East which imported quantities of Oriental lacquer to Italy. In his book Alvar Gonzales Palacios demonstrates how the art of Venetian japanning originated around this time. (Cf. Palacios, 1986 vol. II, figs 719 and 720, p. 337, and fig. 721, p. 338.) One of the few early Venetian japanned pieces that can be dated is a pair of 'Moretti' or Blackamoors at Ham House, Middlesex, which are included in the inventory of 1669 where they are described as 'two Indian stands'.

The fashion for Oriental lacquer was such that soon the demand far outstripped the amount being imported, despite its costliness. Initially the price was regulated by the trading companies, in England, for example, 'Small trunkes or chests of Japan guilded and inlaid with mother of pearle having sundry drawers and boxes' were sold for £4. 5s. and £5 in 1607, and four years later the price had risen to £17 apiece. Thus Venice was compelled to produce its own lacquer. By 1668 it was already a centre for lacquer work when Maximilien Misson remarked that 'La Lacque de Venise est comme on scait en reputation: il y en a à toute sorte de prix.' (Venetian lacquer is exactly like its reputation: you find it at all sorts of prices.)

543 Venice, *c.*1700, carved giltwood with engraved glass
48in (122cm)

544 North Italy, *c.*1700, carved giltwood and japanned
30½in (77cm)

545 Venice, *c.*1700, japanned and parcel-gilt
45in (114cm)

546 Venice, *c.*1700, one of a pair, japanned, parcel-gilt and mother of pearl
42in (107cm)

547 Venice, *c.*1700, carved giltwood and polychrome
51½in (131cm)

548 Venice, *c.*1700, carved giltwood and painted (right)
73in (186cm)

549 Venice or North Italy, *c.*1700, carved giltwood, in the manner of Andrea Brustolon
89½in (227cm)

550 Lombardy, *c.*1710, carved giltwood and painted
78in (198cm)

551 North Italy, *c.*1710, carved giltwood
46in (117cm)

552 North Italy, *c.*1710, green-japanned toilet mirror
7½in (19cm)

553 Venice, *c.*1720, one of a pair, coloured glass and giltwood
37in (94cm) (see colour illustration on p. 242)

554 North Italy, *c.*1715, one of a pair, engraved mirror-glasses
13in (33cm) (see colour illustration of the pair showing the Sacrifice of Isaac on p. 242)

The example here [**545**] differs from the style of decoration found further north in Europe in that the frame is decorated with a combination of chinoiserie as well as European styles. (Cf. Morazzoni, 1945, p. 77, 78a.) Two further mirrors, [**546 and 547**] also betray oriental influence: an almost identical type of frame [**546**] to the previous example, has similar mouldings, and is possibly from the same workshop, the only difference being the introduction of mother-of-pearl. (Cf. Mariacher, 1963, cover illustration; Morazzoni, 1945, pl. between pp. XX/VIII and XXIX.) Venice, as a major seaport, benefitted, as did Antwerp, from trade with the Far East. As a result countries served by such ports, and to a lesser extent England, used etched mother-of-pearl for decorative inlaid work. Again, this example [**547**], uses etched mother-of-pearl and incorporates oriental decoration with European (the latter used in a similar way to the first example [**546**]) but in this case the scrollwork is raised and centred with scarab motifs.

During the fourteenth century the Venetian craftsmen had formed themselves into a Guild called 'L'Arte dei Depentori' which had, in earlier centuries included all painters of pictures 'Pittori' but the latter caused a split in 1691. This break-away faction was led by Pietro Liberi who formed 'il Collegio dei Pittori', and welcomed all decorative painters. An example of the skilled work of members both of the Venetian guilds of 'Intajadori' and 'Depentori' – lacquerers and japanners – is shown here. Heart-shaped chinoiserie decoration could well indicate that this frame was made as a wedding gift.

In contrast, this monumental Venetian frame [**549**] is carved in the manner of Andrea Brustolon (1662–1732). A highly accomplished and influential sculptor in wood, he was born in Belluno in 1662 and was trained in the wood carving tradition of the region. In 1684 he moved to Venice where, during the next ten or twelve years, he is known to have carved a set of eight chairs for the Correr family and a suite for the Venier family (all of which are now in the Palazzo Rezzonico in Venice). Later, in 1700, he worked on a set of twelve chairs, each one carved with emblematic details of the months of the year for the Pisani villa at Etna (now in the Palazzo Quirinale in Rome). He also worked on highly elaborate picture and looking glass frames for which designs exist among his drawings in the Museo Civico in Belluno. (Cf. Palacios, 1986, p. 355, fig. 747.) This drawing incorporates a flight of ten or more putti bearing emblems and representing, according to Brustolon's notes, the Triumph of Love over Valour and Virtue. Perhaps his finest work was a suite of furniture, carved for the Venier family, of chairs with arms and legs in the form of gnarled tree trunks and branches supported by negro boys with ebony heads and arms showing patches of ebony flesh through the slashes in their boxwood carved breeches. The suite also included stands held by negro slaves, naked and with boxwood chains around their necks. Other stands in this form were carved with the Four Seasons and one in particular depicts the figures of Hercules, Cerberus, the Hydra, classical river gods and three young negroes. Brustolon was primarily a sculptor, although he influenced furniture-making, and was more normally employed on ecclesiastical carvings for the city of Belluno. (Cf. Morazzoni, 1945, pp. 16, 18, 196.)

A relatively simple, moulded and painted frame, this example, [**550**] has strapwork and leaf scrolls forming the elaborate decoration. The richly carved florid form of another baroque frame [**551**] may date it a little earlier in that decorative tradition. The cresting, decorated with winged putti masks, probably represents the wind, shown as they are amongst the clouds. Roughly in the form of a cartouche, this particular shape of the mirror plate was popular in Venice throughout the eighteenth century (as will be seen in further illustrations). Roughly contemporary, this early eighteenth-century toilet-glass [**552**] follows a form of design that was also popular in Northern Europe. (Cf. Mariacher, 1963, pl. 10). A combination piece such as this, would have been developed exclusively for the requirements of a lady in her bedroom, and contains a fitted drawer in the frieze with compartments and lidded boxes, designed to take, in some cases, further glass phials and jars of make-up, powder and perfume. Above the frieze drawer is a fall-front bureau with an arrangement of pigeon-holes and drawers surrounding a central cupboard, all in proportion. When fitted the interior cupboard, can conceal further secret drawers and compartments, presumably to hide valuables and private correspondence. From the North of Italy, the mirror may well have been made in Venice by one of the guild of 'Depentori', or 'Depentori alla Chinese'. One such guildsman was Iseppo Tosello, who is mentioned in a document of 1729, and numbered among many who produced japanned work.

555 North Italy, *c.*1720, walnut and parcel-gilt
38in (97cm)

556 Venice, *c.*1720, one of a set of three, with engraved mirror plate
34½in (88cm)

Venetian craftsmen excelled in the production of green lacquer, or more correctly, japanning as the European imitation is called, and with which this example [**552**] is decorated (see p. 42).

There are differences between various types of Venetian japanning, the 'Mobili 'di terra' and 'Venezia d'aqua' were both made in Venice, with slightly poorer quality work produced in other areas. The strictures of the guild ensured that work was of a high standard in Venice, but in other cities it seems that the disciplines were less rigidly observed. Complete rooms were decorated in this way; records show that some sixty lacquered panels were purchased in Rome in 1732 for the Palazzo Reale at Turin for use in a complete decorative scheme devised by the great architect Filippo Juvarra. But the work was not completed until four years later when more panels were provided by Pietro Massia.

Filippo Juvarra (1676–1736) was born in Messina, the son of a goldsmith. He entered the priesthood as well as studying architecture. In 1706 he became a member of the Academy having studied under Carlo Fontana in Rome. He published *Raccolta di Targhe* in Rome in 1722 which contained seventy two plates of designs by Bernini, Borromini, Pietro da Cortona, Algardi, and Carlo Fontana, mainly of Baroque cartouches. He travelled extensively, visiting London, Portugal and Versailles. It was whilst he was in Spain to design the Royal Palace in Madrid that he died in 1736.

During the 1730s Juvarra was the superintendant of all the Court works (apart from the 'Staircase of Scissors' in the Palazzo Reale). But the Chinese cabinet for which the sixty black and gold panels of flowers and animals were purchased was perhaps his greatest achievement. The work, however, was not completed until four years later when Pietro Massia produced the remaining panels for the dado. Massia was only one of the artisans who worked on the cabinet; the framework on the walls and the floor were worked on by Angelo Saniga and a certain Vietto (both of whom are named in the Royal Household Accounts), who are also thought to have produced frames since they form an integral part of the decorative scheme.

Basically, Venetian japanning can be divided into two phases. At the end of the seventeenth century, Venetian japanning, is similar to that of Northern Europe, with gilt relief on a dark background in imitation of oriental examples. By the mid-eighteenth century, Venetian japanning has fewer chinoiserie elements and more floral arrangements together with pastoral scenes inspired by the work of painters like Zais, Zuccarelli, and Ricci. Indeed, designs for japanned work are thought to have been produced by painters like Guardi, Tiepolo and other well-known names and a pair of doors at the Palazzo Rezzonico have tentatively been ascribed to Tiepolo.

One of a pair of typical Venetian looking glasses, made almost entirely of glass with the exception of an inner carved giltwood frame, this mirror [**553**] would originally have been fitted with candlearms. (Cf. Mariacher, 1963, pls 34 and 61.) J.G. de Keysler, who visited Venice during the closing months of 1730, remarked 'The Venetian glass is very pure and ductile when it is in fusion; on which account it is more easily melted, and answers much better than any others for the works of fantasy.' He also commented with admiration on the mirrors, though he also remarked that those 'of any considerable size are extremely dear when other looking glasses at present are so cheap.' The reason for their price and relatively small size is that they were blown and

557 North Italy, *c.*1720, one of a pair, carved giltwood girandoles (candle-arms missing)
34in (87cm)

558 Rome, *c.*1720, carved giltwood
47in (119cm)

559 Venice, *c.*1725, one of a set of four, carved giltwood girandole
42½in (108cm)

560 Venice, *c.*1730, one of a pair, carved giltwood
32½in (83cm)

561 Florence, *c.*1730, one of a pair, carved giltwood
68in (173cm)

562 Florence, *c.*1730, carved giltwood
65in (165cm)

not cast and ground like French mirrors. In this example, [**553**], each central looking-glass plate is decorated with figures shown beneath draped canopies. Such decoration was probably achieved using a diamond wheel as well as acid. Another mirror plate [**554**] one of a pair, is engraved with the finding of Romulus and Remus. This method of etching the glass with hydrofluoric acid, to produce a textured, frosted effect, was also used to create pictorial decorations on a large scale. The method was perfected by Henry Schwanhard who worked in an area bordering Bohemia and Silesia, until his death in 1696. A further link with Bohemia is via Giuseppo Briati, 1686–1772, a craftsman who inherited a glassworks at Murano in the early eighteenth century and who is said to have worked in the Bohemian glass industry. Briati transferred his premises to Venice itself in 1739 and established his business and factory in the parish of S. Angelo Raffaele. From these works he produced mirrors and picture frames, table centres, large chandeliers and panels for the decoration of furniture. (Cf. Mariacher, 1963, pl. 25 for a portrait of Briati.)

Coloured glass panels were used to decorate furniture during the eighteenth century. Later, in 1777, Lady Anna Riggs Miller recorded in her diary, on a visit to Murano, that she had been shown a suite of furniture inlaid with pieces of blue glass and looking glass, commissioned by the Sultan of Turkey for his hareem. Another mirror [**555**] lends further credence to the inability of Venetian looking glass-makers to produce plates of any size, restricted as they were by the blown method. A witness of this process was Charles de Brosses who gave a description of the technique of glassmaking in Murano in a letter to M. de Blancey dated 29 August 1739:

> 'I have just returned from Murano, where I have been to see the glass-house. The glass plates are not as large nor as white as ours but they are more transparent and less faulty. They are not cast on copper tables like ours but blown like bottles. The work demands extremely large and robust workers, especially to swing in the air those great globes of crystal on the end of their blow-pipe. The worker takes from the crucible of the furnace a large quantity of moulten matter, which is then of a gluey consistency, on the end of his blow-pipe. By blowing he makes a hollow globe, then by swinging it in the air and putting it every now and then into the mouth of the furnace so as to maintain a certain degree of fusion, still turning it very quickly so that the matter does not run more on to one side than another, he succeeds in making a long oval of it. Then another worker with the point of a pair of scissors (that is to say they open when the hand is relaxed) pierces the end of the oval. The first worker holding the pipe turns it very quickly whilst the second gradually opens the scissors. In this way the oval is completely opened up at one end on to another specially made pipe. Then it is opened at the other end using the same method I have just described. You have then a long cylinder of glass of wide diameter. Still being turned, it is put once more into the mouth of the furnace to soften it a little again and when it comes out, in a trice it has been cut lengthways with shears and laid out on a copper table. After that, it only has to be heated again in another oven, polished and silvered in the ordinary way.

Another small mirror [**558**] has, however, a carved frame, handled with great life and style and possibly showing a French influence. Looking glasses of this size, and form, some fitted with candle-arms, were made either in pairs or in sets of up to four and six. One of a set of four girandoles made in Venice, the shape of this looking glass [**559**] accentuated by a bevelled edge which is echoed by a line of decoration. Worked on the main field of the glass is Mercury, the typical Greek god, youthful, graceful and athletic, easily identified by his winged sandals and hat. He carries a magic wand or 'cadaceus', entwined with two snakes. As a guide he escorted Psyche to heaven for her marriage, hence the clouds at his feet. In his Roman identity, he was the god of commerce and may have had a purse. Possibly from Florence, this mirror, [**562**] shows a move from the Baroque towards the Rococo, and the influence of France.

The extravagance of the great galleries and state rooms of this time was purely for show, and so impractical that when President Charles de Brosses visited the Palazzo Foscari in Venice in 1739, he complained that there was nowhere to sit because he feared for the safety of the finely-carved chairs under his weight. Of unpretentious design, this gilt mirror (one of a pair) [**564**] was probably made for the family apartments situated above or below the state room in a Palace which would have been furnished in a more domestic way.

The next two mirrors [**566 and 567**] originated in Tuscany and were possibly made in Florence. While both clearly show the gathering momentum of the Rococo

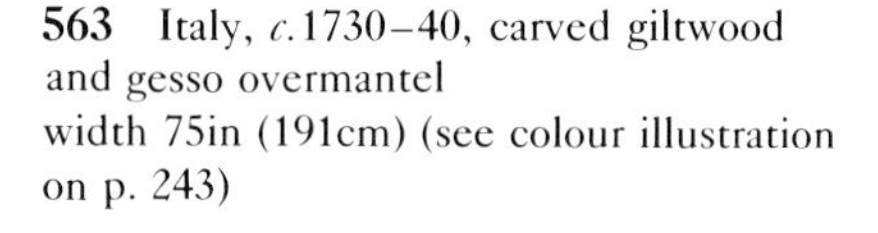

563 Italy, *c.*1730–40, carved giltwood and gesso overmantel
width 75in (191cm) (see colour illustration on p. 243)

563a Detail

564 North Italy, *c.*1730, one of a pair, carved giltwood
31in (79cm)

565 Sicily, *c.*1735, carved giltwood, with matching console-table
51in (130cm)

565a Genoa, *c.*1740, one of a pair, carved giltwood
49in (124cm)

566 Tuscany, *c.*1730, carved giltwood
56in (143cm)

567 Tuscany, *c.*1740, carved giltwood
91½in (232cm) (see colour illustration on p. 243)

568 North Italy, possibly Venice, *c.*1740, carved giltwood (left)
74in (188cm)

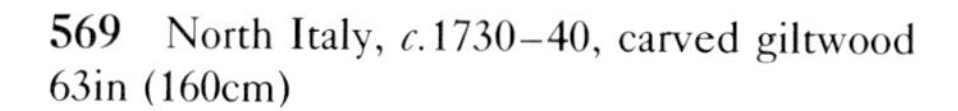

569 North Italy, *c.*1730–40, carved giltwood
63in (160cm)

570 Venice, *c.*1740, one of a pair, carved giltwood
29in (74cm)

571 North Italy, *c.*1740, carved giltwood pier-glass (left)
86in (218cm) (see colour illustration on p. 244)

572 Venice, *c.*1740, 'arte povera', giltwood
29½in (75cm)

573 North Italy, *c.*1740, carved giltwood with etched mirror-plate
56in (142cm)

(although the second mirror is perhaps lighter than the first), the frames still cling to elements of the earlier, Baroque style; both have masks, and those on the second example are so awkwardly placed that they look like an afterthought or a tentative attempt to bridge the stylistic gap. The treatment of the border glasses in this mirror [**536**] is also interesting; there seems to have been a deliberate failure to cover the joins in the glass except in the upper part. The join in the central plate (which is in two parts to achieve the height), is plainly abutted without the bevelled edges that would have been on a mirror of this date from further north. Equally the manner of the carving around the outer frame gives no indication as to whether the design was originally intended to cover those joins in the border plates. Additional observations can be made: the dragons flanking the cartouche and leaf-scrolled cresting are probably derived from decoration on imported Oriental lacquer furniture some forty to fifty years earlier. Equally telling, the extension of the scrollwork of the base of the mirror into lion claw feet would indicate that this frame was originally intended to stand upon a console table as part of a unified scheme, rather than hang in isolation. The same observation can be applied to the another mirror, [**569**]. Here the proportions are unusual and the belief that it may have been intended as an overmantel mirror for one of the smaller family rooms, is reinforced by the lion claw feet indicating that it must stand upon something, possibly the mantel shelf of a fireplace. Carved with a wealth of tightly-drawn decoration, the effect is somewhat cluttered, however the use of a griffin flanking the mirror at the top in such a prominent position is interesting, since its symbolism would have been easily recognized by any viewer.

One of a pair of quite small giltwood mirrors [**570**], this was made in Venice *c.* 1740. A relatively simple frame, it exemplifies perhaps of the lower end of the decorative scale produced in Venice. Not everyone was in the position to furnish a grand palace and the majority of the new bourgeoisie would have required less expensive pieces for their homes. A small hole in the centre of the cartouche at the base of the mirror frame may originally have held a fixing for a candle holder, thus making this pair into girandoles. Again, a more expensive mirror, [**572**] is an example of 'arte povera' (see p. 45). This is probably one of a pair of mirrors [**573**] since the Amazon-like warrior, complete with spear and supported by trophies of war, is facing to the left, probably her companion would have faced the other way.

The next three mirrors [**574–576**] are all examples of majolica, made at Le Nove, Bassano, in Veneto. 'Majolica' was first used to describe the Valencian pottery that was imported into Italy via the island of Majorca. It later became the generic term for a whole range of tin-glazed earthenware, from Spain, Italy and from other countries. The industry in Italy began to flourish and grow during the second half of the fifteenth century at Orvieto in Umbria, Florence and Siena in Tuscany. Each girandole frame is made in three parts, each part separately fired and decorated, hence the slight differences in the depth of the colours in each section. Each one also has an engraved figure, in one example [**575**]there must originally have been a pair with a male and female facing towards each other, beneath a canopy of lambrequins or, in other cases, ribbon-tied foliage. The supports for the figures would appear to be the same in the first and third examples [**574 and 576**], which, combined with the other similarities, points to a common source.

574 Bassano, probably Le Nove, *c.*1740, a pair, majolica girandoles with engraved Venetian mirror-plates
27in (69cm)

575 Bassano, probably Le Nove, *c.*1740, majolica girandole with engraved mirror plate
25½in (65cm) (see colour illustration on p. 245)

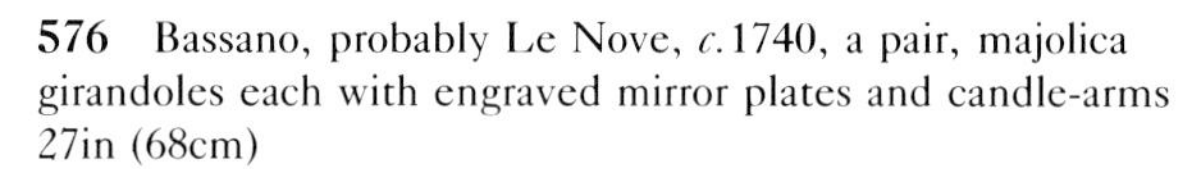

576 Bassano, probably Le Nove, *c.*1740, a pair, majolica girandoles each with engraved mirror plates and candle-arms
27in (68cm)

577 Venice, *c.*1725, one of a pair, carved giltwood with engraved mirror-plate
53in (135cm)

The examples shown here [**577 and 578**] are from a pair and a set of three respectively, the first from the collection of Lady Strickland Constable, the second from the collection of the Duke of Leinster. Both groups are certainly from the same workshop and show interesting differences in the treatment of the carving, for example the lions in the first case appear to be smiling whereas the other lions are unhappy. The similarity extends to the decorated mirror plate, both groups have been decorated by the same man or a group working together using an identical border pattern. The central figures in both examples face in opposite directions, but would have faced towards the companion mirror either as a pair or in a set of four or six.

Typical of mid-eighteenth-century Venetian style of frame, the decorations on the next two examples [**579–580**] are pretty flowers in panels and sprays in bright colours. (Cf. Mariacher, 1963, pls 14–20; II; 21–24; Wannenes, 1984, p. 56.) A swag of leaves centred by a flowerhead [**579**] is a neat way of disguising the join in the two mirror plates, used to fill the frame and re-inforces the prudent use of this expensive commodity. Another Rococo frame carved with lightness [**581**] was possibly influenced by the drawing books of English designers that were published during the middle years of the eighteenth-century. A different approach to hiding the join in two mirror plates is employed in this tall pier-glass, where an exaggerated feature at either side distracts the eye from the carefully disguised join in the mirror plate [**585**]. Carved above the join at each side of the frame is a cornucopia spilling summer flowers. The inner moulded frame of a simple, earlier form that has been elaborated with fashionable mid-eighteenth-century features, all created *c.* 1745 [**586**]. Leafy cabochons at either side of the base of the frame possibly cover flat reserves suitable for the fixings of candle-arms, if the purchaser so wished. Noteworthy in this frame [**587**], though regrettably obscured here, is the top, almost circular plate in the cresting, which is engraved with a young male figure seated on a rock. Conflicting with the harmony and scale of the frame, the carving at the base is probably not original. (Cf. Morazzoni, 1945, p. 48a.) From Tuscany this mirror [**588**] has many similar features and similarities in design to earlier examples. A mirror from the same period from much further south, in this case from Sicily, shows a strong French influence [**589**]. Perhaps the clue to an Italian rather than French maker is the scroll and rocaille carving at the shoulders of the frame topped with carved flowerheads. While the original mirror-plate is heavily distressed, the plate's capacity to reflect can be judged by the slight image of the candle-arms that is visible. To the purist collector the original mirror plate as shown here, is very much part of the value of the whole, whereas a heavily distressed plate may not be acceptable to others. Old plates should only be re-silvered under the guidance of a professional and the old plate should be retained if replaced by new glass. (Cf. Wannenes, 1984, p. 123.)

This small frame [**591**], could well have been converted from a picture frame by the addition of a mirror plate. Imaginative handling of the frame allows the boughs of acanthus, decorated in green, to grow twisting through the carving and finally up through the coronet (the latter cheerfully promulgating the rank of the mirror's owner or the subject of the original painting).

The treatment here [**594**] of the mirror plates in combining regular pieces with abutted joints is not uncommon. Separate pieces are held in place by the outer frame

578 Venice, *c.*1725, one of a set of three, carved giltwood girandole with engraved mirror-plate
51in (130cm)

579 Venice, *c.*1750, one of a pair, painted, carved and giltwood
34½in (87cm)

580 Venice, *c.*1750, carved wood and painted
70in (178cm)

581 Venice, *c.*1750, one of a pair, carved giltwood
42in (107cm)

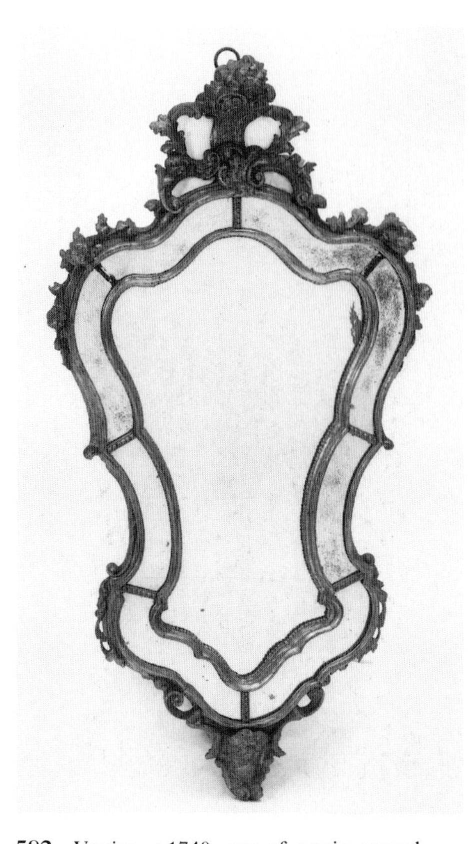

582 Venice, *c.*1740, one of a pair, carved giltwood
39in (99cm)

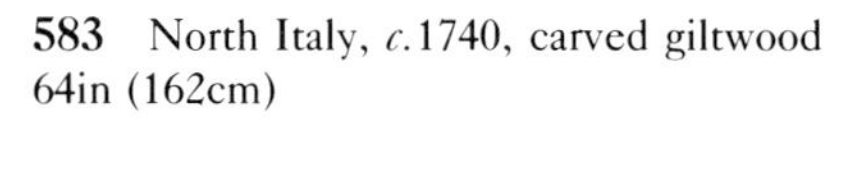

583 North Italy, *c.*1740, carved giltwood
64in (162cm)

584 North Italy, *c.*1740, one of a pair, carved giltwood
45½in (116cm)

585 North Italy, *c.*1730–40, carved giltwood
59in (150cm)

586 South Italy, possibly Sicily, *c.*1745, one of a pair, carved giltwood
37in (94cm)

587 North Italy, *c.*1750, carved giltwood
59in (150cm)

588 Tuscany, *c.*1745, carved giltwood
61in (155cm)

589 Sicily, *c.*1745, carved giltwood
40in (102cm)

590 Venice, *c.*1730, one of a pair, carved wood and painted
53in (135cm)

591 Italy, *c.*1750–50, carved wood, painted and parcel-gilt
35½in (90cm)

592 North Italy, *c.*1750, carved wood and japanned
63in (160cm)

593 Venice, *c.*1750, carved giltwood
57in (145cm)

594 North Italy, *c.*1750, carved giltwood overmantel
95in (242cm) (see colour illustration on p. 246)

595 North Italy, possibly Torino, *c.*1750, carved giltwood
64½in (164cm)

596 North Italy, *c.*1750, painted wood and parcel-gilt (right)
64in (163cm)

597 Tuscany, *c.*1750, one of a pair, carved giltwood
49in (125cm)

598 Sicily, *c.*1750, pair, asymmetrical, carved giltwood
31in (78cm)

and with glass-headed studs at other points. Different head-dresses worn by the figures flanking the frame, and those in a companion mirror, denote the four Seasons or the continents. (The figure on the left is depleted.)

The fact that this pair of mirrors from Sicily [**598**] is handled in a bold, slightly heavy manner, suggests that the new styles and fashions took a considerable time to reach, and become accepted, in the south.

In complete contrast to the somewhat backward state of glass-making in Sicily, the next group of mirrors, [**599 to 601**] are typical of the highly-developed state of the art in Venice. (Cf. Mariacher, 1963, pls 30 and 31.) Two of these frames, [**602 and 603**] are both similar to a Venetian frame sketched by Pietro Longhi (in the Correr Museum in Venice), showing a mother or servant with a child. (Cf. Mariacher, 1963, pl. 64; Morazzoni, 1945, p. 53a.) Another example, [**604**] has engraved border-glass, decorated with trophies and medallions. The mirrored cresting, without embellishment, may have been replaced as the remaining supporting glasses are engraved. As in other countries, the inclusion of Bacchanalian symbols – bunches of grapes and vine leaves – could well point to this mirror having been intended for a dining room. (Cf. Mariacher, 1963, pl. 64.)

One of a set of four girandoles, this example [**608**] is fitted with an iron socket at the base to take the scrolled candle-holder, in addition, each mirror-plate is engraved with a mythological figure depicting either one of the Four Elements or one of the Muses. An insight into the impression such sets of girandoles must have created is given when, a little later in 1765, a Frenchman travelling in Italy described the Royal Palaces at Turin in the following glowing terms:

'The furnishing harmonize with the beauty of the rooms: among other things to be seen there are candle brackets of which the plaques are mirrors set in heavy silver frames wrought most tastefully. We remark upon them only because this particular type of furniture is much used in Italian rooms, usually distributed round the sides so as to throw more light therein.'

599 Venice, *c.*1750, blue and clear glass, originally with a cresting
72in (183cm)

600 Venice, *c.*1750, a pair, reverse-etched *verre églomisé* and giltwood
82in (209cm)

601 Venice, *c.*1750, one of a pair
82in (209cm)

602 Venice, *c.*1750, carved giltwood
57in (145cm)

603 Venice, *c.*1750, carved giltwood
66in (168cm)

604 North Italy, *c*.1750, carved giltwood
92in (234cm)

605 North Italy, *c*.1750, carved giltwood
87½in (222cm)

606 Sicily, *c*.1750, carved giltwood and japanned, with matching console-table overall height 181in (460cm)

606a Detail

607 Torino, *c*.1750, carved silvered wood
83in (211cm)

The back of this *c.* 1760 mirror, [**612**], bears a label dated 1839 with the following inscription: 'Arthur Whitcombe of 23 Coventry Street, Haymarket, London. Carver and gilder' (Cf. Gilbert and Beard 1986, p. 965.) As well as making frames, James Whitcombe may well have repaired and retailed them. One of a pair of chinoiserie mirrors, [**613**] has an apron at the base of the frame carved with scrolls, leaves and flowers, and is centred by a stylized fountain. (Cf. Mariacher, 1963, pl. 79.) Again, one of a pair, these small, natural waxed-walnut frames were probably originally gilded or painted [**614**]. Walnut was used extensively as a carcass timber in Italy because it was in such good supply and therefore was less sought-after than further north in Europe (see p. 92), where walnut tended only to be used when exposed and polished (in some cases it was also used for drawer linings on high quality pieces of cabinet-work). The handling of this overmantel mirror [**616**] combines the rococo and the chinoiserie, particularly in the treatment of the top cresting where a Chinese sage, is seated in a pagoda supported by asymmetrical motifs on each side with the same treatment spreading on to the frame itself. In stark contrast, this example [**618**] is one of a set of four girandoles in the Neo-classical style, which, despite the obviously Venetian flavour introduced by the engraved glass, may have been made elsewhere, possibly in Piedmont. Also from Piedmont, this fine carved fruitwood frame [**619**], can be attributed to Bonzanigo. It has been suggested that this mirror was made for Louis XVI's aunt Madame Adelaide, who lived in Turin after the Revolution. Two comparable frames by Bonzanigo are in the Museo Civico d'Arte Antica, Turin. Both mirrors, roughly the same size as this example, are of comparable quality, and finely carved with similar motifs. (They were exhibited at the Mostra del Barrocco Piedmontese, Turin, June to December 1963, pl. 400, figs A and B.)

Giuseppe-Maria Bonzanigo (1744–1820) was born in Asti, the son of a wood carver. He trained under his father, who specialized in carving organ cases, and later he moved to Turin. There, for the next twenty years, he worked extensively in the Royal Palaces of the House of Savoy and in 1787 Vittorio Amadeo III appointed him wood carver to the Crown, on a salary of 200 lire a year, increased to 300 lire in 1792. His Italianate interpretation of the Louis XVI style included carving of the finest detail. In 1811 A.L. Millin wrote of his work that it 'shows more dexterity than taste'. His work includes a fire screen made in Turin in 1775 with painted decorations by Michele Rapous (now in the Palazzo Reale, Turin).

There is no certainty that the carver of this [**621**] or any other frame that incorporates features, figures and animals, was aware of the symbolism denoted by such decorative detail, but the inspiration clearly was derived from a widely understood source or tradition. In this case the Neo-classical overmantel mirror combines a group of evocative emblems; from a basket of flowers at the top of the frame suspended by a pair of birds (whether eagles or doves, both were strongly representative), to the classical arch supported by a pair of putti or amoretti.

It is unusual to find a table still *en suite* with its mirror, but there can be little doubt that these pieces [**623**] were originally intended to be placed together on a pier-wall, since the decorative motifs physically link together.

Another example of a frame from the Piedmont region of Northern Italy [**625**] reveals a quality of carving and design that is noteworthy. So close is the attention to

608 Venice, *c.*1750, one of a set of four, carved giltwood girandole
28½in (73cm)

609 Italy, *c.*1755, carved giltwood
55in (140cm)

610 Venice, *c.*1755, one of a pair, carved giltwood girandole
36in (92cm)

611 Piedmont, *c.*1760, carved, silvered pier-glass
63in (160cm)

612 North Italy, *c.*1760, carved giltwood
72in (183cm)

613 Venice, *c.*1760, one of a pair, carved giltwood
75in (191cm)

614 Lombardy, *c.*1760, one of a pair, carved walnut
15in (38cm)

615 North Italy, *c.*1750, carved giltwood
46in (117cm)

616 Venice, *c.*1760, carved giltwood overmantal mirror width 37in (94cm)

617 Naples, *c.*1760, carved giltwood
89in (227cm)

618 North Italy, *c.*1770, one of a set of our, giltwood and engraved girandole
39in (99cm)

619 Piedmont, *c.*1785, carved fruitwood, attributed to G.-M. Bonzanigo
19½in (50cm) (see colour illustration on p. 247)

620 North Italy, *c.*1775, a pair of carved giltwood girandoles
26in (66cm)

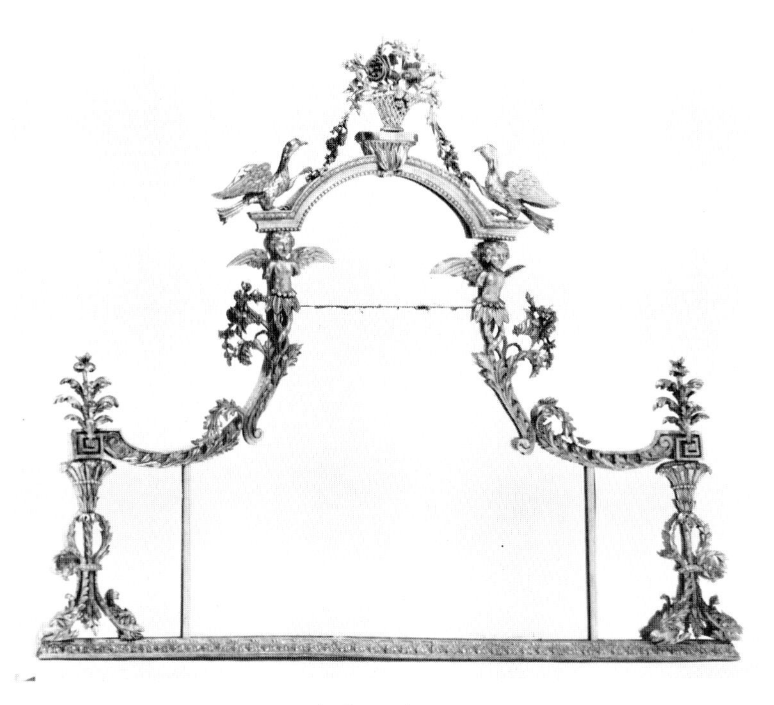

621 North Italy, *c.*1775, carved giltwood overmantel
width 74in (188cm)

622 Italy, *c.*1775, painted and parcel-gilt
width 56in (143cm)

623 North Italy, *c.*1780, painted and silver-gilt, with matching console-table
66 in (168cm)

624 North Italy, *c.*1775, carved giltwood
86in (219cm) (see colour illustration on p. 248)

625 Piedmont, *c.*1775, carved giltwood
$75\frac{3}{4}$in (192cm)

626 Piedmont, *c.*1770, giltwood pier-glass
$92\frac{1}{2}$in (235cm)

627 North Italy, *c.*1785, carved giltwood
80in (203cm)

628 North Italy, *c.*1785, carved giltwood
79in (20cm)

629 Piedmont, *c.*1780, carved and pianted giltwood
67in (171cm)

630 Piedmont, possibly Turin, *c.*1780, carved and painted giltwood
71½in (182cm)

631 Turin, *c.*1780, giltwood and painted overmantel mirror, in the manner of G.-M. Bonzanigo
82in (210cm)

632 North Italy, *c.*1790, carved giltwood
88in (223cm)

633 Tuscany, *c.* 1790, carved giltwood
82in (208cm)

634 Tuscany, *c.*1790, one of a pair, painted and parcel-gilt (see colour illustration on p. 309)
92in (234cm)

635 Tuscany, *c.*1790, carved giltwood
88½in (225cm)

636 Piedmont, *c.*1790, carved giltwood 100in (255cm)

detail that the joints in the border glasses are disguised with carved flowerheads, which would not have been the case earlier in the century. Equally well decorated, this transitional frame [**627**] combines both the Rococo and the Neo-classical styles. In the centre of the cresting is an European interpretation of the Chinese ho-ho bird, while the urns that flank the cresting clearly point to a classical source. The treatment of scrolls that flank the sides of the frame is interesting, the top scrolls begin, or terminate, in a classical flowerhead paterae, whereas the lower scrolls are purely rococo in design. Another frame incorporating an urn is shown here [**629**] where an urn of flowers is flanked by crossed olive branches, these may just have proved useful ingredients to the overall design of the frame, or might have referred to the olive branch being an ancient symbol of peace.

The next group of mirrors, [**632–636**] are all variations of a familiar form of Neo-classical mirror frame all measuring in excess of 79 in, and intended to be placed above a console table. The combined height of between 110 in, and 126 in, of a console table and mirror would point to their use in rooms of palacial proportions rather than in smaller family apartments. Supports for Italian wall mirrors that range from vigorous Rococo scrolls and straight tapered leaf-carved feet during the 1770s are here manifested in the form of a pair of sphinx [**636**]. An ancient symbol of power and vigilance in Egypt, the sphinx (a lion with a human head) was popular as a decorative device during the Regency in England and the Empire in France. In classical Greece the sphinx was given a woman's head, breasts and wings and was regarded as a repository of arcane wisdom. This same use of symbolism as well as allegorical motifs continued to be exploited throughout the period, and across the length and breadth of Italy.

This Sicilian pier mirror, one of a pair, [**638**] is decorated with a panel depicting the figures of Europe and Asia, its companion frame decorated with the figures of Africa and America. On the other hand, the cresting on this example, [**640**] shows a group of features that could be emblematic of the triumph of love: a quiver full of arrows, beneath which is carved a flambeau, or torch, and billing doves surrounded by ribbon-tied flowers. The native Italian interpretation of Empire style, typified in this mirror [**644**] evolved after the restoration of the status quo following 1815, and was adopted for the interiors of the Royal palaces of Naples, Genoa and Turin. In common with so many others in Europe, the Bonaparte family regarded Paris as the fountainhead of taste and brought Parisian styles with them to Italy. The influence of this imported style was felt throughout the country, emanating primarily from the interiors created for the Emperor's brothers, Joseph, the King of Naples, and Lucien, the Prince of Cannino, as well as his sisters, Elisa Baciocchi in Lucca and Florence, the Grande Duchesse of Tuscany, Pauline Borghese in Rome and Caroline Murat in Naples. Just how well this French style was adopted by Italian craftsmen is illustrated by the success of Giovanni Socci, who flourished between 1809–15. An Italian Empire cabinet-maker, he was one of the many artist craftsmen employed by Elisa Baciocchi to redecorate the palaces in the Empire taste. She set up a 'Manufacture Royale' in Lucca and brought the Parisian ébéniste Youf to Lucca in 1806 to work in the premises provided – a secularized Carmelite monastery. There is no evidence that Socci worked under Youf but he soon superceded Youf as the leading exponent of the Empire style

637 North Italy, *c.*1790, carved giltwood
58½in (149cm)

638 Sicily, *c.*1790, one of a pair, carved, japanned and giltwood
89in (225cm)

639 South Italy, *c.*1795, carved giltwood pier-glass
67½in (172cm)

640 Piedmont, *c.*1790, one of a pair, carved giltwood
68in (173cm)

641 North Italy, possible Piedmont, *c.*1820, fruitwood and parcel-gilt
53½in (135cm)

642 North Italy or Switzerland, *c.*1820, mahogany and parcel-gilt
overall height 84in (213cm) (see colour illustration on p. 310)

643 Possibly Naples, *c.*1810–20, painted and parcel-gilt overmantel mirror
width 53in (175cm)

644 Parma, *c.*1830, carved giltwood and painted mirror with matching console-table
96in (244cm)

645 Italy, *c.*1850, carved giltwood
68in (175cm)

646 Italy, *c.*1830, or a more recent copy, one of a set of four, carved giltwood in the Baroque style
43in (109cm)

647 Venice, *c.*1850, one of a pair, carved giltwood girandole in the eighteenth-century style (left)
58in (147cm)

648 Italy, *c.*1850, one of a pair, carved giltwood
42in (107cm)

649 Venice, *c.*1850, carved stripped pine, in the seventeenth-century style
60in (153cm)

650 Italy, *c.*1850, carved giltwood, in the Rococo style
63in (161cm)

651 Venice, *c.*1850, blue and clear glass-panelled
69in (175cm)

652 Venice, *c.*1840, one of a pair, glass and silvered wood girandole
30in (76cm)

653 Venice, *c.*1850, one of a pair, engraved-glass
134½in (342cm)

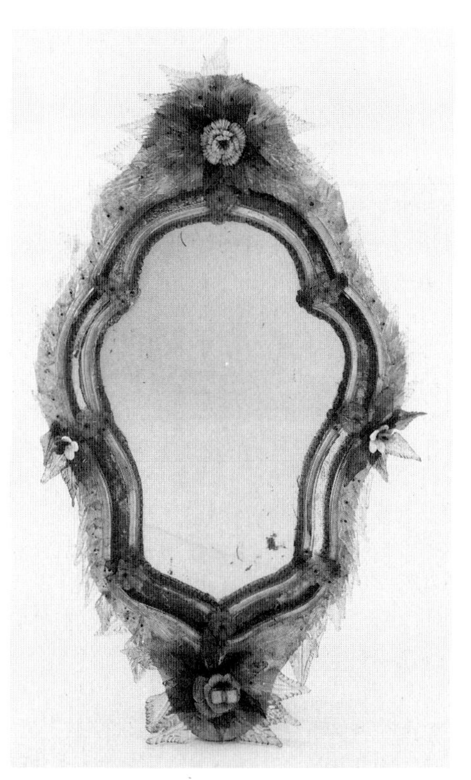

654 Venice, *c.*1850, one of a pair, polychrome wood, clear and coloured glass girandole
43½in (111cm)

655 Venice, *c.*1850, one of a pair, blue painted and giltwood toilet-mirror
32½in (83cm)

656 Italy, *c.*1860, one of a pair, carved giltwood mirrors, part of a drawing-room suite of furniture
76½in (195cm)

657 North Italy, possibly Venice, *c.*1900 one of a pair, carved giltwood in the eighteenth-century style
51in (129.5cm)

658 Venice, *c.*1870, carved giltwood overmantel mirror
78½in (200cm)

in Tuscany. Perhaps the best-known pieces of his work are ingenious, convertible writing desks which, when closed, look like oval chests of drawers on legs, but concealed in the front is a chair which can be drawn out, while the top divides and opens laterally with a section for pens and stationery rising in the centre. Two of these desks are in the Palazzo Pitti, both are signed, and a third is at Malmaison, near Paris, given as a gift to Napoleon by Elisa.

Moving away from the stylistic rigours of the Italian Empire mirror, this unusual romantic rustic style frame [**645**] was probably made for a dining room to be placed above an *en suite* console table.

The nineteenth century in Italy produced a period of revivalism as exemplified by this Venetian-Baroque-type frame [**646**]. Copies such as this were freely available to the English aristocracy and wealthy who, embarking on their Grand Tours, visited Italy in large numbers throughout the century. Highly-skilled Italian craftsmen satisfied this external and domestic demand for 'antiques', undaunted by the diversity of styles required, as shown by the next four mirrors [**647–650**] while others were sold without such precise explanation. Four Venetian glass mirrors [**651–654**], were made around the middle of the nineteenth century or later, after the revival of the Murano glass industry.

The arms shown on [**653**] are those of Don Girolamo Settimo, fifth Principe di Fitalia, first Marchese di Garratana and Barone di Cammaratini, Lord-in-waiting to H.M. Queen Mother of Italy. Before the middle of the century, and having produced such splendid glassware during the previous century, the glass houses declined. Lady Morgan commenting on her travels, noted in 1820 that the Venetian glass pearls ('margaritini', or beads), were:

> 'almost all that remains of that superb "arte vitraria" which rendered Europe independent of the Sands of Tyre, and established at Venice a manufacture which, in spite of Nature, had supplied the world with one of its most brilliant luxuries. The Venetian shops no longer sparkle with girandoles of seeming diamonds, with flowers more brilliant and frail than the blossoms of a Spring shower, which they imitated; and with mirrors, which first replaced the dimness of metal with the reflecting lustre of crystal.'

Some years later another lady visitor, Lady Blessington, remarked on the decline of the glass-works,

> 'It is melancholy to see an art, once arrived at perfection, retrograde, as the trifling, though brilliant ornaments shown to us are the only portion of the trade which now flourishes.'

The revival of the glass factories in the mid-nineteenth century, was in part due to a glass-works owner, Pietro Bigaglia. Many antique dealers used Bigaglia to repair old Venetian glass, in particular two of his workmen, Liberale and Angelo Angaro, who did business with the large number of visitors from overseas. The two craftsmen studied the old glass and based their designs for new pieces upon their studies. Their success was such that new factories started up, producing copies of earlier pieces, including large and colourful chandeliers. An example of such work made to fulfil this demand has unusual cresting in the form of a winged flaming heart [**658**]. A flaming heart is an

659 Venice, *c.*1870, one of a pair, carved giltwood
55in (140cm)

660 Italy, *c.*1870, parcel-gilt walnut, in the Islamic style
78in (198cm)

661 Florence, *c.*1880, carved giltwood, one of a set of four
98½in (250cm)

662 Florence, *c.*1880, carved giltwood
62in (158cm)

663 Florence, *c.*1880, carved giltwood
62in (158cm)

663a Florence, *c.*1880 carved giltwood
95in (241cm)

664 Venice, *c.*1880, carved pine in the manner of Andrea Brustolon
90½in (230cm)

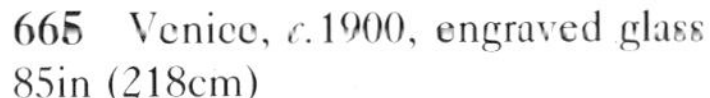

665 Venice, *c.*1900, engraved glass
85in (218cm)

666 Venice, *c.*1880, engraved, clear and blue glass
62in (157cm)

667 Italy, *c.*1880, one of a pair, walnut parcel-gilt pier-glass
86in (220cm)

attribute of Antony of Padua (1195–1231), a Christian Saint and Doctor of the Church. One legend is the finding of the misers heart, when, preaching at a usurer's funeral he quoted the Gospel of St Luke (12:34) 'Where your wealth is, there will your heart be also.' Here the scene shows the opening of the miser's treasure chest in the presence of Antony, in which was found the still-warm miser's heart.

With this moorish frame, [**660**] the exact country of origin is difficult to determine since the use of walnut, so common in Italy, is in itself no proof, but the ports of northern Italy, especially Venice, traded extensively with the Islamic world. The next three mirrors [**661–663**] are from Florence, the first, a large Florentine mirror is in the Baroque revival style, while the other two reflect a typical Florentine style of carving, so popular during the mid-nineteenth century. Another example of Florentine carving is shown here, [**663**] in this case the frame was probably made to celebrate a marriage of two titled families. The two sets of interlaced initials are those of the bride and groom, flanked by putti or 'amoretti'. Revealing a later style of carving in Florence,

669 Venice, *c.*1900, coloured glass mosaic
65in (165cm)

670 Venice, *c.*1900, coloured glass mosaic
39½in (100cm)

671 Venice, *c.*1900, coloured glass mosaic
29in (74cm)

672 Venice, *c.*1900, coloured glass mosaic
57½in (145cm)

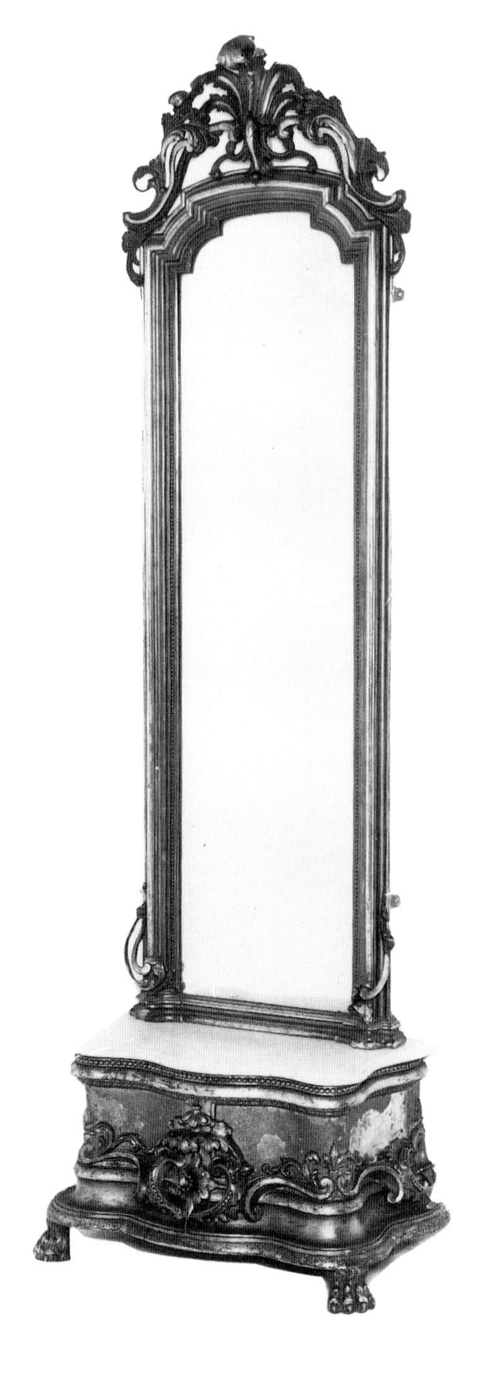

668 Italy, *c.*1890, carved giltwood pier-glass
with matching table
102in (259cm)

this example [**663a**] is less heavy and has tighter scrolling and smaller, more pointed, leaves.

Returning to Venice, this large carved pinewood frame [**664**] was probably originally painted or gilded. Worked in the baroque style it is particularly reminiscent of Andrea Brustolon's work (see also [**549**]).

An example of the success of the Murano glass factories after 1850, this Venetian frame, in an early style [**665**], relies on the skill of the engraver for its effect, since the shaping of the cresting is flat. Taken a stage further, this mirror [**666**], is a more accomplished example, enriched with coloured and clear glass pieces added to a basically asymmetrical frame. Still from Venice, the next five mirrors, [**669–673**] are all examples of late nineteenth-century mosaic work. Glass mosaic work may well have been influenced by the highly successful micro-marble mosaic workers of Rome and Florence who were capable of producing intricate scenes of the highest quality, usually for table tops. During the late nineteenth century, a large number of hotels were built to accommodate the increasing influx of overseas visitors. These hotels vied with the fashionable cities and spa towns of the rest of Europe for business. With the need to please such cosmopolitan tastes, a pan-European style emerged that was equally at home in London, Paris or Rome. The result was an approximation of the styles of both Louis XV and Louis XVI, which would be adapted to the benefits of modern comfort.

673 Venice, *c.*1900, coloured glass mosaic
32in (81cm)

Scandinavia

Scandinavia comprises Norway and Sweden, politically and culturally it also included Denmark and is sometimes considered to include Finland. Sweden's dramatic rise to power and influence lies in the Unification under Gustav Vasa (1520–60). The period under review begins with the Coronation of Queen Christina in 1650. Queen Christina (1632–54) was only six when her father died and Axel Oxenstierna (1583–1654) was appointed Regent. Her education, which included languages, art, music and philosophy under Oxenstierna's guidance gave her an intellectual sophistication and the court which revolved around her aspired to the highest level of European culture. Her enthusiasm was such that she increased spending by the court from some 3 per cent of Royal revenues to 20 per cent at the end of her reign. Crown lands were sold to the nobles to finance the acquisition by her agents of works of art from all over Europe. Under the Regency of Charles XI (1655–97) the second half of the seventeenth century in Sweden was a period of great enrichment for the nobility. Influenced by Germany, after the German wars, wealthy families, like the De la Gardie, Wrangel, Oxenstierna, Bonde and others built castles and palaces with magnificent French gardens.

The basic form of this late seventeenth-century Danish giltwood mirror frame **[674]**, with its relatively simple moulding and pierced and carved cresting, is common to many European countries at this date. Creating a focal point, the cresting is centred by a small oval mirror within a moulded frame. Use such as this of additional mirror-glass, highlights the original owner's wealth in affording both a looking-glass and a mirror with which to decorate it. The glass for this frame could well have been imported from Germany or made locally in Copenhagen by the immigrant Venetian glass-makers who had settled there or by German glass-workers working in the forests of north-west Jutland. In the bevelled or diamonded main plate the name 'C. Lange Ao 1771' is engraved. Since the script is a mature hand, this was presumably done by an adult with a diamond during an idle moment in 1771. (Cf. Wallin, 1931–5, vol. I, pp. 189–90, figs 336 and 338.) Similar in the form to the previous mirror in this example **[675]** the central plate is within decorated border-glasses, while the crest, although decorated in the same way, is surmounted by a crown, possibly the Danish Royal crown. It is not uncommon to see the incorporation of crowns into crestings of mirrors and other furniture. (English chairs made after the Restoration often include a crown at the centre of the toprail.) In this instance it may indicate a royal association or a display of loyalty by the original owner. The individual glass-plates are decorated on the reverse and held in place with lead framing. (Cf. Wallin, 1931–5, vol. II, p. 198, fi.g 751 for an example of engraved border-glasses at this date and p. 199, fig. 753 for an example of a slightly later date.) Reputed to have come from Spottrup castle this early eighteenth-century mirror **[676]** has a japanned frame and carved giltwood

674 Denmark, Frederik IV, *c.*1700, carved giltwood
42½in (108cm)

675 Denmark, Frederik IV. *c.*1700, engraved glass and lead
46in (117cm)

676 Denmark, Frederik IV, *c.*1715, carved giltwood and japanned
49in (124cm)

677 Sweden, Queen Ulrika, *c.*1720, carved giltwood
79in (200cm)

678 Sweden, Charles XII, *c.*1700, engraved glass and gilt metal attributed to Gustav Precht
51½in (131cm)

679 Denmark or North Germany, *c.*1750, walnut and parcel gilt
51in (129cm)

680 Sweden, Frederick, *c.*1750, carved giltwood pier-glass
80in (203cm)

681 Sweden, Adolf Frederik, *c.*1769, carved giltwood (far right)
65in (165cm)

682 Denmark, Frederick V, *c.*1750, walnut and parcel-gilt mirror and console-table
58in (148cm)

683 Denmark, Frederick V, *c.*1750, carved giltwood (far right)
75½in (192cm)

cresting. Speckled with gold dust, the japanning is similar to the finish used for the inside areas of Oriental cabinets.

From the Swedish 'Régence' period this mirror **[677]** is comparable to English Queen Anne mirrors in the use of shaped border-glasses to outline the main plates. The use of two pieces of mirror glass to achieve the required size has already been shown to be common throughout Europe at this time. French mirrors that were made by the process of pouring glass on to a metal bed, would probably have been available to fit the frame but would have been very costly and difficult to transport. Here the join in the glass, as with the edges, is bevelled or 'diamonded', while the joins in the border-glasses are covered by small, shaped plates. The border glasses themselves are secured in place by a lead frame, gilded to match the carved wood. Developed from the late-seventeenth-century rectangular mirror with a separate crest (see 674) the cresting has become more a part of the frame and not an addition, and is balanced by a shaped apron. (Cf. Wallin, 1931–5, vol. II, p. 199, fig. 752.) Also with border-glasses, in this case coloured or engraved, this is one of a group of mirrors with gilt-metal frames **[678]**. (Cf. Roche, 1985, cover and pl. VII for similar mirrors with blue glass bevelled border-glasses and cresting, attributed by Roche to Gustav Precht; Wallin, 1931–5, vol. I, p. 188, fig. 335 and p. 190, fig. 337 for a mirror of similar form with engraved border-glasses and baskets of flowers by Burchard Precht, Stockholm, *c.* 1700.)

Burchard Precht was a sculptor and cabinet-maker from Bremen who arrived in Stockholm in 1674 to work at Drottingholm Palace. His son, Christian (1706–79) became one of Sweden's leading Rococo silversmiths. Christian was apprenticed to a goldsmith in Stockholm in 1721 and travelled to London in 1727, to Paris, Augsburg and Nuremburg, returning home in 1731.

Previously thought to be of Venetian glass, imported into France and framed in gilt-bronze this mirror was formerly in the Wrightsman Collection (Watson, 1966, vol. II, no. 209). It is more likely, however, that frames such as this were the work of the father Burchard Precht working in Stockholm *c.* 1700. In addition to the familiar baskets of flowers, another common feature is a pair of seated putti, each holding variously a flambeau or a trumpet, and both facing in opposite directions. (Cf. Upmark, vol. I, pl. XV, fig. 26.)

In walnut and parcel-gilt this frame **[679]** exemplifies the cross-fertilization of styles from one country to another. Possibly made in one of the Baltic ports of northern Germany or Denmark, they closely resemble English mirrors from *c.* 1740, but can be recognized as having a Northern European place of origin due to the addition of applied giltwood decoration to the veneered surface. Two more mirrors **[680 and 681]** exemplify the transition from the early-eighteenth century form of frame to the mid-eighteenth century and the Rococo. Both frames retain the mirrored border-glasses of the earlier period, (see **[677]**), but the solid cresting of these early frames are now pierced and carved in higher relief and accompanied by a pierced complementary apron. (**[681]** is stamped 'Stockh. Hall 1769'.) (Cf. Upmark, 1912, vol. II, pl. XLVI, fig. 100.)

This Danish mirror and console-table **[682]** is made of walnut and parcel-gilt. Apart from provincial pieces, the use of walnut as a fashionable furniture-making timber had

684 Denmark, Frederick V, *c.*1750, carved giltwood
66½in (169cm)

685 Denmark, Frederick V, *c.*1750, carved giltwood
43½in (110cm) (see colour illustration on p. 311)

686 Denmark, Frederick V, *c.*1750, carved giltwood
71in (180cm) (see colour illustration on p. 312)

687 Denmark, Frederick V, *c.*1750, carved giltwood
38½in (98cm)

688 Denmark, Frederick V, *c.*1755, carved giltwood
40½in (103cm)

689 Denmark, Frederick V, *c.*1750, a pair, carved giltwood pier-glasses
71in (180cm)

690 Denmark, Frederick V, *c.*1760, carved giltwood
69in (176cm)

given way to the 'Age of Mahogany' in much of Northern Europe. Interestingly there has been no attempt to disguise the join in the two mirror plates as one might expect to see in an English frame of this date. (Cf. Clemmensen, 1948, p. 26, fig. 12, 26, fig. 12, for a similar frame with asymmetrical elements.) As with the previous example, this more traditional, carved giltwood frame [**683**] has certain asymmetrical elements and carved features to each side of the frame. The following group of mirrors [**684 to 690**] are all examples of the mid-eighteenth-century Scandinavian Rococo style. In common with many of the courts of Europe, Scandinavia was influenced by French taste, more so in Sweden than in Denmark. Because Swedish architects and designers received their training in Paris, the Swedish Rococo was permeated by current French tastes. On the other hand a necessarily diluted French influence reached the Danes via Germany which gives Danish Rococo pieces less fluidity and vigour. Made of walnut and parcel-gilt, this mirror [**691**] seems old fashioned compared to contemporary European products. If stylistically tied down to English terms, the continued use of walnut is out of step when the main centres of furniture-making had turned to mahogany. The overall form of the frame is Kentian with classical anthemion cresting springing from a common source. Such prominent use of this motif was unusual in mainstream mirror designs before the Neo-classical period, but was particularly favoured by Kent (see p. 83).

Somewhat frivolous after Kentian classicism, this example is one of a pair of girandoles [**692**] with candle-arms decorated with porcelain flowers. Again made of walnut, this parcel-gilt pier-glass [**693**] shows the French influence of the Louis XVI period on Scandinavian craftsmen. The Neo-classical style was well received in Scandinavia and flourished there quite early, promoted especially by the Frenchman Nicholas-Henri Jardin.

Jardin and his brother, who styled themselves 'Architects and Professors' were invited to Denmark in 1755 and were presented to the Academy of Fine Art on the 15 January of that year. Jardin's influence was almost immediate, he supervised the decoration of the Bernstorff Palace in Copenhagen in the latest Parisian style, (complete in 1757).

Despite this importation of French skill, notable Scandinavian designers emerged such as Lorentz Nielson, to whom this curious inlaid mahogany and parcel-gilt mirror [**694**] is attributed. Another designer was Harsdorff and this oval girandole [**695**] is a charming example in the manner of his work from the Danish Neo-classical period. Caspar Frederik Harsdorff (1733–99), a native of Copenhagen, received his training at the Academy of Fine Arts and travelled to Paris in 1757 to further his education. During his five years in Paris he was influenced by Jean-François de Neufforge, one of the first to be seized by Neo-classicism. A year after his return to Denmark in 1764, Harsdorff was appointed Inspector of Works, became a Professor of the Academy, and was made architect to the Court. He carried out extensive work at the Frederiksberg Palace which included many mirrors. (Cf. Wallin, 1931–5, vol. 2, p. 209, fig. 780; Clemmensen, 1948, pl. 65 c and d for examples of two of the elements also present in this mirror.) Again in the manner of C.F. Harsdorff, this pair of mirrors in mahogany and parcel-gilt [**696**], are reputed to have come from the Manor House, Billeshave on the island of Fyn. (Cf. Clemmensen, 1948, pl. 60 b, for a mirror acquired in the 1770s or 1780s for Christianborg, but now missing the applied gilt decoration.)

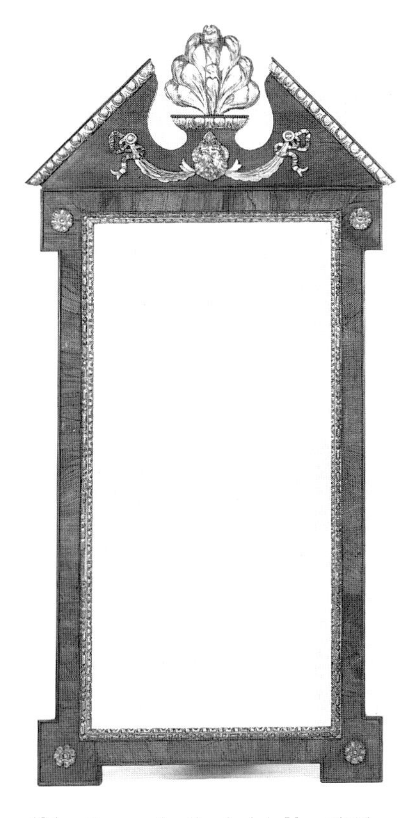

691 Denmark, Frederick V, *c.*1765, walnut veneered and parcel-gilt 58in (147cm)

692 Denmark, Frederick V, *c.*1760, one of a pair, walnut and parcel-gilt girandoles with porcelain flowers
21in (53cm)

692a Denmark, Frederick V, *c.*1760, walnut and parcel-gilt
48½in (123cm)

693 Denmark, Christian VII, *c.*1770, walnut and parcel-gilt
74½in (189cm) (see colour illustration on p. 313)

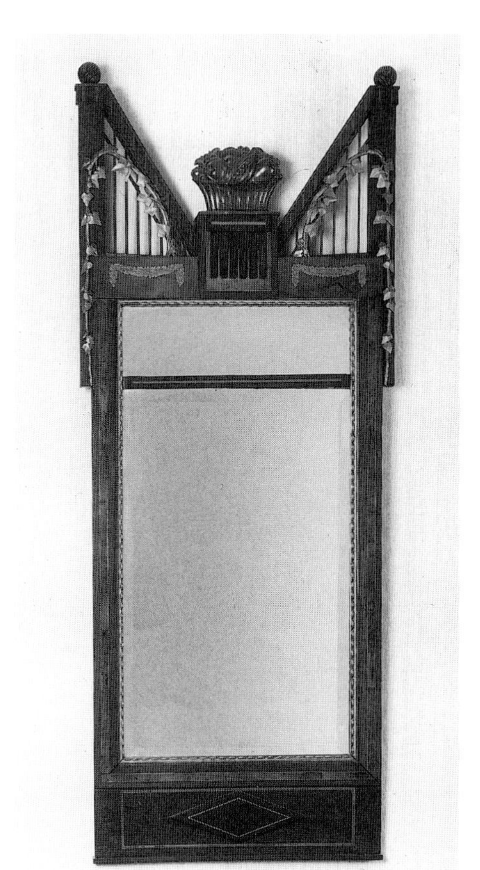

694 Denmark, Christian VII, *c.*1790, inlaid mahogany and parcel-gilt attributed to Lorentz Nielsen (left)
66in (167cm)

695 Denmark, Christian VII, *c.*1785, one of a pair, carved giltwood girandoles in the manner of C.F. Harsdorff
20in (50cm)

696 Denmark, Christian VII, *c.*1790, a pair, mahogany and parcel-gilt
66in (167cm)

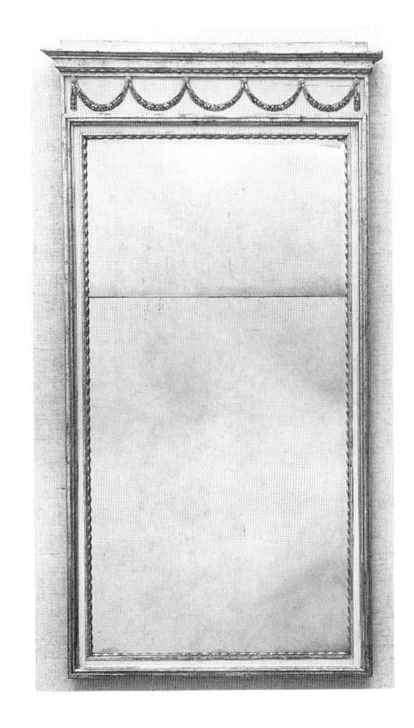

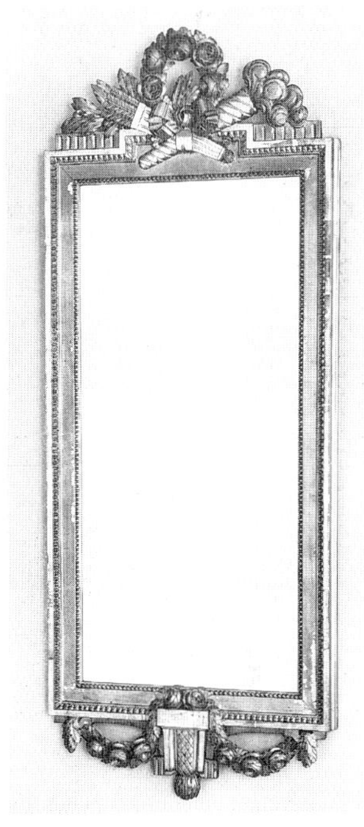

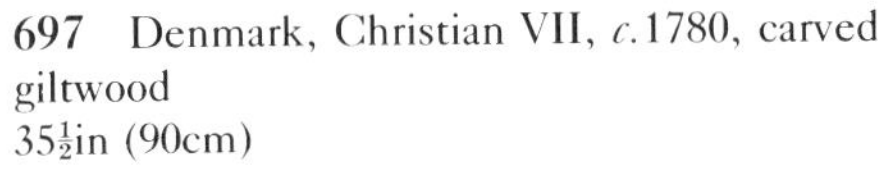

697 Denmark, Christian VII, *c.*1780, carved giltwood
35½in (90cm)

698 Denmark, Christian VII, *c.*1790, one of a pair of pier glasses carved and painted by J.C. Lillie
67in (170cm)

699 Sweden, Gustav III, *c.*1783, carved giltwood, signed *Stockhall Stempel 1783*
66in (167cm)

This is a small oval mirror [**697**] with ribbon-tied cresting. (Cf. Upmark, 1912, vol. I, pl. LXXIV, fig. 158, for a very similar frame fitted with a pair of candle-arms; Wallin, 1931–5, vol. II, p. 209, fig. 780.) Another Scandinavian strongly influenced by other European styles was J.C. Lillie to whom this pier-glass [**698**] can be attributed. Joseph Christian Lillie (1760–1827) was trained at the Copenhagen royal Academy's School of Architecture and was employed by the Royal Furniture Emporium as 'Dessinateur' and inspector. He also ran his father's joinery business. Lillie worked on the decorations at the Christianborg Castle and received the sum of 4,038 rigsdaler from a total of 18,000 rigsdaler allocated to the whole decorative scheme. Although Lillie was fully engaged on commissions for the Royal Family in his capacity as 'Architect and Designer to the Court' (bestowed upon him in 1790), he nevertheless continued to accept work from the nobility. Despite the fact that Lillie considered French decorative art to be his ideal, the influence of English furniture is more pronounced; for instance, this example [**698**] reflects the influence of Robert Adam. As a character, Lillie was very sociable and vigorously pursued the good life. Records show that he owed his vintner a considerable sum of money and was generally slow to settle his debts. He went bankrupt twice, once in 1794 and again in 1799.

Formerly in the collection of Benjamin Sonnenberg, New York, this plain oval plate [**700**] is set within a cross-grained mahogany-veneered frame laid on to a cheaper softwood carcass. The fretwork cresting, which is attached to the top edge of the frame, is made of mahogany ply. The use of laminated woods is by no means a modern day invention, it was a well tried method of making galleries for wine tables during the mid-eighteenth century in England. The use of two or three sheets of fine cut mahogany laid with the grain running counter to each other both strengthens and prevents

700 Denmark, Christian VII, *c.*1785, fretsawn and mahogany veneered 20½in (52cm)

701 Denmark, Christian VII, *c.*1790, carved giltwood, attributed to J.L. Lillie (far right) 81½ (207cm) (see colour illustration on p. 314)

702 Denmark, Christian VII, *c.*1785, silhouette painting on mirror-glass width 14.5in (37cm)

703 Denmark, Christian VII, *c.*1800, silhouette painting on mirror glass width 25in (63cm) (see colour illustration on p. 315)

warping caused by excessive heat or dryness. Almost certainly made by J.C. Lillie this frame [**701**] (now in Klimtholm Castle), may have been made for Liseland which was completed in December 1793. Antoine de la Calmette, the builder of Liseland, would have known about Lillie through his brother who was closely associated with the Court. It seems that A. Kirkerup was the architect of Liseland, as it was he who signed the estimate of the costs of the project, and a strong association developed between Lillie and Kirkerup which continued until the architect left Denmark in March 1799. (Cf. Clemmensen, 1973, pl. 121b for an almost identical mirror, acquired in 1793 for Liseland, designed and supplied by Lillie.)

Both these mirrors, [**702 and 703**] are examples of late eighteenth-century Danish silhouette paintings on glass; the earlier example [**702**], depicts Frederick and Louise, Duke and Duchess of Augustenborg and is signed *Fec:Wietlandt*. Typical of that date the interior scene has zinc plates fitted up to the walls, while the back wall is hung with the silhouette portraits divided by a classical pier-glass with mercury backing to the glass to create the mirror. Of a slightly later date, the second example, has the mercury-backed mirror areas for both the windows and the small looking-glass on the pier wall [**703**]. The ribbon-tied cresting and carved mouldings on this mirror [**704**] are almost identical to those on another mirror by Carl Gustaf Fyrvald. (Cf. Wallin, 1931–5, vol. III, p. 169.) The entablature is centred by a classical figure holding a harp which suggests either that the mirror was made for a music room, or that it is one of a group made to represent the Arts. (Cf. Upmark, 1912, vol. I, pl. LXXIII, fig. 156.) This pair of Danish Empire period mahogany mirrors [**707**] with panels painted *en grisaille* depicting classical figures in chariots, were clearly intended to be hung on pier walls with the horses facing towards each other. Such decoration, after the Antique, is typical of Danish furniture at this period. (Cf. Wilkie, 1987, figs. 100–2.) In addition, the crestings are inlaid with half-paterae or fans and are made up of segments of light timber, probably boxwood, with scorched edges to give the effect of depth. (See p. 46.) These three examples [**709 to 711a**] were made at a time when Britain's naval supremacy had curtailed the trade between Sandinavian countries. Britain objected to the alliance formed between Denmark, Sweden and Russia and attacked the Danish fleet at Copenhagen. As a result the Swedish felt an affinity with France during this period which was reflected in their furniture. A Danish official wrote in 1803 'One day we may well be able to do without English gloves, English silk stockings and English shoes, just as we have become increasingly able to do without English Furniture'. Since the British naval blockade prevented trade, it certainly prohibited imports of exotic timbers, this mahogany frame [**712**] bearing the trade label of P.G. Bylanders, Götheborg is therefore rare. Applied to the surface of the frame are carved giltwood classical motifs including stylized anthemions, lion masks and griffins. The fact that the mirror-glass in this unusual Danish pier-glass and combined base is in two pieces, implies that imported glass was still unavailable [**714**]. The base of stepped form is decorated with applied classical gilt-metal mounts.

This Swedish mahogany and parcel-gilt pier-glass and console [**715**] are attribted to J.H. Dumaths. Such an attribution can be made because the red salon in the Palace of Rosendal, which was decorated by Dumnaths, had red silk wall panels divided by slim ebonized columns with gilded decoration at the capitals, bases and centres which are

704 Sweden, Gustav IV, *c.*1800, carved, painted and giltwood attributed to F.C.G. Fyrvald
65in (165cm)

705 Sweden, Gustav IV, *c.*1800, carved giltwood and painted
63in (160cm) (see colour illustration on p. 315)

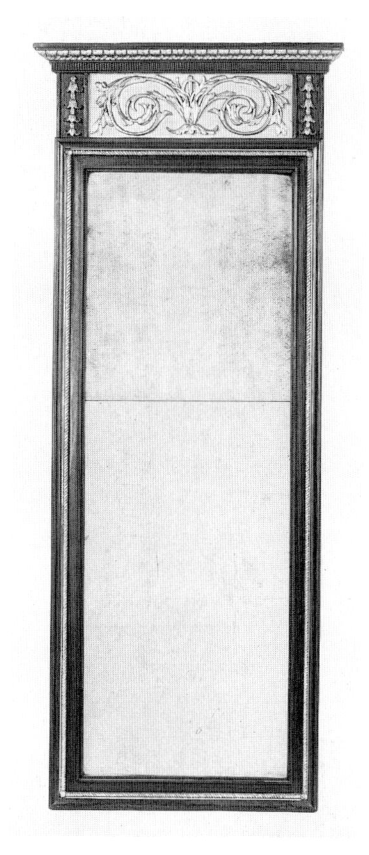

706 Denmark, Frederik VI, *c.*1800, one of a pair, mahogany and parcel-gilt pier-glass
69in (150cm)

707 Denmark, Frederik VI, *c.*1815, a pair of inlaid mahogany pier-glasses with painted panels
66½in (169cm)

708 Denmark, Frederik VI, *c.*1810, a pair of mahogany and fruitwood pier-glasses with painted panels and matching console-tables
overall height 95in (241cm)

709 Sweden, Charles VIII, *c.*1810, carved wood and painted pier-glass with matching console-table
56in (142cm)

710 Sweden, Charles VIII, *c.*1810, painted and parcel-gilt pier-glass
69in (175cm)

711 Sweden, Charles VIII, *c.*1810, painted and parcel gilt
62in (157cm) (see colour illustration on p. 315)

712 Sweden, Gustav IV, *c.*1805, parcel-gilt and mahogany
73in (187cm)

713 Sweden, Charles VIII, *c.*1810, one of a pair, painted and parcel gilt pier-glass
119in (303cm) (see colour illustration on p. 316)

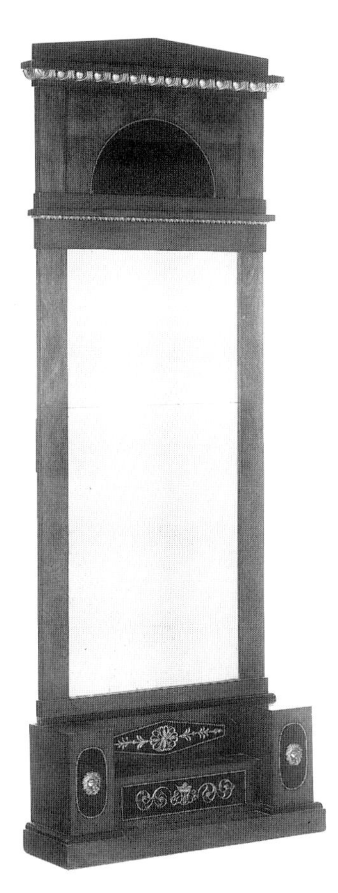

714 Denmark, Frederik VI, *c.*1820, mahogany and gilt metal-mounted pier-glass
104in (264cm)

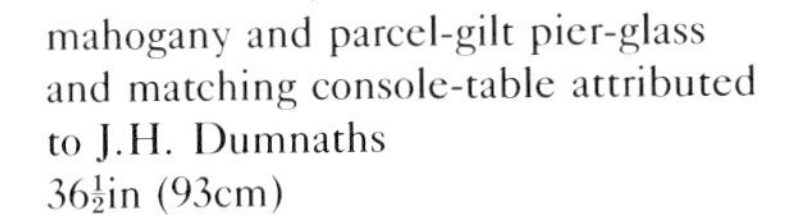

715 Sweden, Charles XIV, *c.*1820, mahogany and parcel-gilt pier-glass and matching console-table attributed to J.H. Dumnaths
36½in (93cm)

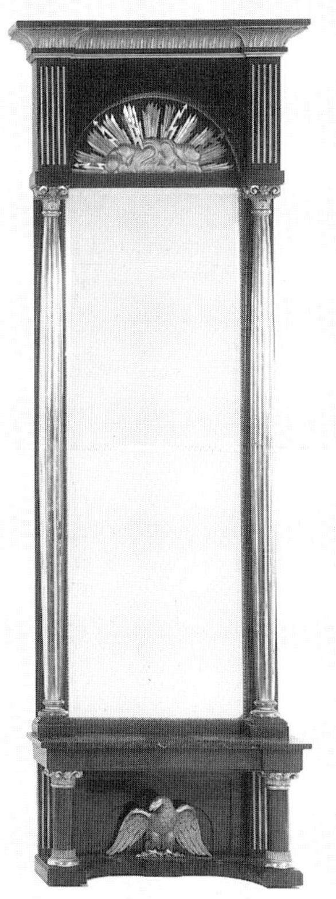

716 Sweden or Russia, *c.*1820 mahogany and parcel-gilt with matching console-table
96½in (245cm)

717 Sweden, Charles XIV, *c.*1820, painted and parcel gilt
74½ in (189 cm)

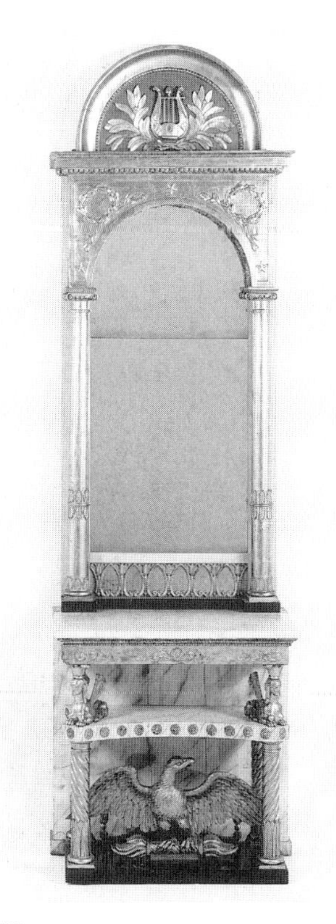

718 Sweden, Charles XIV, *c.*1820, painted and giltwood pier-glasses with matching console table
114in (289cm)

719 Scandinavia, *c.*1825 one of a pair, mahogany pier-glass with matching console-table
110in (28cm) overall height.

720 Sweden, Charles XIV, *c.*1820, carved giltwood pier-glass with matching console-table
79½in (202cm)

721 Sweden, Charles XIV, *c.*1820, carved giltwood pier-glass with matching console-table
75in (190cm)

identical to those on this mirror. (See Vahlneg, ill. on p. 40.) Another mahogany mirror and console-table with free standng columns may well be Russian [**716**] A single sheet of mirror-glass has been fitted to the frame of this pier-glass, [**717**]. Such an extensive plate may well have been made in Sweden or imported from Germany. As an indication of the date, the leaf-carving on the arched upper part is becoming thicker and coaser and generally the amount of decoration on the frame has increased, it is no longer freely drawn and appears cluttered.

Resplendant with sphinxes and an eagle support, this unusual console-table [**718**] combines with a mirror decorated with a lyre. The lyre may well be a convenient decorative device or may have been intended for a music room. (Cf. Wichmann, 1925, pl. 73 and Wallin, 1931–5, vol. III and p. 180, fig. 1262, for a similar mirror.) Based on a similar example bearing his trade label, this pier-glass and console [**722**] are reputed to be by J.M. Bergs.

The 'Late Empire' style of Scandinavian mirrors was guided by Gustav Friedrich Hetsch (1788–1864). Hetsch was German-born but became a naturalized Dane in 1822. Having studied under Eberhard von Etzel in his native Stuttgart, he travelled to Paris where, at the Ecole des Beaux-Arts *c.* 1809, he worked under Charles Percier (1764–1838) and H. Le Bas. From Paris he travelled to Rome in 1812 and in 1815 he arrived in Denmark with P. Malling, the architect, whom he had met in Italy. Working exclusively in the Neo-classical style, Hetsch was an important pioneer of design education in Denmark taught at the Copenhagen Polytechnic. He assisted C.F. Han-

634

642

685

693

701

703

705

711

713

723

724

730

731

732

722 Sweden, Charles XIV, *c.*1820, carved giltwood pier-glass with matching console-table, attributed to J.M. Bergs.
overall height 105in (267cm)

723 Sweden, Charles XIV, *c.*1830, carved giltwood pier-glass and matching table overall height 96in (243cm) (see colour illustration on p. 316)

724 Sweden, Charles XIV, *c.*1835, carved giltwood pier-glass
100in (254cm) (see colour illustration on p. 317)

sen with the redecoration of Christianborg Castle from 1825 and designed for the Copenhagen porcelain factory.

From the end of the 'Late Empire' style Scandinavia enjoyed both the Gothic and the Rococo revivals with less emphasis on national styles. Over-developed interior fashions of the middle of the century led to a reaction spearheaded by Carl Olaf Larsson (1853–1919). From Stockholm, Larsson studied painting at the Academy there under Georg von Rosen from 1866. At the Stockholm Exhibition of 1897 Larsson exhibited watercolours of his home with the aim of improving Swedish taste. These pictures celebrated the joy of domesticity and showed the interiors of his rooms with informal settings, bright colours and flowers. Still popular today, the watercolours were originally published under the titles *A Home* in 1889 and *At Home in the Country* in 1906 and were to have a profound influence on Scandinavian domestic design.

Spain and Portugal

During the sixteenth century Spain became the greatest power in Europe and the mistress of a world-wide empire. The following century, however, saw revolt in the Netherlands and the defeat of the Armada sent against England in 1588. The loss of civil and religious freedom (manifested so cogently in the inquisitions), constant wars, inflation and a corrupt bureaucracy all undermined economic life and led to the country's eventual decline in supremacy. Somehow this political, moral and economic downfall did not prevent the arts from flourishing. This period coincided with the introduction of the new Baroque style from France and Italy found favour with the court and nobility, despite the economic crises, and gave them an opportunity to present a luxurious front to the world. A rather florid style emerged in Spain, typified by the 'Churrigueresque' style, named after the family of architect-sculptors from Barcelona.

The Portuguese meanwhile, rebelled against the Spanish rule in 1640 after Phillip II of Spain had seized the crown in 1580. This placed the Braganza line on the throne, and after a long war forced Spain to recognize their independence in 1688. Brazil was recaptured from the Dutch in 1654 as well as some of her former empire in the Far East. All of these events laid the foundations for the prosperity of the next century.

Of finely-worked giltwood this frame encloses a relatively small mirror plate [**725**]. The richly carved decoration includes flowers and scrolls as well as pomegranates, the *impresa* (symbol) of the Holy Roman Emperor Maximilian I (1459–1519) and of Isabella of Portugal, the wife of his grandson, Charles V of Spain. Carved with the arms of the J'auregui family of northern Spain, the cresting implies noble associations. A member of this noble family, Don Miguel de J'auregui y Guzm'an, Knight of the Military Order of Calatrava, was created Marqués de Gandul by King Charles II of Spain on 29 October 1699.

A crowned female mask centring the apron of this baroque mirror, [**726**] may indicate that it was also originally owned by a noble family. Vigorously handled, gilded scrolls and leaves are punctuated by putti painted in flesh tones.

On this extremely unusual embossed silver frame, [**727**] trumpeting angels decorate the shoulders beneath a coronet forming the cresting, (the latter, again indicating the rank of the original owner). This example was probably not originally intended as a mirror-frame and the mirror-glass that it now contains is a modern, hard-bevelled plate. Flowers and foliage growing from a pair of classical urns, decorate the sides of the frame and entwined amongst the foliage is the familiar mannerist strapwork of designers such as Bérain and Marot, whose work was to have an almost pan-European influence (see p. 161 and 205). As with the preceding examples, this carved giltwood frame [**728**] may well originally have been made for a picture. Such extravagance of style reflects the influences of France and Italy, particularly the latter, in late seventeenth-century Spain, where the court and nobility seemed unperturbed by the fast-

725 Spain, Philip IV, *c.*1650, carved giltwood
79in (201cm)

726 Spain, Philip IV, *c.*1650, carved and painted giltwood
51in (130cm)

727 Spain, Charles II, *c.*1690, embossed silver
41in (104cm)

728 Spain, Charles II, *c.*1700, carved giltwood
31½in (80cm)

729 Spain, Ferdinand VI, *c.*1750, carved giltwood (left)
63in (160cm)

730 Portugal, John V, *c.*1750, carved giltwood pier-glass (far left)
121½in (308cm) (see colour illustration on p. 318)

731 Portugal, John V, *c.*1750, one of a pair, carved giltwood pier-glass and console-table (left)
overall height 121in (308cm) (see colour illustration on p. 319)

732 Spain, Charles III, *c.*1760, one of a pair, carved giltwood girandole
39½in (100cm) (see colour illustration on p. 320)

733 Portugal, Joseph I, *c.*1760, carved giltwood pier-glass (far left)
109in (277cm)

734 Spain, Charles IV, *c.*1790, one of a pair, carved giltwood
54½in (138cm)

approaching economic crisis and were instead delighted by this display of ostentation.

The Spanish-made mirror-glass for this frame [**729**] possibly came from one of the three main glass-producing areas of Spain, but not from La Granja de San Ildefonso in Castille where production from the Royal factory was reserved for the royal palaces. Mirror produced at the factory was silvered in Madrid, but it was not until *c.* 1760 that a retail store was opened in the Puerta del sol in Madrid to sell glass to the public. This frame shows the French influence over Spanish styles during the reign of Philip V, (1700–46) who was a grandson of Louis XIV of France. He inherited the crown in 1700 but was not recognized until 1714.

An almost inexhaustable wealth in precious stones and metals was yielded by Portugal's colonies, which gave rise to a period of luxury and decadence in the early eighteenth century. It was during this period that the royal palace at Queluz was designed by Mateus Vicente (1710–86), the interior by J.B. Robillion. In common with the rest of Europe, the fashion for mirrored rooms spread to Portugal and the rooms of the palace that were decorated with mirrors, including the Throne room, the Ambassador's room, the Queen's room and Boudoir, described as some of the finest examples in Europe.

Joseph I (1750–77) with his chief minister, Pombal, introduced an enlightened programme of political and economic reforms. As a result, and despite the devistation caused by the destruction of Lisbon and other cities in the earthquake of 1755, the wealth and stability of the nation was condusive to creativity on an extravagant scale. Mirrors such as this [**730**], and the elaborate mirror and console-table [**731**], reflecting a strong French influence, were popular during the middle years of the eighteenth century in Portugal.

Made during the middle of the century, this small Spanish girandole has two mirror-plates [**732**]. Technical skill was available in Spain at this date to make large plates, especially at the Royal factory of La Granja, and the method used for casting mirrors was described by a visiting Italian in 1755

> 'The process of pouring them is altogether ingenious. From the large furnace they draw a clay crucible containing moulton cyrstal and pour it on a great brass frame that has been heated red-hot. Carried to the edge of the frame by a machine to which it is held by four iron chains, the crucible is tipped skilfully and all the crystal, which is of a thin consistancy, spreads and begins to harden. Then it (is) drawn into a little oven at the end of the table and left there as long as necessary to anneal.'

Another example of a mirror originally made with a matching console-table, this frame [**733**] continues the tradition of mid-eighteenth-century Portuguese pier-glasses and is fitted with an oil painting depicting a harbour entrance.

Drawing upon a different culture, the octagonal border-glasses on this mirror [**734**] reveal a strong Moorish influence. Moors were the people from what is now Algeria and Morocco, from north of the Sahara and west of Tripoli who were conquered by Arabs in the seventh century. The Arabs who then occupied southern Spain from 711–1492 were called Moors, hence the Islamic influence on Spanish architecture.

Attached to the reverse of this mirror by José Anicetol, [**735**] is a printed label: 'Na

735 Portugal, Maria I, *c.*1810, mahogany pier-glass and console-table by José Aniceto
103in (262cm)

736 Portugal, Maria I, *c.*1795, one of a pair, carved giltwood pier-glass in the manner of José Francisco de Paiva
overall height 114in (290cm)

737 Spain, Ferdinand VII, *c.*1820, mahogany dressing-mirror
27½in (70cm)

739 Spain, Isabella II, *c.*1860, carved giltwood and composition
71in (181cm)

738 Spain, Isabella II, *c.*1840, one of a pair, giltwood
57½in (146cm)

740 Spain, Alfonso XII, *c.*1890, carved giltwood
62½ in (159cm)

5 fabrica de marce Lisboa Naria de Jose Aniceto RA/PO20 as Bairro alto fronte do chafaris do loureto/No. 8.' The pier-glass and its console-table are rare due to the use of Chinese decorated mirror-plates, (see p. 309), the lower panel of which depicts figures on a veranda overlooking a winter townscape. As these console-tables and mirrors were made in pairs, and perhaps sets of four, for grand palaces, the other three may have been decorated with the remaining seasons. (In this example the console-table is missing the marble top.) A late eighteenth-century pier-glass, this time in carved giltwood [**736**] is in the manner of José Francisco de Paiva, (1744–1824), who published designs for similar consoles and mirrors. (Cf. Mendes Pinto, 1973, p. 163.) According to the designs, this example, one of a pair, would have had a matching console-table with a marble-top and pierced trellis-style friezes decorated with swags of flowers. These swags are repeated at the base of the frame and the urns are used, singularly, as a centre to the curved stretchers. This mirror [**737**] illustrates the artistic ideas that were brought to Spain by the French, (who left in 1811) and were popular until the middle of the century. Known as Fernandino, the style was derivative of the French Empire and directoire forms, but evolved in Spain in a heavy and ponderous way. Fernandino frames were predominantly composed of mahogany, often enriched with carved giltwood or gilt-metal mounts, but the result lacked the quality of their French counterparts.

Girandoles were usually smaller and made for the less grand family rooms. This Spanish example from the mid-nineteenth century [**738**] forms part of that pan-European Rococo revival style that found its inspiration in France and was almost universally adopted. Another form of the mid-century revival is shown here [**739**]; lighter in style, it points to the advent of Neo-classicism that was to follow.

Included among the various revivals of the nineteenth century was an interest in the seventeenth century as exemplified by this mirror, [**740**] which can be compared to an original piece from this date [**726**].

It is interesting to see the method for hanging large mirrors at this date. (Cf. Payne, 1981, p. 374, for two Spanish interiors showing mirrors in gilded frames hung with the top edge out from the wall as was fashionable during the seventeenth century.)

Following the Fernandino style, so called after Ferdinand VII, Queen Maria Mercedes Isabella (1833–68) gave her name to the revival of French eighteenth-century styles during her reign. 'Isabellino' often posed a more exuberant revivalist style than in other European countries. The revival of the 'Churrigueresque' style in the seventeenth-century taste took place *c.* 1870.

In the cities of Madrid and Barcelona, the Art Nouveau movement finally brought a revolutionary rather than reactionary taste. Barcelona produced a purely Catalan interpretation called simply 'Stile Modernista' or 'Arte foren'. On the other hand, in Portugal, the French occupation had left a strong influence which led to a heavier interpretation of the Empire style. The international Exhibition in Oporto in 1865 was a showcase for the revival of French eighteenth-century styles, favouring the Louis XIV – XVI period. Portugal fell in line with the rest of Europe in following further revival styles until the end of the century.

United States of America

Despite attempts to establish a glass industry in America as early as 1607, there were no craftsmen in the country capable of producing mirror-glass of quality or in quantity before the nineteenth century. A statement in *The Great Industries of The United States* published in 1872, confirms this:

> 'Though some of the modern processes, as for example, the making of mirrors, are not yet carried on in this country, and we have to depend still upon Europe for the supply of many articles of glassware to meet the demands . . .'

So it was not until after 1893 that America had eight plate-glass manufacturers with the possible exception of isolated and unrecorded production of mirror-glass before that date. There is a reference to one Stephen Whiting of Boston as an example of isolated glass production when he advertised in *The Boston News Letter*, 12 November 1767 that the

> 'Said Whiting does more at present towards manufacturing Looking-Glasses than any one in the Province, or perhaps on the Continent, and would be glad of Encouragement enough to think it worth while to live.'

American mirrors fall into four main groups, unlike the earliest surviving American furniture that was made by the early settlers. The first group of mirrors, was composed of prized possessions taken out to the New World by the immigrants. The second group consisted of mirrors that were imported by wholesalers and retailers both from England and Europe and were often labelled by those traders as their own. There are many references to a brisk trade importing mirrors. *The Boston News Letter* for 10 August 1719, advertises 'Looking-glasses of divers sorts and sizes lately imported from London to be sold at the glass shop Queens Street'. Imports were not confined to England as is revealed by the following advertisement from *The Pennsylvania Gazette* for 12 May 1784: 'Just imported and to be sold by James Reynolds at his Looking-Glass Store, The Golden Boy . . . A great variety of English, French and Dutch Looking-Glasses . . .' Another advertisement from the *Baltimore Daily Repository* for 25 May 1792 included a reference to '. . . an assortment of German Looking-Glasses' imported by Valck Adrian for resale. These merchants would almost certainly have labelled the imported mirrors, in fact James Reynolds (1736–94) was the first of a long line of carvers and gilders supplying labelled looking-glasses from various addresses in Philadelphia until the nineteenth century. He and his wife had arrived from London on the brig *Mary and Elizabeth* commanded by Captain J. Sparks on 21 August 1766. By 4 September Reynolds was advertising in *The Pennsylvania Gazette:*

> 'James Reynolds carver and gilder. Just arrived from London (by Captain Sparks) at his house in Dock Street opposite Lodge Alley . . . Undertakes to execute all the various Branches of Carving and Gilding in the newest neatest and genteelest Taste . . .'

741 'Queen Anne', New England, *c.*1700–25, painted pine
17½in (44cm)

742 'Queen Anne', probably New York, *c.*1730–50, japanned, attributed to Geradus Duyckinck
28in (71cm)

743 'Queen Anne', *c.*1735, carved walnut and giltwood 40 in (102cm)

744 English, *c.*1740, carved walnut and giltwood
53in (135cm)

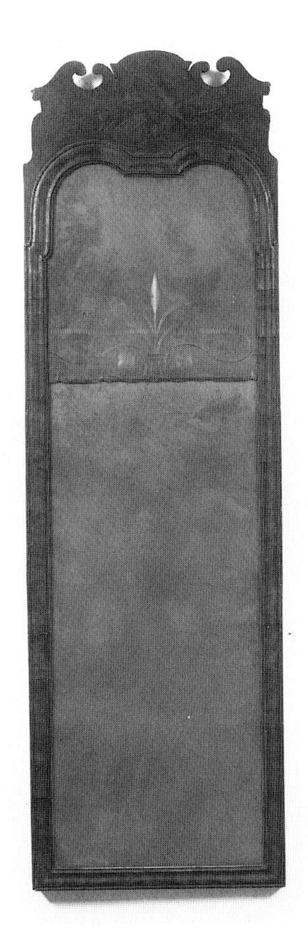

745 English, *c.*1750, simulated walnut engraved mirror-plate.
61in (155cm)

746 American possibly Philadelphia, *c.*1750, carved walnut and parcel-gilt
59in (150cm) (see colour illustration on p. 345)

The third group, and the largest, is formed of the vast numbers of mirrors imported mainly during the eighteenth and early nineteenth centuries, either by wealthy individuals or merchants and not marked in any way.

Mirrors in the fourth group are probably the first true American mirrors. It would seem likely that since framed mirror-glass was imported at considerable expense, unframed mirror-plate would also have been imported to be framed locally. Indeed plain glass was imported from France, Holland and England, and was in some cases unsilvered. As late as 1817 Henry Bradshaw Fearon wrote to a friend of his visit to New York '. . . Silvering looking-glasses is a separate trade; there is but one silverer in New York and he is not constantly employed . . .' Despite Fearon's claim, in his letter, that the best glass came from England, the French supplied the finest glass. John Doggett of Roxbury Massachusetts who had the largest looking-glass frame-making business, recorded in a daybook for the years 1802–9 that his best glass (plate) came from the Royal Plate Glass Manufactory in Paris, whose director he instructed on one occasion, to: 'have them very well packed with flannel between them'. As for the timber needed to frame the glass, the early joiners found domestic walnut in abundant supply: 'Black walnut is mightily esteem'd by the Joiners for its grain and colour.'

Skilled craftsmen were also available to refurbish unfashionable frames; in 1730 James Foddy offered 'to alter and amend old looking-glasses'. Another, Stephen Dwight of New York, advertised his ability to carve picture and mirror frames in 1755. These early American frames consisted at first of simple mouldings or flat frames, made purely to protect the valuable mirror-glass. As the eighteenth century progressed, local craftsmen would copy the imported fashionable frames, although often at a slightly later date and in an earlier style, using local as well as imported timbers.

747 'Queen Anne', *c.*1755, mahogany and giltwood toilet-mirror 27in (69cm)

The use of the terms 'Federal' and 'Chippendale' when associated with American mirrors requires some explanation. When applied to furniture, 'Chippendale' usually refers to the years *c.* 1755–85 and was preceeded by the 'Queen Anne' period *c.* 1702–45. The former can be a confusing term, however, because this same period in England embraced the work of Chippendale (and the publication of his *Gentleman and Cabinet Maker's Director*) as well as the work of Hepplewhite and Adam. 'Federal' is a chronological rather than strictly stylistic description which is applied to American arts during the period from the establishment of the Federal government in 1789 to *c.* 1830.

From New England, this painted pine mirror is in the form and style of decoration popular in England *c.* 1690 [**741**]. In shape and form, this type of cushion frame is now more often associated with walnut and in rare cases olive or laburnum wood. From an inventory of 1678 in Virgina, two mirrors are recorded: '1 Olive wood glass, 1 large walnut tree glass £4.14s', while another inventory, taken in Philadelphia in 1687, lists, 'an olive wood diamond cut looking-glass', ('diamond cut' refers to the bevelled edges of the glass). During the closing years of the seventeenth century and throughout the reign of Queen Anne, (1702–14) the japanned-style of decoration was popular in Europe. As exemplified here, this imitation of Oriental lacquer was also popular in America, although in common with most styles, slightly later than Europe. There is a record of an advertisement in 1735 in *The New York Weekly Journal* by Geradus Duyckinck at the sign of the Two Cupids; 'Looking-glasses new Silvered and Frames plain,

748 'Queen Anne' or English, *c.*1755, mahogany and giltwood sconce
23in (58cm)

749 'Chippendale', *c.*1760, carved mahogany and giltwood
45½in (116cm)

750 English or Baltic, *c.*1765, carved mahogany and giltwood
56in (143cm)

751 'Chippendale', *c.*1765, carved mahogany and giltwood
68in (173cm)

752 'Chippendale', *c.*1765, carved mahogany and giltwood
55in (140cm)

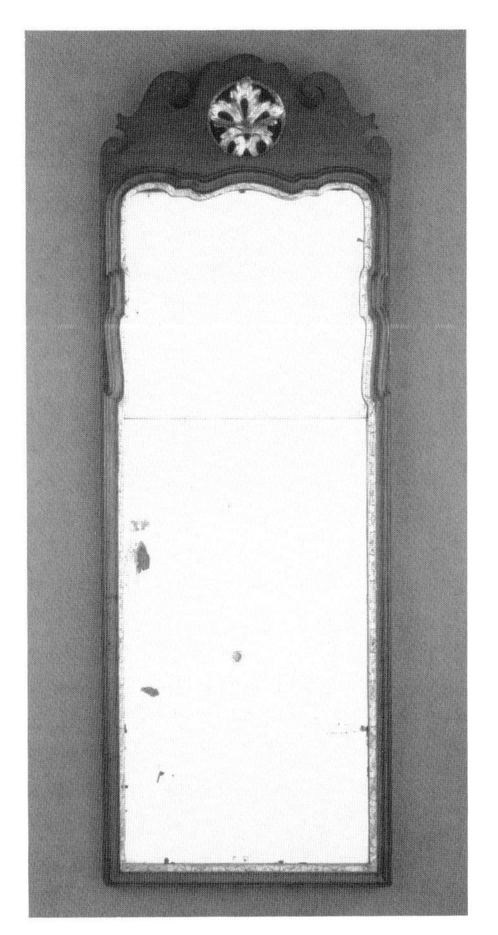

753 'Queen Anne', Philadelphia, *c.*1765, carved mahogany and giltwood, labelled *John Elliott*
51in (130cm)

Japan'd or flowered'. After Duyckinck's death his son, Gerardus Duyckinck, Jr announced in a 1746 New York paper that he was continuing the family business. 'Limning, Painting, Varnishing, Japanning, Gilding etc.' Believed to be an example of his work, this frame [**742**] shows Duyckinck's japanning skills. (For another example of japanning reputed to be by Duyckinck, Snr, cf. Davidson, 1979, vol. I, fig. 197).

From the Queen Anne period in England, this [**743**] frame is from that group of frames taken to American by an early settler. In overall shape, the frame is a development of the late seventeenth-century form with a separate, sometimes removable cresting. In this permutation, the cresting has become an integral part of the frame and is complemented with an apron. There are indications on the apron lobes of screw holes which would have attached the backplates of candle-arms, a common feature of this period. This form of small, early mirror fitted with a candle-arm or a pair of candle-arms are sometimes referred to as sconces. An advertisement of a slightly later date for a mahogany frame but with gilt moulding and carved shell, appears in the *Newport Mercury*, 13 May 1765. 'To be sold by Peckham and Gould at their shop in Thames Street, an assortment of looking-glasses, *viz.*: mahogany, sconce, gilt edge and shell, thirty inches by seventeen . . .' An inventory of Mayor Charles Willing double house of Third Street Philadelphia between 1746 and 1755 included 'In the S.W. room up One pair of stairs . . . 1 Walnut Fram'd Sconce Glass with gilt shell.'

The frame of this English walnut pier-glass with divided mirror-plate [**744**], (slightly damaged) is comparable to mahogany mirror made for Charles Norris in 1755 by John Elliott of Philadelphia and (Cf. Hornor, Jr. 1935, pl. 455). John Elliott, Sr (1713–91) was a Quaker born in Bolton, England, who arrived in Philadelphia with his wife and five children in 1753. He is known to have used three different labels from the addresses at Chestnut and then Walnut Street, each printed in both English and German. He registered as a cabinetmaker and advertised looking-glasses in *The Pennsylvania Gazette* of December 1756. His children and grandchildren continued the business into the nineteenth century as looking-glass merchants and later as druggists. Charles Norris's pier-glass was one of three purchased from Elliott at a cost of £44.10s in December 1755. Plain, but expensive, these pier-glasses were quite twenty years behind the London fashions, but were considered acceptable in leading Philadelphia homes of the time. (See also [**753**].)

With a divided and decorated mirror-plate [**745**], the frame of this English pier-glass is in simulated walnut. Fitting the frame with more than one mirror-plate was a common practice, purely based on cost. Large mirror-plates were available from English glass-works, (made by the cylinder process), or from France, (made by the cast process) that could have fitted such a frame, however there was a definite saving in using two plates, even taking into consideration the cost of engraving. Here engraved decoration is not merely decorative, but it helps to draw the eye away from the harsh line dividing the two plates. Another walnut frame, this time with parcel-gilt, [**746**] can be compared with a frame veneered with English walnut on a spruce or pine base in The Jonathan Sayward House (Cf. Jobe and Kaye, 1984, p. 455, no. 146). Jonathan Sayward, the York, Maine trader and judge, probably purchased his mirror between 1761–67 when he was enlarging his home and acquiring additional furniture.

An example of a toilet-mirror [**747**]; they were also known in America as 'Dressing

Boxes and Swingers'. The *Boston News Letter* of 22–9 September 1737 advertises 'Swinging glasses with draws and without'. An inventory of Thomas Flankin's house taken in 1725 records in the front chamber, '1 large Looking Glass £12, One handsome Dressing Ditto £3'.

The candle-arm is missing from this mahogany and parcel-gilt sconce [**748**]. Originally this may well have been one of a pair of sconces, imported from England by a private American individual, a merchant, a wholesaler or a ships captain. English dealers in furnishings were able to supply suitable items for export from stock. One such dealer was Lake Young of James Street, Covent Garden, who offered his wares from his James Street address and from his warehouse near the Pump in Watling Street London. His card reads as follows:

> 'Where Merchants, Captains of Ships, Country Chapmen etc. may be supply'd on reasonable Terms with all Sorts of Looking Glasses Viz Sconces, Pier and Chimney Glasses, Dressing Boxes and Swingers, in mahogany, walnut-tree and Painted, or in rich carv'd and gilt frames in the neatest Taste and newest fashion. All sorts of Window Glass, wholesale and Retail or for Exportation.'

A relatively simple form of mahogany frame [**749**] this example is decorated with a pierced, carved Oriental ho-ho bird and a shell. Carefully incised leaves and branches as here often feature on mirrors in American collections and it is possible that this detail was added to frames exported to America since few mirrors with this type of decoration are found in England. It is also a possibility that dealers exporting mirrors to the United States during this century embellished the frames to increase their value, since it would have been a relatively easy process to incise the line and leaf decoration with a V-shaped chisel to the depth of the veneered surface and infill with gold leaf. To add credence to the originality of this decoration, however, the backboard of a mirror purchased in Boston by Johnathan Bowman from the merchant William Jackson in 1770, bears a number of inked inscriptions. Possibly applied before the shipment from England, the inscriptions read: '30.17', designating the size of the glass, while 'Sham Pediment/flower potts & sprigs' describing the decoration. Certainly one of the imported group of mirrors, [**750**] but whilst the overall shape and gilt decoration has an English appearance, this frame could have been made in northern Germany or Denmark. Extensive trade links between England and the Baltic ports meant a cross-fertilization of styles, which was especially applicable to mirrors.

The next two examples [**751 and 752**] are a form of mirror referred to by collectors of American furniture as 'Constitutional Mirrors'. Veneered in walnut their overall design is purely English and would date from *c*. 1730 if 'à la mode' in a London drawing-room. Perhaps the only real difference, other than the fact that English examples would have been in mahogany, is the use of an eagle centering the swan-neck pediment, where an English example could well have had a cartouche. Standing well above the pediment, the bird that often features on these mirrors is either an eagle or more often a version of the ho-ho bird. (Cf. Hornor, 1935, pl. 448; Sack, 1950, p. 208.) The next example, [**753**] is an American mirror labelled by the well-known John Elliott, (see also [**743**]). After the style of 'Chippendale' this mahogany and parcel-gilt mirror [**754**], is similar to an example bearing the label of James Stokes (cf.

754 'Chippendale', *c*.1770, carved mahogany and parcel-gilt
47in (120cm)

755 'Chippendale', Philadelphia, *c.*1760–80, carved mahogany and giltwood, labelled *John Elliott*
46in (117cm)

756 'Queen Anne', Philadelphia, *c.*1760–70, walnut and parcel gilt
61in (155cm)

757 'Chippendale', *c.*1770, veneered walnut and parcel-gilt
53in (56cm) (see colour illustration on p. 346)

758 English, *c.*1765, carved mahogany and giltwood
43in (110cm)

759 'Chippendale', *c.*1765, carved mahogany and giltwood (left)
41½in (105cm)

760 'Chippendale', *c.*1780, carved mahogany and giltwood
38in (97cm)

Strickland, April 1978.) Stokes (*c.* 1755–1831) was a looking-glass, hardware and dry-goods merchant in Philadelphia between 1785 and 1804 and again for a year in 1810. Stokes's name is more often associated with a later style of mirror, with *verre églomisé* panels, popular towards the end of the eighteenth and early nineteenth centuries. Two trade labels are recorded for him, the second, when he resumed business after T. and J. Fassit had taken over in 1804. The label reads 'James Stokes/At his long established Store Southwest Corner of Market and/Front Streets' and is dated 14 March 1810. He married twice, his first wife, Sarah Magill Stokes, died in 1815 and he married Mrs Hannah Weaver Piehlo in 1817. He was succeeded in business by his sons-in-law, Caleb Parry Wayne and Charles Biddle, Jr in 1811, from when, until his death in 1831, he lived in Germantown.

An American origin for this mirror [**756**] is indicated by the fact that it was found in the presence of nine similar mirrors in the home of a Philadelphian family near Germantown. Compared to English parcel-gilt frames of the English walnut period, this frame is much higher at just over five ft. (Cf. Schiffer p. 138, fig. 331 for an American made frame veneered in mahogany of similar pier-glass height and outline of cresting.) A walnut mirror of a similar height, with inner shaped moulding and carved sides has an eighteenth-century inscription inked on the backboard 'For/Mr Charles Treadwell' (Cf. Jobe and Kaye, 1984, pp. 453–4, fig. 145). As Treadwell (1705–93) was a successful merchant, the mirror bearing his name could have been for retail or for his own use; Schiffer, 1983, p. 152, fig. 378, for a frame with a similar outline to the cresting bearing the label of Joseph White. White, who died in 1798, was a druggist and looking-glass merchant in Wilmington Delaware. He is known to have purchased looking-glasses from John Elliott which may explain the similarities in design for frames labelled and sold by each man. Although used as a veneer, this walnut and parcel-gilt mirror [**757**] is similar to [**751** and **752**]. (Cf. Sack, 1950, p. 208.) In The Henry Francis du Pont Winterthur Museum there is a frame of almost identical outline to this one, [**763**]. (Cf. Schiffer, 1983, p. 154, fig. 385.) The Winterthur frame retains the fourth label of John Elliott Jr (*c.* 1739–1810), who used six different labels between 1784 and 1803 from a location on the West side of Front Street, Philadelphia. Another similar example is at the Colonial Williamsburg Foundation, Williamsburg, Virginia, (Cf. Greenlaw, 1975, pp. 128–9, no. 109).

Compared to others in this style, this mirror [**764**], seems austere; while the basic inner parcel-gilt and cross-grained moulding, together with the incised fretwork outline, is common to others, this one lacks additional decoration. The cost of the frame would have been raised by the extras available, for example giltwood scrolls overlying the cresting and giltwood swags at each side. (Cf. Sack, 1950, p. 208; Schiffer, 1983, pp. 136 and 137.) The following mirror, [**766**], is an embellished example of an earlier mirror [**764**]. From New England this mirror [**765**] bears a paper label on the backboard 'The Washington mirror belonged to Samuel Leavenworth Hurd (born 1762). He had two wives, two Clark sisters and the mirror probably came through them – 1744–1780.'

Probably of English origin, this frame was quite possibly sold in New York by William Wilmerding [**767**]. Wilmerding (1762–1832) from Brunswick in Germany arrived in New York in 1783 and married Catherine van Falkenam two years later.

761 'Chippendale', *c.*1780, carved mahogany and giltwood
41in (104cm)

762 'Chippendale', *c.*1780, mahogany and giltwood
34½in (88cm)

763 'Chippendale', Philadelphia, *c.*1785, carved mahogany labelled *John Elliott*
44in (112cm)

764 Probably English, *c.*1780, carved mahogany and giltwood
51in (130cm)

765 'Chippendale', New England, *c.*1780, carved mahogany and giltwood
45½in (116cm) (see colour illustration on p. 346)

766 'Chippendale', possibly New York, *c.*1780, carved mahogany and giltwood
44in (112cm)

767 'Chippendale', New York or English, *c.*1790, mahogany and parcel-gilt, attributed to William Wilmerding
45in (114cm) (see colour illustration on p. 346)

768 Federal, *c.*1795 inlaid mahogany and giltwood
55½in (141cm)

769 Federal, possibly New York *c.*1790, inlaid mahogany and giltwood
57in (145cm)

770 Federal, possibly New York *c.*1800, carved mahogany and giltwood, surmounted by a *verre églomisé* panel
59in (150cm)

771 Federal, possibly New York *c.*1795, carved giltwood and mahogany
56in (142cm)

772 Federal, *c.*1800, carved giltwood
51in (130cm)

Wilmerding was a looking-glass merchant and importer whose name has been associated with similar mirrors to this for many years. This association is based on an original bill for one of these closely connected mirrors: 'bot from William Wilmerding in New York, August 15, 1794 for £8.0.0 by Jacob Everson' (Cf. Downs, 1946). Since Wilmerding was a merchant it is unlikely that he made these mirrors, but he may have had a 'line' especially produced for him. (Cf. Montgomery, 1966, p. 260, no. 212; Mus. of The City of New York, exhib. cat., 1956–7, p. 50, no. 71.) The carved leaves and flowers to the sides of this frame [**769**] have a naïve quality in comparison to earlier examples. (Cf. Montgomery, 1966, fig. 216 for a frame which probably came from the same workshop. It would seem that the captions for figs 216 and 217 have been transposed.)

From New York City or Albany, this example [**770**] is fitted with a *verre eglomisé* panel. (See p. 56 *The Argus, Greenleaf New Daily Advertiser* for 2 January 1797 carried an advertisement from Anthony Renault of New York that

> 'He makes all sorts of frames, rich and common, whether for pictures, engravings or looking-glasses. He also gilds upon glass and writes inscriptions upon it in such a mode or taste as may be pointed out.'

This example, is similar in conception to a looking-glass also made in New York or Albany which bears a stencilled inscription 'From Del Vecchio Looking-Glass and Picture Frame Manufacturers New York'. This family were in business in New York between *c.* 1800 and 1847. The Del Vecchio brothers, Francis, Joseph, John-Paul and Charles were natives of Moltnasio, a small town on Lake Como in northern Italy, who arrived in New York from London on 24 September 1800.

This oval Federal giltwood mirror [**772**] has an ornate and delicately carved swagged cresting. It is interesting to compare this with an oval frame illustrated by Luke Beckerdite in his article 'Philadelphia Carving Shops' *Antiques*, May 1984, p. 1132, Fig. 17. The article is one of three and discusses the work of James Reynolds, an Englishman who settled in Philadelphia in 1766, and to whom Beckerdite attributes the oval mirror.

773 Federal, *c.*1800, mahogany toilet-mirror
27in (69cm)

Adjustable toilet-glasses were probably introduced into England from France, and this Federal mirror of *c.* 1800 betrays its European origins [**773**] (See p. 181) (Cf. Lockwood, 1957, p. 331, Fig. 397; Miller, Jr, 1966, p. 688, Figs 1260 and 1262). In the 'Academie of Armoire' of 1688 Randle Holme describes a toilet glass and adds 'these sorts of glasses are most used by Ladys to look their faces in, and to see how to dress their heads and set up their top knots on the foreheads upright'. In America this popular form of mirror became known as a 'swinger'. The term was used in 1784 by the firm Willing, Morris and Swanwick in an advertisement 'Two oval Swinging Glasses with mahogany frames and black and white string edges – one marked on the back 52s 6d, the other 35s.' These had been stolen from their counting house. An earlier reference to them was in 1737. This form of Federal mirror [**774**] displays a late use of the pediment top with swan-neck scrolls. Although this example is reputed to have been made in New York, other similar examples were made in Massachusetts and on the trade card of Nathan Ruggles of Hertford Connecticut, *c.* 1810, is a drawing of a similar frame enclosing his advertisement. (Cf. Lockwood, 1957, p. 306, fig. 348; Miller, Jr, 1966, p. 644, fig. 1159; Schiffer, 1983, p. 171, fig. 442.) This group of

775 Federal, possibly New York *c.*1805, inlaid mahogany
41½in (105cm) (see colour illustration on p. 346)

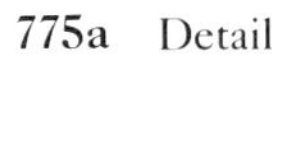

775a Detail

774 Federal, New York, *c.*1800, inlaid mahogany and giltwood
43in (109cm)

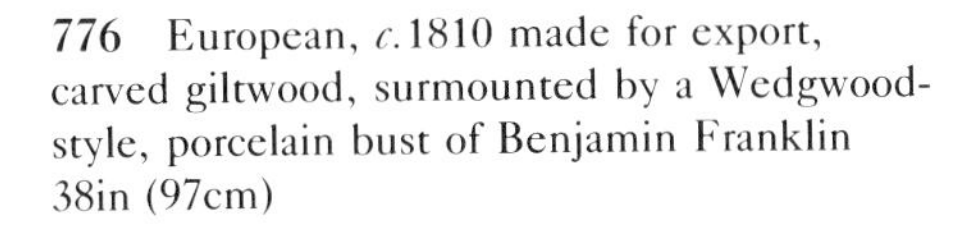

776 European, *c.*1810 made for export, carved giltwood, surmounted by a Wedgwood-style, porcelain bust of Benjamin Franklin
38in (97cm)

777 Federal, possibly New York, *c.*1820, carved mahogany cheval-mirror (far right)
65in (165cm)

778 English, *c.*1810, carved giltwood with *verre églomisé* panel
55in (140cm)

779 Federal, *c.*1800, giltwood pier-glass with *verre églomisé* panel
65in (165cm) (see colour illustration on p. 347)

780 Federal, *c.*1810, giltwood with *verre églomisé* panel
73in (186cm)

781 Federal, *c.*1810, giltwood with *verre églomisé* panel (far left)
36½in (93cm)

782 Federal, *c.*1810, giltwood with *verre églomisé* panel, labelled *Barnard Cermenati, Newburyport, Massachusetts*
48in (122cm)

mirrors frequently have histories of New York or Hudson Valley family ownership and share many common features. A number have inlaid eagle paterae on the frames as well an inlaid line stringing and most, if not all, have white pine as the secondary timber. Other examples have panels of *verre églomisé* beneath the cresting, usually depicting pastoral scenes. Almost certainly of European origin, giltwood frames of this type [**776**] were common in northern Europe particularly the north of Germany and Scandinavia in the late eighteenth century. Inspired by French design, the frames recall those from the reign of Louis XVI. In the centre of the cresting is a Wedgwood or Wedgwood-style porcelain medallion bust of Benjamin Franklin in white relief on a blue ground. It is perhaps convenient to believe that this Danish or Scandinavian frame was fitted with an English-made medallion of this statesman, scientist and writer, before the frame was shipped to America, where it was fitted with a piece of English or european mirror-glass. Franklin was already a rich scientist and a member of the Pennsylvania Assembly when he acted as agent for the State in London between 1764–75 and was therefore well-known in England. A related mirror with an oval, reverse painting on glass of George Washington is in the Karolik Collection in the Museum of Fine Arts in Boston (Cf. Hipkiss, 1941, p. 207, fig. 140).

In America this form of giltwood mirror with a decorated panel above the mirror-plate is known as an 'Albany' mirror [**778**]. Numerous examples exist of this type of mirror, which was principally composed of white pine and thought to have been made in Albany or New York. This example, however, is English and bears the label of William Gould & Son, London. William Gould, Jr was apprenticed to his father, also William Gould, in July 1781 and completed his time in August 1788. Gould Snr, of 78 Gracechurch Street, London, was an upholder, glass grinder and looking-glass manufacturer between 1758 and 1812. After 1795 father and son were in partnership at the same address and their label is recorded on another frame of pier-glass proportions with a Wedgwood plaque and a blue and white decorative panel: 'Gould & Son's Looking & Coach Glass Manufactory, No. 78, 6 Church Street, London, Wholesale and for Exportation'. A. Henry Gould is also recorded as working as an upholder and looking-glass manufacturer from 78 Gracechurch Street at the same time, 1782–95. Since insurance cover on stock and utensils in1812 amounted to £1,500, the business was substantial.

Again, probably from New York or Albany, this frame [**779**] has eagle cresting and classical urns to each side of the frame, united by pairs of chains. (Cf. Montgomery, 1966, p. 278, figs 236 and 237.) A variation upon this theme of chains is shown here [**780**] where the balls are graduated. Another mirror from the Federal period has a reverse painted and *verre eglomisé* panel depicting a battle between two ships, the *Constitution* and the *Gurriere*, (the names of which are inscribed in gilt). Whilst this style of frame, as mentioned before, implies an American origin, many were imported. Another advertisement in the *Argus, Greenleaf new Daily Advertiser*' on 2 January 1797, placed by William Voight of 92 Maiden Lane, New York reads

> '. . . by the latest importations from London and Hamburg, a superb assortment of Looking-Glasses, made after the newest London fashion . . . Elegant Gilt Frames, with pillars, balls, enamelled frieze and eagle top of all sizes.'

There seems to be no foundation to the theory that the sizes of the gilt balls changed at, or after, 1800. John Doggett (1780–1857), a gilder, looking-glass-, and frame-maker of Roxbury and Boston, recorded in his day book covering the years 1802–9, sales of four sizes of gilt balls. His records show sales to other frame-makers such as Barnard Cermenati from Newbury port and Salem Massachusetts, of different sizes on the same occasion. Charges were made for balls of four sizes at 5, 6, 7 and 8 dollars per gross. An 1815 inventory of William I Tillman of New York, looking-glass manufacturer, records:

'Gilt 468 feet Twist	$4.68
5 patterns balls	$17.50'

The patterns are probably moulds for the production of composition balls that were gilded later. The 468 ft of twist refers to the twist-moulding at each side of the frame as in this example [**781**] and others. Frames of this type were composed of pine covered with gesso and gilded, whereas the ornaments, including the balls, were either carved in softwood or made of composition imported from England. Within the first twenty years of the nineteenth century American-made composition was also available, as Tillman's inventory records. An advertisement in the *Philadelphia Advertiser* for 1818 by a R. Welford, announces: 'Philadelphia manufactory of composition ornament'. (Cf. Lockwood, 1957, p. 325, fig. 383; Schiffer, 1983, p. 214, fig. 562.) Another mirror [**782**] retains the label of Barnard Cermenati. An Italian, Bernard Cermenati (*c*. 1783–1818) was a carver, gilder, looking-glass frame-maker who traded in Newburyport (1807–9) and in Salem, Massachusetts in 1810. Later, in 1812, he was in Portsmouth, New Hampshire, moving on to Boston in 1811, where he returned in 1813–18. There he died aged 35 years old on 22 April 1818, leaving his wife Mary with five small sons; she was to die the following year.

Referred to as an overmantel, or 'mantle glass' in contemporary inventories, this type of mirror [**783**] was the prerequisite of every fashionable early-nineteenth-century parlour. As an example of a contemporary interior see *The Tea Party c*. 1821–5, by Henry Sargent illustrated by Jane Nylander, '*Henry Sargent's Dinner Party and Tea Party*', (see Antiques, May 1982, p. 1180). The relatively high cost of such a mirror would certainly mean that it was intended to be placed in a room used by visitors. In

783 Federal, *c*.1810, giltwood and *verre églomisé* overmantel (below) width 52½in (133cm) (see colour illustration on p. 348)

784 Federal, *c*.1815, giltwood and painted overmantel (right) width 56in (142cm)

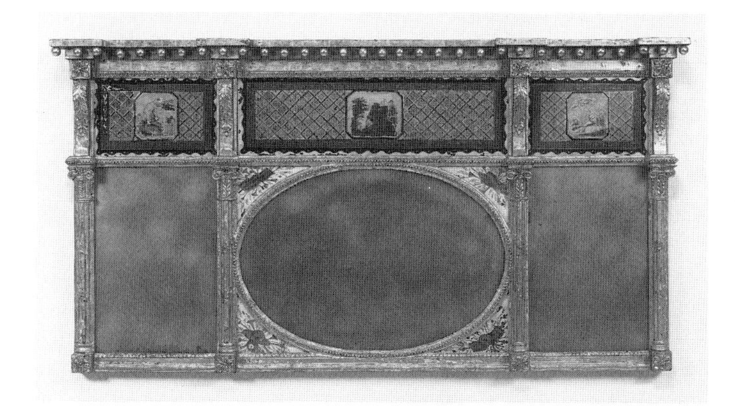

785 Federal, *c.*1815, giltwood and *verre églomisé* overmantel (left)
width 46in (117cm) (see colour illustration on p. 348)

786 Federal, *c.*1820, carved giltwood and *verre églomisé* (above)
60in (153cm)

this case the spandrels of the oval central plate are decorated with musical instruments and sheet music in *verre eglomisé*. Conceivably these symbols may have been included to imply that the owners were musical and cultured people, possibly from the leisured class who would have been able to afford such decoration, (see also 785). In his diary for 24 October 1801, the Reverend William Bentley of Salem refers to a visit to Mr Nathaniel West's house. 'Mirrors were very large and gave full view of every one who passed . . .' An inverted, moulded cornice placed above a classical scene is flanked by double pilasters in this mirror [**787**]. Either the candle-arms are unusual original features, or later additions. In the next two cases [**788** and **789**], the inverted break front cornice is decorated with acorns instead of the more conventional balls. Probably made in New York, two mirror-plates have been used to achieve the required height. Possibly from Philadelphia this frame can perhaps be attributed to Wayne and Biddle [**791**]. Caleb Parry Wayne and Charles Biddle, Jr were married to the daughters of James Stokes. Stokes *c.* 1755–1831, a looking-glass, hardware and dry goods merchant in Philadelphia who was succeeded in business by his sons-in-law after he restablished his business in 1809 (see p. 335). (Cf. Schiffer, 1983, p. 222–3, figs 587–8.) Also attributed to a Philadelphia maker, the frames of this rare pair of mirrors [**793**] are richly decorated with double columns and flowerhead paterae corners; the mirrors also have elaborately-carved crestings centred by opposing eagles.

This Federal dressing-mirror, [**794**] bears the stencilled label of Rufus Pierce on one of the interior drawers. Pierce was a furniture dealer from Boston and New York City, *c.* 1825–30. (Another dressing-glass with a Pierce stencilled label, 17 Market Street, Boston, is illustrated, *Antiques*, May 1976, p. 1008 and p. 1010, fig. 9.)

Of Regency, or early nineteenth-century form, this is a typical convex mirror [**796**]. The term 'Looking Glass' is commonly found during the eighteenth and ninteenth centuries on invoices and inventories. The word 'Mirror', used today to describe a

787 Federal, possibly New York, *c.*1815, carved giltwood
53in (134cm)

788 Federal, possibly New York, *c.*1815, carved giltwood
62in (158cm)

789 Federal, *c.*1820, giltwood with *verre églomisé* panel
67in (170cm)

790 Federal, possibly New York, *c.*1815, carved giltwood with *verre églomisé* panel
46in (117cm)

791 Federal, Philadelphia, *c.*1820, carved mahogany with *verre églomisé* panel
35in (89cm)

792 Federal, *c.*1820, carved giltwood
59in (150cm)

746

757

765

765

767

775

775

779

783

785

816

817a

b

818

822

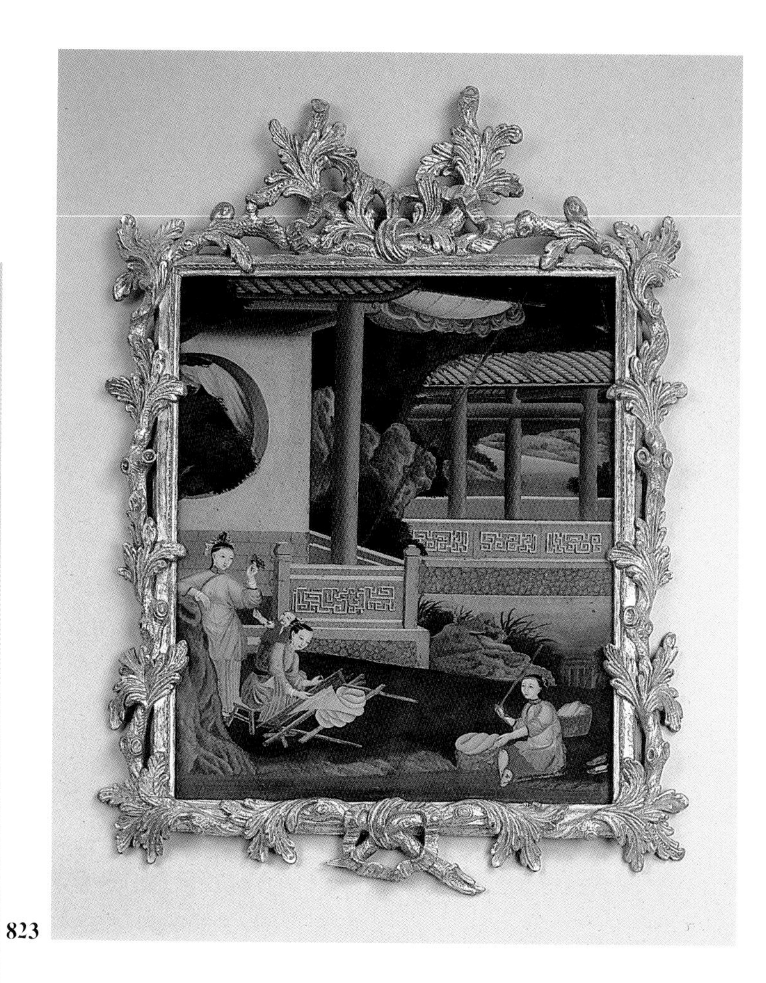

823

824

793 Federal, possibly Philadelphia, *c.*1825, a pair, carved giltwood and gesso mirrors with ebonized surrounds
72½in (184cm)

794 Federal, *c.*1815, mahogany toilet mirror, labelled *Rufus Pierce, Boston*
16½in (42cm)

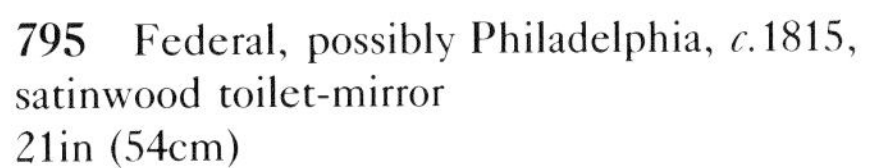

795 Federal, possibly Philadelphia, *c.*1815, satinwood toilet-mirror
21in (54cm)

796 Federal, *c.*1805, giltwood, convex girandole
40in (102cm)

797 Federal, *c.*1815, one of a pair, giltwood convex mirror
43in (110cm)

798 Federal, *c.*1815, carved giltwood convex mirror
39in (99cm)

looking-glass and its frame, was in 1803 used by Thomas Sheraton in his *Cabinet Dictionary* to describe convex mirrors (see p. 143). Sheraton's description of the 'agreeable effect' led to them being 'universally fashionable'. This example is fitted with double candle-arms and a dragon as a cresting. Another fine example has the rare feature of a clock fitted into the apron [**799**]. Although the clock is signed *K. Agnew, Manchester*, Agnew is not recorded as a clockmaker. It is possible, however, that he was the retailer of this clock and possibly of the mirror as well. 'Extras' such as the double set of candle-arms fitted with drop-hung glass drip-pans, (two missing) as well as glass candle-holders would have placed this mirror in luxury class. The cresting in this example has a pair of crossed cornucopia which spill fruit giving a clear indication of Abundance and Plenty. Behind the mirror is a vertical metal strap which would certainly have supported a further feature, instead of, or possibly as well as, the carved fruit and leaves shown. Another Philadelphian example, this is one of a rare pair of convex mirrors that have been in the Newbold family for at least four generations[**800**]. Some indication of the value of these mirrors is given by an inventory made in 1814 of the estate of Elizabeth Derby, daughter of Elias Hasket Derby. Wherein the valuer estimated a convex mirror as being worth $75 and five looking-glasses ranging in value from $75 to $150.

Probably made in New York, the design of this Federal mahogany cheval glass [**803**] is based on early nineteenth-century French Empire models with classical columns to each side. More typically English, however, are the downswept moulded legs, together with the traditional Regency brass lion-paw castors. (Cf. Bridwell, Bates and Fairbanks, 1981, p. 245 for a similar pediment on a mirror in the Metropolitan Museum of Art, New York.) Both Duncan Phyfe (1768–1854) and Charles-Honoré Lannuier (*fl. c.* 1803–19), produced designs for this type of mirror. An illustration on Lannuier's label shows a similar cheval glass with pillars, legs and cresting. (Cf. Wiedman, 1984, fig. 108, for a similar example of a cheval glass attributed to Lannuier.) This toilet mirror, [**804**] bears the label of Thomas Natt of Philadelphia. Thomas J. Natt, (1805–59) was the son of Thomas Natt (*c.* 1779–1842), carver, gilder, looking-glass maker, importer and merchant who is first recorded at 25 South Fourth in 1809, then at 76 Chesnut and at 134 High Street. His son, Thomas J. Natt, first appears as a looking-glass maker and merchant at 134 High Street in 1837. There is some confusion, however, as a bill of sale at the Historical Society of Pennsylvania from Thomas J. Natt to Charles Graff is dated 16 February 1833, some four years before the son is recorded. This can be explained if both father and son had the same middle initial (Cf. Lockwood, 1957, p. 333, fig. 401).

Probably from Pennsylvania this frame [**805**], is made from curly maple. John Evelyn, the celebrated English seventeenth-century diarist and author of *Sylva* (see p. 39), recorded his findings on maple: 'The knot', he stated 'was the most esteem'd'. His theory was that 'pretty undulations and chyamfers' were caused by 'the rain distilling along branches'. He was full of praise for maple and added 'above all notable for these extravagant damashings and characters, is the maple; and tis notorious, that this tree is very full of branches from the root to its very summit.'

Belonging to a relatively late pair of pier-mirrors [**808**], this frame has lost that finesse of earlier examples and has become a little heavier and thicker. Some decora-

799 English, *c.*1815, giltwood and gesso convex girandole
29in (74cm)

800 Federal, *c.*1815, one of a pair, giltwood convex girandole
25in (63cm)

801 Federal, *c.*1815, carved giltwood and gesso girandole
53½in (139cm)

802 Federal, *c.* 1820, one of a pair, ebonized and giltwood convex mirror
48in (122cm)

803 Federal, probably New York, *c.*1820, giltwood and mahogany cheval-mirror with brass feet
67½in (177cm)

805 Federal, probably Pennsylvania, *c.*1820, curly maple toilet-mirror
23in (58cm)

804 Federal, Philadelphia, *c.*1820, mahogany toilet-mirror, labelled *Thomas Natt, Philadelphia*
18in (46cm)

806 Federal, *c.*1820, curly maple toilet-mirror
19in (48cm)

807 Federal, *c.*1825, mahogany veneered with ivory roundels
21in (53cm)

808 Federal, *c.*1830, one of a pair of giltwood mirrors and composition pier mirrors
66in (168cm)

tive details, particularly on the base, point to a French Empire influence which explains why this period is referred to as 'American Empire'. The mirrors would have been hung in such a way as to have the eagles' heads turned towards each other. While the predominance of the eagles reinforces the patriotic theme, the olive branches that they grasp are emblematic of Peace.

In his book, *Colonial Furniture in America* Lockwood records that during the eighteenth, and presumably the nineteenth century as well, it was the custom to support looking-glasses on small enamelled and brass looking-glass rosettes (Cf. Lockwood, 1957, p. 328, fig. 390). The frame would have required support at the top on chains or cord and the base would have been supported at each corner by a rosette. As a result the top of the frame tilted forward away from the wall in much the same way as framed paintings during the seventeenth century in Europe. (Lockwood also mentions larger, matching rosettes used to hold back curtain drapes.)

By the mid-nineteenth century, although an element of the Empire style persists, especially in the column supports, fashion has changed and, as shown here [**809**] the mirror-plate frame has become arched. By contrast, this Rococo-style giltwood overmantel [**810**] is in the manner of those produced by Belter, *c.* 1850. John Henry Belter (1804–65) was born in Würthemberg, Germany, and established a business in New York, which flourished between 1844 and 1861. Belter patented a process of laminating and steaming panels. This involved glueing together layers of wood, one-sixteenth of an inch thick, in such a way that the grain of one layer ran in the opposite direction to that of the next. The layers varied in number from three to as many as sixteen. These panels were then steamed in moulds so that they could be bent into any desired shape. For an example of the unified Rococo style of interior, of which this mirror might once have been a part, there is a room setting at the Metropolitan Museum of Art, New York, displaying furniture by Belter. (Cf. Hayward *et al.*, 1965, p. 253, fig. 968, for a similar mirror made by Berkey and Gay Co. of Grand Rapids, Michigan, *c.* 1876 and probably exhibited at the 1876 Centennial Exposition in Philadelphia.)

With the exception of overmantel mirrors, cheval glasses and the occasional wall mirror, the use of mirror-plate during the second half of the nineteenth century tends to be combined with furniture. There are numerous examples such as mirror-backed wash-stands and dressing tables, sideboards with mirrors above and below, hall stands, side and console tables. This large mirror-plate, the product of well established American glass industry by this time, exemplifies just such use [**811**]. Following the European fashion for Renaissance revival pieces, the frame was made by Thomas Brooks. Brooks (1811–87) was a cabinet-maker working between 1850 and 1870 in the Gothic, Rococo and Renaissance styles. His recorded address was 127–9 Fulton Street, Brooklyn, New York, where he was in partnership for a short time between 1841–2 with Lorenzo Blackstone. He is known to have exhibited two sideboards at the Crystal Palace that are reputed to have been designed by Gustave Herter. This example displays the fine figuring of the burr or burl walnut, contrasting well with the carved surfaces. This mirror, [**811**] forms a part of a bedroom suite including a bedstead, bureau and marble-top dressing bureau, two pieces of which are stencilled 'T. Brooks & Co. Furniture and Upholstery Warehouse, 127 & 129 Fulton Street Cor. Sands, Brookylyn NY.'

809 Federal, probably New York, *c.*1825, mahogany cheval-mirror
69in (175cm)

810 American 'Renaissance', *c.*1865, giltwood overmantel mirror in the manner of John Henry Belter
width 61in (155cm)

811 American 'Renaissance', *c.*1865, carved, burr-walnut, by Thomas Brooks, Brooklyn, New York (right)
overall height 91in (231cm)

812 American 'Renaissance', *c.*1865, carved mahogany
92in (234cm)

813 American 'Renaissance', *c.*1870, ebonized walnut and parcel-gilt by Robert Renwick & Son, Baltimore
155½in (395cm)

814 American 'Eastlake', *c.*1880, giltwood pier-glass
94in (239cm)

Combined with a low table or bench, this massive mirror, [**813**] was made by Renwick of Baltimore. Robert C. Renwick (*fl.* 1848–90) worked principally in the Gothic Revival style. He traded as R. Renwick & Son, Cabinet Manufacturer, 92 N Howard St Baltimore. Born in Scotland, Renwick came to Baltimore in 1848 where he established himself as a leading cabinet-maker, to be joined by his son in 1865. Stencilled on the back of this piece is the company name and address and the inscription 'J. Wilson Potts, Jr', perhaps for whom it was made. The best examples of his Gothic Revival furniture can be seen in the First Presbyterian Church on Park and Madison Avenues in Baltimore, Maryland.

The style of a particular group of pieces of furniture made in America was influenced by the Englishman Charles Lock Eastlake. Born in Plymouth, Eastlake (1836–1906) was the scion of an affluent Devon family. As such he embarked upon a Grand Tour as a young man and travelled extensively through Europe where he cultivated his taste for medieval architecture. In 1855 he became the Secretary of the Royal Institute of

British Architects. It was during his time with the R.I.B.A. that he published his most famous work, *Hints on Household Taste* in 1868. The work was to become the 'Bible' of the design movement that included William Morris (1834–96) and William Burgess, Bruce Talbert and Alfred Waterhouse. Following its publication in America in 1872, *Hints on Household Taste* was so successful that by 1876 examples of 'Eastlake' furniture were being exhibited at the Philadelphia Centennial Exhibition. An example of this appreciation is reflected in the style of this pier-glass [**814**].

The American furniture-making industry expanded during the closing years of the 1860s and during the 1870s. New machinery was designed for woodworking including 'Boults Carver and Moulder' patented in 1869 by M.T. Boult's Battle Creek Machinery Company and many other inventions which out-paced traditional methods. Unhappily, the term 'Eastlake' soon appeared in trade catalogues illustrating examples of factory-carved ornament that were a violation of Eastlake's principles and his adoption of incised geometric ornament was to influence, not just furniture-makers, but many gadgets including early refridgerators and the mechanical furniture and iron furniture industries.

Chinese mirror and reverse-glass paintings

The arrival in Europe of Chinese mirror and reverse glass paintings owes much to the exploratory ambition of the Portuguese, the well-developed commercial sense of the Dutch, English and French and the skills of the looking-glass makers of Europe.

A sea route to the East was not available until 1497 when the Portuguese explorer, Vasco de Gama, established a route via the Cape of Good Hope. Up until that time, long and difficult overland expeditions were made in search of spices and silks. Over a century after De Gama, both the English and the Dutch sent expeditions, which rounded the Cape and sailed across the Indian Ocean, (avoided the Portuguese presence) and landed in Java. In time the expeditions returned to Europe loaded with cargoes of pepper, cloves, nutmeg and mace. As a direct result of these voyages, the English East India Company was founded in 1599 and the Dutch Vereenigde Oostindische Compagnie, more conveniently called the V.O.C., was founded three years later. France also became involved in the growth of trade and the Compagnie des Indes was established towards the end of the century.

Although the volume of French trade was not as large as that of the Dutch or English, the French exerted great influence due to the presence of their Jesuit missionaries. The Jesuits helped to introduce the European language into China therefore making communication easier and reducing the need to hire interpreters. They also gained the sympathies of the Emperor K'ang-Hsi (1662–1722) and introduced Western taste into court circles. As early as 1687 Jean de Fortaney, the Superior of the first mission, wrote from Peking asking for 'peintures en émail' and 'des ouvrages d'émail' as gifts for members of the Emperor's court. Influenced by the arrival of Jesuit artists such as Giovanni Gheradini, in 1698, and Guiseppe Castiglione, some years later, the oriental porcelain made for export was decorated in a European style.

Due to the market demand in Europe, as well as spices, export porcelain became a valuable part of any trading ship's cargo. It has been estimated that between the years 1604 and 1657 the Dutch imported no fewer than three million pieces of porcelain into Europe. Such success was clearly reflected in the profits of the European trading companies. The Honorable East India Company, despite being limited by the seasons and the winds of the Indian Ocean, was paying an annual dividend of 20 per cent on its stock, in the 1680s, and was responsible for 14 per cent of the value of England's total imports. Perhaps the most surprising aspect of this trade was the Company's policy of allowing its captains, and other officers as well as the crews of its ships to engage in private trading.

'Supercargoes', or negotiators, who were sent from London, were required to have a detailed knowledge of all goods to be traded and act as diplomats and arbitrators. They were responsible for the importation of many of the mirror pictures and other artefacts which made considerable fortunes for the sailors concerned. Many stayed in Macao and wintered there instead of making two sea journeys in a year.

The variety of goods exported from Europe for private sale were extensive and included, in the case of one Captain Thomas Cooke on the ship *Earl of Elgin* in 1764, '80 tons of flints in lieu of ballast for sale in China'. Later in 1768 Captain William Baker of the *Cruttenden* exported such items as 15 chests of clocks and jewellery, 250 boxes of tin plates, 7 chests of glassware, 24 tons of lead, as well as 6 chests of window glass among many other items. This importation into China of glass objects and window glass is interesting since glassmaking has a long history in China.

The use of glass in ancient China as a substitute for jade and as a material for making decorative items such as hairpins, bracelets and earrings, has long been known to historians. Glass coloured with minerals was used to simulate precious and semi-precious stones. An example of this is the insignia worn by the palace officers; a third class officer would use one of clear blue glass, a fourth class officer, opaque blue glass and a fifth class, clear, uncoloured glass.

The development of glass-making in China springs from the Emperor K'ang-Hsi's interest in Western science and craft. Mirrors and objects made from glass as well as clocks, wine, herbs and scientific instruments were among the gifts that were brought to the Emperor by emmissaries and missionaries. One particular tribute that was brought by a Dutch mission in 1686 included two large mirrors, 581 glass cups of various shapes, a large glass lamp (chandelier) and a large striking clock as well as herbs and spices. These Western gifts appealed immensely to the Emperor, the majority by virtue of their technical achievement, and stimulated him to create the Imperial glass-works. The glass workshop was established within the Forbidden City by Imperial edict in 1696. The Imperial glass-works produced large quantities of ritual utensils, articles of display as well as snuff-bottles and ornaments, but no flat glass, (hence the shipments of window glass). Local Chinese glass was described by one Leang Tong-shu (1723–1815) as being 'thin and brittle' in contrast to 'foreign glass' which was praised as 'thick and crystal-like'. In 1756 birthday gifts to the Emperor from the Customs in Canton included mirrors and covered bowls.

Although foreign craftsmen were employed to provide technical assistance in the Palace workshop the import of flat glass was still necessary. An explanation of this continuing need is provided by Breton de la Martinière in his book, *China, its costume, arts etc*, (translated in 1813).

> 'Looking-glasses and glass mirrors have been manufactured there (Canton), quicksilvered in the European manner, but this undertaking has not proved successful. The manufacturers do not know how to manufacture it with the proper materials.'

Mirror pictures, made for export, were some of the products of the cultural exchanges between the European and the Chinese. The earliest mention of a painted mirror appears in *Mercurius Rusticus*, 30 August to 6 September 1660, No. 36,

> 'Stolen the second of September out of a Dining Room in Holborn, a large looking-glass set in an ebony frame, a landskip being drawn at the bottom of the glass with a shepherdess, a lamb, a goat and several other figures, there being a flaw at the top of the glass.'

Another reference to a mirror painting is quoted in Savary des Bruslon's *Dictionnaire Universal de Commerce* (1745) where a French writer speaks of the difficulty of back painting and states that the practice was almost unknown in France at that time:

> 'When I was in Port Louis in 1745 I saw a Chinese mirror which had been sent to the Marquis de Rotumier, whereon was seen a Chinese lady at her toilet; above her in one corner a parrot on its perch and behind it a monkey . . . Overcome by the beauty of the mirror and the skill of the workmanship, I tried eagerly to discover by what means I could imitate it. When after much careful thought I believed I had solved the problem, I secured the help of Monsieur Desnagem, manager of the magazine at the citadel of Port Louis who was a very skilful painter. Together we worked out my idea and had the happiness to achieve a result which seemed to both of us highly satisfactory.'

The process whereby imported mirror plates were used to create mirror pictures is thought to have been developed by the Jesuit missionary Father Castiglione (1688–1766). Guiseppe Castiglione is believed to have arrived in Peking in 1715, where he was to remain for the rest of his life. He was favoured by both Emperor Yang Cheng and Emperor Ch'ien Lung, and was entrusted with the decoration of the Imperial Garden in Peking. Castiglione learnt to paint in oil on glass as well as in watercolour on silk, and specialized in painting trees, fruit and animals but rarely figures. The technique of 'back painting', (painting on the back of glass panels), was known in Europe. Painting on the reverse of glass with silver and gold leaf was used for decoration by the Italians in the fourteenth century, and later by the English in the sixteenth century (see p. 57). The *Dictionarium Polygraphicum*, 1735, describes it as 'quite contrary to that of limning [miniature painting] or painting on cloth or wood, for in this, the paint being put on one side is plainly visible on the other.' The Chinese artists first traced the outlines of their designs on the back of the mirror-plate, and with a special steel implement removed the mirror backing of tin and mercury to clear a space for their painting.

Alvarez Semedo, the Portuguese writer, who lived in China for twenty-two years, explained that the Chinese had no knowledge of painting in oils. In his *The History of the Great and Renowned Monarchy of China*, (translated in 1655), he remarked 'in painting they have more curiosities than perfection. They know not how to make use of oyles or shadowing in this art and do therefore paint figures of men without any grace at all.' The technique is said to have been introduced by another missionary, Father S.J. Gheradini, who reached Peking in 1699 on the ship *Amphitrite*. Gheradini was especially brought to China by French missionaries on the orders of the Emperor K'ang-Hsi.

The subjects featured in mirror painting fall into four groups. Still life, including flowers, shrubs, trees, utensils and birds; figures, either in groups or alone in a Chinese setting, usually including a river; Chinese scenes with Chinese figures of courtiers or the Emperor and Empress and finally Chinese paintings of European scenes or portraits. Mid-eighteenth century examples often show Chinese men and women of a leisured class seated in gardens or landscapes wherein a river or lake is represented by mirrored areas.

Towards the end of the eighteenth century the fashion changed to favour the copying of European prints. J. Barrow, in *Travels in China,* 1804, mentions 'A case of prints after Poussin', and a writer in the same year states that 'coloured prints of Europe that are carried to Canton are copied with the most wonderful fidelity.'

Sir George Staunton, Chief of Council at Canton in 'Embassy to China' 1798, records the Cantonese craftsmen's ability to copy: 'The Canton artists are uncommonly expert in imitating European works, they mend and even make watches, copy paintings and coloured drawings with great success.' He also mentioned a 'gentleman eminent for his taste in London' who had in his possession a coloured copy made in China of a print from a study of Sir Joshua Reynolds which he felt was worthy of a place in his collection.

The majority of Chinese mirror paintings are anonymous; none have been recorded with a signature. There is, however, a painting of *c.* 1800 in a heavy Chinese frame decorated with gilt over red lacquer, perhaps after Reynolds it depicts a frantic cherub trying to alert a sleeping lady to the danger of a snake. On the wooden back of this painting, is the original maker's label, one of only two recorded, showing an artist's easel, with a ship in the background and paint pots in the foreground. It reads: 'Fatgua, PAINTER in Oil and Water Colours, and on Glass, China Street, Canton. Prepares boxes of assorted colours for drawings at the lowest terms.'

Canton, the great port situated on the delta of the Pearl River or Chu Kiang, on the South coast of China, was the sole point of commercial contact between the Chinese Empire and the rest of the world. There had been a settlement of Arab merchants there since at least the Tang Dynasty of A.D. 618–907, and it was a deliberate act of Imperial policy to attempt to restrict trade to Canton from 1729. An official of the Imperial Household supervised the port for the Emperor who was the main beneficiary of this trade. Along a section of the Canton waterfront sprang up factories, combined offices, warehouses and living quarters of all the major trading countries, inluding the Dutch, English, Swedish, Imperial (for the Holy Roman Empire), the French and Danish, and in 1715 an English factory was established there. Thus Canton developed as a centre for reverse-glass and mirror glass painting. William Hickey (*c.* 1749–1830), the English writer who was 'packed off' by his family to the East wrote his 'Memoirs' from 1769–75. Hickey records that when he was in Canton he was taken to see the 'most celebrated painters upon glass'. This observation was upheld by C. de Gaigne in his *Voyages à Peking 1784–1801*, in which he refers to Canton as a centre for painting on glass.

Frames for Chinese mirror paintings vary from simple oriental hardwood and lacquered softwood frames to elaborate European-made carved giltwood examples. The backboards which hold and protect the glass, are secured by small sliding tongues that fit into slots in the frames. These frames were designed for both decoration and protection during the long sea voyage. As with some of the porcelain, the finished mirror pictures may well have been packed in sago, itself a major export in the China trade. The risk of breakage, as with porcelain, must have been very high, and as early as 1658 the Dutch stipulated 'against breakage please add 10 more of each.'

The Chinese domestic market for mirror-painting was limited since the only place they were used was in their 'Maisons de tolèrence and their theatres.

825

826

827

828

832

833

834

839a

839b

840

b

844

844a

815 China, Qianlong, *c.*1750, one of a pair, mirror painting in contemporary George II giltwood frame
29½in (75cm)

816 Qianlong *c.*1750, mirror painting in carved giltwood frame
14in (36cm) (see colour illustration on p. 349)

817 Qianlong, *c.*1750, a pair of mirror paintings in Contemporary George II Carved giltwood frames
29½in (75cm) (see colour illustrations on p. 350)

818 Qianlong, *c.*1760, mirror painting in eighteenth-century giltwood frame
13in (33cm) (see colour illustration on p. 351)

In 1793 the Emperor of China pointed out to George III that 'the great productions of our Empire are manifold, and in great Abundance, nor do we stand in the least Need of the Produce of other Countries.'

Against this background, many of the European trading companies had very successfully been both importing and exporting to and from China throughout the eighteenth century. Amongst that vast trade, and probably carried as 'private trade' for crew members, were mirror and reverse-glass pictures, (see p. 59).

There is little doubt that it is very difficult, if not impossible, to give accutate dates for mirror and glass pictures from China. Since the mirror and plain glass that was shipped from Europe cannot be dated, one is left with two elements with which to pin down the mirrors: the style of painting and the frame. Examples from the early group of reverse-glass paintings show Oriental scenes which are less affected by Western influence and incorporate areas of mirrored glass. Paintings from the later group are frequently copies from European prints. One of a pair, this example [**815**] falls into the earlier group of pictures. Its pair, (not illustrated), shows a lady dozing in a chair on a balcony overlooking a garden, she is attended by a female servant carrying a ewer and before her is a vase of flowers on a rustic table. Both pictures illustrate members of a leisured class, probably ladies of the court, set in idyllic surroundings and reveal the Chinese artist's wish to convey an impression of the perfect life in China. Originally the paintings would have been given simple, but sturdy, hardwood frames which would have been replaced by the time they were hung in the fashionable drawing-rooms of Europe. Assuming these replacement frames were contemporary, they give an indication of the period during which the paintings were imported. In the first example, the English style of giltwood frame with pierced rocaille work outlined with continuous scrolls dates the pair *c.* 1750. Another pair of paintings [**817**], is in a similarly early oriental style to the example to above, [**815**]. Had the land- or riverscapes been painted later they would have been treated in the horizontal format of European art.

Since Canton was the centre of the glass-painting industry it is not surprising that the artists derived inspiration from the estuary and tributeries of the Pearl River which flows through the city for five or six miles. Macao, a two-mile long peninsula, eight miles south of Canton, was first settled by the Portuguese in 1556–7. Because Western merchants were only allowed to remain in Canton during the trading season they spent the remaining months of the year in Macao. Up to the end of the eighteenth century, it was very unusual for any European woman to live in Macao and they were forbidden to visit Canton. The first record of such a visit, however, was when Mrs Page, wife of a Captain Page, RN, inspected the factories with her husband in 1804. By September 1810, Mrs Elliott, wife of the Master of *HMS Modeste* was with her husband in Macao and two years later The East India Company was recording births, deaths and marriages in their register.

Every educated person in China would have painted. Painting and calligraphy played an important part in the life of the nation, with famous paintings being copied over and over again. It is therefore significant that this court lady or princess, [**818**] wearing a blue dragon robe, is holding a paint brush. Beside her is a vase of chrysanthemums which were probably emblematic of long life. Of a slightly later date,

819 Qianlong, *c.*1760, mirror painting in contemporary George III giltwood frame 53in (135cm)

820 China, Qianlong, *c.*1760, one of a pair of mirror paintings in contemporary George III carved giltwood frames
43½in (110cm)

821 China, Qianlong, *c.*1765, one of a pair, mirror painting in contemporary George III carved giltwood frame
75in (190cm)

822 China, Qianlong, *c.*1770, reverse-glass painting in George III carved giltwood frame
13½in (35cm) (see colour illustration on p. 352)

823 China, Qinalong, *c.*1770, mirror painting in George III carved giltwood frame
31in (79cm) (see colour illustration on p. 352)

824 China, Qianlong, *c.*1765, mirror painting in later George III Chippendale-style frame
28in (71cm) (see colour illustration on p. 352)

825 China, Qianlong, *c.*1775, mirror painting in George III giltwood frame
24in (62cm) (see colour illustration on p. 365)

826 China, Qianlong, *c.*1775, mirror painting in George III giltwood frame
width 17in (43cm) (see colour illustration on p. 366)

827 China, Qianlong, *c.*1770, mirror painting in lacquer and gilt frame
10in (25.5cm) (see colour illustration on p. 367)

828 China, Qianlong, *c.*1770, mirror painting in lacquer and gilt frame
10½in (27cm) (see colour illustration on p. 368)

829 China, Qianlong, *c.*1760, mirror painting in George III japanned frame
11in (28cm)

830 China, Qianlong, *c.*1770, mirror painting in George III japanned frame
21½in (67cm)

831 China, Qianlong, *c.*1760, mirror painting in George III japanned frame
16in (40cm)

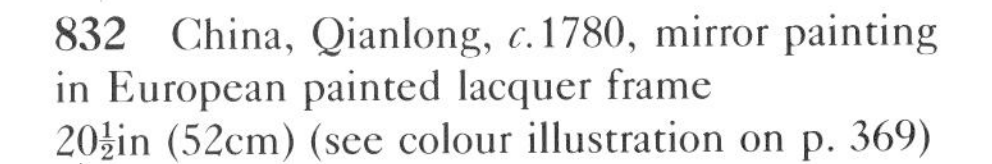

832 China, Qianlong, *c.*1780, mirror painting in European painted lacquer frame
20½in (52cm) (see colour illustration on p. 369)

c. 1760, the George III carved giltwood frame has a lighter and more open feel than the earlier examples. Of about the same date this frame [**819**], is in the full English Rococo style with C-scrolls, acanthus leaves and a ho-ho bird cresting and serves to accentuate the unusual proportions of the painting. Probably the origin for the stylized ho-ho bird, are Chinese golden pheasants, shown here among flowering trees [**820**], one of a pair, this carved giltwood frame has many English Rococo features including scrolls, foliage, rockwork and dripping water or icicles. (Cf. Wills, 1965, p. 117, fig. 133 for an example of similar birds.) Unusually this mirror painting, one of a pair, [**821**] is centred on a George III mirror. Its pair (not shown) depicts a bird of paradise scolding a falcon which is devouring its prey on a lower branch. Here, lotus-blossoms flank an oramental pool as well as a pair of mandarin ducks, while peacocks stand beneath a flowering prunus with finches perched among its branches. The painted central plates are surrounded by shaped border-glasses within contemporary carved giltwood frames. (Cf. Edwards, 1964, p. 368, fig. 55 for an example fitted with scrolling candle-arms.) If this George III giltwood frame is original, [**823**] then it dates the reverse-glass painting (without mirrored area) to *c.* 1770. The scene shows three ladies in front of a pavilion working with silk. Another George III frame, althought slightly later, encloses a picture from the early group of Chinese mirror glass pictures that has a mirrored area [**824**].

Reclining in a boat, this courtesan has a teapot and cup with her [**825**]. It is amusing to see this reference to tea since for two Centuries it was the mainstay for trade between East and the West. Tea drinking in China is recorded as early as the fifth century A.D. but is not mentioned in Europe until 1559 in Ramusio's *Navigatione et Viaggi*. Catherine of Braganza, who came to marry Charles II in 1662, stimulated the fashion for tea in England. The first record of an advertisement for tea was four years earlier and quoted by Dennys Forrest in his *Tea for the British* (p. 23) 'that excellent, and by all Physicians approved *China* drink to be sold at the Sultaness-head, a cophee-

833 China, Qianlong, *c.*1785, mirror painting in a Chinese lacquer frame
40in (102cm) (see colour illustration on p. 370)

834 China, Qianlong, *c.*1785, mirror painting in George III giltwood frame 11½in (29cm) (see colour illustration on p. 371)

house'. While Steward to the Dutch Embassy in China in 1655, Jan Nieuhof recorded that tea-drinking was not only pleasurable, but also beneficial: it drives away drowsiness, aids digestion, counteracts an excess of alcohol, prevents gout and gallstones, and promotes powers of memory. So by 1756 it is not surprising to read that Dr Johnson confessed himself to be a 'hardened and shameless tea-drinker'. The similarities between these two mirror pictures are striking [**827 and 828**] and both retain their original Chinese export lacquer frames, (see p. 40). Allowing direct comparison, the flat-fronted frame of the next picture, [**832**] is decorated with English japanning, in imitation of Chinese lacquer. Possibly made for a dressing-table, the shaped mirror picture is supported by a rear strutt. Following the line of the frame, especially the draped curtains at the top, the decorative scene depicts a courtier in a red hat offering a fan to a courtesan, while an attendant offers her a robe. An interesting detail is the boy seated on the left of the picture holding an opium pipe.

'Foreign Mud' as opium was called by the Chinese, was not introduced into China by the British but they were responsible for the huge increase in its consumption there. In 1797 the East India Company monopolized the production of Bengal opium. By the early nineteenth century opium was responsible for one-eighth of the total revenue of British India. Although traffic in opium was banned by the Chinese the trade flourished. *The Canton Register* of March 1828 carried a proclamation from the Chinese against the drug. It explained that it was addictive, expensive and destructive of health and life and led to a 'longing for luscious and savoury food' and warned that the faces of addicts 'became as sharp as sparrows, adding that 'their heads sunk between their shoulders in the form of a dove'.

Again this fine oval mirror picture [**833**], has an original Chinese lacquer frame

835 China, Qianlong, *c.*1780, mirror painting in George III giltwood frame 8½in (23cm)

836 China, Qianlong, *c.*1780, mirror painting in giltwood frame 8½in (23cm)

837 China, Qianlong, *c.*1780, mirror painting in ebonized and parcel-gilt frame
26in (66cm) high

838 China, Qianlong, *c.*1790, reverse-glass painting in modern carved giltwood frame
15in (38cm)

839 China, Jiaqing, *c.*1790, a pair of reverse-glass paintings in ebonized and parcel-gilt frames (see colour illustrations on pp. 372 and 373)
18in (45cm)

840 China, Jiaqing, *c.*1800, reverse-glass painting in giltwood frame
17½in (44cm) (see colour illustration on p. 374)

841 China, Jiaqing, *c.*1800, reverse-glass painting in carved giltwood frame
width 18in (45cm)

842 China, Jiaqing, *c.*1800, a pair of reverse-glass paintings in white and gilt frames

843 China, Daoguang, *c.*1810, a pair of reverse-glass paintings in giltwood and composition frames
11½in (29cm) (see colour illustrations on p. 375)

844 China, Daoguang, *c.*1825, a pair of Chinese school paintings
18in (46cm) (see colour illustrations on p. 376)

845 China, Daoguang, *c.*1840, reverse-glass painting in Chinese hardwood frame
29in (74cm)

846 China, Daoguang, *c.*1800, Islamic-style mirror painting in giltwood frame
39½in (10cm)

decorated in gilt on a black ground. With the majority of decoration at the base thus allowing it to be used as a mirror, the painting has been carefully composed to accentuate the oval shape. After Henry Moorland's *The Fair Nun Unmasked* this example [**834**], comes from the later group of reverse-glass paintings copied from European prints. J. Barrow in his *Travels in China* of 1804, (p. 327), states that the 'coloured prints of europe that are carried out to Canton are copied there with the most wonderful fidelity'. Also copied from an European picture or print, this painting [**835**] depicts a European lady, possibly French, but of an earlier date, *c.* 1740. It seems strange that the fashion-conscious Europeans would have required pictures of an out-moded style to be copied. Perhaps they were chosen 'on spec' by Chinese artists who had no idea of their original date or could be dated earlier as with [**836**].

In Chinese art it was considered a great compliment to copy the old masters and a much respected pastime. Two examples shown here [**836 and 837**] have drawn upon panel painting, the first, is a copy of an English woman, strongly reminiscent of the style of the English portraitist Sir Geoffrey Kneller bt. (*c.* 1700–20). The second shows an Oriental interpretation of a classical subject, Diana and her attendants, rendered in the style of the Flemish painter Cornelius Polenburg who worked in the late seventeenth and early eighteenth centuries. Drawing upon more local sources of inspiration, this example [**838**] depicts a courtesan playing the part of a shepherdess against a river scene, possibly the Pearl River. (The carved, giltwood frame is modern.)

Executed in pale pink, blue and grey, the softness in colouring, combined with a lack of mirrored water or sky, places this reverse-painted mirror [**840**] in the Jiaguing period (1769–1820). Somewhat later, the fairly simple, English, moulded giltwood frame is late eighteenth century.

Stressing the enormous social and cultural dissimilarities, the next two examples [**841 and 843**] show moments from the lives of an Oriental and a European woman. The first, [**841**] may illustrate a Courtesan in her palace-room on an opium bed playing the flute. While the second, [**843**], one of a pair of early nineteenth-century reverse-glass paintings, depicts a European woman seated at a table, perhaps reading a letter from, and later writing a letter to, her sailor husband or lover. If the wood based frames, decorated with composition are original, it would place this pair of pictures in the 1840s or 1850s.

Chinese artists were more commonly found working in oils on canvas to fulfil the export demand. This pair of paintings [**844**] represents the familiar scenes used by both painters working on canvas and those using plain or mirror glass.

This relatively large mirror painting [**846**] was produced for the Middle Eastern market. Amiot, in her *Memoires concernant l'histoire les sciences, les arts, les moeurs, les usages etc des Chinois*, (Paris 1786) refers to pornographic painting on glass: 'Les Chinois n'ont que trop hein réssi à peindre sur de grandes et de petites glaces, les saletés et les infamies cyniques dont on leur avait donné des modèles.' (The Chinese have only too well succeeded in painting on large and small mirrors, the filth and abjectness of the models they have been given.) These paintings of diaphanously clad women were used by the Chinese to decorate the interiors of their maisons de tolèrance or theatres.

Symbols and emblems

Art historians and connoisseurs have for many years derived a deeper understanding of paintings from a knowledge of emblems and symbols. As a corollary to this, many of the frames of paintings are decorated in the same way with emblems or symbols that reinforce the meaning of the paintings. The same, however, is not necessarily appreciated by the connoisseurs of frames of a different kind, those used to enclose, what was for some, as important as a painting, the mirror plate.

The period covered by this book begins in the middle of the seventeenth century at a time when the language of the sign and symbol was well understood. The craftsmen who carved the earliest examples illustrated would have been well aquainted with the language of symbolism found in European art since the renaissance, especially Christian symbolism. Nor can the repeated use of these symbols to decorate eighteenth-century mirror frames be attributed to chance, since there was clearly a continuity of decorative detail. Whether this re-use of symbolic motifs was, however, a conscious act on behalf of the craftsman is a matter for speculation in each example.

The following list has been compiled from the symbols which appear on mirror frames illustrated throughout the book. There is no certainty that any of the meanings read into them would have applied at an earlier date, or that the motifs have any relevance other than pure decoration, however, it may enhance the enjoyment of a frame and may be worthy of further investigation.

Acanthus An ubiquitous decorative form used on classical architecture during the English rococo period, the acanthus leaf developed into a major decorative feature for looking-glass frames and furniture generally.

Acorn The fruit of the oak tree and sacred to Jupiter, the acorn represents faith and is also associated with Charles II of England who hid in an oak tree after the battle of Worcester.

Anchor While obviously used as a decorative motif on nautical frames, the anchor is a symbol of hope and steadfastness, and an emblem of the Templar Knights.

Armour A symbol of chivalry, armour was often used with other military trophies on French frames of the late seventeenth century.

Arrow Often accompanied by a bow or assembled in a quiver, the arrow symbolizes Cupid, the god of love; a group of arrows is an attribute of harmonious relations.

Ball Used singly or in pairs, on moulded Regency looking-glass frames, they probably derive from cannon balls. Suspended on a chain from eagles' beaks, they are reputed to represent cannon balls that were chained together and fired simultaneously to demast enemy shipping.

Basket Baskets of flowers are often used as cresting to English giltwood mirrors; while a basket of flowers is a symbol of Hope, a basket of fruit is a symbol of Taste, one of the five senses.

Bow The archer's bow, representes America, one of the four continents (see also *arrow*).

Butterfly Emerging from a chrysalis, it stood in antiquity for the soul leaving the body at death. The life cycle of the butterfly, caterpillar – chrysalis – butterfly symbolizes life, death and resurrection.

Caduceus Carried by Mercury, this magical wand, winged and entwined with snakes has the power to induce sleep (see *Lyre*).

Camel A representation of Asia, one of the four continents.

Carnation A *dianthus* or pink, is a symbol of betrothal.

Cock A symbol of lust.

Cornucopia The cornucopia or horn of plenty is emblematic of the earth's abundance, whose origin probably lies in the ancient belief that power and fertility resided in the horns of goats and bulls.

Crane A long-legged wading bird, the crane represents female vigilance and symbolizes the virtue of monarchs and those in public places.

Crocodile Used as a decorative device during the early years of the nineteenth century in England, it referred to Nelson's victory at the battle of the Nile.

Crown Emblematic of sovereignity, the crown is often shown supported by cherubs on late seventeenth-century English furniture as a celebration of the restoration of Charles II. Coronets on mirror cresting can denote the rank of a titled owner.

Dog Man's best friend, the dog alludes to fidelity.

Dolphin A symbol of velocity and agility, dolphins are found on frames with nautical associations and were used during the English Regency period as a further tribute to Nelson's naval victories.

Dove The sacred symbol of the Holy Ghost and peace personified, in secular use a pair of billing doves represents the lovers' embrace used on mirrors included for a bedroom or boudoir. The high cost and variety of looking-glass throughout the seventeenth and eighteenth centuries rendered them suitable as wedding gifts and so many alluded to matters of the heart.

Dragon The dragon is a representation of vigilance, as a decorative device it is often seen on English Regency looking-glass frames and furniture. This style incorporates many oriental influences, especially where the dragon is associated with water.

Eagle An ancient symbol of power and victory as well as generosity, it has been incorporated into the arms of numerous nations. Its significance was appreciated by Napoleon and it was widely used both in France and England, as well as America, where the bald eagle became the national symbol.

Father Time Often winged, holding a scythe and hour-glass and dressed in a loin cloth, he notes in his book the records of heroes and adds to the burden of man.

Fish An early symbol of Christianity, baptism and of Christ.

Flag Bearing a red cross it is the Christian symbol of victory over death and the banner of the Resurrection. Flags were used during the eighteenth and nineteenth centuries to decorate frames of paintings with nautical and military subjects.

Flaming heart Symbolic of passion extreme ardour and charity personified.

Fleur-de-lys A stylized lily used in heraldry, it was the emblem of the French kings and also of the city of Florence; a fleur-de-lys also represented a direct line of succession.

Fountain The fountain of life is a symbol of spiritual life and salvation and is generally represented by an ornamental fountain. There is also, of course, the fountain of love.

Garden tools Tools used in an enclosed garden represent fecundity.

Globe A symbol of power; in the hand of a monarch it signifies sovereignty. It is an attribute of truth, fame and ascendancy, and perhaps also of wisdom, since it was used on frames intended for libraries.

Grapes A symbol of the eucharistic wine – the blood of Christ – grapes are often shown together with ears of corn representing bread. Since it is also an attribute of Bacchus the god of wine, it is used for decorative features in eighteenth-century dining rooms. The harvesting of grapes refers to September.

Griffin Usually depicted with the head, wings and claws of an eagle, and the body of a lion, it symbolizes the combined qualities of both beasts – watchfulness and courage. The griffin is also represented as a guardian of gold and an emblem of immortality.

Harp Played by the angels, the harp is also emblematic of Ireland.

Head Winged heads represent the winds.

Hippocampus A fabulous marine creature with the fore parts of a horse and the hind parts of a fish. Hippocampi drew the chariots of Neptune and Galatea and, so allude to the sea.

Ho-ho birds A European interpretation of a mythological bird, the ho-ho bird is possibly based on the native golden pheasant, which was used in plenty of European, as well as American frames.

Ivy Sacred to Bacchus, it may be shown entwining his head; as an evergreen it also symbolizes immortality.

Knot A symbol of union, possibly between families or nations, the knot can refer to ties of love, and if interlaced with initials, commemorates a marriage.

Lamb A lamb, sheep or ram is a symbol of Christ in his sacrificial role – the Agnus dei, accordingly the lamb also represents innocence, gentleness, patience and humility.

Laurel Used to make the victor's crown, the laurel therefore denotes victory.

Lily A symbol of purity associated with the Virgin Mary.

Lion Emblematic of strength, majesty, courage and fortitude, it was a medieval belief that the lion slept with its eyes open, for which reason it also became a symbol of watchfulness.

Lyre The attribute of poetry. The lyre is again a product of Greek mythology. Having stolen sheep from under the gaze of Apollo, Mercury was ordered to return them. In doing so Mercury and Apollo were reconciled and they sealed their friendship by exchanging gifts. Mercury received the caduceus from Apollo, (see *Caduceus*) giving in return a lyre which he was said to have invented.

Medusa The petrifying severed head of Medusa, with snakes for hair, was used as a protective talisman on a warrior's sheild.

Mitre The head-dress of a bishop and a symbol of episcopal office.

Monkey Used during the Renaissance, the monkey represented taste, one of the five senses.

Musical instruments Different instruments have precise meanings as symbols of love. Equally they are often contrasted with the weapons of war as 'love the conqueror'. Many frames have individual or groups of instruments on console table supports beneath mirrors. They may have been used on frames intended for music rooms or ballrooms where music was played.

Oak The tree of knowledge, also a symbol of strength, faith and endurance, Charles II hid in an oak tree and so it, its fruit (see *acorn*) and leaves became symbols of the Restoration in England.

Palm Conversely the palm was a symbol of military victory and medieval chastity. Palms were also laid on the road during Christ's entry to Jerusalem (recalled on Palm Sunday). It was also associated with Nelson's Egyptian victories.

Peacock A symbol of immortality; the hundred eyes of the peacock's tail are sometimes used to symbolize the 'all seeing' church.

Phoenix A mystical bird with a life-span of some five hundred years, the phoenix supposedly rose from its own ashes and so came to represent the triumph of eternal life over death and

Pineapple A symbol of welcome associated with hospitality.

Plumes A head-dress of feathers is a symbol of America, three plumes are the personal device of the Prince of Wales, and three feathers, resembling those of the ostrich, sometimes red, white and green, symbolize faith, hope and charity when shown passing through a ring.

Pomegranate A symbol of fertility and of union, usually of the church.

Putto Amoretto, the winged infant found in Renaissance and Baroque art, is an angelic spirit or a harbinger of profane love.

Rabbit A symbol of lust, interchangeable with the hare, the rabbit was often used on needlework looking-glass frames.

Rose Associated with the Virgin Mary – the rose without thorns – it is also a symbol of England.

Scales Symbolic of judgement.

Seasons The four seasons: Spring has a young woman holding flowers, young lovers with flowers in their laps or birds in a cage. Summer has a sickle and a sheaf of corn; Autumn has grapes and vine leaves; Winter is shown protected against the cold, or as an old man wrapped in a cloak.

Senses The five senses are generally represented by five women, each engaged in some apposite activity. For hearing she plays music; for sight she holds a mirror; taste has a basket of fruit; smell has a bunch of flowers; touch may have a bird, a hedgehog or an ermine, to conjure up images of soft and hard sensations. (See also monkey.)

Sheep (See also lamb), the sheep received and restored to the flock symbolizes the repentant sinner, while they also refer to Christ as the shepherd.

Shell Notably the scallop shell is used in Christian art to signify a pilgrim, especially of St James of Compostella. In antiquity, the shell was one of the attributes of Venus who was born of the sea and whose other attribute, with which she is frequently shown in compositions, was a mirror. (*Venus with a mirror*, Titian, National Gallery of Art, Washington).

Snail Thought to represent laziness.

Snake The snake or serpent can signify fertility, wisdom and is a symbol of re-birth and of healing. Encircling a tree, however, the snake refers to the serpent in the Garden of Eden.

Sphinx Regarded by the Greeks as a repository of arcane wisdom and in ancient Egypt a symbol of power and vigilance.

Squirrel Perhaps the squirrel represents prudence since it stored food for the winter months.

Stag An attribute of the godess Diana, the huntress, it is also known for its swiftness and sharp sense, which make it difficult to capture. The stag is also associated with Julian the Hospitaller. A nobleman fond of hunting, Julian mistakenly killed his parents and to atone for this he founded a hospice by a river-crossing. He once gave his bed to a leper who was dying of cold after he had carried him across the river.

Sun The attribute of truth, all is revealed by sunlight. The sun was the emblem of Louis XIV of France.

Sunflower Used by Van Dyck as a symbol of his unswerving devotion to his patron Charles I.

Swan Because of its beauty, it is an attribute of Venus. Fable records that the soul of the poet entered into a swan. Leda, on the other hand, was seduced by Jupiter in the form of a swan.

Thunderbolt Lightning, perhaps forming zig-zag shapes with heads at each end in a bunch, is an attribute of fire, one of the four elements.

Torch A torch or flambeau signifies the fire of love.

Tree The tree of knowledge.

Trident A three-pronged fork, an attribute of Neptune.

Urn Lying on its side spilling water is an indication of river themes.

Vine A common symbol of Christ as the vine. Bacchus also wore a crown of vines and they can also represent autumn.

Well A biblical meeting place, the well or fountain is the symbol of baptism and of life and rebirth. The flowing fountain symbolizes the waters of eternal life. (See also fountain.)

Wheat ears The attribute of Ceres and the classical goddess of agriculture, representative of abundance. Also, one of the seasons.

Glossary

Anthemion The Greek word for flower, the anthemion is a single motif resembling the leaves and flowers of the honeysuckle and is derived from a continuous, classical decoration composed of alternating palmettes and lotus motifs.

Appliques Carved wood, wall-mounted decorative panels without the benefit of candle-arms or mirror backing.

Apron Integrated with the mirror frame, the apron is a raised and decorated panel, normally placed immediately below the mirror surround.

Bevel An angled edge ground into mirror plate, also known as a diamonded edge from the eighteenth-century word for the process: 'diamonding.'

Bezel A metal band enclosing and containing loose or fragile parts of a frame.

Breakfront The term used to describe a frame where the central section projects beyond the lateral sections.

Cartouche Usually designed to bear an inscription or arms, a cartouche is a decorative panel, sometimes in the form of an elaborately-carved scroll, which is often part of the *cresting* or *apron*.

Chamfer The effect created when the sharp corner of two meeting surfaces is cut off at an angle of about 45 degrees.

Corbel Singly or in a series, a corbel is the projecting block or bracket placed beneath a horizontal member for support.

Cornice Based on classical architectural decoration, the cornice is the final or crowning layer of projecting moulding which surmounts a frieze or any other finishing layer of decoration.

Curl A form of vigorous graining found in mahogany.

Cresting Normally composed of carved or pierced wood, cresting is the decorative, terminal feature present on many frames.

Cross-graining This is normally found around the outer edges of the top of cabinet furniture and drawer-fronts and is intended to protect the main body of veneer from damage, while also being decorative. Cross grained mouldings are made up of sections of timber, usually walnut, taken across rather than along the grain.

C-scroll A rococo ornament, c-shaped as its name suggests, which normally terminates in a leaf-tip and incorporates foliate elements.

Corona Decorative cut-glass 'crowns' hung with glass drops.

Egg-and-dart moulding Also called 'egg-and-tongue', this is a convex (or ovulo) moulding with a relief pattern of alternating eggs and arrow heads.

Gadroon A decorative, relief pattern composed of a series of radiating, convex ridges or lobes.

Girandole Derived from the Italian word for a type of firework, 'girandola', the word was used in eighteenth-century England to describe a carved wood sconce in the Rococo style.

Grisaille Worked entirely in monochrome, grisaille, as implied by its name, is a painting executed in neutral greys.

Guilloche Used to embellish convex moulding, the plaited effect of a guilloche pattern is composed of interlaced bands.

Ho-ho birds Probably based upon an Oriental bird, perhaps the Chinese pheasant, ho-ho birds are a common feature on rococo mirrors.

Lambrequin Originally a piece of draped fabric, when in carved wood on a mirror frame, a lambrequin appears as a decorative rendering of a scalloped edge.

Menuisier The French term for a joiner or carpenter.

Ormolu The method, both expensive and dangerous of gilding metal (usually bronze or brass) by applying mercury and gold as an amalgum; after the former is driven off by applied heat, the gold is left adhering to the metal.

Out-set Squared, projecting corners found on rectangular frames.

Oyster veneers Developed in Holland during the latter half of the seventeenth century, oysters are transversely cut veneers taken from small branches of olive, laburnum and walnut trees which, because they reveal the whorl pattern of the grain, create a distinctive oyster-effect and are often placed side by side.

Parcel-gilt Areas of timber overlaid with gold leaf associated with walnut and occasionally mahogany frames.

Patera (pl. paterae) a small, flat, round or oval motif of classical origin often decorated with flower-heads or acanthus leaves.

Pier wall The interior area of a wall between two windows on which pier-glasses were hung.

Pilaster Derived from classical decoration, a pilaster resembles a flattened column, rectangular in section, which projects only slightly from the surface to which it is applied.

Pip moulding A decorative effect created by what appears to be a series of tiny, halved balls laid side by side in a continuous string.

Repousée Relief ornament that is hammered from the inside of the metal and is often given added sharpness of form by surface-chasing of the detail and outline.

Rocaille Embracing stylized *rockwork* and shellwork from *c.* 1734 onwards, the term was originally used to describe the decoration used in grottoes. From *c.* 1796 the derogatory term 'Rococo' was used.

Rockwork A rock-like effect carved as a decoration in wood and often found with stalactites and waterfalls.

Sconce A small, wall-light fitted with a candle-arm, a sconce also has a mirror or polished metal backing to reflect the light.

Shagreen A form of untanned leather with a rough, granular surface, later this came to refer to highly polished shark skin (from the French word for this type of leather – 'Chargrin'.)

Spandrel The triangular field created between two or more arches.

Strapwork Of Flemish origin, but adopted in Elizabethan England and elsewhere, strapwork is raised decoration composed of interlaced bands or straps resembling cut leather or fretwork and incoporated with foliate or grotesque decoration. A more delicate form of strapwork was revived by the French Baroque designer Jean Bérain.

Tabernacle Originally intended for sacred images, a tabernacle is a form of canopied recess or ornamental niche. The term is also used to describe an American mirror of architectural form, usually with a decorative panel, often painted, above the main plate.

Term A pedestal, tapering towards the base, surmounted by a bust or the upper half of a human, mythological figure or animal.

Trumeau Derived from French architecture, the term was originally used to describe the space between two windows and later referred to the pier-mirror itself. (See *pier wall.*). By the mid-eighteenth century, the word was used to describe an overmantle mirror.

Vernis Martin Named after the Martin Brothers, who worked in the Palace of Versailles during the mid-eighteenth century, the technique involved the decoration of carefully prepared wood surfaces with painted scenes of a romantic nature in the style of Watteau or Boucher. The decorated surface was then 'antiqued' by creating a heavy craquelure pattern which was then lacquered. In some cases the ground was sprinkled with gold dust to imitate Japanese lacquer.

Bibliography

Technique

Collard, Frances, *Regency Furniture*, Antique Collectors Club, 1985

Jourdain, Margaret, *Regency Furniture 1795–1930*, (revised edition by Ralph Fastnedge), London, 1965

Spaulding Devoe, Shirly, *English Papier Mâché of the Georgian and Victorian Periods* London, 1971

Symonds, R.L., *Masterpieces of English Furniture and Clocks*, Batsford, 1940

Yorke, James, 'Paper Assets', *Traditional Homes*, March 1988

Cennini, Cennino d'Andrea, (trans. Thompson, Jr., Daniel) *The Craftsman's Handbook*, Dover, New York, 1960

Glass

Burgogne, Ian, *Two Thousand years of Flat Glass Making*, Pilkington glass, 1985

McDonald, L.J., *Ravenhead: the first cast plate glass company*, Pilkington Glass Company publication

Neuburg, Frederic, *Ancient Glass*, (trans. M. Bullock and Alisa Jaffa), Barrie and Rockliff, 1982

Polak, Ada, *Glass, its makers and its public*, Weidenfeld and Nicholson, 1975

Seligman, Gustav Wein, *The Book of Glass*, (trans. J. Seligman) Barrie and Jenkins, 1971

Wills, Geoffry, *English Looking Glasses*, Country Life, 1965

Wilson-Frothingham, Alice, *Spanish Glass*, Faber and Faber, 1983

England

Aldrich, Megan, 'Looking Glasses in the Chippendale Style', *Antique Collecting* vol. 21, Oct. 1986

Bracket, Oliver, *An Encyclopedia of English Furniture*, Ernest Benn Ltd, 1927

Coleridge, Anthony, *Chippendale Furniture*, Faber & Faber, 1968

Collard, Frances (see under Technique)

Edwards, Ralph, *The Shorter Dictionary of English Furniture from the Middle Ages to the Georgian Period*, Country Life, 1954

Edwards, Ralph, 'A Chinoiserie Lacquered Mirror', *Apollo Magazine*, vol. 29, 1939

Fitzgerald, Desmond, 'A Family of Looking Glass Merchants', *Country Life* Jan. 29, 1971

Fitzgerald, Desmond, 'Dublin Directories and Trade Labels', *The Furniture History Journal*, 1985

Gilbert, Christopher, *The Life and Work of Thomas Chippendale*, Studio Vista, 1972

Gilbert, Christopher, *Furniture at Temple Newsam House and Lotherton Hall*, National Art Collections Fund and Leeds Art Collection Fund, 1978

Gilbert, Christopher and Beard, Geoffrey, *The Dictionary of English Furniture Makers 1660–1840*, The Furniture History Society, 1986

Hackenbroch, Yvonne, *English and other Needlework Tapestries and Textiles in the Irwin Untermeyer Collection*, Thames and Hudson, 1958

Hall, Ivan, 'Burton Constable', *The Furniture History Journal*, vol. VIII, 1972

Hayward, Helena, *Thomas Johnson and the English Rococo*, Alec Tiranti, 1964

Hayward, Helena, 'The Drawings of John Linnell in the Victoria and Albert Museum', *The Furniture History Journal*, vol. V, 1969

Hayward, Helena and Kirkham, Pat, *William and John Linnell*, Studio Vista, 1980

Hayward, John, 'Furniture by Mathias Lock for Hinton House', *The Connoisseur*, Dec. 1960, vol. CXLVI *Apollo Magazine*, vol. 671, 1958

Hinckley, Lewis F., *Directory of the Historic Cabinet Woods*, Crown Publishers, New York, 1960

Jourdain, Margaret, *Georgian Cabinet Makers*, Country Life, 1955

Joy, Edward, *English Furniture 1800–1851*, Sotheby Parke Bernet, 1977

Joy, Edward, *Pictorial Dictionary of British nineteenth Century Furniture and Design*, the Antique Collectors Club, 1977

Kimball, Fiske and Dunnell, Edna, *The Creators of the Chippendale Style*, Metropolitan Museum Studies II, Nov. 1929

Lenygon, Francis, *Furniture in England from 1660 to 1760*, (pub. not known) 1914

Lunsingh Scheurleer, Th.H., *Silver Furniture in Holland*, Hermmark, Stockholm, 1966

Macquoid, Percy and Edwards, Ralph, *The Dictionary of English Furniture*, (revised edition), Country Life, 1954

Mortimer, Martin, 'The Irish Mirror Chandelier' *Country Life*, 28 Jan. 1971

Musgrave, Clifford, *Adam Hepplewhite and other Neoclassical Furniture*, Faber & Faber, 1966

Payne, Christopher, *Nineteenth Century European Furniture*, The Antique Collectors Club, 1985

Rieder, William, 'Furniture Smuggling for a Duke', *Apollo Magazine*, 1965

Saville Seligman, G. and Hughes, Talbot, *Domestic Needlework*, Country Life, 1926
Schiffer, Herbert F., *The Mirror Book*, Schiffer Publishing, Pennsylvania 1983
Symonds, R.W., *English Furniture from Charles II to George II*, The Connoisseur Ltd, 1929
Symonds, R.W., *Masterpieces of English Furniture and Clocks*, Batsford, 1940
Symonds, R.W., 'Carved and Gilt Carolean looking-glasses' *The Antique Collector*, Nov. and Dec. 1948
Symonds, R.W., *Rococo Art Design in Hogarth's England*, The Victoria & Albert Museum, exhib. cat. 1984
Ward-Jackson, Peter, *English Furniture Designs of the Eighteenth Century*, H.M.S.O., 1958
Wills, Geoffrey, *English looking Glasses*, Country Life, 1965
Wills, Geoffrey, 'Furniture Smuggling in the Eighteenth Century, *Apollo Magazine*, 1965

France

de Bellaigne, Geoffry, *Furniture, Clocks and Gilt-Bronze, The James A. de Rothschild Collection at Waddeston Manor* vols I and II, Office du Livre, for the National Trust, 1974
Dumonthier, Ernest, *Le Meuble-toilette*, Paris, Editions Albert Moracé, Paris, 1923
Eriksen, Svend, *Early Neo-Classicism in France*, Faber & Faber, 1974
Frégnac, C., *Les Styles Français de Louis XIII à Napoléon III*, Hachette, 1975
de Groër, *Les Arts décoratifs de 1790 à 1850*, Fribourg, Office du Livre, 1985
de Ricci, Seymour, *Louis XIV and Regency Furniture and Decoration*, Batsford, 1929
Verlet, Pierre, *French Furniture and Interior Decoration of the Eighteeenth Century*, Barrie & Rockliff, London, 1967
Wannenes, Giacomo, *Mobili di Francia il Settecento, Storia, Stili, Mercato*, Mondadori, Milan 1984
Watson, F.J.B., *Wallace Collection Catalogues, Furniture*, London, 1956
Watson, F.J.B., *The Wrightsman Collection Catalogue*, New York, 1966

Germany

Ehret, Gloria, *Deutsche Möbel des 18 Jahrhunders, Barock, – Rokoko – Klassizismus Keyser*, Munich 1986
Freytak, Claudia, *Möbellechen*, 1978
Hinz, Sigrid, *Innenraum und Möbel*, Berlin, 1976
Jervis, Simon, *Printed Furniture Designs before 1650*, Furniture Historical Society, 1974
Kreisel, Heinrich, *Die Kunst des Deutschen Möbels*, vols I and II, Beck, Munich 1968
Schmitz, Hermann, (ed.) *Deutsch Möbel des Barock und Rokoko*, Hoffmann, Stuttgart, 1923
Wichman, Heinrich, *Kunst und Kunsthandwerk im Hause Basner in Zoppot*, Klinkhardt & Biermann, Danzig, 1925

Italy

Alberici, Clelia, *Il Mobili Lombardo*, Gorlich, Milan, 1969
Bacceschi, *Mobili Genovese*, Gorlich, Milan, 1962
Bacceschi, *Mobili Piemontesi del Sei e Settecento*, Gorlich, Milan, 1963
Chiesa, G., *Il Settecento In Italia*, Gorlich, Milan, 1974
Mariacher, Giovanni, *Specchiere Italiane*, Gorlich, Milan, 1963
Mazzariol, Giuseppe, *Mobili Italiani, Seicento e Settecento*, Villardi, Milan, 1964
Morazzoni, Giuseppe, *Le Cornici Veneziane*, Luigi Alfieri, Milan 1945
Morazzoni, Giuseppe, *Le Cornici Bolognesi*, Luigi Alfieri, Milan 1953
Odom, William, *A History of Italian Furniture*, The Archive Press, New York, 1967
Payne, Christopher, *The Price Guide to Nineteenth Century European Furniture*, Antique Collectors Club, 1981
Palacios, Alvar Gonzales, *Il tempo del Gusto*, 2 vols: Rome and Central Italy 1984, Northern Italy 1986, Longanesi, Milan, 1984
Quaglino, Elio, *Mobili Regionali Italiani, Il Piemonte*, Gorlich, Milan, 1966
Rosa, Gilda, *I Mobili nelle civiche raccolte artistiche di Milano*, Aldo Motello, Milan, 1963
Vitale, Vittorio, *Mastra del Barocco Piemontese*, Turin, 1963
Wannenes, Giacomo, *Mobili d'Italia*, Mondadori, Milan, 1984
Wannenes, Giacomo, *Mobili d'Italia, Il settecento, Storia, Stili, Mercato*, Mondadori, Milan, 1984
Furniture History Society, *The Dictionary of English Furniture Makers*, Maney, 1986

Scandinavia

Clemmensen, Tove, *Danish Furniture of the Eighteenth Century*, Copenhagen, 1948
Clemmensen, Tove, *Furniture by N.H. Jardin, C.F. Harsdorff and J.C. Lillie and examples of their decoration*, National Museum of Denmark, Copenhagen, 1973
Thornton, Peter, *Authentic Decor, The Domestic Interior (1620–1920)*, Weidenfeld & Nicholson, 1984
Upmark, Gustaf, *Möbler*, Stockholm, 1912
Vahlneg, Bo *Catalogue of the Royal Palace of Rosendal*, (date not known)
Wallin, Signord, *Nordiska Museet Möbler Fran Svenska Herremansherm*, vols I–III, Stockholm, 1931–5
Wichmann, Heinrich (see Germany)
Wilkie, A., *Biedermeier Furniture*, London, 1987
Washington, National Gallery of, *Royal Treasures of Sweden 1550–1700*, exhib. cat. 1988

Spain and Portugal

Arte Antiga, Museu Nacional de, *Artes Decoratives Portuguesas séculos XV–XVIII*, Lisbon, 1979

Byne, Arthur and Stapley, Mildred, *Spanish Interiors and Furniture*, Dover, New York, 1921–5

Guimaraes, Alfred, *Mobiliário Do Pago Ducal de Villa Vicosa*, Lisbon, 1949

Mendes Pinto, Maria Helena, *José Francisco de Pavia: Ensamblador e Arquitecto do Porto (1744–1824)*, Museu Nacional de Arte Antiga, Lison, 1973

Payne, Christopher, (see England).

America

Albany, Institute of History and Art, *Furniture by New York Cabinetmakers*, exhib. cat., (date not known)

Beckerdite, Luke, 'Philadelphia Carving Shops: Part 1: James Reynold's', *Antiques*, May 1984

Bridwell, Bates, Elizabeth and Fairbanks, Jonathan L., *American Furniture to the Present*, Richard Marek, New York, 1981

Comstock, Helen, *The Looking Glass in America 1700–1825*, Viking, New York, 1964

Davidson, Marshall, B., *The American Heritage: History of Colonial Antiques*, New York, 1979

Down, 'Two Looking Glasses', *Antiques*, vol. XLIX, May 1946

Dubrow, Eileen and Richard, *Furniture Made in America 1875–1906*, Shiffer, Pennsylvania, 1982

Dubrow, Eileen and Richard, *American Furniture of the Nineteenth Century, 1840–1880*, Schiffer, Pennsylvania, 1983

Greenlaw, Barry A., *New England Furniture at Williamsburg*, Williamsburg, 1972

Heckscher, Morrison H., *American Furniture in the Metropolitan Museum*, Metropolitan Museum of Art, New York, 1985

Hinckely, F. Lewis, (see England)

Hipkiss, Edwin, J., *Eighteenth Century American Arts: The M and M Karolik Collection*, Cambridge, Massachusetts, 1941

Hornor, jr., William Macpherson, *Blue Book of Philadelphia Furniture*, Highland House, Washington, 1935

Jobe, Brock and Kaye, Myrna, *New England Furniture: The Colonial Period*, Houghton Mifflin, Boston, 1984

Lockwood, Luke Vincent, *Colonial Furniture in America*, Castle Books, New York, 1957

Madigan, Mary Jean Smith, *Eastlake-Influenced American Furniture 1870–1890* Hudson River Museum, New York, 1974

Miller, Edgar G., *American Antique Furniture*, vol. II, Dover, New York, 1966

Montgomery, Charles F., *American Furniture: The Federal Period*, Viking, New York 1966

Otto, Celia Jackson, *American Furniture of the Nineteenth Century*, Viking, New York, 1965

Ring, Betty 'Check list of looking-glass and frame-makers and merchants known by their labels', *Antiques*, May 1981

Sack, Albert, *Fine Points of Furniture, Early American*, Crown Publishers, New York, 1950

Schiffer, Herbert F., (see England)

Strickland, Peter L.L., 'Documented Philadelphia Looking Glasses, 1810–1850', *Antiques*, April 1976

Weidman, Gregory, R., *Furniture in Maryland 1740–1940*, Maryland Historical Society, Baltimore, 1984

Chinese Mirror and Reverse Glass-Painting

Brown, Claudia and Rabiner, Donald, *Chinese Glass of the Qing Dynasty 1644–1911*, exhib. cat., Phoenix Art Museum, Phoenix, 1987

Cohen, William, 'A Study of Chinese Paintings', *Burlington Magazine*, Jan. 1942

Conner, Patrick, *The China Trade, 1600–1860*, The Royal Pavilion Art Gallery and Museum, exhib. cat., Brighton 1986

Fell, Granville, 'Chinese Mirror Paintings of the XVIIIth Century', *Apollo*, Dec. 1933

Godden, Geoffrey A., *Oriental Export Market Porcelain*, Granada, 1979

Jeryns, R.S., and Jourdain, M., 'Chinese Mirror Pictures on Glass', *Apollo Annual*, 1948

Wills, Geoffrey, (See England, first entry under Wills)

General

Ferguson, George, *Signs and Symbols in Christian Art*, Oxford University Press, 1954

Hall, James, *Subjects and Symbols in Art*, John Murray, London, 1974

Hayward, Helena *et al. World Furniture*, Paul Hamlyn, London 1965

Roche, Serge, *Miroirs*, Ernst Wasmuth, Tubingen, 1985

Photographic acknowledgements

Apart from the cases cited below, all the illustrations in this book have been supplied by Sotheby's London, Sotheby's New York or Sotheby's Monaco.

William Bedford Plc, London 164a

Fisher Bohler, Munich 477, 479, 480, 495, 498

Peter Hempson Fine Art, London 538

Bob Huffham fig. 10

Mallets, London 173a, b and c

Edmund Peel Associates, Madrid 727–42

Arne Bruun Rassmussen, Copenhagen 674, 677, 681–4, 686, 688–90, 694–6, 698, 699, 701, 704, 705, 707, 712

Spelt Doon et fils, Brussels 349

Victoria and Albert Museum, London, Prints and Drawings Department 442a and b, 458a

List of names

Figures in *italics* refer to captions.